Advance praise for *Energy Transition and Economic Sufficiency*

For decades, we have dealt with energy consumption and carbon emissions by increasing efficiency; the result was bigger pickup trucks, cheaper flights, and rising carbon emissions. The contributors to this volume explain why it is time to stop thinking so much about efficiency and start thinking about sufficiency: how much do we really need? What's the best tool to do the job? What is enough? They describe a future that is not just sustainable but is regenerative, and where there is enough for everyone living in a low-carbon world.

– Lloyd Alter, Design Editor at treehugger.com, Contract Lecturer at Ryerson University, and author of *Living the 1.5 Degree Lifestyle: Why Individual Climate Action Matters More Than Ever*

Energy descent is crucial to stopping climate and ecological breakdown, both by greatly reducing the magnitude of transition and by increasing the odds that it is a just transition. This is a key conversation to have as we lurch toward ecological civilization.

– Peter Kalmus, climate scientist, author of *Being the Change: Live Well and Spark a Climate Revolution*

This lively and insightful collection is highly significant for identifying key trends in transitioning to low-energy futures. Cutting carbon-emitting activities will drive economies towards de-urbanisation. Using less, and renewable, energy will turn current relations between agricultural and high tech sectors upside down. Weaknesses of global supply chains highlighted in the 2020 pandemic will be overtaken by 21st century low-energy institutions. Goods produced locally or moved by wind-powered ships and cargo bikes, solar commons, regenerative organic agriculture and consumer food cooperatives are all critically and acutely analysed as practical solutions to the twin challenges of energy descent and climate change.

– Anitra Nelson, author of *Small is Necessary: Shared Living on a Shared Planet*,
co-author of *Exploring Degrowth: A Critical Guide*

Whether as a result of climate action or fossil fuel depletion, our future will almost certainly be shaped by energy scarcity. However, very few policy makers or academics are preparing for, or thinking about, life with less energy. Cheap, abundant energy gave us the industrial food system, consumerism, and a growing middle class. Might we see that gravy train reverse itself? Declining energy may stress-test our economy and political system, pushing them to their limits and forcing us to adapt quickly and uncomfortably. The contributors to this volume have done us all a tremendous service by surveying the terrain ahead and by identifying the easiest and best low-energy paths to a survivable, sustainable future.

– Richard Heinberg, Senior Fellow, Post Carbon Institute, author of
Power: Limits and Prospects for Human Survival

It is nearly half a century since the seminal *Limits to Growth* provided the context for considering human prospects beyond continuous growth on a finite planet. Permaculture was one response that has proliferated and spread as the multiple crises facing humanity converge. It is nearly two decades since I first clarified permaculture ethics and design principles as thinking tools for responding to "energy descent" futures.

For those already applying permaculture in their lives and livelihoods, this collection of essays is affirmation that we are on the right track for creative adaption to a world of less.

This book helps fill the conceptual black hole that still prevails in academia, media, business and politics about how a world of less is inevitable.

For those articulating "energy descent" futures; whether to friends, colleagues, teachers, students, employees, policy makers or political representatives, this collection by writers across a range of fields helps paint the picture of how a world of less is possible by design rather than collapse.

– David Holmgren, co-originator of Permaculture, author of *RetroSuburbia*

Energy Transition and Economic Sufficiency

Food, Transportation and Education in a Post-Carbon Society

edited by Bart Hawkins Kreps and Clifford W. Cobb

ISBN-13: 978-0-9895995-6-6

Cover design by Carrie Cockburn and Bart Hawkins Kreps
Book design and layout by Bart Hawkins Kreps
Text is Adobe Garamond Pro

Post Carbon Institute
800 SW Washington Ave., Suite 5
Corvallis, Oregon 97333
United States
postcarbon.org

Contents

Preface

Clifford W. Cobb and Bart Hawkins Kreps

This project began as an issue of the *American Journal of Economics and Sociology* (AJES). The journal dates back to 1941. From the beginning, its aim was to apply the lessons of the social sciences to problems faced by society, not to the artificial intellectual problems often created within academia. Energy and resource issues are among the many categories of topics that AJES addresses.

The idea for this book came about when Cliff, editor of AJES, read Jason Bradford's 2019 report *The Future is Rural: Food System Adaptations to the Great Simplification*, published by Post Carbon Institute. That report explains the qualitative changes in agriculture that will result from rising energy prices and especially from the declining availability of gasoline and diesel fuel to operate the equipment currently used on farms. Among other changes, agriculture will have to become more labor intensive, which means that rural populations are going to have to grow. That scenario suggests, of course, that there will be widespread changes affecting all aspects of social and economic organization.

Cliff envisioned an issue of AJES examining those issues under the general theme, "Problems of transition to a world of climate instability and rising energy costs." He contacted Bart, who had written many articles on related topics, to ask if Bart would serve as guest editor for this issue for AJES.

Bart found that many scholars and activists are grappling with how to live in a world of climate instability, but relatively few are discussing the coming decline in per capita energy availability. Fewer still are dealing with the two challenges as a simultaneous reality. Many people both inside and outside academia, however, are working out solutions that will be relevant in the coming energy transition. Their work may not focus on either the climate crisis or energy descent, but they nevertheless help us understand how specific social sectors and practices can be transformed for true sustainability.

We were able to assemble a diverse group of writers who address a wide range of these issues, including how and where food is produced, and how food is distributed; how goods are transported, both within cities and around the world; how education can better equip students for the intertwined technical and social challenges in energy transition; and how a commons model for renewable energy resources can promote economic democracy and equity. The articles were made available to the scholarly community in the May 2020 issue of AJES. With the help of Post Carbon Institute and the permission of AJES publisher Wiley, we are happy to make this collection available to the wider public now.

CHAPTER I

Editors' Introduction: Energy Transition and Economic Sufficiency

Bart Hawkins Kreps and Clifford W. Cobb

Until the spring of 2020, it was possible for many people to picture the global economy as a well-oiled machine. Some of its flaws were well known—physical scientists have warned for decades that reliance on fossil fuels threatens the survival of our species, and social scientists increasingly see income and wealth inequality as threats to political stability. Yet corporate and political leaders projected continuing economic growth as both necessary and highly desirable. This faith in "business as usual" was echoed in mainstream media. Progress in communications, bioengineering, and nanotechnology promised a future in which human ingenuity could finally overcome the last barriers imposed by natural limits.

Like the scratching sound of a needle on a phonograph record, the COVID-19 pandemic suddenly stopped the music. The fragility of a complex global supply chain was laid bare as never before. Economies around the world shrank dramatically, almost overnight, and formerly radical ideas were suddenly on the lips of national leaders and on the op-ed pages of prestigious newspapers. The tragedy that hundreds of thousands experienced in hospitals, and hundreds of millions faced as they struggled to pay rent or buy groceries, also called into question conventional wisdom about politics, economics, and ways of life. Regardless of what happens after the pandemic is over, it seems unlikely that we will return to the same world we left behind.

Work on this collection of articles began almost a year before the pandemic, guided by the belief that "business as usual" cannot and will not continue for decades into the future. Our belief that major changes are coming is founded in two realities. First, our climate is increasingly unstable and will present increasingly severe challenges to human life even if we immediately embark on a rapid and sustained reduction of carbon emissions. (This reduction is something that, prior to the pandemic, we had never achieved in spite of the chorus of warnings from climatologists. Even at the height of the pandemic, many business leaders were determined to reverse as soon as possible the temporary reduction in fuel use.) Second, the global economy relies increasingly on energy that is costly, in the very basic sense that it now takes greater investment to extract or produce a given amount of usable energy. As a result, there is less net energy surplus available to sustain economic growth. We believe that both these trends are becoming more pronounced as we move into the 21st century, and our preparations for the future must take these trends into account.

Urbanization or De-Urbanization?

The proportion of people living in the world's non-rural areas has increased over the past century, and it is common to simply plot a trend line and draw conclusions such as "by 2050, 68 percent of the world's population is projected to be urban" (UN-DESA 2019: xix). We see things differently. There are good reasons to believe that the challenges of climate instability and high energy costs will slow or even reverse the trend towards urbanization.

Cities arose in history because the surplus created

by agriculture made it possible for some people to shift from primary production to the role of artisans, toolmakers, educators, and administrators. Food production was the first—and is still the most fundamental—energy sector. Over many centuries, the gradual improvements in food-production systems provided a greater net energy surplus, supporting more complex economies and allowing more people to live and work with no direct personal connection to food production.

That slow gain in net energy jumped by orders of magnitude when civilizations learned to use fossil fuels effectively. The massive increase in per capita energy availability supported a vast array of new industries, creating new products as well as services and supporting the construction of large cities around the globe. At the same time, fossil fuels transformed food-provisioning systems. Fossil-fueled engines drastically reduced the need for farm labor; artificial fertilizers derived from fossil gas allowed dramatic gains in harvests even as soil resources were being depleted; and fossil-fueled food-processing and transportation systems allowed food to be shipped rapidly around the world. Relatively few primary food producers were needed, therefore, to provide the food consumed by large numbers of urban citizens. Agricultural areas around the world have lost population, while cities have swelled.

In recent decades, however, the basis of urban expansion has been stifled. The production of *net* energy (net of energy used to produce it) is in decline, even though *gross* energy production continues to climb. It takes more work to get the same amount of usable energy than it used to. In the United States, fracking is temporarily masking the larger trend toward costlier energy because of implicit subsidies, but fracking yields little *net* energy and is thus unprofitable (see Chapter 3). Canada, likewise, celebrates an illusory energy boom in a massive program of extracting heavy bitumen from the Alberta tar sands. The sudden market price plunge of oil during the pandemic highlighted the poor economic viability of these unconventional resources. But it is equally important in the long run that easy-to-extract conventional fossil fuels* are steadily depleting. It has been decades since new conventional oil discoveries have matched current consumption.

Since aggregate economic output is directly related to the availability of *net* energy, rising energy costs will force the entire economy to shrink. Labor will become relatively *less* expensive as energy becomes *more* expensive. One result will be that more people will be employed in primary food production, reversing a trend of the past 200 years, while rising costs of transportation mean economic activity will have to be located closer to sources of supply to reduce transmission losses. As discussed later in this chapter, and in detail in Chapter 5, we expect this will result in the gradual decline of urban life and the growth of rural activity.

Climate change will be another important cause of large-scale population shifts. Models of how climate change will affect different regions are imprecise, but we can predict with some confidence that rainfall is going to be excessive at some times and places, even as drought conditions arise in others. Cities that experience repeated hurricanes, floods, or droughts are likely to lose population over time, particularly as those events accelerate in frequency and severity. Miami, New York, Mumbai, Shanghai, and

* "Conventional" oil and gas resources are those found in relatively easy-to-access geological formations, and which flow up through the well mostly or entirely due to the pressure found within these formations. Due to relative ease of access, conventional oil resources were exploited first and have been the primary sources of petroleum since the late 1800s. Discoveries of conventional petroleum resources have fallen off drastically in recent decades. "Unconventional" resources do not flow readily, requiring more complicated extraction methods such as fracking – in which oil- and gas-bearing shale rock is fractured through injection of high-pressure fluids – or tar sands mining – in which oil-soaked sands are heated in order to retrieve heavy bitumen which can then be further refined.

even London could become partially uninhabitable because of rising sea levels combined with higher storm crests. Urban water crises (such as affected Capetown, South Africa in 2019) are likely to become more common on every continent. Over time, climate variability will make many cities less hospitable places to live.

These sources of social and economic disruption come on the heels of other damage from humanity's interactions with nature, especially over the last few decades. First, the loss of humus-rich soils has begun to exacerbate the problems of food production at the same time that fossil-fuel-based fertilizers have become more expensive. Second, overfishing and climate change are beginning to cause the decline of the oceans as a source of food. Third, depletion of ancient aquifers is making human populations more dependent on variable rainfall and thus more vulnerable to drought. Fourth, rapid extinction reduces species diversity, making every ecosystem vulnerable to external disturbance. Fifth, mass human migrations, set in motion by drought, energy decline, and other factors, are already testing the capacity of societies to respond humanely.

What is not speculative is the lesson that the COVID-19 pandemic demonstrated: sudden, unexpected discontinuities can occur beyond human control. System change is nonlinear, and the pandemic is only one example of the kind of system change the world is likely to experience. After decades of integrating everyone on earth into a global economic system, we have learned the fragility of tightly coupled systems that lack redundancy.

The Energy Descent and Flawed Economic Optimism

The articles assembled here help us think through just a few of the challenges that modern societies face during the transition to a low-energy future. As explored in several of this book's chapters, we expect an *energy descent* – a rise in energy costs and the concomitant decline of the economy. A "low-energy future," we are aware, is a concept that is scarcely even whispered in mainstream media. Optimism about the future of energy production and conservation still holds sway, not only among fossil fuel diehards, but also among many who believe that we will transition to all-renewable energy sources within just a few decades.

Various cheerful scenarios have been presented about how electric vehicles, solar electricity, wind turbines, and carbon-capture schemes can save the planet without demanding any significant behavioral changes by the public. There is widespread hope that economic disruption caused by the decline of fossil fuels can be avoided with a relatively smooth transition to renewable energy. If that optimism turns out to be unwarranted, we will be left with an economy crippled by various energy bottlenecks and a planetary trajectory of excessive warming. Thus, it is of utmost importance to gain clarity about whether it is reasonable to expect renewable energy to provide a solution to dual crises of economic and environmental health.

We return to a question that has periodically haunted modern societies since the 19th century: What are we going to do when the energy supply runs short? Economists have long viewed that question as naïve. They have argued that a reduced supply of any valuable commodity will cause the price to rise, which will lead to conservation, technical changes, and substitution of alternatives. For that reason, they say, resources are never depleted. It is true that there will always be some oil in the ground; but there is nothing in economic theory that prevents the price from rising to levels that restrict other economic activity. Nevertheless, economists tend to be technological optimists, believing that a *deus ex machina* will always prevent economic collapse, just as they blame "exogenous forces" for periodic economic contractions. This amounts to an admission that economic theory is useless in analyzing a disequilibrium system.

The optimism inherent in modern economic arguments is thus naïve. It hinges on technological change coming to the rescue. But all of the technical fixes to our energy descent conundrum that have been proposed in the past several decades 1) become competitive only when oil prices reach a minimum threshold, 2) still require hidden energy subsidies from fossil fuels, and 3) often produce negative net energy when the full supply chain and life-cycle of the production process is considered. Even when new technologies operate at a financial loss, they are still deemed viable. For example, nuclear power – electricity generated via nuclear fission reactors – has operated in the United States only because of implicit subsidies. Perhaps the largest subsidy is a legal cap imposed by the U.S. Congress on potential liabilities. Without that cap, the cost of liability insurance would be prohibitive, and nuclear power would have failed the test of market viability.

We believe it is no less naïve to imagine that renewable-energy sources can simply replace the fossil-fuel system while providing equally high net-energy returns. It cannot, as explored at length in Chapter 4. The transition to a renewable-energy system is critically important in the short term as we try to limit the catastrophic consequences of climate change. The transition is inevitable in the long term, since the remaining high-energy-return fossil resources are rapidly depleting and even unconventional fossil resources, which provide marginal amounts of net energy, are finite. But if we want that transition to provide reasonable and equitable prosperity for all, we must understand that the economy of the future will run on lower per capita energy.

Fixing Nordhaus's error

The policy community will take seriously the problem of energy descent only when one bit of accounting is cleared up. It is the same accounting error that leads senior economist William Nordhaus (2007) to imagine that the future costs of climate change are a tiny portion of global GDP because the loss of agricultural output represents only a small part of current economic output.* Farming is currently a small part of gross world output because of positive natural conditions. The reduced availability of irrigation water in dry regions as a result of climate change will make some land barren. Reduced fuel supplies for farm equipment will also reduce the geographic scale of food production. If the productivity of high-value arable land declines by 20 percent due to those factors, food costs will not rise by a mere 20 percent; they might rise by 200 or 400 percent or more. The effects are not linear or incremental. There would be bottlenecks in many parts of the economy

* Nordhaus, like most economists, is accustomed to models that examine large-scale changes by breaking the consequences into a series of isolated effects, each of which can currently be managed at low cost by importing resources from elsewhere, as needed. But what if "elsewhere" is on fire or under water? The underlying bias of these models is the assumption of equilibrium conditions. Even Nordhaus (2007: 14–15) recognizes that some disequilibrium will result from climate change:

> However, those human and natural systems that are "unmanaged," such as rain-fed agriculture, seasonal snow packs and river runoffs, and most natural ecosystems, may be significantly affected. ... The damages are likely to be most heavily concentrated in low-income and tropical regions such as tropical Africa and India. While some countries may benefit from climate change, there is likely to be significant disruption in any area that is closely tied to climate-sensitive physical systems, whether through rivers, ports, hurricanes, monsoons, permafrost, pests, diseases, frosts, or droughts. (emphasis added)

Five-year droughts in one region may not be catastrophic as long as other areas of the world are in healthy condition, but not if they are also faced with floods, insect infestations (such as locusts in India and East Africa in 2020), pandemic, or other natural disasters. What the models ignore in their sanguine predictions is the rising likelihood that *simultaneous* crises will set in motion cumulative causation and interactive effects that create disequilibrium conditions for prolonged periods. Recovery of "normal" conditions will not be assured.

as resources shifted among alternative uses.

In 2007 and 2008, the world already witnessed riots when prices tripled or quadrupled in a tight grain market, in part due to price increases in fossil-fuel feedstocks for fertilizers (Barbet-Gros and Cuesta 2015; Headey and Fan 2010). The reduced stability of weather conditions over the next 50 to 80 years will have the same effect.

Nordhaus engaged in an error typical of economists of using stable current prices as a guide to unstable future events. He recognizes that demand elasticities of both food and fuel are quite low, which means that small quantity changes can have disruptive price effects. But he fails to account for the disruptive effects of low elasticities by assuming equilibrium conditions and ignoring the effects of cumulative "shocks" from climate change that will repeatedly ripple through the world economy. These disequilibrium conditions need to be incorporated in accounting for future consequences of present behavior.*

The importance of an economic sector cannot be assessed simply by its relative size in the economy. We cannot argue, as Nordhaus has done, that changes in a small sector of the economy will have small effects in the future, if the changes themselves cause a large imbalance among sectors. In a recursive system with large discontinuities, it is meaningless to draw conclusions from current experience.

We already got a taste of those discontinuities in the 1970s. When the price of petroleum rose sharply, households not only reduced driving and lowered thermostats; they also bought new energy-saving equipment. Older cars—the "gas guzzlers" with low fuel efficiency—lost value overnight. Even though, as machinery, they had many years of useful life, economically they were too expensive to operate. In this way, a small change in the supply of energy caused a large increase in the rate of capital depreciation and shortened the time-frame of household and corporate investment in equipment. In a similar fashion, when the artificial glut of oil and fossil gas from fracking runs its course, energy prices will rise again and that will have a devastating effect on capital goods, such as vehicles and machinery, bought when fuel was cheap.

Lower labor productivity, energy bottlenecks, and lost capital value will probably result in a prolonged economic depression. Unlike previous depressions, which were caused by a misalignment of credit with real production potential, the future depression will be caused by a decline in real productivity caused by the reduced amount of useful work provided by each unit of primary energy available.

Everyone born before 1980 grew to adulthood in a world of rising expectations. Economists promised that whatever problems existed could be solved eventually by an increase in the scale of economic activity. As long as a small energy input could leverage a large energy output, the additional energy could be put to work satisfying private whims and public purposes. In short, it seemed that growth of GDP was a natural process that would continue forever. That optimism, which still prevails in the economics profession, consistently ignored the many civilizations in the last 6,000 years that grew beyond the limits of their resource base and then crashed.

For a little over a century, fossil fuels created the illusion that humans were no longer earth-bound creatures—that we could deplete the resources of this planet and then escape to other planets. But the illusion is gradually becoming apparent as the United

* An equilibrium system in economics means one that will return to normal prices and supply levels within a short period of time after a disruptive event. An economy in equilibrium is one in which businesses can make contracts that they can reliably fulfill based on other reliable contracts. Disequilibrium refers to a condition that lacks normal prices and quantities because disruptive changes become the new norm. Events are not statistically distributed around a "bell curve." The economic models and straight-line predictions that work under equilibrium conditions are no longer valid. Prices may rise suddenly without explanation. Supply-chain disruptions become standard. Every aspect of life becomes haphazard.

States pours increasing subsidies into energy production in a failing attempt to close the gap between rising consumption and the declining energy value of new discoveries. Rather than working to find a soft landing for the inevitable energy descent, our society is devoting the last vestiges of our energy endowment to keeping the illusion alive for another decade.

A Better Way

Do the views in this volume add up to "gloom and doom?" We forecast a future of lower energy availability, less high-speed and long-distance mobility, economic contraction, and a renewed emphasis on local industries, including food production. These developments might sound dismal to some readers. In our view, these changes *need not* be disastrous, though they very well *may* be disastrous if our societies are unprepared. We need to work out new ways of living—on individual, local, regional, national, and international scales—to prosper without economic growth and to develop our human potential without robbing the opportunities of future generations.

The assembled authors here have analyzed some of the problems we face and pointed in the direction of some possible solutions. We hope these articles can contribute to the sense of urgency needed to begin reorienting society and the economy in ways that address the twin crises of energy and climate.

Authors Leading Us Out of the Labyrinth Ahead

Collaboration on this project began with a conversation between the two editors. The selection of authors and initial work with them was conducted entirely by the primary editor, Bart Hawkins Kreps. In the process of gathering the articles assembled here, not every potential author who was contacted was able to make a contribution in the time-frame of publication. Thus, the collection offers a less comprehensive scope than our original hope. In particular, we deal primarily with changes in the economies of wealthy industrialized nations, and we are aware that perspectives and needed solutions will look much different from the Global South. Nevertheless, we have assembled a diverse array of thinkers who are considering creative responses to the restrictions imposed by nature.

Not surprisingly, no two authors envision the world ahead in the same terms or on the same scale. But as fossil fuels are phased out in the coming decades, most choices will need to be made by local jurisdictions. The emphasis of the authors is on institutional responses by cities, suburban enclaves, cooperative associations, solar commons, universities, shipping companies, and farmers. There is probably universal agreement among the authors that it would be a giant mistake to await the leadership of central governments. Everywhere in the world, central governments are following initiatives by citizens rather than taking the lead in devising innovations.

Part I: The Major Challenges—Climate Change and Energy Descent

The first part deals with the overall situation faced by humanity from the combination of climate change and energy descent.

Climate change is an unprecedented challenge that is disrupting the material systems on which modern societies depend. Rising sea levels, hurricanes, disease vectors, droughts, forest fires, and ocean acidification spell disaster for a large portion of the world's population. They will interfere with crop production, forestry, fishing, transportation, water supply, mosquito abatement, electricity production, healthcare, and many other essential services. But national leaders have avoided either mitigation (cuts in emissions) or adaptation (projects to deal with the consequences) in a meaningful way. Instead they have focused on crafting diplomatic language to delay a serious response.

In addition to the climate crisis, we are also suffering a second global problem: the decline of *net energy* and the resulting constraints on the operation of industry and agriculture. A decline in net energy will restrict the ability of nations to resolve problems that were previously manageable. Even adaptation to climate change will be impeded by lack of net energy.

Thus far, the problem of global warming has been acknowledged, but the challenges posed by a decline in net energy are underestimated. Even most advocates of "green energy" have yet to take seriously the problem that sources of renewable energy will not serve as a full substitute for fossil fuels. An economy powered by renewable energy will necessarily be much smaller than a fossil-fuel economy. The longer we hold on to the habits of a high-energy economy, the harsher will be the consequences when change is imposed by the limits of nature.

Chapter 2 – Adaptation and Mitigation Amid the Consequences of Failure

Paul Cox and Stan Cox

Since the 1990s, when world leaders began to take climate change seriously, there has been a tension between restricting carbon emissions (mitigation) and dealing with the damage that is inevitable (adaptation). Mitigation means either using less fuel for heating, cooking, and transportation or developing technology to use it more efficiently. Political leaders have been wary of mitigation because it hurts today even though it reduces harm in the future. Thus, a cottage industry of analysts emerged to twist language and policy to make it seem as if adaptation was the better choice and could be done without effort. If people's houses are destroyed in hurricanes and government does not help them, then adaptation does not show up as either a business cost or a public cost. This is the sort of cowardly way world leaders have been avoiding the reckoning imposed by climate change—through intellectual sleight-of-hand tricks that deny responsibility.

Paul Cox and Stan Cox provide a detailed guide to how world leaders have appeared to be taking action when they have been doing little more than manipulating language. Even in 2020, after decades of powerful hurricanes and typhoons harming relatively powerless people around the world, leaders are still primarily oriented toward protecting economic growth, and thus against activists who would slow or stop it for the sake of future generations. Mitigation would limit economic growth the most, so international treaty negotiations have done little more than express hope that nations might cut emissions. Even adaptation, which was originally envisioned as a back-up plan if mitigation failed, has been transformed into an economy-friendly process that places the burden on the "resilience" of individuals and local jurisdictions. Negotiators have found ways to quietly sideline any reference to the gargantuan public spending that would be needed to provide effective adaptive measures. In the process, the leaders of nations in the Global North have also been able to deflect demands for compensation for damage caused by the effects of cumulative CO_2 emissions during the decades when the Global South was still colonized. The entire diplomatic apparatus to solve the climate problem has been twisted into a method of protecting economic interests.

Yet, since the costs of climate change are already materially present in the lives of billions of people, there is one factor that climate diplomacy has been unable to suppress: popular resistance. Climate change is an immanent and existential threat to the world's poor, who have chosen to fight back with a global movement for climate justice. In effect, the nations of the Global North have abdicated climate leadership to the low-income nations that are being forced to design programs of mitigation and adaptation on their own. The specific example presented by Cox and Cox is Puerto Rico. Faced with devastation from Hurricane Maria in 2017 and the prospect of more disasters to come, this island territory of the United States, to which President Trump refused to provide meaningful disaster assistance, has been developing innovative, decentralized strategies for coping with climate change. It seems that this crisis is going to determine who the true leaders are in shaping a workable plan for the future of the planet.

Chapter 3 – The Rising Costs of Fossil Fuel Extraction: An Energy Crisis That Will Not Go Away

Bart Hawkins Kreps

In the first of two articles by Bart Hawkins Kreps, he explains the general conditions of energy scarcity and why those conditions will increasingly restrict economic activity in the near future. We are accustomed to thinking about the availability of energy to power the economy in terms of barrels of oil, tons of coal, or megawatts of electric capacity from alternative fuels, including wind and solar. But accounting for energy capacity in terms of those metrics gives a flawed result. As in financial accounting, where the crucial figure for a company is its net revenue or profit, the relevant consideration in energy accounting is net energy. For this purpose, Kreps works from the concept of energy return on investment (EROI): energy available for useful work from a given input of energy. While most analysts have been measuring energy supply for decades in terms of gross quantities, the more insightful analysts have been showing that global average EROI has been declining from around 80:1 in the 1950s, to 37:1 in 1990, to 13:1 in 2013. In energetic terms, that means we have to work harder to stay in place. When the EROI finally falls to unity (1:1), a point where we get back only what we put in, there will be no *net* energy to operate tractors, cars, or machines in factories—which means that energy production will be pointless. Long before we arrive at that point of collapse, the decline of net energy will create a drag on the economy, raising costs in real terms that cannot be circumvented. The concept of "peak oil" is often caricatured and means different things to different people, but what we actually need to be concerned about is "peak EROI," and that point was passed decades ago. EROI climbed rapidly in the early fossil fuel age as industries learned to extract, refine, and utilize fuels more efficiently, but average EROI has dropped more recently as we rely on increasingly difficult-to-extract fossil fuel deposits. Growing investment in gross energy production has compensated for the decline of net output, but the subsidies to the energy sector are becoming less politically viable.

In the second part of the article, Kreps points to specific places around the world where the consequences of declining EROI have brought about conflict. Syria, Egypt, and Yemen are examples of nations in which the government has been destabilized by rising energy costs and by the declining ability of the government to subsidize food and energy consumption in urban areas. The United States has seemingly escaped the fate of other nations by permitting the use of hydraulic fracturing (fracking) to extract oil and gas from otherwise unproductive shale formations. But, as Kreps shows, the glut of shale oil and shale gas is a result of a special circumstance: the zero-interest-rate policy in the wake of the economic crisis of 2008. That policy enabled banks to lend to fracking companies at low interest rates in spite of high risk. Nevertheless, those companies have yet to turn a profit; their success depends on ever-growing subsidies.

Even if such enterprises are kept artificially afloat, an economy running on low-EROI resources cannot sustain economic growth—a predicament that has bedeviled Western governments unwilling to accept that the era of economic growth has passed.

If a falling rate of net energy production from fossil fuels puts the brakes on economic growth, it may be hoped that renewable energies, such as solar photovoltaics and wind energy, can compensate. Not likely. To burst that bubble, we now turn to the second article by Kreps that examines precisely this question: Can renewable energy produce the level of net energy that we are accustomed to using?

Chapter 4 – Energy Sprawl in the Renewable-Energy Sector: Moving to Sufficiency in a Post-Growth Era

Bart Hawkins Kreps

There has been considerable enthusiasm about renewable energy in the past few years, as the price of electricity generated with solar and wind power has been dropping rapidly. This sudden increase in the efficiency of renewable-energy systems has given rise to a fantasy that they can quickly replace fossil fuels. If that is true, then both the energy crisis and the climate crisis can be solved with a simple shift from one technology to another.

Like most dreams, this one is evanescent. In his second article, Bart Hawkins Kreps dashes the hopes of an easy transition to a 100-percent renewable-energy economy by pointing out the limits of the technology. The central concept he employs is "energy sprawl," a term that refers to the required expansion of the energy-production sector of an economy as the EROI falls. Just as the net energy derived from fossil fuels is declining, the net energy from renewables is inherently low. At present, the true energy cost of renewables is being masked by the use of fossil fuels with a relatively high EROI to produce the components of the instruments for capturing energy from wind and sun. When we reach the point that the entire life-cycle of renewable energy is unsubsidized by fossil fuels, the low EROI of renewables will become clear. (At the moment, any precise measure of that EROI is difficult because the energetic benefits of fossil fuels permeate the economy.)

Renewable energies, like fossil fuels, have "sweet spots"—areas with long sunny days or nearly constant winds. Sweet spots tend to be tapped first for solar-photovoltaic or wind-turbine installations. As we try to produce the same quantity of net energy that currently drives our economy, while also eliminating fossil-fuel use, the renewable-energy industry will need to expand far beyond the sweet spots. This is a vicious cycle, as a dependence on low-EROI renewable-energy installations will accelerate energy sprawl and lower the net energy available to the economy as a whole.

A crucial problem with renewable energy is its poor suitability, under most conditions, to replace industrial heat, thereby making it difficult and expensive to continue producing cement, steel, chemicals, and numerous other components of an industrial economy. Another characteristic of renewable energy is the delay in returning the energy that is put into creating its infrastructure. In contrast to a timeless analysis of "energy return," a calculation of "power return" takes into account timing. With photovoltaics and wind turbines, almost 100 percent of the energy investment is upfront, while the energy return follows gradually over 20 years or more. This poses a serious problem for the transition to renewables because there will be little or no gain in available net energy during rapid expansion phases. The energy invested in new construction will be as great or greater than the energy output of the relatively small, older, installed base. Although a transition to renewable energy is inevitable because of declining stocks of high-EROI fossil fuels, the transition is not going to be smooth. Dramatic changes in ways of life will be essential in a post-growth era.

Part II: How Will We Feed Ourselves?

Farming was the occupation of most people during the past six millennia. That changed in the past century as urban economies absorbed most agricultural labor, even as population grew. Food production and distribution will be deeply affected as the world responds to the joint challenges of climate and energy change. The expectation that a small rural population can provide enough sustenance to feed a growing urban population will be overturned as rising energy costs filter through the economy, reducing mechanization and demanding more labor-intensive forms of production at shorter distances from urban areas. Climate instability will add to the difficulties faced by farmers, foresters, and fishers. Without the availability of cheap fertilizers from natural gas, the importance of natural soil fertility will become more evident, and soil regeneration will become a significant aspect of an economy based on renewable energy. In addition, the distribution of food will become more decentralized, creating an advantage for cooperatives, which are currently operating in the shadows of large grocery chains.

Chapter 5 – The Future Is Rural: Societal Adaptation to Energy Descent
Jason C. Bradford

On a global basis, the world transformed in the 20th century from being primarily rural and agrarian to being urban. Employment shifted from farming to industrial production and service occupations. Cheap, abundant fossil fuels made that transition possible. As the age of readily accessible hydrocarbons begins to wane, that transformation will begin to slow down and eventually reverse. As Jason Bradford entitles his article: the future is rural.

The global pandemic of 2020 has raised doubts about never-ending globalization, but faith in urbanization remains prevalent. Most prognostications about the future consist of little more than straight-line projections of previous patterns. On that basis, it seems self-evident that a greater proportion of the population will live in cities in the future. It requires a leap of imagination to question the trend and claim that urbanization will soon peak and begin a reversal, perhaps quite suddenly.

Bradford's analysis is based initially on a biological metaphor in which cities are similar to organisms. Like organisms, cities make use of energy to survive and grow. The more urbanized a country, the more energy per capita it uses. In the last century, growing cities have consumed vast quantities of energy to operate at a very high rate of metabolism, similar to mammals and other endotherms that maintain a constant internal temperature. Bradford argues that, as cities experience energy descent, they will be forced to adopt a metabolism that is similar to fish, reptiles, and other exotherms that require far less energy because they do not maintain a constant metabolism. The analogy is not perfect, as mammals cannot become exotherms. But it indicates the magnitude of the challenge faced by cities in their relation to the hinterlands from which they draw the raw materials that provide the basis of external trade. Most modern urbanists have lost sight of those hinterlands, picturing cities as concentrations of people, buildings, and economic activity, making scant reference to the raw materials from the countryside that make city life possible. Bradford's analogy redefines the city as an organism that includes both hub and periphery—with the city gathering surplus labor and materials from the surrounding region to sustain itself. Globalization has distorted that image in recent decades, but energy descent will bring the relationship of city and hinterland once again into stark relief.

Bradford shows in detail why reliance on renewable energy will not stave off the inevitable decline of cities. Renewable sources of energy are not one-for-one substitutes for fossil fuels. Fossil fuels have six characteristics that will be lost in an economy based on renewables: reliability of uninterrupted service, mobility of fuel, industrial-thermal uses, concentration of sources of energy, universality (not location specific), and aggregate energy availability. All of these factors contribute to the dilemmas the food sector will confront as renewables replace fossil fuels.

For the past century, farming has become increasingly industrialized as a result of intense use of fossil fuels. Under those conditions, natural factors such as soil carbon, nitrogen-fixing bacteria in the soil, erosion control, natural pest management, and animal husbandry as an element of crop production have been ignored and replaced with standardized procedures for managing monocultures. In response to energy descent, agriculture will have to become more diverse, adaptive, and aligned with natural processes.

The sorts of integrative farming methods that can persist without large inputs of fossil fuels will require the renewal of older forms of agriculture. The change will involve a high demand for labor, the use of grazing animals to provide fertilizer and as buffers to balance the variance between good and bad harvests, the encouragement of natural predators, the diversification of crops, and the management of soils to capture atmospheric carbon and nitrogen. All of the elements add up to renewed complexity of biological interactions in relatively small areas. We are accustomed to global complexity on the basis of specialization or division of labor. But that actually entails simplification of each local area. In the rural future envisioned by Bradford, complexity will return to the farming community.

The final dilemma with which Bradford leaves us is how it might be possible to simplify social organization at the macro level in order to create the conditions for local, decentralized complexity. Since the members of industrial societies are far from understanding the need to reverse the current growth trajectory, the most likely scenario is that we will hold onto high-energy modernity until there is a sudden system collapse. But if enough people begin reorienting life to a rural future, beginning with existing suburbs and urban food cooperatives, perhaps a relatively soft landing is possible.

Chapter 6 – Why Regenerative Agriculture?
Courtney White

The transition to a low-energy, low-impact future depends in large part on agriculture: the culture that expresses our practical relationship with nature. Courtney White insists that regenerative agriculture needs to be central to the process, not only in terms of specific farming methods but as a general philosophy that can guide other human activities.

As a practical matter, the most important question facing modern society is whether its farming techniques will continue to deplete the carbon content of soil or increase it. The future of civilization hinges on the answer to that question. Modern agriculture treats soil as nothing but dirt—a medium that holds plants in place so that inputs may be added in the form of seeds, fertilizer, pesticides, and other additives. This approach to farming is not only destructive of soil structure and composition; it also imposes heavy economic burdens on farmers. The solution is relatively simple. Regenerative agriculture lets nature do the heavy lifting by producing soil that captures essential nutrients for free, so additional inputs can be minimized. The first step lies in recognizing that soil is alive, not mere dirt. The metabolism of the soil involves the work of myriad microorganisms along with grazing animals, birds and other predators, as well as humans who plant seeds to be harvested. If human action is oriented in ways that release the productive power of soil, it will sustain plants, animals, and humans.

It might seem, at first, that regenerative agriculture is merely a set of platitudes about good cultivation. But it goes far beyond that into controversial territory. One of its radical principles is that farmers should not plow the soil. Although it might seem that plowing is necessary to remove competitive plant species and to prepare a field for seeds, the actual effect of breaking the soil is to cut the connection between surface and deep roots, reduce the capacity of soil to hold water and release it slowly to plants, and to destroy the interaction of organisms that are crucial to the health of the soil. When soil is left intact, it is an even more effective sink for carbon than the plants growing in it. Plowing releases carbon instead of capturing it.

No-till agriculture is not a novel idea. It has been adopted by thousands of farmers in the United States, but it does not qualify as regenerative unless it is combined with other practices designed to improve the complexity of life within the soil, which is not the case when no-till is combined with intense use of herbicides to control weeds.

The second radical principle of regenerative agriculture is the importance of animals. The need for habitat for birds and other predators to keep insects and rodents in check is an old idea, but it has been ignored for at least half a century in the industrial model of agriculture. The more surprising feature of regenerative agriculture is the premise that grazing animals are essential to the formation of soil. Not only do their urine and feces serve as fertilizer spread across a field without machinery, the indentation of their hooves in the soil creates variations in the surface that enable it to hold water. In addition, grazing itself stresses plants in positive ways and encourages deep root growth, which draws nutrients from subsoil minerals.

Modern agriculture has largely succeeded in training farmers to think of land as an inert substance to be managed entirely according to human designs. That approach ignores ecosystem complexity and destroys it by imposing mechanistic models on living systems. White stresses that regenerative agriculture is more than a set of good farm practices. It is a way of developing an attitude that the land can teach us how to live, if we will take the time to listen. The prevailing modern assumption that technology can solve all problems needs to be questioned. The philosophy of regenerative agriculture reminds us that we need to adapt human systems to the limits imposed by nature.

Chapter 7 – Differing Visions of Agriculture: Industrial-Chemical vs. Small Farm and Urban Organic Production
Heather Gray and K. Rashid Nuri

Although there is mounting evidence that the industrial-chemical model of agriculture is harming the planet and the lives of both farmers and food consumers, the corporate interests that continue to promote that model around the world often seem impervious to change. In recent decades, they have added genetically-modified organisms (GMOs) and hybrid seeds to the technologies that are forcing farmers to become more dependent on the inputs supplied by agribusiness.

Heather Gray and K. Rashid Nuri put the contemporary situation in perspective by taking us on a tour of deep history. They remind us that agriculture began in the region that is now within the territory of Iraq. The farmers there have been following traditional methods of seed selection, planting, and harvesting for countless generations. Like other farmers around the world, they recognize that the health of their families and communities depends on preservation of seed diversity and fertile soils.

Thus, it was particularly ironic that one program sponsored by the occupying U.S. military in Iraq after 2003 was agricultural modernization. It is possible that some of the techniques presented by U.S. agronomists were ones that Iraqi farmers would have willingly adopted. Instead, the Iraqis were forced to accept changes imposed by U.S. agribusiness companies that were backed by raw power. Corporate interests that were put in charge of the U.S. programs were not motivated by finding methods that would help the local farmers. Instead, their only aim was to clear away tradition in order to create a clean slate on which a new agricultural policy would be written, one that made farmers increasingly dependent on seeds and chemicals from U.S. suppliers. Here we see that the social side of industrial agriculture is as indifferent to the diversity of culture as the biological side is indifferent to genetic and ecosystem diversity. Agribusiness can only maximize profits if diversity is swept aside. The procedures followed in Iraq are a condensed and extreme form of agribusiness practices around the world. In the name of progress, farmers in most nations have become economically dependent on foreign interests for the inputs used on farms.

While recognizing the ubiquity and power of agribusiness, Gray and Nuri do not counsel despair. They point out that there is also resistance to industrial-chemical agriculture from farmers and health-conscious consumers. In the United States, the authors are among the activists who are promoting small farms and urban-organic food production to restore local control over farming and provide healthy jobs, healthy food, and a healthy environment. Nuri's Truly Living Well Center for Natural Urban Agriculture in Atlanta, Georgia is one of the leading institutions in the southern United States in this effort.

Chapter 8 – Consumer Food Co-ops in the Age of Grocery Giants
Jon Steinman

While agribusiness ignores the importance of soil in its pursuit of industrial efficiency on farms, the corporate chains that sell food to households are committed, first of all, to shareholder profits rather than to the health of households and communities. Jon Steinman takes us on a tour of the many ways in which giant grocery store chains stand as obstacles to short supply chains between food producers and the consumer who wants to buy healthy, locally produced food. If concentrated ownership of food retailing is a problem in times of prosperity, it will become even more severe as changes in climate and energy supply constrict the economy and drive up food prices along every step of the supply chain. Although energy and climate crises will initially affect the ability to grow, store, process, and transport food, their consequences will alter economic and political relationships, an event for which we should begin planning.

The grocery giants use their market dominance to control both suppliers (food producers along the supply chain) and customers. In many metropolitan areas in the United States and Canada, three to five grocery chains control 70–80 percent of the retail food market. Although antitrust laws and state regulations once limited the power of grocery chains, deregulation and lax antitrust enforcement in the 1980s gave the chains virtual control over what producers would be able to sell and at what price.

As a result of growing retail power, when food prices have risen in recent decades, retail prices have increased far more than the price of food as it leaves the farm or ranch. Retail grocers have devised various strategies for extracting income from food producers even before their products are bought by consumers. For example, producers must pay initial and ongoing fees to grocers merely to have their products displayed on the shelf. At the other end of the process, grocers can cause great hardship to their suppliers by delaying payments to them for many months. The size of grocery giants thus allows them to exploit food producers in a variety of ways.

As increasing energy costs raise the price of food in coming decades, closing the gap between farms and consumers will be necessary to keep food affordable and to provide small farmers with enough income to stay in business. One of the best ways of connecting producers and consumers is consumer cooperatives. This is a subject that Jon Steinman knows exceptionally well, since he has served co-ops as a board member and he has conducted research with co-ops across the continent.

At a minimum, consumer co-ops provide a venue for local producers to sell their food. Since chain grocers have rules that effectively block the entry of small, local suppliers, the co-ops are often the only means for small vendors to remain viable. Co-ops do not require advance payments or long-term contracts from local suppliers. This makes it possible for struggling producers to find a market at an early stage of operations. At the same time that this benefits producers, it also benefits consumers, who consequently have access to healthier food choices than are normally found in grocery stores.

In addition to serving as an alternative to the grocery giants in providing diverse and affordable products to consumers, co-ops also function as incubators for the formation of new businesses. One might argue that this is true capitalism at work: the kind of innovative capitalism that works for everyone by promoting the creation of small business. One of the foremost problems of transitioning to a low-energy society is how to facilitate the renewal of rural economies. Acting as catalysts in the creation of small regional businesses may be the most important function that co-ops will play in the economy of the future.

Part III: Generation, Transportation, and Education

As we move into an energy-challenged future, our ability to rely on cheap energy to create convenient ways of living will be called into question. We may need to organize our economic life on a seasonal basis, as our ancestors did. We will need to rethink daily travel and the possible substitution of local products for distant ones. In coping with these changes, it will be essential for more citizens and policymakers to have a wide-ranging understanding of energy issues; energy provision will go beyond technical issues for engineers.

Most motorized transportation today is powered by fossil fuels. Cities have been built or transformed with as much or more space devoted to vehicles as people. Yet a large number of trips are short enough for walking or cycling, and even much of what we call "freight" can be delivered by bicycle within cities. Long-distance and heavy freight is more challenging. Maritime shipping was once powered by wind, and we may need to revive such ancient technologies, though that will likely mean the annual volume of goods shipped across the oceans will drop substantially.

In transitioning to systems that generate and distribute electricity produced with renewable energy, we are likely to face many new challenges, with implications for economics, politics, and organization of work and home lives. Specialists in electrical engineering will have an important role to play, but other students will need some basic knowledge of energy science, and electrical engineers will need to understand the social implications of their work. Developing a renewable-energy system will also call into question the ownership models built for electrical utilities during the past century of industrial capitalism. Solar radiation is a "commons" resource. Our legal traditions still retain the centuries-old framework of "trusts" that can be used today to set up "solar commons" for community benefit.

Chapter 9 – Reorienting the Economy to the Rhythms of Nature: Learning to Live with Intermittent Energy Supply
Kris De Decker

We tend to think of the industrial age as contemporary with the fossil-fuel age. But though industrial production accelerated exponentially with fossil-fuel exploitation, Kris De Decker points out that many industrial processes—sawing timber, grinding grain, weaving textiles, to name a few—were powered by wind and water for centuries before coal- and oil-powered engines took over. We also think of global trade in terms of today's combustion-engine ships, but a major global shipping industry operated on renewable energy—the trade winds—for centuries.

There are important lessons to be learned from these older technologies, De Decker writes. The primary renewable-energy sources are inherently intermittent. Solar radiation is stronger in summer and absent at night, wind power is seasonal in many areas and changeable in all areas, and water-powered turbines in rivers produce less power during dry seasons when river flows drop. If we try once more to "run the economy based on the weather," we will need to adjust demand to energy supply in a much more flexible way than we do at present. But a flexible approach would make the transition to renewable energy far less daunting. If we can accept seasonal and hourly variations in energy supply, we will need much less long-term storage and long-distance transmission in our energy systems, compared to the infrastructure needed to run our 24-hour, 365-day economy on renewable energies.

Building an economy that again adapts to seasonal changes need not mean abandoning all 20th- and 21st-century technologies. De Decker argues that we can greatly benefit from technologies like photovoltaic panels and electric motors to use renewable energies to best effect, while still organizing our societies around a gracious acceptance of the intermittency of energy supply.

On the other hand, if we assume that renewable-energy infrastructure must operate by the rules of the current industrial economy we are in danger of exchanging short-term gain for long-term pain. De Decker offers a cautionary tale in his examination of the wind-turbine industry. The towering wind turbines that have been constructed by the tens of thousands are widely believed to be highly efficient exemplars of "clean" energy. But they achieve their economic and thermodynamic efficiency through the use of composite rotor blades. The longer the blade, the stiffer the blade must be. The dominant designs today have many layers of artificial materials, sandwiched together in ways that preclude effective recycling. If we ramp up wind-power production dramatically throughout the next 25 years, then societies 25 years from now may be chopping up and landfilling hundreds of thousands of tons per year of these composite materials.

De Decker writes that windmill blades were made entirely from renewable materials for centuries and were used very effectively. He calls for more research on construction of new windmills and wind turbines that not only harness renewable energy but are built from renewable materials. Though we will likely sacrifice some short-term economic efficiency, we should focus on long-term sustainability rather than leaving another big waste management problem for our descendants to deal with.

Chapter 10 – Suburban Practices of Energy Descent
Samuel Alexander and Brendan Gleeson

Discussing the inevitability of energy descent may prepare for the changes ahead at an abstract level, but we also need detailed guidance about what actions to take to make the transition as smooth as possible. As Samuel Alexander and Brendan Gleeson point out in their article about what suburban communities can do, it is foolish to wait for guidance from national governments. Pioneering households must start the transition process without a roadmap.

Before they get under way, Alexander and Gleeson offer several caveats. They recognize that measures to reduce energy consumption and increase self-sufficiency of suburban households are only one part of a much bigger transition. They also remind us that there are many households, even in rich countries, that do not have the luxury of overconsumption. A comprehensive transition program would need to include structural changes that would create a more just and equitable economy that enables everyone to be a full participant.

They then turn to the practical measures that suburban households with discretionary income could begin to take. The measures include older ideas about turning the thermostat down in the winter or up in summer, improving home insulation, or eating less meat. But they extend their proposals to new and more radical actions, such as making investments in biogas digesters, solar-photovoltaic panels, composting toilets, and heat pumps, as well as using suburban land for farming. Until around 1950, most suburban households in Australia were oriented toward self-sufficiency. Only the past few generations have become adjusted to buying rather than making. What is now needed is the restoration of that mindset and the habits that went with it. If enough households adopt an ethic of sufficiency and frugality, it becomes possible to envision neighborhood projects and methods of sharing that advance the level of collective services at low cost. The aim is not merely to conserve energy but to create a culture that is resilient in the face of adversity.

To some critics, it seems that personal action is irrelevant in the face of structural impediments to change. However, Alexander and Gleeson explain that one of the purposes of developing practices of household frugality is the development of a political constituency. Cultural movements to prepare for energy descent need advocates with experience of voluntary simplicity who can fight against the prevailing orthodoxy that favors endless economic growth. Unless enough households make a voluntary commitment to a simple life, there will never be a base of support for a smooth transition to a low-energy society when nature eventually imposes change on us.

Chapter 11 – What Makes a Good Cargo Bike Route? Perspectives from Users and Planners

George Liu, Samuel Nello-Deakin, Marco te Brömmelstroet, and Yuki Yamamoto

While wind power can be used to transport freight long distances across oceans, cities are going to need other forms of renewable energy to transport goods within cities. Electric cars will meet part of that demand, but there is an even more efficient method: a cargo bike, which is a bicycle designed to carry either freight or additional passengers. These bikes, which are heavier and often wider than standard bicycles, can be partially motorized, or they can be propelled entirely by pedaling. They are already in use in a number of European cities, not to mention in countries outside of Europe. As part of a concerted effort to reduce carbon emissions, they are likely to be used far more in the future. But they are not as popular as they might be if road conditions were more favorable. Thus, it is important to determine which factors influence the use of cargo bikes and the routes they take through cities.

George Liu, Samuel Nello-Deakin, Marco te Brömmelstroet, and Yuki Yamamoto investigate the conditions that deter cargo bike operators from using specific roads and paths when traveling across a city. Rather than examining the experience of cargo bike operators in only one city, they compare two cities. Amsterdam, in the Netherlands, is flat and seldom has snow. Stockholm, in Sweden, has more complex terrain and has snow part of the year. Despite these differences, the concerns of cargo bike riders in the two cities are generally similar. The biggest problem they face is traffic: trucks and other heavy vehicles pose a big hazard to bicyclists of all types but particularly to cargo bikes that cannot always be accommodated on designated bike paths. Other important factors are the number of cars, the smoothness of streets, the number of parked cars, and the type of infrastructure that is intended to help cyclists.

City planners have been taking the concerns of cyclists into account for a number of years, particularly in Europe. But they have largely ignored the different concerns of cargo bikes, which cannot as easily be ridden on pedestrian walkways or through parks. The authors used the occasion of this study to demonstrate to planners that the subjective views of cyclists are often at variance with the objective measures used by planners. The actual routes chosen by cargo bike operators are often different from what one might assume by looking at a map; the conditions on the ground include variables that are not easily included in representations. Unfortunately, this means that there is often no best route choice for cargo bikes because each rider will weigh traffic, infrastructure, traffic lights, and other factors in a way geared to individual considerations. Though it is difficult to create infrastructure that meets the preferences of all cyclists, the increasingly diverse modes of human-power transportation highlight a need for a more inclusive planning process.

Chapter 12 – Winds of Trade: Passage to Zero-Emission Shipping

Nicola Cutcher

Global trade existed for thousands of years before the invention of the steam engine and the use of fossil fuels. The basis of ocean-going cargo transportation was sailboats, which made use of solar power in the form of wind energy. Nicola Cutcher explains how some companies are already moving in the direction of restoring wind power, albeit with the use of modern technologies.

For thousands of years, cargo was shipped on sailing craft. Only for the past century or so have we come to rely on fossil fuels to power shipping. Around 80 percent of all goods travel by sea at some point. Shipping creates 2–3 percent of greenhouse gases. Because petroleum-powered shipping is faster, allows larger volumes of freight, and arrives on a schedule, we have become dependent on it. It will take decades to build or retrofit wind-powered ships to carry cargo on a large scale and it will involve longer transit times that depend on prevailing winds.

Nevertheless, climate change and declining supplies of fossil fuels make the transition necessary. A step forward is to find ways to retrofit existing vessels with special sails or rotors to make hybrids that use both wind power and fossil fuels. That will enable existing ships to reduce emissions by anywhere from 5 to 35 percent. The higher end of the scale can only be reached by relaxing the demand for travel speed, which is possible for cargos that go from one warehouse to another, but not for just-in-time manufacturing processes.

Some ships are being built today that rely entirely on wind power. Thus far, the purists who favor this approach are in the minority, and the hybrid approach is the one most shipbuilders are taking. Since ships take years to build and even more years to repay the cost of construction, the uncertainties surrounding the future of fuel prices make any investments very risky. The long-term prospects seem to favor those who invest now in ships that are mostly dependent on wind for propulsion. But if the decline of low-cost energy does not become fully evident for another decade, gambling on a wind-power future could be a losing bet in the meantime. Thus, for the sake of long-term market stability, governments should adopt incentive-oriented taxes and regulations that shorten the timeline of renewable-energy benefits. If that occurs, the wind-power crusaders will be vindicated in their choice of investments.

Chapter 13 – Energy-Transition Education in a Power Systems Journey: Making the Invisible Visible and Actionable

Jonee Kulman Brigham and Paul Imbertson

The transition from fossil fuels to renewable energies will have major implications for the electric grid. As we embark on this transition, Jonee Kulman Brigham and Paul Imbertson write: "The grid can no longer remain effectively invisible to society, for every sector of society is affected by the transition and has a role to play in accelerating its implementation."

Guided by this insight, they lead students on a Power Systems Journey. Their course is part of the University of Minnesota's Grand Challenges Curriculum, which takes on thorny systemic problems that, by their very nature, cannot be solved effectively by any one specialty. Each course in this curriculum has instructors from more than one university department, while students are recruited from across the university.

In the Power Systems Journey, an energy transition for the electric grid is seen not just as a technical problem but as a project in how to communicate scientific issues to the public. The students work together in this project. Whether they are engineering students or arts students, they need to develop a basic science literacy. Likewise, they develop ways to communicate their knowledge of the grid in accessible ways, so that members of the public can understand the implications of grid transformation for the economy, for civic life, for the natural environment, and for individuals' daily lives.

Brigham is an artist and educator affiliated with the University of Minnesota's College of Design. Imbertson teaches in the university's Department of Electrical and Computer Engineering. But, as they explain, interdisciplinary learning involves much more than having alternating lectures by people from two different disciplines. They follow a course framework of *contextual frames*, which includes: theories of systemic change; history of previous energy transitions; the climate crisis, which lends urgency to the energy transition; the physical, financial, and regulatory aspects of the grid; and, last but not least, *communications and humanities* frames through which people understand and experience the implications of the grid in their lives.

Throughout the course, students keep their own journals in written and visual form. Students draw on this work as they create a suite of public communications, including a public website. Thus they gain hands-on experience in communicating complex technical and policy issues in language and imagery that are accessible to a wider public. Brigham and Imbertson give us a detailed description of the course process and content, illuminated with examples of student drawings and writings.

The transformation of our electric grid during a move away from fossil fuels is a "wicked" problem, with implications for and from every component of society. There are many other wicked problems as well. So while the Power Systems Journey offers thought-provoking insights on education and communications about the electric grid, Brigham and Imbertson's model has clear relevance to interdisciplinary learning about many other issues as well.

Chapter 14 – Solar Commons: A "Commons Option" for the 21st Century
Kathryn Milun

Granting utilities monopoly powers over the production and distribution of electricity has created a new sort of serfdom in which all of us participate today. That is the startling thesis of Kathryn Milun, a legal anthropologist who interprets modern institutional behavior in terms of influences arising over the past millennium. But as utilities work behind the scenes to preserve a collapsing fossil-fuel economy, Milun and others are restoring a different institution from the past—trusts as a form of common ownership. They are seeking to create a solar economy based on trust agreements that will displace the monopoly power of utilities.

The Solar Commons Project is a prototype of a trust agreement that can provide solar power to neighborhoods, strengthen local institutions, and create a stream of revenue to help a low-income beneficiary invest in energy-saving equipment. Already a demonstration project has been completed in Tucson, Arizona to create a small-scale act of resistance to the dominant economy. The basic principle that drives the project is the concept of a solar commons—a legal framework that enables the value of the commons (solar radiation, in this case) to be captured and shared by multiple stakeholders. In legal frameworks rooted in European traditions, we owe this institutional capacity to recognize common property to medieval peasants who resisted aristocratic power and claimed rights-in-common to fish, game, and other sources of food and fuel required for sustenance.

A similar ongoing battle today against what Milun calls "modern managerial feudalism" involves recognizing the ways in which electric utilities abuse their power. In one of her classes, Milun teaches students to read regulatory documents to find out what the local utility, Minnesota Power, is doing that it does not mention on its website. Her students have learned that, while the utility tells the public about its "green energy" program, it leases its rights-of-way to pipelines carrying fossil fuels that have been extracted by fracking. In an open forum called Power Dialog, which students in her class host as a public service, they seek to expose the truth. When the press revealed that Minnesota Power belonged to the Utility Air Regulatory Group, an industry lobby that actively promotes fossil-fuel subsidies and the relaxation of environmental regulations, the utility withdrew its membership. Thus, public pressure can make a difference.

Milun understands, however, that fighting against modern managerial feudalism is not enough. Since utilities are not going to design a solar economy, it is up to ordinary citizens to do that. To gain active support from people who are accustomed to being passive consumers of energy, programs of resistance need to do more than provide factual information. They also need to appeal to emotions and aesthetic values. For that reason, the Solar Commons Research Team recognizes that artistic representation of the commons is just as important as legal instruments. In Tucson, the children in the Garden District, which is the beneficiary of the trust created by the Solar Commons Project, worked with local artists to design what they call the Solar Commons Game, a tile board game to teach the principles of common ownership. Milun envisions that similar artistic projects will serve as a basis on which beneficiary communities will be able to claim equitable ownership in future solar commons.

References

Barbet-Gros, Julie, and Jose Cuesta (2015). *Food Riots: From Definition to Operationalization.* Washington, DC: World Bank. https://www.world bank.org/content/dam/Worldbank/document/Poverty%20 documents/ Introduction%20Guide%20for%20the%20Food%20Riot%20Radar.pdf

Headey, Derek, and Shenggen Fan. (2010). *Reflections on the Global Food Crisis: How Did it Happen? How Has it Hurt? And How Can We Prevent the Next One?* Washington, DC: International Food Policy Research Institute. http://cdm15738.contentdm.oclc.org/utils/getfile/collection/p15738coll2/id/5724/ filename/5725.pdf

Nordhaus, William. (2007). *The Challenge of Global Warming: Economic Models and Environmental Policy.* New Haven, CT: Yale University (private manuscript). http://www.econ.yale.edu/~nordhaus/homepage/ OldWebFiles/DICEGAMS/dice_mss_072407_all.pdf

U.N. Department of Economics and Social Affairs (UN-DESA). (2019). *World Urbanization Prospects: The 2018 Revision* (ST/ESA/SER.A/420). New York: UN-DESA. https://population.un.org/wup/ Publications/Files/WUP2018- Report.pdf

Part I
The Major Challenges: Climate Change and Energy Descent

CHAPTER 2

Adaptation and Mitigation Amid the Consequences of Failure

Paul Cox and Stan Cox†*

Abstract. Societies once could choose between changing direction or dealing with climatic disaster; now it is necessary to do both at once. The best-laid plans for mitigation would be hard enough to fulfill in a stable climate, but they will be vastly harder in the climate chaos ahead. If simultaneous mitigation and adaptation are still achievable, such a difficult balance cannot also take on the burden of supporting unrestrained economic growth. The failing efforts so far have been dominated by a search for synergistic ways to mitigate, adapt, and grow economies at the same time, while wishing away the predictable trade-offs between these goals. Wealthy polluting countries have enforced this optimistic spirit in international climate debates, in part to counter the language of loss and damage, which they have seen as a direct challenge. Key to their effort has been a reframing of adaptation that flips the focus from the vulnerability of exposed populations to their resilience. However, the reality of implementing plans for resilience is running into problems, and those populations are instead taking up the banner of climate justice. Debt- and disaster-plagued Puerto Rico illustrates the failure of both adaptation and mitigation through growth and the promise of climate justice as a means to articulate other forms of balance.

Introduction

In October 2018, a year and a month after Puerto Rico lay devastated in the tracks of Hurricane Maria, and just two months after electricity was fully restored, the territorial Senate declared the island's will to decarbonize. The Energy Public Policy Act would require Puerto Rico to transition to 40 percent renewable energy within seven years, eliminate coal power outright within 10 years, and use nothing but renewable energy by 2050 (PREB 2019). Signed into law the following April, it was an extraordinary statement of commitment to climate change mitigation, come what may, from a highly vulnerable place. This was Puerto Rico, which had just suffered the worst storm in its recorded history, with uncounted thousands of deaths and $90 billion in economic wreckage (Milken Institute 2019; National Hurricane Center 2018). It was a territory with more than $100 billion of public debt, subjugated to a federally appointed austerity board. Anthropogenic climate change had already doubled or tripled the chance of more Maria-scale disasters in each coming year

*Anthropologist and freelance writer on climate and disaster. He is co-author, with his father Stan, of *How the World Breaks: Life in Catastrophe's Path, from the Caribbean to Siberia* (New Press 2016). Email: paul@tpaulcox.com

†Stan Cox is a research fellow in ecosphere studies at The Land Institute in Salina, Kansas. His most recent book is *The Green New Deal and Beyond: Ending the Climate Emergency While We Still Can* (City Lights 2020). Email: cox@landinstitute.org

(Keellings and Hernández Ayala 2019). Every resident knew that the president who controlled their fate was openly contemptuous of them and would be loath to provide the slightest federal assistance. This wounded and vulnerable island was responsible for only 0.38 percent of U.S. fossil-carbon emissions (US-EIA 2019). Nevertheless, with the Energy Public Policy Act, Puerto Rico became a national leader in the ambition to end the use of fossil fuels for generating power.

Puerto Rico's Act is part of a trend that spans the planet: some of the most vulnerable countries and territories are declaring some of the most drastic actions in the interest of mitigation. To say that their actions are inspiring (or shaming) the rest of the world is not to say that they are a solution. After all, their sacrifices alone are not going to stop the changes that are threatening their destruction. The storms are only going to worsen. How will Puerto Rico's transitioning power system hold up if disaster begins to strike repeatedly—then regularly? What if the island can expect no help at all in future disasters, not just because of an antagonistic federal administration, but because other parts of the United States are getting hit just as hard and federal emergency funds are stripped to the bone? How much stress can the island's ambitious green plans handle? For that matter, how much climate chaos can a national Green New Deal handle, or a global course of action?

Societies once could choose between changing direction or facing catastrophe; now it is necessary to do both at once. Future success will come amid the consequences of past and present failure, or not at all. There are many ideas for post-carbon transitions that would be challenging to pull off in a stable and forgiving climate, but they will be immensely harder in the climate that lies ahead. Here, we review the terms of this historic dilemma. The framing efforts taking place on every side of international climate debates have persistently codified the challenge as one of balancing mitigation and adaptation, putting vulnerable places like Puerto Rico in the position of carrying both burdens together. This framing has also been persistently optimistic, celebrating the idea of economically rewarding synergies while showing a distaste for potential trade-offs. Yet as the consequences pile up in vulnerable places, the economic case falls apart. The impetus for action in the time of consequences must be forceful; it must upset balance in the name of justice.

Solar Panels in the Wind

Hurricane Maria was an energy crisis. The storm dealt a heavy blow to Puerto Rico's housing and transportation, but it was the breakdown of the electric power system that became the overriding concern. Loss of power led, in turn, to loss of safe water supplies and access to medical care, accounting for a large share of the storm's high death toll (Kishore et al. 2018). The island's power plants and transmission and distribution systems had long been ill-maintained by the Puerto Rico Electric Power Authority. As the utility struggled to survive on decreasing revenue flows, service disruptions, including large-scale blackouts, became more frequent in the years leading up to Maria. The storm did not, in fact, inflict critical damage on the island's four large thermal power plants, but it did fell almost 850 transmission towers and 50,000 distribution poles, plunging the island into darkness. An estimated 80 percent of power lines went down. Even two months after the storm, 60 percent of Puerto Rico's residents remained without power. Restoration of 95 percent of service took more than six months, far longer than had been the case following any other U.S. hurricane since 2004 (Kwasinski et al. 2019).

In October 2019, Puerto Rico's government took steps toward funding the transformation of the island's electric power system, announcing a 10-year, $20 billion plan to strengthen the still-fragile grid by putting in buried lines and building aboveground transmission and distribution lines that can withstand winds of 250 km/hr. The network would incorporate eight smaller grids, each of which could function independently if others go down. This classic adaptation effort was shadowed by a nagging worry that future big storms might strike before the decade-long project is complete. Ottmar Chávez, director of Puerto Rico's Central Office for Reconstruction, Recovery and Resiliency, told the press: "We're not where we would like to be" (AP 2019). It turned out to be a magnitude-6.4 offshore earthquake in January 2020 that next brought down the grid, revealing just how unpredictable the island's perilous future is going to be. The feared tsunami did not materialize, and that was especially fortunate for the people of Puerto Rico's south coast. Approximately half of the island's emergency sirens, crucial elements of disaster adaptation, had been knocked out of service by Maria and had not been repaired. The government's emergency management commissioner Carlos Acevedo told the *New York Times* that the sirens were still down "because insurance companies denied municipalities' insurance claims" (Ayala et al. 2020).

Researchers at the University of Puerto Rico Mayagüez have developed much more decentralized plans under which clusters of approximately 10 households each would form throughout the island, each group having its own solar photovoltaic generating system with battery storage. These "microgrids" would be integrated with the main power grid, but in the event of any interruption of the main power supply, the microgrids would each operate in isolation (O'Neill-Carrillo and Irizarry-Rivera 2019). Before Maria, Puerto Rico was generating 2 percent of its electricity from wind and solar sources. In the first year and a half of the recovery, the number of rooftop solar installations doubled. Once in place, decentralized solar and wind generation with a more robust, compartmentalized grid would be less vulnerable to a Maria-scale event than the old system. Damage is nevertheless to be expected. Maria inflicted serious harm on solar and wind installations in several locations (Kwasinski et al. 2019). Widespread rooftop solar generation, as envisioned in microgrid planning, will be highly vulnerable unless both the equipment and the roofs on which it is installed are capable of withstanding winds at least as strong as Maria's.

It is estimated that 230,000 Puerto Rican residences were damaged by Maria, and countless roofs throughout the island were damaged or lost in the storm (Hinojosa and Meléndez 2018). The U.S. Federal Emergency Management Agency (FEMA) and the U.S. Army together distributed approximately 185,000 roof tarps of various kinds, and those were not enough to meet demand (Quiñones 2019). The rebuilding effort must ensure that all construction meets rigorous code requirements and that safe, affordable housing becomes available to all who still live in homes that are not constructed to code.

While such an effort would be an enormous step forward in adaptation terms, a far more dramatic escalation in rooftop solar panels and other non-carbon sources would be necessary to achieve 40 percent renewable electricity by 2025 and the elimination of fossil fuels by 2050, as called for in the mitigation-oriented Puerto Rico Energy Public Policy Act. P. J. Wilson, a solar industry spokesperson, told reporters in 2019: "I don't think anybody has a clear answer for exactly how to get there" (Gupta 2019). Wilson was speaking about Puerto Rico, but his statement could stand for the whole global question of how sufficiently deep mitigation and sufficiently rapid adaptation will "get there," simultaneously and under intense pressure from the crises of the present.

The Ideological Life of Adaptation and Mitigation

The distinction between climate change mitigation actions and adaptation actions is an old one, and the effort to articulate a balance between the two has multiple decades behind it, too. All of those years of discussion could have been about confronting the kinds of severe futures that are now arriving, as they have sharpened in severity with each passing year. Instead, there has been a long history of crafting inventive language to wish it all away. The rhetorical proving ground for that is the annual Conference of Parties (COP) to the U.N. Framework Convention on Climate Change (UNFCCC).

The meaning of mitigation has not changed much; the meaning of adaptation has. There was a time, through the 1990s and a bit beyond, when the word adaptation was regarded as a flag of surrender—or at least a moral hazard that would license the worst of instincts. Al Gore, for one, made this charge in his 1992 book *Earth in the Balance*. Years before his "inconvenient truth," Gore (1992) derided adaptation as an "imprudent hope":

> Believing that we can adapt to just about anything is ultimately a kind of laziness, an arrogant faith in our ability to react in time to save our skin. ... In my view this confidence in our quick reflexes is badly misplaced.*

Kates (2000) identified two opposing biases that together worked against putting adaptation on the agenda in the 1990s. His name for Gore's stance was the "limitationist" bias, the suspicion of those who wanted to keep limitation of emissions on the front page. The other he identified as an "adaptationist" bias. Kates (2000) wrote:

> Many "adaptationists" see no need to study adaptation in any special way, simply trusting the invisible hand of either natural selection or market forces to encourage adaptation.

They adopted that view without recognizing the likely social costs or the original message from natural selection: that adaptability is defined by its limits. Adaptationism was what Gore was critiquing when he expressed doubt about "confidence in our quick reflexes." Researchers in 1992 were inclined to regard adaptation as a sort of ingrained reflex that would kick off in response to the stimulus of climate change. The whole idea was, after all, freshly transplanted from the sciences of biology and ecology. Other species adapted to environmental change without anyone writing an international convention for them. At least they sometimes adapted. Other times, species just went extinct. The relevant policy questions were therefore not about how to adapt, but about identifying the limits of societal adaptation, and then slowing down greenhouse-gas emissions to keep the planet's warming within those red lines. It was this tricky business of emissions that was the sole and proper remit of the freshly inked UNFCCC. If it went well, nobody would have to adapt at all (Schipper 2006; Kongsager 2018).

Of these early factions, the adaptationists won. Parties who wanted to ignore limitation (which is now almost exclusively referred to under the broader term mitigation) found a safe subject in adaptation, and those who preferred to treat adaptation as an emergent property found ample opportunities to do so as the discourse evolved. This all became clear on the day in 2001 when George W. Bush pulled the United States out of the Kyoto Protocol. The subsequent Third National Communication to the UNFCCC—the report in which the United States was to lay out a vision that would somehow place it ahead of the Kyoto Protocol it had just abandoned—hinged on a particularly red-blooded-American style of adaptation language. Adaptation would be a big job, but it would be better for America than the onerous bonds of enforced mitigation. Besides, Americans were good at it. As the U.S. State Department (2002: 88–89) explained in the report:

> In considering the potential impacts of climate change, however, it is also important to recognize that U.S. climate conditions vary from the cold of an Alaskan winter to the heat of a Texas summer, and from the year-round near-constancy of temperatures in Hawaii to the strong variations in North Dakota. Across this very wide range of climate conditions and seasonal variation, American ingenuity and resources have enabled communities and businesses to develop, although particular economic sectors in particular regions can experience losses and disruptions from extreme conditions of various

* This early suspicion around adaptation can still be observed surrounding some of today's more faith-based techno-solutions, like geo-engineering and carbon capture and storage—and in backlash against the resilience paradigm, described below.

> types. … This adaptation to environmental variations and extremes has been accomplished because the public and private sectors have applied technological change and knowledge about fluctuating climate to implement a broad series of steps that have enhanced resilience and reduced vulnerability. For example, these steps have ranged from better design and construction of buildings and communities to greater availability of heating in winter and cooling in summer, and from better warnings about extreme events to advances in public health care. Because of this increasing resilience to climate variations and relative success in adapting to the modest changes in climate that were observed during the 20th century, information about likely future climate changes and continuing efforts to plan for and adapt to these changes are likely to prove useful in minimizing future impacts and preparing to take advantage of the changing conditions.

This report is a particularly interesting example because it by no means played coy about climate change or its impacts. For example, the U.S. State Department (2002: 110) correctly predicted this for Puerto Rico, the Southeast Atlantic Coast, and U.S. Virgin Islands:

> Rising sea level and higher storm surges are likely to cause loss of many coastal ecosystems that now provide an important buffer for coastal development against the impacts of storms. Currently and newly exposed communities are more likely to suffer damage from the increasing intensity of storms.

According to Bush doctrine, economic growth could be harnessed to solve any such problems and reach for the advantages beyond. Adaptation seemed destined for such a laissez-faire approach because, whereas mitigation is a long-lasting and global undertaking, adaptation is local and immediate. Successful mitigating countries can worry about others free-riding in their shared atmosphere (the enduring American paranoia), but adaptation appears, on the surface, more aligned to the simple self-interest of those who adapt (Frey and Gasbarro 2019; Biesbroek et al. 2009).* As Tol (2005) observed: "Local mitigation is often defended under the slogan 'think global, act local'; the equivalent slogan for adaptation would be 'think local, act local,' [which] really is not much of a slogan."

But slogan or no slogan, all of this was set to change. Schipper (2006) observed how the meaning of the term "adaptation" changed for political reasons:

> Within the policy context of negotiations and the UNFCCC, adaptation has gone from being understood as a spontaneous adjustment that would determine the limits of how much climate change could be tolerated, and hence how much mitigation was necessary, to being seen as a fundamental policy strategy to promote the attainment of sustainable development.

Indeed, the word that entered the UNFCCC process as a descriptive, ecological concept had, by the mid-2000s, "practically become a synonym for development" (Schipper 2006). What happened? The Bush administration's open rebellion was part of the story, and so was a whole lot of other bad news. Researchers came to understand that with or without American cooperation, mitigation simply was not happening fast enough to make adaptation easy or even possible, let alone automatic (Tol 2005; Anderson and Bowes 2008). Discussions about adaptation became discussions about its alarmingly mounting costs and then about funding

* In one example, Bayramoglu et al. (2018) analyzed this in game-theory terms as a public-good (mitigation) versus private-good (adaptation) problem, and found no reason to fear "crowding out" of one by the other.

those costs in poor countries that could not bear them alone.* It did not stop with poor countries, either; extreme weather events—each one seemingly bearing clearer fingerprints of anthropogenic climate change than the last—hit rich countries, too, with astounding damages. Hurricane Sandy's $70 billion strike on the U.S. East Coast in 2012 closed the chapter for good on adaptation as a wholly developing-world challenge, a local challenge, a cheap challenge, or a challenge that would solve itself through the sum total of simple human pluck (Denton et al. 2014; Kongsager 2018).† With disaster in the air, mitigation and adaptation became fixed for good as a linguistic duo—the yin and yang, the offense and defense of climate action. The balancing act began in earnest.

The most basic form of relationship between adaptation and mitigation was easy to see. The Intergovernmental Panel on Climate Change (IPCC) laid it out in a single sentence in its very first Assessment Report in 1992: "For example, the more net emissions are reduced and the rate of climate change potentially slowed, the easier it would be to adapt" (IPCC 1992). Terminology proliferated from this common-sense beginning. Landauer et al. (2015) collected a long list of words from papers published between 2005 and 2013: in neutral language, the dance of adaptation and mitigation was one of interrelationship, interaction, inter-linkage, integration, response capacity, trade-off, or substitutability. With a more positive outlook, the dance promised synergy, balancing, or harmonization. On bad days there was conflict, trade-off, or negative synergy (Landauer et al. 2015). (On the double-counting of "trade-off" in the neutral and negative columns, more below.) Picking from this list, "substitutability" was a popular starting point in the 1990s and 2000s. This formalizes the IPCC's 1992 statement in economic terms; add mitigation, and you can subtract some adaptation. More controversially, add some adaptation and subtract mitigation. Working with this concept brought in the field of global cost-benefit analysis. Tol (2005) described the question in this way: "If the world were ruled by a benevolent dictator, a philosopher-queen who is in control of the entire planet and is up to speed with the latest scientific insights, what would she do about climate change?"‡

By 2007, the philosopher-queen had not yet arrived, and everything was getting worse. The chapter by Klein et al. (2007: 747, 748) in the IPCC's Fourth Assessment Report on "inter-relationships between adaptation and mitigation" framed the issue in business terms:

> It is therefore no longer a question of whether to mitigate climate change or to adapt to it. Both adaptation and mitigation are now essential in reducing the expected impacts of climate change on humans and their environment. ... Creating synergies between adaptation and mitigation can increase the cost-effectiveness of actions and make them more attractive to stakeholders, including potential funding agencies (medium confidence).

That medium confidence came with a long list of caveats.

> However, such synergies provide no guarantee that resources are used in the most efficient

* Schipper (2006) traces this back to COP6 President Jan Pronk in 2000, who grouped adaptation on the negotiating table together with technology transfer, capacity-building, and funding, branding it a developing-country issue.

† For an account of adaptation and resilience discourses in the response to Hurricane Sandy, see Cox and Cox (2016).

‡ Tol identifies a number of influential 1990s studies with this approach, including his own: Manne et al. (1995); Nordhaus (1991, 1993); Peck and Teisberg (1992); Tol (1999). Nordhaus, the Nobel-Prize-decorated master of this analysis, famously argued with it that 4.5°C of global warming could be macroeconomically bearable, shaving only 2-4 percent off per-capita GDP.

> manner when seeking to reduce the risks to climate change. In addition, the absence of a relevant knowledge base and of human, institutional and organizational capacity can limit the ability to create synergies. Opportunities for synergies are greater in some sectors (e.g., agriculture and forestry, buildings and urban infrastructure) but are limited in others (e.g., coastal systems, energy, health). A lack of both conceptual and empirical information that explicitly considers both adaptation and mitigation makes it difficult to assess the need for and potential of synergies in climate policy.

The uncertainties did not slow the ascendancy of the positive notion of synergies. Today, smart, synergistic, pro-development plans that aim for both mitigation and adaptation are almost a prerequisite for participating in climate action (or at least accessing funding). The UNFCCC Adaptation Fund, originally set up back in 2001, finally went live in 2007. In 2010 it was joined by the Green Development Fund, which attempts to provide balanced funding to both adaptation and mitigation in developing countries. The year 2010 also saw the launch of a U.N. Global Adaptation Network for knowledge sharing and collaboration. The IPCC Fifth Assessment Report put an unprecedented focus on the adaptation-mitigation balance (IPCC 2015).* Later, Article 7 of the Paris Agreement codified the aim of adaptation in support of sustainable development:

> Parties hereby establish the global goal on adaptation of enhancing adaptive capacity, strengthening resilience and reducing vulnerability to climate change, with a view to contributing to sustainable development and ensuring an adequate adaptation response in the context of the global temperature goal. (United Nations 2015: 9)

Countries committed to develop national adaptation plans and report them to the United Nations. The plans were to be integrated with their mitigation plans. There has been an ongoing hunt for real-world examples of synergy in action, and some exist: a waste-to-compost project in Bangladesh (Ayers and Huq 2009, cited in Suckall et al. 2015), water-saving irrigation systems in China (Denton et al. 2014), and pilot programs in "climate-smart agriculture," an umbrella term for a suite of farming practices like minimal tillage and agro-forestry (FAO 2009, cited in Suckall et al. 2015).

Yet synergy was never really an empirical concept. It has been propelled less by real-world experiences than by a highly attractive idea about economic development. Klein et al. (2007: 767) made this case in their chapter for the IPCC:

> Response capacity is often limited by a lack of resources, poor institutions and inadequate infrastructure, among other factors that are typically the focus of development assistance. People's vulnerability to climate change can therefore be reduced not only by mitigating greenhouse-gas emissions or by adapting to the impacts of climate change, but also by development aimed at improving the living conditions and access to resources of those experiencing the impacts, as this will enhance their response capacity.

No longer simply paired in synergy, adaptation and mitigation are now bundled up in promises like "climate compatible development" and "green growth," complete package deals with highly speculative benefits (Suckall et al. 2015; Kongsager 2018).

> [D]uring the last decades, the notion of adaptation has evolved in the direction of making societies more robust and flexible in general, which will facilitate the robustness to climate change and variability, but also to socio-economic

* Of the report's four topics, see Topic 3, Future Pathways for Adaption, Mitigation and Sustainable Development, and Topic 4, Adaptation and Mitigation.

> changes, many of which are more rapid than global warming. … [T]he overlap with development becomes very natural, as the two have many cross-cutting issues that would contribute to both objectives, for instance, poverty reduction and food security. This involvement with development has made the goals of adaptation less clear-cut, as the actions consist of a wide palette of arrangements, for example, agricultural and land tenure policies, infrastructure, irrigation systems, and livelihood diversification programs. (Kongsager 2018: 7)

It is very telling that these synergistic pitches for mitigation, adaptation, and development are often described as "win-win," "win-win-win," "triple win," or even "green-win" opportunities (Denton et al. 2014; Suckall et al. 2015; Thornton et al. 2019).* This reveals the influence of other triple-win narratives that have held sway in the same era, promising to balance various global needs, and always assuming steady economic growth would be one of them. The narratives have been expressed in many ways, but the original proponent, John Elkington (1994), made as clear a statement as any:

> In contrast to the anti-industry, anti-profit, and anti-growth orientation of much early environmentalism, it has become increasingly clear that business must play a central role in achieving the goals of sustainable development strategies.

To this end, Elkington (1994) considered "some of the ways in which business is now developing new 'win-win-win' strategies … to simultaneously benefit the company, its customers, and the environment." This was a tailor-made model for the age of corporate-backed sustainable development, and its trinitarian form became a template for other difficult planning efforts. One was the effort to balance simultaneous mitigation, adaptation, and development—despite very limited examples showing these kinds of hat-tricks being accomplished in practice.

The Dreary World of Trade-Offs

Above all, the fixation on synergies and triple wins is about staying positive in the face of projections that should, by all rights, trigger fear and despair. With these positive ideals leading the way, acknowledging the existence of possible trade-offs is a betrayal of the spirit of winning. This does not have to be the case; trade-off is basically a neutral word, describing a balance found through compromise. In the context of allocating climate funding at a national or international level, this may simply be a budgetary compromise. But in some arenas, trade-off has become the major antonym of synergy and a synonym of conflict (Landauer et al. 2015).

If synergy and trade-off are antonyms, then they are opposite in the sense that synergy is a rare and precious phenomenon in climate action, while trade-offs are drearily common:

> Some climate measures have no complementarity or synergy, maybe even trade-offs, but if they are essential, they have to be implemented nevertheless, and disfavoring these measures in the pursuit of linking adaptation and mitigation should be avoided. (Kongsager 2018: 13)

After all, preventing climate catastrophe was never going to be about the easy choices.

Kongsager was unsurprised when his review of studies revealed a tangle of positive, neutral, and negative effects. For the IPCC's Fifth Assessment Report, Denton et al. (2014) found a similarly

* The search for win-win outcomes was still alive and well in 2019 at the "Global Conference on Strengthening Synergies between the Paris Agreement on Climate Change and the 2030 Agenda for Sustainable Development," which revolved around positive links between climate-related nationally determined contributions to the UNFCCC and individual Sustainable Development Goals. According to the outcome statement, the most apparent links were to the goals on food, water, energy, cities, and life on land (UN-DESA 2019).

messy story in the Clean Development Mechanism (CDM), a Kyoto Protocol mechanism intended to fund projects with wins for both emissions reduction and development (adaptation was not included). An indicative study of 16 CDM projects showed that they could meet 72 percent of their mitigation goals but fewer than 1 percent might contribute to sustainable development, and trade-offs were amply evident (Denton et al. 2014; Sutter and Parreño 2007). More recently, Frey and Gasbarro (2019) collected examples from agriculture, energy, construction, and other sectors. The trade-offs they identify all follow the theme of adaptation actions that come with high energy bills: coastal protection infrastructure, air conditioning, synthetic fertilizers, irrigation, wastewater treatment and reuse, deep-well pumping, desalination, and even artificial snowmaking. Such measures will incur mitigation trade-offs so long as fossil fuels are powering them. This complication is well recognized. The trade-offs were already discussed in the chapter of the IPCC report by Klein et al. (2007: 760):

> [M]any effects of adaptation on greenhouse-gas emissions and their mitigation (energy use, land conversion, agronomic techniques such as an increased use of fertilizers and pesticides, water storage and diversion, coastal protection) have been known for a long time.

Most adaptation assessments at the time did not take emission consequences into account, but that could perhaps be excused, wrote Klein et al. (2007: 760): "[T]he emissions generated by most adaptation activities are only small fractions of total emissions, even if emissions will decline in the future as a result of climate-protection policies."

Does that conclusion still hold up? Perhaps it did so long as the balancing act was between local, targeted adaptation measures and global mitigation needs. But it became highly debatable once development, wholesale, became part of the act. When development is treated as one of the winners in triple-win ambitions or as a prerequisite for adaptation—or even another word for adaptation—then the trade-offs become a serious question indeed. At this point it is fundamentally a question about how much economic growth can be sustained and expanded within the planet's limits, and that is the biggest question of all.

Profit and Damage

Governments of the Global North have long avoided taking effective action on climate precisely because they fear that doing so would jeopardize economic growth. This fear is fed by economists' use of integrated assessment models to estimate the social cost of carbon and to conduct global cost-benefit analyses. The exercise is aimed not at learning how to halt greenhouse warming but at determining how much warming governments will need to accept in order to sustain economic growth (Nordhaus 2018). Growth is the non-negotiable goal; it is acknowledged that greenhouse warming should also be curbed, but only to the extent that GDP growth can be protected by improving efficiency and fully "decoupling" growth from greenhouse emissions (Fischer-Kowalski et al. 2011). Decoupling, unfortunately, is a mirage. No national economy has yet managed to achieve sustained economic growth along with sustained decreases in consumption of material resources and in production of greenhouse emissions and other wastes (York and McGee 2017; Hickel and Kallis 2019; Ward et al. 2016; Parrique et al. 2019; Knight and Schor 2014). The building of wealthier, faster-growing economies in some parts of the world has increased the number and strength of hazards that threaten communities throughout the world, and the pursuit of triple wins through growth in the Global North will likewise continue to fuel hazard creation, making adaptation even more difficult. The reason is simple: simultaneous pursuit of mitigation, adaptation, and economic growth will require large inputs of energy and other resources. Most strategies rely on the assumption of rapid increases in efficiency; unhappily, growth soon undermines such efficiency gains (Ward et al. 2016). Improvements in the quantity of economic output per unit of resource input may impress at first, but they proceed asymptotically, necessarily slowing and eventually ceasing as they bump up against physical limits. At some point, therefore, as exponential economic growth proceeds, the material and energy resources required to support that growth will inevitably increase. Ward et al. (2016) conclude that "GDP ultimately cannot plausibly be decoupled from growth in material and energy use, demonstrating categorically that GDP growth cannot be sustained indefinitely." Decoupling is just another offering to the insatiable appetite for optimism in a time of crisis and consequences.

In the climate debates of the UNFCCC, optimism is, among other things, a buffer built up by polluting countries against the litigious language of loss and damage. The loss and damage fight is as old as the UNFCCC itself, with the phrase first coming on the table as an intervention by the Alliance of Small Island States in 1991. The plight of disappearing island states illustrates the concept in high contrast: if mitigation is insufficient, there are some consequences to which these countries simply cannot adapt. The possibilities that lie beyond both mitigation and adaptation are catastrophic damage and tragic, permanent loss. Before long, the loss and damage phrase became associated with an insistence on polluters' liability and calls for compensation; it has been a signature of vulnerable developing countries, and a quick way to make U.S. negotiators try to change the subject. Nongovernmental organizations have joined vulnerable countries in keeping the discourse going. WWF-UK published one particularly tough and influential discussion paper in 2008, titled "Beyond Adaptation: The Legal Duty to Pay Compensation for Climate Change Damage" (Verheyen and Roderick 2008). This made the case that an orderly agreement on loss and damage was the only way for polluting countries to prevent a raft of messy individual lawsuits that was on its way in the near future. This raft has since begun to land, with public health cases being brought against fossil-fuel companies and an equal-protection lawsuit on behalf of children against the U.S. government, among others (Wallace-Wells 2019: 149–151). It could get much worse as polluters lose their first line of defense: attribution uncertainty. Attribution science is becoming an ever more incisive tool for assigning responsibility for impacts, including very specific impacts like hurricanes. The limits of this science are not clear, and as it improves, liability may creep up on the responsible from all sides (Mace and Verheyen 2016).

The recurring alternative to the liability-and-compensation frame has been a risk-management-and-insurance frame, much preferred by the United States and other major polluting countries. Although risk-management and insurance foster an atmosphere of security, they are evidently limited in their application to climate change loss and damage (Adelman 2016). Furthermore, the United States has gone beyond wrangling over the right tools for dealing with loss and damage to disputing the very meaning of that phrase: U.S. negotiators prefer not to see loss and damage as that which lies beyond adaptation, but as just another way of talking about adaptation. The optimist's starting point is that adaptation is *always* possible; loss and damage is not an inevitability of climate change, but a failure to adapt as quickly, thoroughly, and creatively as possible. To the optimist, then, failure lies with the countries and individuals that do not adapt, not with any polluters.

Vanhala and Hestbæk (2016) have documented these opposing frames (liability and compensation vs. risk management and insurance), and how, starting in 2008, they softened into a productive ambiguity that allowed both sides to feel like loss and damage meant whatever they wanted. This ambiguity presided over the formation, in 2013, of the Warsaw International Mechanism for Loss and Damage Associated with Climate Change Impacts, and the inclusion, in 2015, of an article on loss and damage in the Paris Agreement. But the passage came with a significant rider: "Article 8 of the Agreement does not involve or provide a basis for any liability and compensation." That particular frame was now out the window—at least so long as the United States remained in the

Agreement.* Meanwhile, the question of whether loss and damage is something beyond adaptation, or just another adaptation issue, has also drifted toward the latter interpretation. In 2019, at the generally inconclusive COP26 in Madrid, a review of the Warsaw International Mechanism did not produce an outcome. The parties did, however, "[reaffirm] the role of the Warsaw International Mechanism in promoting the implementation of approaches to avert, minimize and address loss and damage associated with climate change impacts in a comprehensive, integrated and coherent manner" (UNFCCC 2020). The key words "avert" and "minimize," before addressing loss and damage, put the mechanism in adaptation territory; their inclusion was motivated by a pragmatic hope among vulnerable countries that this might be a route to accessing streams of *adaptation* finance—as the prospects for loss and damage finance ever coming forth were looking dim.†

Can Societies Really Adapt to Anything?

Thanks to human-induced greenhouse warming, Earth's average atmospheric temperature today is about 1.2°C (2.2°F) higher than it was in the pre–fossil-fuel era. The IPCC reported in 2018 that if warming is allowed to surpass 1.5°C, the world will risk widespread ecological destruction and human suffering. To keep temperatures below that limit, it concluded, global greenhouse emissions will have to be cut almost in half before 2030, and net-zero emissions will have to be achieved by 2050 (IPCC 2018). The report describes devastating impacts that will be risked if warming is allowed to rise past 2°C: irreversible loss of the Greenland and West Antarctic ice sheets (which would raise sea levels by one to two meters); loss of 25 to 50 percent of all permafrost, which will release, irreversibly, a surge of stored carbon, further warming the atmosphere; an acceleration of species extinction, especially in marine and coastal ecosystems; and loss of all coral reefs worldwide. Forest dieback will accelerate because of storms, wildfires, and pest outbreaks. The number of people exposed to frequent severe heat waves will rise to 1.7 billion. The number of people living in the midst of severe habitat degradation will increase eightfold, to 680 million, and the number of farmers hit with crop failure will see a tenfold increase. The report projects that food shortages triggered by global warming will dramatically raise the rate of childhood undernutrition, stunting, and mortality, with Asia and Africa suffering the most. *Anopheles* and *Aedes* mosquitoes will expand their ranges to the north and south, extending the risk of malaria, dengue fever, chikungunya, yellow fever, and Zika. These and other disruptions will lead to massive waves of human migration. The IPCC (2018) projects that human conflict will spread as large-scale movements occur:

> Tropical populations may have to move distances greater than 1,000 km if global mean temperature rises by 2° … A disproportionately rapid evacuation from the tropics could lead to a concentration of population in tropical margins and the subtropics, where population densities could increase by 300 percent or more. …

* The United States also pushed in Madrid to keep the Warsaw International Mechanism under the Paris Agreement, which the United States was in the process of leaving, rather than under the whole UNFCCC, which the United States is not leaving (Timperley 2019).

† UNFCCC (2019) and Hirsch (2019) were prepared before COP25 and advised vulnerable countries to seek funding in this way. The interest was answered from the other side when the Green Climate Fund's executive director announced in Madrid that the Fund would expand its support to certain kinds of actions under this broad loss and damage heading that also constitute adaptation—such as "early warning systems, weather insurance or infrastructure resilient to climate stresses." As the Paris Agreement's major funding mechanism, the Green Climate Fund only has a mandate to support mitigation and adaptation, with 50 percent of its funding aimed at each (Rowling 2019).

> Populations at disproportionately higher risk of adverse consequences ... include disadvantaged and vulnerable populations, some indigenous peoples, and local communities dependent on agricultural or coastal livelihoods.

If 2°C of warming is reached despite best efforts, all is not lost—yet—but further warming must be avoided at all costs. Published in 2007 and based on the scientific literature of the time, Lynas's (2007) book *Six Degrees* argued that warming beyond 3°C would bring an end to what would still be left of human civilization. Wallace-Wells (2017, 2019) has presented further horrific possibilities. At 2.5°C, drought could plunge the world into shortages of fresh water and food, with famine becoming common. With 3°C, many of the world's major cities would eventually go entirely underwater, along with 97 percent of Florida and Delaware, and more than half of Louisiana, New Jersey, South Carolina, Rhode Island, and Maryland. Arkansas and Vermont would have seacoasts. At 4°C, land area burned annually by wildfires in the western United States could increase from today's maximum of 4 million hectares to an appalling 64 million hectares. Already, hundreds of thousands around the world die annually from inhaling the smoke of wildfires; with further warming, millions could die every year. If greenhouse emissions are not curbed, ozone pollution will increase to the point that approximately one-fourth of the world's population will breathe air that exceeds the WHO "safe" level. The oceans' current death spiral will accelerate. Melting of Arctic ice could potentially release the smallpox and bubonic plague pathogens, or even the strain of influenza virus that killed 50 million people worldwide in 1918 and 1919.

An array of 17 scientists sharply criticized Wallace-Wells' (2017) *New York* magazine article "The Uninhabitable Earth" as "alarmist." Wallace-Wells, they wrote, exaggerated the projected impacts of greenhouse warming and portrayed low-probability events as being likely (Climate Feedback 2017). However, the article and book served to warn the general public that the possible global and local consequences of continued greenhouse-gas production, even those with low probability, are so dreadful that humanity cannot take the risk (Guenther 2017). Australia's horrific bushfire emergency of 2019–2020 showed that the nightmare future may be arriving sooner than even Wallace-Wells imagined. Citing the increasing risk of so-called tipping points, such as landscape-transforming megafires, the loss of the Amazon rainforest, or the collapse of the West Antarctic ice sheet, Lenton et al. (2019) have emphasized the inestimable urgency of reining in emissions, even if 1.5°C warming is racing into sight. "In our view, the clearest emergency would be if we were approaching a global cascade of tipping points" that could result in a "global tipping point" and runaway warming, they wrote. Lenton et al. conclude:

> We argue that the intervention time left to prevent tipping could already have shrunk towards zero, whereas the reaction time to achieve net zero emissions is 30 years at best. Hence we might already have lost control of whether tipping happens. A saving grace is that the rate at which damage accumulates from tipping—and hence the risk posed—could still be under our control to some extent.

While humanity has full control over the rate of carbon emissions from fossil fuels and can conceivably reduce that rate to zero, any control humanity may have over the rate of damage accumulation may be slipping away. For example, in 2020 the U.K. Meteorological Office projected that the fires then raging in Australia would contribute significantly to one of the largest annual increases in atmospheric CO_2 concentration ever recorded (Green 2020). Those emissions, of course, would help generate more hot, dry conditions of the sort that were fostering such catastrophic fires in the first place. This and other feedback loops will narrow the window for both mitigation and adaptation, eventually to a pinprick. As vulnerable populations around the world face runaway wildfires, storms, floods, droughts, and heat waves, they will be tasked with repairing or rebuilding significant portions of their economy and infrastructure, repeatedly. It will not be a choice between adaptation, mitigation, or development; it will merely be a choice between what to save and what to give up.

Blessed Are the Resilient

Balanced on the rim of these profound dangers, the phrase "loss and damage" sounds not alarmist but wholly insufficient. How, at this juncture, is it possible to speak of humanity's vulnerabilities to such severe, spiraling damage and permanent loss as merely adaptation issues to iron out? How can the likelihood of mass suffering not itself be the core of the issue of balancing mitigation and adaptation? There is, of course, a history and a politics to the blindness. Starting in the early 2000s, optimistic polluting nations vigorously steered discussions away from the vulnerabilities associated with climate change and other disasters, seeking a counter-discourse to define success in adaptation. It emerged in the idea of resilience. Over the past two decades, the term resilience has come to be deployed seemingly everywhere in the policy world, with a wide variety of intended meanings (Olsson et al. 2015; Ruszczyk 2019). The term had been used for decades in the discipline of systems ecology, where it signifies an intrinsic property of natural systems (Walker and Cooper 2011; Grove 2018). But when it is invoked in the context of communities' responses to climate change or other disasters, resilience appears to slip back and forth between signifying, on the one hand, an inherent capacity of social or social-ecological systems to respond to disturbances and, on the other hand, a goal toward which societies must aspire if they are to navigate an increasingly hazardous world—what Grove (2018) calls a "will to design." (See also Olsson et al. 2015.) Both of these understandings play on a central idea of resilience that was repurposed from ecology: that systemic adaptability is achieved through smaller-scale fragility and feedback. Anderies et al. (2013) of the Resilience Alliance have called this the concept's "modularity," explaining that "transformation at one scale in a system, which may be related to an inherent fragility in a system module, is a necessary part of maintaining resilience at other scales in the system." Here lies the appeal: periodic catastrophe in one locality or another might just be a sign that adaptation is happening. Each extreme event will allow society as a whole to learn, respond, and build back better. Resilience therefore goes a step beyond earlier forms of adaptationism, mainstreaming the idea that disaster is not just a part of adaptation but its driving force.

In 2019, the Trump administration officially withdrew the United States from the Paris Agreement, displaying an optimism rooted in resilience thinking. Secretary of State Mike Pompeo (2019) explained that the United States would continue to develop its capacity to adapt, while other nations would be left to fend for themselves:

> We will continue to work with our global partners to enhance resilience to the impacts of climate change and prepare for and respond to natural disasters. ... [W]e will continue to offer a realistic and pragmatic model—backed by a record of real-world results—showing innovation and open markets lead to greater prosperity, fewer emissions, and more secure sources of energy.

At the following World Economic Forum, President Donald Trump (2020) stood and railed against "prophets of doom" like Greta Thunberg, who sat in the audience awaiting her turn to speak:

> In America, we understand what the pessimists refuse to see: that a growing and vibrant market economy focused on the future lifts the human spirit and excites creativity strong enough to overcome any challenge—any challenge by far.

Flying in the face of a climate panic that had gripped much of the rest of the Forum (WEF 2020), it was an expression of the unconditional faith that buoys the doctrine of resilience, and a glimpse of the kind of governmentality that could answer the devastation of Puerto Rico with a shrug.

Braggadocio aside, the ubiquity of resilience as a concept can only be sustained if it can be operationalized, which is to say if countries, donors, and international institutions can track it and set targets for their resilience-building projects. Such a need implies a set of resilience indicators or even something like a Human Resilience Index. This may turn out to be the undoing of the resilience era; its endlessly modular indefinability, threatening always to slip into a mélange of buzzwords, has caused some exhaustion in the development community. Ruszczyk (2019) has done a recent review of this area of work, including her own fieldwork in Nepal, and found that ambivalence is running high. Among the studies she reviewed, Schipper and Langston's (2015) comparison of 17 resilience measurement frameworks concluded that "universal indicators cannot exist"; Levine's (2014) overview of the five major approaches finds that "[t]he attempt to find the perfect resilience index is not so much a difficult quest as a search for a holy grail"; and Mochizuki et al.'s (2018) investigation of community resilience measurement efforts underlined the point that a resilience indicator cannot be both universal and always good. In reality, many undesirable properties of a system are resilient too, bringing resilience measurement back to the kind of normative judgments (what should be resilient to what?) that the discourse generally disavows. Ruszczyk (2019) concludes:

> This is a damning summary of the state of resilience thinking among donors and practitioners and of efforts to operationalize the concept. While the drive to operationalize resilience may be of some value to donors and practitioners, it does not appear to offer much in the way of significance to people who live with and manage risk in daily life or when a disaster unfolds.

All of this might sound like a technical issue for the big development donors to figure out, but it is a real problem; after all, resilience-building is supposed to be the path to adaptation, so if resilience cannot be measured, how can anyone know if they are adapting?

Climate Justice: The Rogue Frame

Ignored in all of this, still, are the inordinate suffering and uncompensated labor of resilient people, and their lack of power to choose how adaptation-through-resilience is defined. These are all non-issues in the study of natural systems where resilience was first modeled. But in the human world, resilience is a global shadow economy of hard work: anticipating disaster, surviving disaster, recovering from damage, mourning loss, piecing together new livelihoods, caring for others, making do with less and less. This work is what makes global capitalism resilient and adaptable—and what lets it stay "focused on the future," to use Trump's phrase, not on the demands of mitigation. Two leading critics of the resilience discourse, Evans and Reid (2013), put it like this:

> Accepting the imperative to become resilient means sacrificing any political vision of a world in which we might be able to live better lives freer from dangers, looking instead at the future as an endemic terrain of catastrophe that is dangerous and insecure by design.

So vulnerable people, communities, and countries are rejecting that imperative, refusing to make that sacrifice. Indeed, no longer diplomatic enough to simply call themselves vulnerable, they are taking up the banner of climate justice with resolve. Building on older traditions of environmental justice, social justice, and human rights, and on the battles that communities, activists, and civil society groups have been fighting for generations, the shout for climate justice is what the polluters and win-win optimists most feared from the beginning: a narrative that is spinning out of their control. Climate justice spans adaptation and mitigation issues, but not in the name of balance. Instead of optimizing the cost-benefit equilibrium of mitigation and adaptation, climate justice treats these as the distributional issues that they really are. Instead of seeing "people vs. climate" conflicts of interest as something to manage away, climate justice endorses the legitimacy of the people who fight back.

The International Monetary Fund (IMF), for example, has long argued that the trillions of dollars governments extend every year in fossil-fuel subsidies are hugely detrimental to mitigation, and this is patently true. In 2019, it calculated that efficient fossil-fuel pricing in 2015 would have lowered global carbon emissions by 28 percent, increased government revenue by 3.8 percent of GDP, and smoothed all kinds of price distortions (Coady et al. 2019). In the IMF's free-market outlook, cutting subsidies has stood as the foremost, no-brainer win-win solution: it is good climate policy and good economic policy. So, the IMF asked the government of Ecuador to end decades of fuel subsidies in the negotiations for a $4.2 billion loan to the country. This would not prove to be such an easy win: protests, with the mass participation of Indigenous groups and the poor, took over the streets of Quito. Things got so heated that the government had to flee to the city of Guayaquil. Ultimately, the government was forced to back down and negotiate a peace deal that would trade the subsidy abolishment decree for "a new one that has mechanisms for directing its resources to the people who need it the most" (Valencia and Munoz 2019; Cabrera and Krauss 2019). (The IMF's cutting of consumer fuels subsidies was not aimed specifically at emissions reduction; rather, it was part of a sweeping imposition of austerity on Ecuador's poor. The IMF has reported on the size of subsidies going to energy companies worldwide, but it can take no action to reduce those subsidies, since the IMF is a creation of the governments that are giving them.)

The year 2019 was one of fierce and inspiring protests, and Ecuador was not the only country where government decisions to raise fuel and transport prices were the match that lit the fire. Iran and Chile also saw the largest mass protests in years; in neither case was the rise in prices a mitigation policy, but the explosive responses sent the same message: that unequal burdens would not be taken up quietly. In a historic irony that will not soon be forgotten, the protests that swept over Santiago, touched off by an increase in public transit fares, shut down the government's plans to host COP25, relocating the conference to Madrid at short notice (Planelles et al. 2019). It was only the sudden restrictions of the COVID-19 pandemic that shut down the global wave of dissent, for a time, in 2020.

Climate justice is challenging mainstream frames of mitigation and adaptation head-on, but it is also creeping close to the boundaries of the mainstream. The Paris Agreement shows this; it was the first global climate instrument to reference human rights as a guiding principle. Although it went into little detail on what this means, simply making the connection was a leap into new terrain for the UNFCCC (Ajibade 2016). The Agreement also mentions climate justice, if only in scare quotes:

> *Noting* the importance of ensuring the integrity of all ecosystems, including oceans, and the protection of biodiversity, recognized by some cultures as Mother Earth, and noting the importance for some of the concept of "climate justice," when taking action to address climate change. (UN 2015)

If in Paris it may have held importance only "for some," then in 2018 the IPCC 1.5°C report pushed justice more boldly, insisting that:

> Social justice and equity are core aspects of climate-resilient development pathways that aim to limit global warming to 1.5°C as they address the challenges and inevitable trade-offs, widen opportunities, and ensure that options, visions, and values are deliberated, between and within countries and communities, without making the poor and disadvantaged worse off. (IPCC 2018)

Is this a welcome switchback in the policy discussion, or just another addition to the wish list for a perfect and probably impossible climate solution?

The long history of climate justice and its precedents operating through protest movements, civil disobedience, courtroom challenge, and desperate rebellion has given the whole concept an air of the radical and not necessarily of the workable. Resilience may prove impossible to put into practice, but climate justice does not even *sound* as if it could be applied.

The preconception that climate justice cannot be put into practice is, however, unfair. There has been no shortage of justice-rooted proposals that are wholly down to earth. In this ever-advancing and context-sensitive field, one can find plentiful ideas from 2019 and early 2020 alone. The ACT Alliance turned a justice lens on possible financing for loss and damage, identifying an international-airline-passenger levy, a bunker-fuel levy, a financial-transaction tax, a climate-damages tax, and carbon levies among the possible sources that could bring some sense of justice to the issue (Hirsch 2019). Participants in the "Global Conference on Strengthening Synergies between the Paris Agreement on Climate Change and the 2030 Agenda for Sustainable Development," held in Copenhagen in April 2019, double-underlined the relevant areas of human rights that demand respect: the right to health; the rights of Indigenous peoples, local communities, migrants, children, persons with disabilities, and people in vulnerable situations; the right to development; and gender equality, empowerment of women, and intergenerational equity (UN-DESA 2019). Hjorthen (2019), elaborating on Caney's (2014) distinct principles of harm-avoidance justice and burden-sharing justice in the context of humanitarian action, showed how they can be reconciled under institutions that distinguish between the duty to take action (driven by what is effective) and the duty to pay for it (driven by what is fair). Researchers injected grassroots justice into city-scale resilience discourses in Philadelphia (Shokry et al. 2020), Phoenix (Harlan et al. 2019), and Washington, DC (Ranganathan and Bratman 2019), with a common focus on histories of racial segregation. Undoubtedly, other cities have engaged in similar dialogue. In 2019, popular support grew for the U.S. Green New Deal and its European predecessors, which attempt to integrate economic and social justice fully with climate mitigation and adaptation; indeed, their proponents give as much or more attention to the former as they do the latter (Bhattacharya 2019; Rogers 2019). In 2020, the arrival of a pandemic ripped up the script for what politicians and voters considered politically thinkable, possible, and necessary.

Justicia Climática

Puerto Ricans were waiting, and fighting, for justice long before the wait for post-Maria relief, recovery, and adaptation funds began.

> The crisis is the consequence of the years of mismanagement and neoliberalization that have driven the Puerto Rican livelihood to precarity. However, these factors enter the discussion only to further justify why the population needs more discipline. Caribbean residents are, therefore, redirected toward risk responsive modes of citizenship in which they are to develop independence from federal assistance. (Moulton and Machado 2019)

This sort of resilience amounts to no more than learning how to live with already inadequate resources that continue to diminish. In response, Puerto Ricans have also rebelled against their assigned role.

In the aftermath of Maria, even before it became clear that assistance from the mainland would be wholly inadequate, Puerto Ricans organized wide-ranging mutual aid and political organizing efforts based on justice principles (Crabapple 2017). Mutual aid groups, the most well-known of which were the network of Centros de Apoyo Mutuo, pooled their limited resources and established road-clearing brigades, health clinics, free community kitchens, meal delivery systems, solidarity networks, discussion spaces to generate critical thinking, communication webs, and community solar generation. According to Crabapple (2017):

> Many of these groups honed their activist skills fighting the punishing austerity cuts that the U.S. imposed to address Puerto Rico's debt crisis.

Cabán (2019) writes that the disaster "exposed the failings of the current colonial system and has created new space for the people to reimagine Puerto Rico's political future." Arturo Massol González, who heads the ecological community center Casa Puebla, told Klein (2018): "We look at crisis as an opportunity to change." Not coincidentally, in July 2019, tens of thousands of Puerto Ricans took control of central San Juan in what may have been the largest demonstrations in the island's history, demanding the resignation of Governor Ricardo Rosselló. The groundswell began as a response to the leak of group-chat messages by Rosselló and other officials in which, among other outrages, they attacked San Juan Mayor Carmen Yulín Cruz (a prominent critic of the Trump administration's response to Maria) and joked in unbelievably bad taste about the hurricane's high death toll. On the territorial capitol's steps, protesters laid out pairs of shoes left behind by people who had died in Maria's wake (Weissenstein 2019). By the time of the demonstrations, the movement's target list had broadened to include the federal oversight board that Congress has empowered to control the government's finances; the territory's continued economic crisis; the closing of hundreds of schools; and the government's weak response to Maria, especially the botched restoration of electric power (Hernández and Epstein 2019). The organizing and protests succeeded in securing Rosselló's resignation (Gerber and Carrero Galarza 2019). However, the other problems continue to plague the island.

Unfortunately, grassroots efforts toward climate justice in Puerto Rico are swimming against the strongest of institutional undertows. With one-third of the mainland U.S. median household income and only 37 percent of the per-capita carbon emissions (Guzman 2019; CIA 2019), and with centuries of Spanish and U.S. colonial history behind it, the commonwealth fits the profile of many places around the world that have been rendered highly vulnerable to climatic disasters by the Global North's greenhouse emissions and its acts of economic domination. By the time Maria struck, Puerto Rico's struggle to make debt payments and the economic decline triggered partly by those payments had produced increasing poverty, a home-foreclosure epidemic, involuntary migration, and relentless contraction of public services. Pre-Maria Puerto Rico was spending more on debt service than on education, health, or security. Results included the shuttering of 150 schools, the gutting of health care, increased taxes, splitting of families between the island and the mainland, and increased food insecurity (Ora Bannan 2015). Those existing problems were exacerbated by the inadequate federal response to Maria, which was far weaker than the responses to mainland disasters caused by Hurricanes Harvey and Irma that same year (Willison et al. 2019). Adding to the problem was the imposition of harsh fiscal austerity by the federally appointed Financial Oversight and Management Board (known locally as *la junta*), which took effective control of the island's economy a year before Maria. These and other forces are not only standing in the way of Puerto Rico's rebuilding; they are rendering the island even more vulnerable to future disasters. Cabán (2019) predicted, even pre-COVID-19, that the island's economy would continue to shrink:

> The situation for Puerto Ricans will deteriorate further when federal transfers are reduced in five years and hurricane-related funding is exhausted. The austerity measures will lead to further emigration of the most skilled and valued workers. ... Through no fault of its own, Puerto Rico is no longer regarded as an advantageous possession by the United States.

Crabapple (2017) found recognition of this fact everywhere:

> Many Puerto Ricans told me that they believe the poor response from the federal government and the slow pace of the recovery are deliberate, part of a strategy to depopulate the island, so that it can be remade as a luxury hotel-filled playground for the rich.

Puerto Rico lost 8 percent of its population between 2015 and 2018 (Puerto Rico Report 2016; Census Bureau 2019). Some communities have lost a much larger share. Homes in the six-square-block Sierra Brava neighborhood of the Salinas municipality on the south coast, for example, were almost all occupied before Maria. Eighteen months after the storm, almost none of the flood-damaged homes had been repaired, and three-fourths of the neighborhood's houses stood empty (Cox and Cox 2019; Cox 2019). A community with most of its homes vacant and most schools closed is highly vulnerable to any economic shock or disaster, and it is difficult to imagine how such communities can recover from such vulnerability. But imagine they do.

Better examples are not far away. Puerto Rico's Caribbean neighbor Cuba has developed, in Moulton and Machado's (2019) words, "a decidedly distinct manifestation of resilience" in recent decades with its much-celebrated successes in disaster preparedness, emergency response, and rebuilding efforts following storm events. "The metric for legitimate governance in Cuba has long been tied to the government's ability to provide for its citizens, especially in the context of tropical storms and hurricanes" (Moulton and Machado 2019). When Hurricane Sandy, the island's second-strongest recorded hurricane, struck in 2012, its sustained winds of 175 km/hr blew for six hours, leaving Cuba's second city, Santiago, in ruins. A staggering 170,000 homes were damaged, and a half million inhabitants were left in dire straits; nevertheless, the death toll was held to 11 (Poole 2013). By 2015, with help from the United Nations, Santiago and the rest of eastern Cuba had been largely restored (UNDRR 2019). The recovery was yet another example of what Moulton and Machado (2019) call Cuba's "decolonial model of resilience," in which the state is engaged "not only [in] support and provisioning before and after large storms and disaster events, but also in ... non-disaster provisioning, specifically through its national food and agricultural system."

If U.S. federal departments and agencies wanted to show the legitimacy of their governance in Puerto Rico, Brown et al. (2018) have recommended specific actions they could take that would actually help the commonwealth adapt while also meeting mitigation goals. In their proposal, the Energy Department would begin "rapid development of decentralized grid structures" and foster community solar generation. Working with residents and local organizations, FEMA would improve emergency preparedness and prevention. Housing and Urban Development would ensure that rebuilt houses are "hurricane-proof, environmentally friendly, chemically safe, and affordable," while halting foreclosures and providing assistance to those who are struggling to make mortgage payments. The Agriculture Department would help address Puerto Rico's vulnerability in the realm of food, up to 90 percent of which is imported from the mainland or other countries, by restoring and increasing agricultural production capacity based on ecological principles. The Labor Department would establish a large job training program. Health and Human Services would build up a network of emergency clinics, "similar to military zone clinics." EPA would kick off "a massive increase in cleanups of Superfund and other hazardous waste sites." The Defense Department would launch a thorough cleanup of Vieques Island, which was used by the military as a bombing range for 60 years, is contaminated with heavy metals and toxic chemicals, and has some of the highest illness rates in the Caribbean (Pelet 2016). All of these actions would be expensive, of course, which is why an indebted and austerity-bound commonwealth cannot take them alone. Worse, there is no easy economic pitch to the federal government; the investments will not necessarily help the U.S. economy and may not even have a great return for Puerto Rico's economy. Still worse, if the United States really wants to make a better future for Puerto Rico it will have to make deep, painful cuts in emissions on a national scale. Why, U.S. politicians are implicitly asking, should a world-class polluting country, having mastered the game of protecting itself from economic burdens by only entertaining win-win solutions, take on a losing prospect like that?

The Language of Consequences

For Puerto Rico, for the country, and for the world, a balancing act may still be possible. Mitigation (beyond the mitigation that has already failed) and adaptation (within the limits of what is possible to adapt to) may still be achievable together. But that is all. Such a balance cannot support unlimited economic growth, too. Therefore, as good as action plans for mitigating and adapting may be, there may simply not be a case for them that will appeal to the proponents of the dominant economic system. There is an appeal to justice, though. Climate justice favors action over equilibrium; it is a rejection of the demand to work perpetually at maintaining the balance and growth of global capitalism atop a collapsing ecosphere. Everyone looking for ideas, even climate scientists and engineers and economists, needs to take the language of climate justice seriously because it might contain the dictionary for ideas that cannot be articulated in the market's language.

What will we do with those ideas? As a final note, it is worth reflecting on the difficulty of writing about climate action without using the pronoun "we." Up to this point, we have been writing without reference to "we," "our," or "us." Of course, climate action is collective action, and there are many reasons to address everyone together. But it can be a danger when writing about balancing priorities, costs, and responsibilities, and making the real judgment calls, because that easy pronoun obscures all the uneven and inequitable truths of climate change. When Gore (1992) wrote, "[b]elieving that we can adapt to just about anything is ultimately a kind of laziness"; when Lenton et al. (2019) warned that "we might already have lost control of whether tipping happens"; and when Trump (2020) said, "[i]n America, we understand what the pessimists refuse to see," each "we" was a rich fiction far removed from how belief, control, and understanding—and the consequences of belief, control, and understanding—are really distributed. Our collective actions depend foremost on our collectives. Ideas travel, not to sell the whole world a win-win-win solution, but to find the right collectives, at the right times, to make something in the ruins of others' failure.

References

Adelman, Sam. (2016). "Climate Justice, Loss and Damage and Compensation for Small Island Developing States." *Journal of Human Rights and the Environment* 7(1): 32–53.

Ajibade, Idowu. (2016). "Distributive Justice and Human Rights in Climate Policy: The Long Road to Paris." *Journal of Sustainable Development Law and Policy* 7(2): 65–80.

Anderies, John, Carl Folke, Brian Walker, and Elinor Ostrom. (2013). "Aligning Key Concepts for Global Change Policy: Robustness, Resilience, and Sustainability." *Ecology and Society* 18(2): 143–160.

Anderson, Kevin, and Alice Bowes. (2008). "Reframing the Climate Change Challenge in Light of Post-2000 Emission Trends." *Philosophical Transactions of the Royal Society A* 366: 3863–3882.

Associated Press (AP). (2019) "Puerto Rico to Spend $20 Billion to Modernize Power Grid Hit by Hurricane Maria." *AP* October 24. https://apnews. com/1bc72e84f242479095fd96cec3266879

Ayala, Edmy, Patricia Mazzei, Frances Robles, and Sandra E. Garcia. (2020). "'Scarier' Than Hurricane Maria: A Deadly Earthquake Terrifies Puerto Rico." *New York Times* January 7. https://nytimes. com/2020/01/07/us/ puerto-rico-earthquake.html

Ayers, Jessica M., and Saleemul Huq. (2009). "The Value of Linking Mitigation and Adaptation: A Case Study of Bangladesh." *Environmental Management* 43(5): 753–764.

Bayramoglu, Basak, Michael Finus, and Jean-François Jacques. (2018). "Climate Agreements in a Mitigation-Adaptation Game." *Journal of Public Economics* 165: 101–113.

Bhattacharya, Tithi. (2019). "Three Ways a Green New Deal Can Promote Life Over Capital." *Jacobin* June 10. https://jacobinmag.com/2019/06/ green-new-deal-social-care-work

Biesbroek, G. Robbert, Rob J. Swart, and Wim G. M. van der Knaap. (2009). "The Mitigation-Adaptation Dichotomy and the Role of Spatial Planning." *Habitat International* 33(3): 230–237.

Brown, Phil, Carmen M. Vélez, Colleen B. Vega, Michael Welton Murphy, Hector Torres, Zaira Rosario, Akram Alshawabkeh, José F. Cordero, Ingrid Y. Padilla, and John D. Meeker. (2018). "Hurricanes and the Environmental Justice Island: Irma and Maria in Puerto Rico." *Environmental Justice* 11(4): 148–153.

Cabán, Pedro. (2019). "Hurricane Maria's Aftermath: Redefining Puerto Rico's Colonial Status." *Latin American, Caribbean, and U.S. Latino Studies Faculty Scholarship* 34. Albany: State University of New York. https:// scholarsarchive.library.albany.edu/lacs_fac_scholar/34

Cabrera, José María León, and Clifford Krauss. (2019). "Deal Struck in Ecuador to Cancel Austerity Package and End Protests." *New York Times* October 13.

Caney, Simon. (2014). "Two Kinds of Climate Justice: Avoiding Harm and Sharing Burdens." *Journal of Political Philosophy* 22(2): 125–149.

Central Intelligence Agency (CIA). (2019). "Puerto Rico." *CIA World Factbook.* Langley, VA: CIA. https:// cia.gov/library/publications/resources/the-world-factbook/geos/rq.html

Climate Feedback. (2017). "Scientists Explain What New York Magazine Article on 'The Uninhabitable Earth' Gets Wrong." *Climate Feedback* July 12. https://climatefeedback.org/evaluation/scientists-explain-what-new-york-magazine-article-on-the-uninhabitable-earth-gets-wrong-david- wallace-wells/

Coady, David, Ian Parry, Nghia-Piotr Le, and Baoping Shang. (2019). "Global Fossil Fuel Subsidies Remain Large: An Update Based on Country-Level Estimates." *IMF Working Papers* 19(89). Paris: International Monetary Fund. https://doi.org/10.5089/9781484393178.001

Cox, Priti Gulati. (2019). "Living Here and Not in the Street Is Worth Gold." *SMoC – Sidewalk Museum of Congress* March 10. https://pritigcox.wordp ress.com/2019/03/10/ living-here-and-not-in-the-street-is-worth-gold

Cox, Stan, and Paul Cox. (2016). *How the World Breaks: Life in Catastrophe's Path, from the Caribbean to Siberia.* New York: New Press.

________. (2019). "In Salinas, Puerto Rico, Vulnerable Americans Are Still Trapped in the Ruins Left by Hurricane Maria." *CounterPunch* March 15. https://counterpunch.org/2019/03/15/ in-salinas-puerto-rico-vulnerable- americans-are-still-trapped-in-the-ruins-left-by-hurricane-maria

Crabapple, Molly. (2017). "Puerto Rico's DIY Disaster Relief." *New York Review of Books* November 17. https://nybooks.com/daily/2017/11/17/puerto- ricos-diy-disaster-relief

Denton, Fatima, Thomas J. Wilbanks, Achala C. Abeysinghe, Ian Burton, Qingzhu Gao, Maria Carmen Lemos, Toshihiko Masui, Karen L. O'Brien, and Koko Warner. (2014). "Climate-Resilient Pathways: Adaptation, Mitigation, and Sustainable Development." In *AR5 Climate Change 2014: Impacts, Adaptation, and Vulnerability.* Geneva, Switzerland: Intergovernmental Panel on Climate Change. https://ipcc.ch/report/ar5/ wg2

Elkington, John. (1994). "Towards the Sustainable Corporation: Win-Win-Win Business Strategies for Sustainable Development." *California Management Review* 36(2): 90–100.

Evans, Brad, and Julian Reid. (2013). "Dangerously Exposed: The Life and Death of the Resilient Subject." *Resilience* 1(2): 83–98.

Fischer-Kowalski, Marina, Mark Swilling, Ernst Ulrich, Yong von Weizsacker, Yuichi Moriguchi Ren, Wendy Crane, Fridolin Krausmann, Nina Eisenmenger, Stefan Giljum, Peter Hennicke, Rene Kemp, Paty Romero Lankao, Anna Bella Siriban Manalang, and Sebastian Sewerin. (2011). *Decoupling Natural Resource Use and Environmental Impacts from Economic Growth: A Report of the Working Group on Decoupling to the International Resource Panel.* Nairobi, Kenya: U.N. Environment Program. https://wedocs.unep.org/handle/20.500.11822/9816

Food and Agriculture Organization of the United Nations (FAO). (2009). *Harvesting Agriculture's Multiple Benefits: Mitigation, Adaptation, Development and Food Security.* Rome, Italy: FAO. http://fao.org/3/a-ak914e.pdf

Frey, Marco, and Federica Gasbarro. (2019). "Adaptation and Mitigation Synergies and Trade-Offs." In *Good Health and Well-Being.* Eds. Walter Leal Filho, Tony Wall, Ulisses Azeiteiro, Anabela Marisa Azul, Luciana Brandli, and Pinar Gökcin Özuyar, pp. 1–9. Cham, Switzerland: Springer.

Gerber, Marisa, and Milton Carrero Galarza. (2019). "Puerto Rico Gov. Ricardo Rossello Announces Resignation amid Mounting Protests." *Los Angeles Times* July 25.

Gore, Al. (1992). *Earth in the Balance.* New York: Taylor & Francis.

Green, Matthew. (2020). "Australia Bushfires Contribute to Big Rise in Global CO_2 Levels: UK's Met Office." *Reuters* January 24. https://reuters.com/ article/us-climate-change-australia-emissions-idUSKBN1ZN0BT

Grove, Kevin. (2018). *Resilience.* London: Routledge.

Guenther, Genevieve. (2017). "A Defense of Climate Tragedy, or What the Scientists Got Wrong About 'The Uninhabitable Earth'." *Medium* November 14. https://medium.com/@DoctorVive/a-defense-of-climate-tragedy-or-what-the-scientists-got-wrong-about-the-uninhabitable- earth-e220090ea3e5

Gupta, Anand. (2019). "Puerto Rico Is Targeting 100% Renewable Energy. The Trump Administration Has Other Ideas." *EQ Magazine* April 18. https://eqmagpro.com/puerto-rico-is-targeting-100-renewable-energy- the-trump-administration-has-other-ideas

Guzman, Gloria. (2019). *U.S. Median Household Income Up in 2018 from 2017.* Washington, DC: U.S. Census Bureau. https://census.gov/libra ry/stories/2019/09/us-median-household-income-up-in-2018-from-2017. html

Harlan, Sharon L., Paul Chakalian, Juan Declet-Barreto, David M. Hondula, and G. Darrel Jenerette. (2019). "Pathways to Climate Justice in a Desert Metropolis." In *People and Climate Change: Vulnerability, Adaptation, and Social Justice.* Eds. Lisa Reyes Mason and Jonathan Rigg, pp. 23–50. New York: Oxford University Press.

Hernández, Arelis, and Kayla Epstein. (2019). "Puerto Ricans Shut Down Major Highway, March Toward Capitol to Demand that the Governor Resign." *Washington Post* July 22.

Hickel, Jason, and Giorgos Kallis. (2019). "Is Green Growth Possible?" *New Political Economy.* https://doi.org/10.1080/13563467.2019.1598964

Hinojosa, Jennifer, and Edwin Meléndez. (2018). *The Housing Crisis in Puerto Rico and the Impact of Hurricane Maria.* New York: Centro de Estudios Puertorriqueños, Hunter College, City University of New York. https://centropr.hunter.cuny.edu/sites/default/files/data_briefs/HousingPuertoRi co.pdf

Hirsch, Thomas. (2019). *Climate Finance for Addressing Loss and Damage: How to Mobilize Support for Developing Countries to Tackle Loss and Damage.* Berlin: Brot fur die Welt. https://actalliance.org/wp-content/uploads/2019/11/ClimateFinance_LossDamage.pdf

Hjorthen, Fredrik D. (2019). "Humanitarian Intervention and Burden-Sharing Justice." *Political Studies.* https://doi.org/10.1177/0032321719882607

Intergovernmental Panel on Climate Change (IPCC). (1992). *Climate Change: The IPCC 1990 and 1992 Assessments.* Geneva, Switzerland: IPCC. https:// ipcc.ch/report/climate-change-the-ipcc-1990-and-1992-assessments

________. (2015). *AR5 Synthesis Report: Climate Change 2014.* Geneva, Switzerland: IPCC. https://ipcc.ch/report/ar5/syr

________. (2018). *Special Report: Global Warming of 1.5°C.* Geneva, Switzerland: IPCC. https://ipcc.ch/sr15

Kates, Robert. (2000). "Cautionary Tales: Adaptation and the Global Poor." *Climatic Change* 45(1): 5–17.

Keellings, David, and José J. Hernández Ayala. (2019). "Extreme Rainfall Associated with Hurricane Maria Over Puerto Rico and its Connections to Climate Variability and Change." *Geophysical Research Letters* 46(5): 2964–2973.

Kishore, Nishant, Domingo Marqués-Reyes, Ayesha Mahmud, Matthew V. Kiang, Irmary Rodriguez Rivera, Arlan Fuller, Peggy Ebner, Cecilia Sorensen, Fabio Racy, Jay Lemery, Leslie Maas, Jennifer Leaning, Rafael A. Irizarry, Satchit Balsari, and Caroline O. Buckee. (2018). "Mortality in Puerto Rico After Hurricane Maria." *New England Journal of Medicine* 379(2): 162–170.

Klein, Naomi. (2018). *The Battle for Paradise: Puerto Rico Takes on the Disaster Capitalists.* Chicago: Haymarket.

Klein, Richard J. T., Saleemul Huq, Fatima Denton, Thomas E. Downing, Richard G. Richels, John B. Robinson, and Ferenc L. Toth. (2007). "Inter-Relationships Between Adaptation and Mitigation." In *AR4 Climate Change 2007: Impacts, Adaptation, and Vulnerability,* Chapter 18. (Working Group II Contribution to the Fourth Assessment Report of the Intergovernmental Panel on Climate Change.) Geneva, Switzerland: Intergovernmental Panel on Climate Change. https://ipcc.ch/report/ar4/wg2, https://www.ipcc.ch/site/assets/uploads/2018/03/ar4_wg2_full_report.pdf

Knight, Kyle, and Juliet Schor. (2014). "Economic Growth and Climate Change: A Cross-National Analysis of Territorial and Consumption-Based Carbon Emissions in High-Income Countries." *Sustainability* 6(6): 3722–3731.

Kongsager, Rico. (2018). "Linking Climate Change Adaptation and Mitigation: A Review with Evidence from the Land-Use Sectors." *Land* 7(4): 158. https://www.mdpi.com/2073-445X/7/4/158

Kwasinski, Alexis, Fabio Andrade, Marcel J. Castro-Sitiriche, and Efraín O'Neill- Carrillo. (2019). "Hurricane Maria Effects on Puerto Rico Electric Power Infrastructure." *IEEE Power and Energy Technology Systems Journal* 6(1): 85–94.

Landauer, Mia, Sirkku Juhola, and Maria Söderholm. (2015). "Inter-Relationships Between Adaptation and Mitigation: A Systematic Literature Review." *Climatic Change* 131(4): 505–517.

Lenton, Timothy M., Johan Rockström, Owen Gaffney, Stefan Rahmstorf, Katherine Richardson, Will Steffen, and Hans Joachim Schellnhuber. (2019). "Climate Tipping Points—Too Risky to Bet Against." *Nature* 575(7784): 592–595.

Levine, Simon. (2014). "Assessing Resilience: Why Quantification Misses the Point." *HPG Working Paper.* London: Overseas Development Institute. https://www.odi.org/sites/odi.org.uk/files/odi-assets/publications-opinion-files/9049.pdf

Lynas, Mark. (2007). *Six Degrees: Our Future on a Hotter Planet.* London: Fourth Estate.

Mace, M. J., and Roda Verheyen. (2016). "Loss, Damage and Responsibility After COP21: All Options Open for the Paris Agreement." *Review of European, Comparative & International Environmental Law* 25(2): 197–214.

Manne, Alan, Robert Mendelsohn, and Richard Richels. (1995). "MERGE—A Model for Evaluating Regional and Global Effects of GHG Reduction Policies." *Energy Policy* 23(1): 17–34.

Milken Institute School of Public Health. (2019). *Ascertainment of the Estimated Excess Mortality from Hurricane Maria in Puerto Rico.* Washington, DC: Milken Institute of Public Health, George Washington University. https:// publichealth.gwu.edu/sites/default/files/downloads/projects/PRstudy/Acertainment%20of%20the%20Estimated%20Excess%20Mortality%20from%20Hurricane%20Maria%20in%20Puerto%20Rico.pdf

Mochizuki, Junko, Adriana Keating, Wei Liu, Stefan Hochrainer-Stigler, and Reinhard Mechler. (2018). "An Overdue Alignment of Risk and Resilience? A Conceptual Contribution to Community Resilience." *Disasters* 42(2): 361–391.

Moulton, Alex, and Mario Machado. (2019). "Bouncing Forward After Irma and Maria: Acknowledging Colonialism, Problematizing Resilience and Thinking Climate Justice." *Journal of Extreme Events* 6(1): 1940003. https://www.worldscientific.com/doi/10.1142/S2345737619400037

National Hurricane Center. (2018). *Costliest U.S. Tropical Cyclones Tables Updated.* Washington, DC: U.S. National Oceanic and Atmospheric Administration. January 26. http://nhc.noaa.gov/news/Updated-Costliest. pdf

Nordhaus, William. (1991). "To Slow or Not to Slow: The Economics of the Greenhouse Effect." *Economic Journal* 101(407): 920–937.

________. (1993). "Rolling the DICE: An Optimal Transition Path for Controlling Greenhouse Gases." *Resource and Energy Economics* 15: 27–50.

________. (2018). "Projections and Uncertainties About Climate Change in an Era of Minimal Climate Policies." *American Economic Journal: Economic Policy* 10(3): 333–360.

O'Neill-Carrillo, Efraín, and Agustín Irizarry-Rivera. (2019). "How to Harden Puerto Rico's Grid Against Hurricanes." *IEEE Spectrum* 56(11): 42–48.

Olsson, Lennart, Anne Jerneck, Henrik Thoren, Johannes Persson, and David O'Byrne. (2015). "Why Resilience Is Unappealing to Social Science: Theoretical and Empirical Investigations of the Scientific Use of Resilience." *Science Advances* 1(4): e1400217.

Ora Bannan, Natasha. (2015). "Puerto Rico's Odious Debt: The Economic Crisis of Colonialism." *CUNY Law Review* 19(2): 287–311. https://acade micworks.cuny.edu/clr/vol19/iss2/5/

Parrique, Timothée, Jonathan Barth, François Briens, Christian Kerschner, Alejo Kraus-Polk, Anna Kuokkanen, and Joachim Spangenberg. (2019). *Decoupling Debunked: Evidence and Arguments Against Green Growth as a Sole Strategy for Sustainability.* Brussels: European Environmental Bureau. https://eeb.org/library/decoupling-debunked

Peck, Stephen C., and Thomas J. Teisberg. (1992). "CETA: A Model for Carbon Emissions Trajectory Assessment." *Energy Journal* 13(1): 55–77.

Pelet, Valeria. (2016). "There's a Health Crisis on This Puerto Rican Island, but It's Impossible to Prove Why It's Happening." *Atlantic* September 3. https://theatlantic.com/politics/archive/2016/09/vieques-invisible-health-crisis/498428

Planelles, Manuel, Carlos E. Cué, Rocío Montes, Noor Mahtani, and A. Ponce. (2019). "Madrid to Host UN Climate Summit After Chile Cancels amid Protests." *El País* November 1. https://elpais.com/elpais/2019/11/01/inenglish/1572600094_630306.html

Pompeo, Michael. (2019). *On the U.S. Withdrawal from the Paris Agreement.* November 4. Washington, DC: U.S. Department of State. https://www.state.gov/on-the-u-s-withdrawal-from-the-paris-agreement

Poole, Lisette. (2013). "A Year After Hurricane Sandy Hit Cuba." *Havana Times* October 24. https://havanatimes.org/features/a-year-after-hurricane-sandy-hit-cuba

Puerto Rico Energy Bureau (PREB). (2019). *Notice About Proposed Regulation Adoption.* September 5. San Juan, PR: PREB. http://energia.pr.gov/en/notice-about-proposed-regulation-adoption-5

Puerto Rico Report. (2016). "New Census Data on Puerto Rico." December 19. https://puertoricoreport.com/new-census-data-puerto-rico

Quiñones, Ivelisse Rivera. (2019). "Sheet Roofs: Puerto Rico Reels 2 Years After Hurricane Maria." *Phys.org* September 20. https://phys.org/news/2019-09-sheet-roofs-puerto-rico-reels.html

Ranganathan, Malini, and Eve Bratman. (2019). "From Urban Resilience to Abolitionist Climate Justice in Washington, DC." *Antipode*. https://doi. org/10.1111/anti.12555

Rogers, Adam. (2019). "The Green New Deal Shows How Grand Climate Politics Can Be." *Wired* February 8. https://wired.com/story/the-green-new-deal-climate-politics

Rowling, Megan. (2019). "Green Climate Fund Stepping Up on 'Loss and Damage', Head Says." *Thomson Reuters Foundation* December 13. https://news.trust.org/item/20191213111118-mifuq

Ruszczyk, Hanna. (2019). "Ambivalence Towards Discourse of Disaster Resilience." *Disasters* 43(4): 818–839.

Schipper, E. Lisa F. (2006). "Conceptual History of Adaptation in the UNFCCC Process." *Review of European Community & International Environmental Law* 15(1): 82–92.

Schipper, E. Lisa F., and Lara Langston. (2015). "A Comparative Overview of Resilience Measurement Frameworks: Analysing Indicators and Approaches." *Working Paper* 422. London: Overseas Development Institute. http://pdfs.semanticscholar.org/2d45/b8f15d521051d7af464e607b465b164f03cc.pdf

Shokry, Galia, James J. T. Connolly, and Isabelle Anguelovskia. (2020). "Understanding Climate Gentrification and Shifting Landscapes of Protection and Vulnerability in Green Resilient Philadelphia." *Urban Climate* 31100539.

Suckall, Natalie, Lindsay C. Stringer, and Emma L. Tompkins. (2015). "Presenting Triple-Wins? Assessing Projects That Deliver Adaptation, Mitigation and Development Co-Benefits in Rural Sub-Saharan Africa." *Ambio* 44(1): 34–41.

Sutter, Christoph, and Juan Carlos Parreño. (2007). "Does the Current Clean Development Mechanism (CDM) Deliver its Sustainable Development Claim? An Analysis of Officially Registered CDM Projects." *Climatic Change* 84(1): 75–90.

Thornton, Thomas, Diana Mangalagiu, Yuge Ma, Jing Lan, Mahir Yazar, Ali Kerem Saysel, and Abdel Maoula Chaar. (2019). "Cultural Models of and for Urban Sustainability: Assessing Beliefs About Green-Win." *Climatic Change.* https://doi.org/10.1007/s10584-019-02518-2

Timperley, Jocelyn. (2019). "COP25: What Was Achieved and Where to Next?" *Climate Home News* December 16. https://climatechangenews.com/2019/12/16/cop25-achieved-next

Tol, Richard. (2005). "Adaptation and Mitigation: Trade-Offs in Substance and Methods." *Environmental Science & Policy* 8(6): 572–578.

________. (1999). "Kyoto, Efficiency, and Cost-Effectiveness: Applications of FUND." *Energy Journal* 20(SI-6): 130–156.

Trump, Donald. (2020). *Remarks by President Trump at the World Economic Forum, Davos, Switzerland.* January 21. Washington, DC: White House. https://whitehouse.gov/briefings-statements/remarks-president-trump-world-economic-forum-davos-switzerland/

United Nations. (2015). *Paris Agreement.* New York: United Nations. https://unfccc.int/files/essential_background/convention/application/pdf/english_paris_agreement.pdf

U.N. Department of Economic and Social Affairs (UN-DESA). (2019). *Global Conference on Strengthening Synergies Between the Paris Agreement on Climate Change and the 2030 Agenda for Sustainable Development: Maximizing Co-Benefits by Linking Implementation of the Sustainable Development Goals and Climate Action.* New York: UN-DESA. https://sustainabledevelopment.un.org/content/documents/25236un_bookletsynergies_v2.pdf

U.N. Framework Convention on Climate Change (UNFCCC). (2019). *Elaboration of the Sources of and Modalities for Accessing Financial Support for Addressing Loss and Damage: Technical Paper by the Secretariat.* Bonn, Germany: UNFCCC. https://unfccc.int/sites/default/files/resource/01_0.pdf

________. (2020). "Decision 2/CMA.2: Warsaw International Mechanism for Loss and Damage Associated with Climate Change Impacts and its 2019 Review." In *Report of the Conference of the Parties Serving as the Meeting of the Parties to the Paris Agreement on its Second Session, Held in Madrid from 2 to 15 December 2019: Addendum Part Two: Action Taken by the Conference of the Parties Serving as the Meeting of the Parties to the Paris Agreement at its Second Session Contents Decisions Adopted by the Conference of the Parties Serving as the Meeting of the Parties to the Paris Agreement.* FCCC/PA/CMA/2019/6/Add. 1. Bonn, Germany: UNFCCC. https://unfccc.int/sites/default/files/resource/cma2019_06_add.01_.pdf#page=4

U.N. Office for Disaster Risk Reduction (UNDRR). (2019). "2019 *Global Assessment Report.* Geneva, Switzerland: UNDRR. https://gar.undrr.org/sites/default/files/reports/2019-05/full_gar_report.pdf

U.S. Census Bureau. (2019). *QuickFacts: Puerto Rico.* Washington, DC: U.S. Census Bureau. census.gov/quickfacts/PR.

U.S. Energy Information Administration (EIA). (2019). *Puerto Rico.* Washington, DC: US-EIA. http://eia.gov/state/data.php?sid=RQ#CarbonDioxideEmissions

U.S. State Department. (2002). *U.S. Climate Action Report: Third National Communication of the United States of America Under the United Nations Framework Convention on Climate Change.* Washington, DC: Government Publications Office. https://unfccc.int/resource/docs/natc/usnc3.pdf

Valencia, Alexandra, and Ignacio Munoz. (2019). "Ecuador's President Strikes 'Peace' Deal, Agrees to Change Fuel Subsidy Cuts." *Reuters* October 14. https://reuters.com/article/us-ecuador-protests-idUSKBN1WS0ND

Vanhala, Lisa, and Cecilie Hestbaek. (2016). "Framing Loss and Damage in the UNFCCC Negotiations: The Struggle Over Meaning and the Warsaw International Mechanism." *Global Environmental Politics* July 7.

Verheyen, Roda, and Peter Roderick. (2008). *Beyond Adaptation: The Legal Duty to Pay Compensation for Climate Change Damage.* London: World Wildlife Fund UK (WWF-UK). https://assets.wwf.org.uk/downloads/beyond_adaptation_lowres.pdf

Walker, Jeremy, and Melinda Cooper. (2011). "Genealogies of Resilience: From Systems Ecology to the Political Economy of Crisis Adaptation." *Security Dialogue* 42(2): 143–160.

Wallace-Wells, David. (2019). *The Uninhabitable Earth: Life After Warming.* New York: Tim Duggan Books.

________. (2017). "The Uninhabitable Earth." *New York* July 10.

Ward, James, Paul Sutton, Adrian Werner, Robert Costanza, Steve Mohr, and Craig Simmons. (2016). "Is Decoupling GDP Growth from Environmental Impact Possible?" *PloS One* 11(10): e0164733.

Weissenstein, Michael. (2019). "Puerto Ricans Try to Forge Movement to Oust Governor." *Associated Press* July 18. https://apnews.com/f2062d610de94669b18d4ee8c73b7553

Willison, Charley E., Phillip M. Singer, Melissa S. Creary, and Scott L. Greer. (2019). "Quantifying Inequities in US Federal Response to Hurricane Disaster in Texas and Florida Compared with Puerto Rico." *BMJ Global Health* 4: e001191.

World Economic Forum (WEF). (2020). *The Global Risks Report 2020.* Geneva, Switzerland: WEF. https://www.weforum.org/reports/the-global-risks-report-2020

York, Richard, and Julius McGee. (2017). "Does Renewable Energy Development Decouple Economic Growth from CO_2 Emissions?" *Socius* 3: 2378023116689098.

CHAPTER 3

The Rising Costs of Fossil Fuel Extraction: An Energy Crisis That Will Not Go Away

*Bart Hawkins Kreps**

ABSTRACT. In biophysical terms, such as energy return on investment (EROI), energy sources for the global economy have grown more expensive over the last few decades. This trend is likely to be more pronounced in the near-term future as conventional oil and gas are depleted and difficult-to-extract unconventional oil and gas become a larger part of the fossil-fuel supply. On the one hand, this will lead to "energy sprawl"—the growth of the energy sector, as this sector consumes a much larger portion of the energy it extracts—leaving less energy surplus for other sectors. On the other hand, we will see an unsustainable imbalance between the fuel prices that fossil-fuel companies will need to meet their costs and the fuel prices that the larger economy can afford to pay. This article reviews the historical role of inexpensive energy in economic growth, discusses the declining availability of conventional oil resources, and examines the increasing reliance on expensive, unconventional petroleum resources such as shale oil in the United States.

Introduction

The world now faces a huge challenge: *how to make the transition to a world of climate instability and rising energy costs.* The need to adapt to climate change is widely accepted. Nearly all climate scientists, and a majority of citizens in most countries, accept that the global climate is warming and that collective responses are required. By contrast, the need to adapt to rising energy costs is neither widely accepted nor widely understood. While business media usually focus on the short-term gyrations of the market price for fuels, there is little attention given to the more fundamental long-term issue of the increasing difficulty of extracting energy in the quantities the world economy has come to expect. This article will explore this long-term ongoing rise in energy costs and its implications, particularly a decline in per capita energy consumption.

The first section of this article will explore the foundational role that energy production and consumption plays in the global economy—a role that is downplayed or misunderstood in dominant schools of economic theory in recent generations. The second section will summarize evidence that inexpensive fossil fuels are growing scarcer both on a global basis and in North America, while much more expensive fossil fuels are becoming proportionately more important. Rising costs are already having ripple effects throughout economies and societies, presenting severe challenges to national governments in many countries as well as to the global financial order.

Section One: Energy Return on Investment as an Economic Fundamental

The economic boom of the past two centuries relied on readily accessible fossil-fuel sources. The

*Worked as newspaper editor, and as financial controller and geographic information manager for the Gwich'in Tribal Council in the Canadian arctic. Four-season cyclist for 40 years. BA in philosophy from Calvin College, Michigan. Lives near Toronto. Email: bart@anoutsidechance.com

extraction of that fuel required very little energy input compared with its high energy output. The resulting energy surplus facilitated nearly continuous economic growth. The most energy-rich and accessible fossil fuels have been extracted, and the world has begun an energy descent pathway. As a result, economic growth is faltering and cannot be sustained.

The viewpoint expressed in that short summary of the energy descent pathway is a world apart from the mainstream economic theories that have guided policymakers. So, a brief explanation of the guiding economic principles of energy descent is in order.

The views expressed here are strongly informed by researchers working under the rubrics "biophysical economics" and "ecological economics."* A key concept for this discussion is "energy return on investment" (EROI), an idea pioneered by Charles A. S. Hall and explored at length by Hall and Klitgaard (2018). (Some authors prefer "EROEI" or "energy return on energy invested," which clarifies that energy, not money, is the investment metric here.) The concept is rooted in biology and ecology. All living creatures require energy in usable forms, and getting that energy also requires an expenditure of energy. It is essential that the energy returned from the effort is greater than the energy expended in the effort. For example, a fox needs to catch and eat another animal. But if the fox continually expends more calories chasing rabbits than it gets from eating the ones it catches (an EROI below 1), then that fox will not survive. Extending the analysis one small step, a family of foxes needs to gather enough energy cumulatively to more than cover their energy expenditures in raising fox kits to an age when they can gather their own food. The need for an EROI above 1 is just as important for human societies, although the energy system dynamics can become very complicated.

Because the concept of EROI is fundamental to biophysical economics and is fundamental to so much of the analysis in this article, I will review the basics of this theory here, and then discuss refinements to the theory, where needed, later in this article and in the article following this one (Chapter 4).

EROI is a simple ratio, and does not in itself indicate anything about the *amount* of energy produced. An oil field that produces 1 million barrels of oil a day could have the same EROI as a single oil well producing 1,000 barrels a day. That EROI could be high or low or in-between.

EROI indicates the ratio between the total energy output of a source—for example, an oil well or a whole complex of wells—and the amount of energy expended in drilling and operating the wells (the energy investment). As a ratio, EROI is sometimes specified as "10:1" or "10 to 1," but the concluding "1" is often assumed and EROI values are referred to simply by values such as "30," "15," or "2.5."

In the example above, if the whole field and the single well each had an EROI of 10, then for each 10 barrels of oil output, the energy equivalent of one barrel of oil was invested to drill the wells and keep them operating. Therefore the *net energy output* would be nine barrels of oil—9/10 or 90 percent of the *total energy output*. The net energy output is the part that can fuel other economic activity, and the net energy output—also sometimes referred to as energy surplus—drops dramatically for EROI values under 10. This is often illustrated in a simple graph (Figure 1) known as the "energy cliff," a concept first introduced by Euan Mearns (2008) as a "net energy cliff." The key relationships to keep in mind are these:

energy return on investment (EROI)
= total energy output ÷ energy investment

net energy output = total energy output − energy investment

total energy output = energy investment + net energy output

As shown in Figure 1, when EROI is very

* The differences in approach, and reasons why writers might prefer one label over the other, are not essential to the discussion here. See Biophysical Economics Policy Center (2017) for a brief summary of differences.

high—anywhere from 50 down to about 10—net energy output (shown as dark blue) is, by far, the biggest share of total energy output. The consequence is that, in societies with high-EROI energy systems, the energy sector uses only a small proportion of its own energy output, and almost all the output of this sector is net energy output, or energy surplus for other economic activities.

Energy provisioning systems with extremely high EROI were a very recent development in human history. Both our global economic systems and our dominant economic theories have been developed during this brief period of very high EROI. As we discuss in subsequent pages, both the onset of high-EROI values and the gradual decline of EROI in recent decades have had and will have major economic implications.

Economic Orthodoxy as an Artifact of a High-EROI Economy

During long periods of history when agrarian societies dominated, farmers relied on high levels of skill

Figure 1
The Energy Cliff

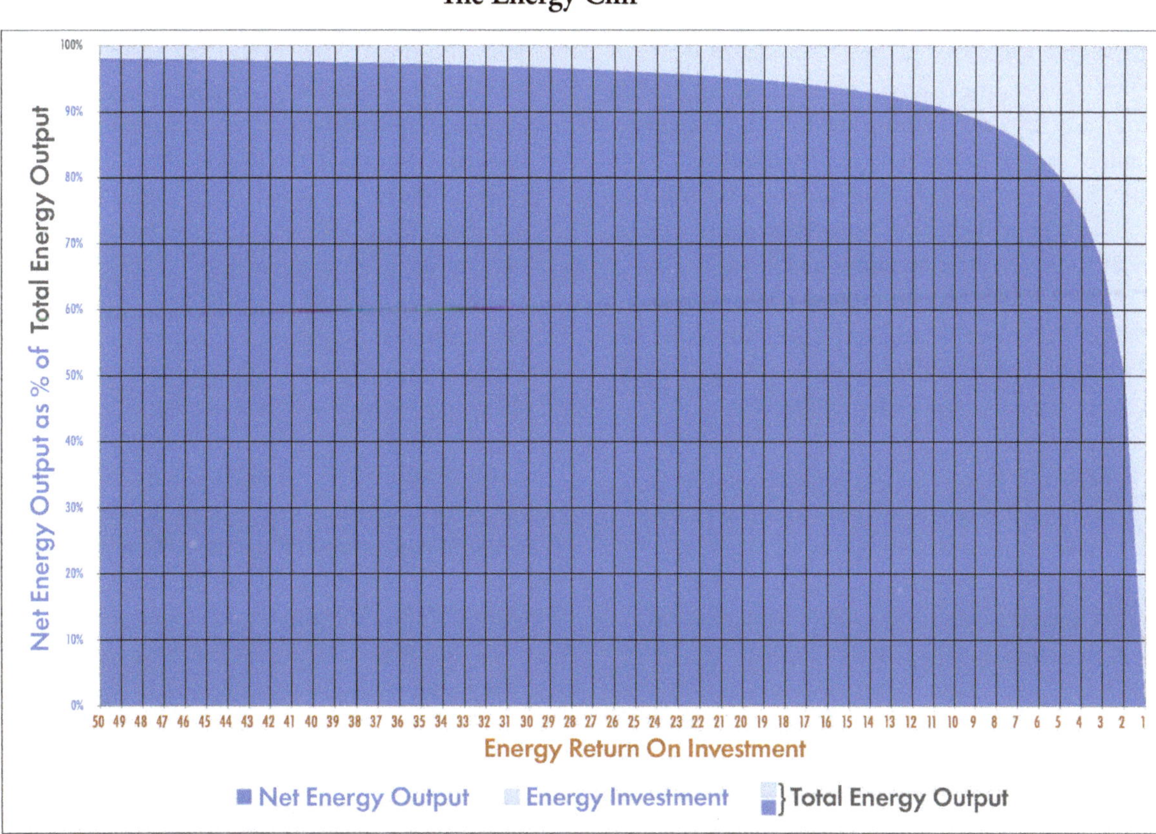

NOTE: The "energy cliff" refers to the rapid drop-off in net energy output for low energy return on investment ratios (with lower EROI values at the right side of the graph). The net energy output is 98 percent of total energy output when EROI is 50, and 90 percent when EROI is 10, but net energy output plummets for EROI values less than 8. At the far right edge of this scale, an EROI of 1 means the total energy output = energy investment, leaving a net energy output of 0.

SOURCE: Author, based on standard mathematical relationships.

and soil fertility to harvest food-energy in excess of energy expended in growing the crops. Energy use took the forms of people's dietary consumption, the consumption of crops by animals raised for pulling plows and carts, and biomass burned for cooking or heating.

The EROI in such societies was low, estimated by one Cornell University researcher as ranging from 1.1 to 1.6 (Staniford 2010). Taking the mid-point of that range—an EROI of 1.35—we can calculate both energy invested and net energy. Total energy is 1.35 times energy invested. Taking total energy output as 100 percent, invested energy can be calculated as 100/1.35 or 74.1 percent, leaving 25.9 percent as net energy. The proportion available as net energy thus ranges from 9.1 percent of the total (for an EROI of 1.1) to 37.5 percent (for an EROI of 1.6 percent). Thus, the majority of labor was devoted to producing (through farming and forestry) the energy required simply to maintain the agrarian labor force (the "energy sector"). A small surplus—from 9.1 to 37.5 percent of the total—supported others: priests, royalty, soldiers, artisans, and toolmakers.

A further consequence of low-EROI economies was that most people received their subsistence directly from their own work, as there was little surplus to support buying and selling in markets:

> The small energy surplus that could be extracted from solar flow produced only a small economic surplus. This small surplus was exchanged infrequently. What we know as the marketplace was not a part of daily life for most in the medieval era and before. (Klitgaard 2013: 279)

In contrast, the discovery of ways to extract and to use fossil fuels led to economies based on very high EROI. Hall and Klitgaard (2018) cite a range of EROI estimates for fossil-fuel extraction in the second half of the 20th century, ranging from 80 for some coal resources, to the high 60s for some conventional oil and gas resources (Hall and Klitgaard 2018: 398–399).

In a society running on such high-EROI resources, a small number of people employed in energy procurement can provide a large energy surplus that can fuel many other economic sectors. The goods and services produced with this surplus can be exchanged in the market, which thus can assume a very prominent role. As Klitgaard (2013: 278) explains, currently dominant economic theories were conceived during this brief period of extraordinarily high energy availability and rapidly growing surplus. Historian Timothy Mitchell (2013: 123, 124) further explains that today's widely accepted view of the economy only took hold in the mid-20th century, at a time when EROI levels were at a historical peak and fossil-energy resources seemed, to many people, practically inexhaustible:

> John Maynard Keynes, the economist who played a leading role in devising the postwar apparatus for tying the value of money to the movement of oil, helped formulate and describe another innovation of the mid-twentieth century: the modern apparatus of calculation and government that came to be called "the economy." … In the era that Keynes's thinking helped to define, the supply of carbon energy was no longer a practical limit to economic possibility. What mattered was the proper circulation of banknotes.

Until around 1950, biophysically-oriented economists were able to raise concerns about resource exhaustion in economic discussions. After that, they lost the battle for influence to the price theorists. Mitchell (2013: 132) summarizes these trends:

> Many economists were concerned to measure the exhaustion of the earth, … [but after 1950] economics became instead a science of money; its object was not the material forces and resources of nature and human labour, but a new space that was opened up between nature on one side and human society and culture on the other—the not-quite-natural, not-quite-social space that came to be called "the economy."

The overwhelming emphasis on market exchange

was crystallized in three letters: GDP or gross domestic product—the sum of all goods and services bought and sold, as measured in currency. Everyone—financiers, politicians, and voters alike—"knows" that in a healthy economy, the GDP is always growing.

But this economic orthodoxy is a poor framework to explain what is actually happening in the world, for many reasons, including the following two.

First, bank notes and the money supply can grow infinitely—but physical resources and the carrying capacity of our ecosystems do not. The fixation on the measurement of productive activity in monetary terms has fed a widespread belief in both the possibility and necessity of infinite economic growth.

Second, the simple-minded emphasis on the market value of energy resources drastically underestimates the foundational role of those resources in the economy. As long as energy resources remain cheap (and as long as we do not count the social and environmental externalities), orthodox economics measures the energy sector as a small part of the overall economy. But that misses the point, say Hall and Klitgaard (2018: 77):

> Curiously, energy's low price is the reason for its importance, not its unimportance. For 200 years the economy has received huge benefits from energy without having to divert much of its output to get it. This is because basically we do not pay nature for energy, but only the cost of exploiting it.

When the best energy resources are exhausted and it takes substantially more resources and workers to secure adequate energy supplies, then there will be less energy surplus and fewer workers to grow other sectors of the economy. This is summed up by financial analyst Tim Morgan (2016: 137) as "energy sprawl":

> In physical terms, the infrastructure required to access energy and deliver it to where it is needed is going to expand exponentially. At the same time, the proportion of GDP absorbed by the energy infrastructure is going to increase as well, which means that the rest of the economy will shrink. … Far from being a prediction, energy sprawl describes what is already happening.

Declining EROI and the End of Economic Growth

Energy historians who have studied economies in terms of EROI have documented a significant drop in EROI since a high point in the 20th century. Hall and Klitgaard (2018: 97) conclude that "[i]n the case of petroleum from the United States … the EROI has declined from at least 30 to 1 in 1970 to 18 to 1 in the late 1990s." Tim Morgan (2016: 128) adds:

> We are now experiencing a sharp deterioration in the availability of surplus energy, a trend evident in a decline in the global average EROEI [energy return on energy invested] to about 13:1 [in 2013] from 23:1 in 2000 and 37:1 in 1990.

At this juncture it is important to make clear the difference between "peak oil" and "peak EROI." The key is recognizing that not all of the energy "produced" by our energy sectors is useful to us. The only part of energy *output* that is useful is the part that is in excess of the energy *inputs*. Theoretically, fossil-fuel extraction could expand into more and more difficult areas and continue to grow until it was producing vast amounts of energy output that just equaled the energy inputs. In that absurd situation, fossil-fuel outputs would be at an all-time high, but the *net* outputs or usable energy surplus would be zero. Nevertheless, it is possible to operate individual projects with *negative* net energy (EROI less than 1) with an energy subsidy from elsewhere. Such projects can currently exist, but an entire civilization that operates with negative net energy would collapse quickly.

In our current world, fossil-fuel energy output is still growing, so we have not reached "peak oil" in terms of total output. But if the above-cited analysts are correct that we have reached "peak EROI," then the useful energy surplus has either stopped growing, or it is growing at a slower pace than the extractive industry requires to produce this surplus. In other words, the effects of a declining EROI are currently being masked by the high influx of capital into projects to extract oil and gas from marginal sources. Because the world petroleum market is increasingly dependent on difficult-to-extract resources, including shale oil and gas, tar sands, and deep-water, offshore wells, it seems reasonable to expect average EROI ratios to continue dropping. We will look at this trend and its implications through a survey by Nafeez Mosaddeq Ahmed and through a look at the brief history and uncertain future of fracking in the United States.

Section Two: Consequences of the Depletion of Conventional Fossil Fuels

Ahmed (2017) looks at major changes in oil production both in terms of the dramatic effects in specific countries and in terms of impact on the global economy. For decades we have heard about the vast and cheap oil resources in the Middle East, but Ahmed (2017: 50) finds that several countries in the region have already passed their peak production, with drastic consequences.

> Prior to the onset of war, the Syrian state was experiencing declining oil revenues, driven by the peak of its conventional oil production in 1996. Even before the war, the country's rate of oil production had plummeted by nearly half, from a peak of just under 610,000 barrels per day (bpd) to approximately 385,000 bpd in 2010. (Ahmed 2017: 50)

The drop in fiscal revenues forced steep cuts in social services, which combined with severe environmental pressures to make life intolerable for much of the population.

Turning to Yemen, Ahmed (2017: 53) found a parallel situation in which a decline in oil revenues is undermining the capacity of the state to serve citizens:

> Around 2001, Yemen's oil production reached its peak, since then declining from 450,000 barrels per day (bbd), to 259,000 bpd in 2010, and as of 2014 hitting 100,000 bpd. ... This has led to a drastic decline in Yemen's oil exports, which has eaten into government revenues, 75% of which had depended on oil exports. ... The decline in post-peak Yemen state revenues has reduced the government's capacity to sustain even basic social investments.

Likewise, in Egypt, Ahmed (2017: 64) discovers that energy descent is the culprit behind social and political fragmentation: "The unsung villain of political turbulence in Egypt is the peak of its conventional oil production." From 1993 to 2009, Egypt's oil production dropped by about 24 percent, while the annual increase in domestic oil consumption was about 3 percent. Again, the resulting revenue crunch for the Egyptian government led to damaging social service cuts for the population.

This region, in Ahmed's terms, is suffering simultaneous "environmental system destabilization" and "human system destabilization." The result for millions of inhabitants has been hellish, and the turmoil has reached far beyond individual nation-state borders.

On a global scale, oil production in Syria, Yemen, and Egypt was never a large part of world trade. The same cannot be said of Saudi Arabia. Ahmed (2017: 57) cites one study that predicts a peak in Saudi oil production by 2028. A peak in Saudi *production* is just part of a bigger problem for the global economy because the steadily increasing internal *consumption* of oil in Saudi Arabia will mean Saudi oil *exports* drop faster than its production drops. By the early 2030s, Ahmed writes, net oil revenues for the Saudi regime may decline to zero. With the country 80 percent dependent on imported food, this would mean a severe internal crisis. Externally, this would also mean that there would be little of the low-cost, high-EROI Saudi oil on the world market.

Countries like China and India, whose economies have continued to grow rapidly up to now, will compete for that oil with an increasingly needy

Europe: "Around 2000, Europe produced up to 25% of its own oil, but today this has declined to 13%" (Ahmed 2017: 77).

The projections of future oil demand presume, of course, that the world community continues a pattern of delaying serious climate action and continues to rely on fossil-fuel energy sources. It is unknown whether or when intensifying ecosystem crises will shake the hegemony of the fossil-fuel interests. Likewise, it is unknown how long a sufficient number of people will be able to afford increasingly expensive fossil energy. In economic terms, there is no "demand" for things that people simply cannot afford. We will touch on these questions later in this essay and in the following article (Chapter 4).

First, though, we will look at a country that has been one of the globe's biggest oil producers, biggest consumers, and biggest importers—a country whose boosters now like to call "Saudi America."

The Unsustainable Economics of Saudi America

In just over 10 years, the rapid growth of shale oil and gas became one of the biggest business stories in the United States. The fuel in shale deposits is referred to as "tight oil" and "tight gas" because it must be freed from shale rock layers through hydraulic fracturing—"fracking." The shale revolution boosted U.S. petroleum production dramatically, giving rise to the nickname "Saudi America" and to claims that the United States was becoming "energy independent." The following discussion summarizes the view that the shale revolution is a case of turning to much lower EROI oil than the U.S. and world economies used in the past century. In biophysical economics terms, "low EROI" is another way of saying "high cost." Thus, the shale revolution cannot produce a large *net* energy surplus for the United States, no matter how high *total* energy output might become.

The shale revolution also highlights a scenario where the true, high cost of a resource in EROI terms may not be reflected in its market or financial price, at least in the short term. This is vividly illustrated by the drastic plunge in the market price of oil in the COVID-19 pandemic; this was caused by a temporarily dramatic mismatch between market demand and the current supply of oil, but the low price does not at all reflect the high energy cost of producing much of that oil supply.

At the outset of this discussion, however, it is important to note that accurate estimates of the EROI of shale oil and gas are particularly hard to establish, for several reasons. The fracking boom—particularly fracking for oil—has happened primarily in areas where conventional oil was discovered and tapped decades ago. Some of the required infrastructure was already in place; and, furthermore, the fracked oil and gas may be combined with conventional petroleum in production reports.

To estimate the EROI of an oil or gas well, or of a field of wells, requires data on all the energy inputs. For fracked wells, that would require good data on the energy to prepare drill pads and sometimes new roads to the pads; energy to drill the well; energy to truck hundreds of loads of water and specialized sand to the well; energy to force water, sand, and chemicals into the well at high enough pressure to fracture the shale; energy to haul away the contaminated water that comes back up; and energy to truck the oil to collection points. (The thousands of scattered wells do not facilitate collection by pipeline.)

These energy *investments* have been managed by many different companies working as contractors in a fast-moving business environment, so data collection is a challenge. As for the energy *return* part of the ratio, that too is a fast-moving target.

In contrast to production in major conventional oil fields, where a well might yield approximately the same number of barrels each year for decades, it quickly became clear that fracked wells deplete far more rapidly—70–90 percent within three years. Production can only be maintained by drilling new wells continuously, but frackers keep trying new drilling techniques, and move to areas that may or may not be "sweet spots." So a figure as basic as "average output per well per year" is hard to nail down.

It is possible to estimate that the overall EROI of U.S. petroleum extraction has been dropping during the same period that the fracking boom developed, but it is much harder to pinpoint how much of the decline in EROI is due to the growing proportion of fracked resources. We may not have good answers on the EROI of fracked oil and gas until the fracking boom is over.

There is indirect evidence, however, to suggest that the fracking boom is producing poor returns—evidence from financial reports and markets that should, over the longer term, reflect falling energy return on investment.

Cambridge University economist Helen Thompson looked at this evidence with a view to answering two big questions: Why did global oil production increase only slowly from 2000 to 2008 in spite of a record oil price spike? and Why did the fracking boom occur only after the 2008 financial crash, and then continue in spite of dramatic swings in oil prices?

Thompson (2017: 18, 20) notes that the George W. Bush administration "appeared from the onset to conceive of oil supply as an urgent strategic problem." But in spite of delegating Vice President Dick Cheney to chair a task force on this problem, and in spite of rapid price increases that should have led to a boost in supply, "the Bush, Jr. administration's energy strategy did little to increase the supply of oil over the first eight years of the twenty-first century."

Central bankers in Western nations were preoccupied after 2008 with maintaining steady economic growth and staving off inflation. The rapidly climbing price of oil made this difficult, if not impossible. High oil prices stifled economic growth, but even high prices for oil were not enough to make the exploitation of unconventional oil profitable.

The problem went deeper than financial markets. The problem was as deep as geology. In order to significantly expand production, oil companies needed to turn increasingly to bitumen sands, shale oil, and deep-water offshore resources.

Thompson (2017: 48) writes that shale oil "has heavy extraction costs and requires continuous capital investment and ongoing drilling to prevent rapid decline since each individual well produces only a small amount of oil." Mere high prices were not enough to spark a significant growth in fracked oil production: "it is dependent on high prices *and cheap credit"* (emphasis added).

Before the new "Saudi America" (the name for the U.S. fracking boom) could be born, difficult geology needed a partner in improbable finance: the zero-interest-rate policy (ZIRP) that came into being following the financial crash and subsequent recession of 2008. Thompson (2017: 49, 50) writes:

> Without the extraordinary monetary expansion over which Western central banks have presided since 2008 the post-crisis world as we have known it would be unrecognizable, and the rise of non-conventional oil production would not have been possible. ... QE [quantitative easing] and ZIRP hugely increased the availability of credit to the energy sector. ZIRP allowed oil companies to borrow from banks at extremely low interest rates, with the worth of syndicated loans to the oil and gas sectors rising from $600 billion in 2006 to $1.6 trillion in 2014. Meanwhile, in raising the price and depressing the yield of the relatively safe assets central banks purchased, QE created incentives for investors to buy assets with a higher yield, including significantly riskier corporate bonds and equities. ... This rise of high-yield bond funding for the energy sector tied the shale boom from the outset to financial dynamics in which the incentives for investment were out of proportion to the risks entailed.

The long-sought boom in U.S. oil production did not mean, however, that ZIRP had solved the Western economic crisis. In the years since 2008, GDP growth has remained sluggish while income inequality has grown more extreme (Oxfam 2019). Though the new monetary policies led to asset inflation and wealth accumulation by the rich, "the general consequences of QE and ZIRP have been deep and profound not least for savings, pension prospects, and the distribution of wealth" (Thompson 2017: 50).

These policies resulted in a big flow of oil—but

not a flow of profits. Thompson (2017: 73) thus concludes:

> By the second quarter of 2015, more than half of all distressed bonds across investment and high-yield bond markets were issued by energy companies. Under these financial strains, a wave of shale bankruptcies began in the first quarter of 2015, and by the end of the year, 42 U.S. oil and gas companies had filed for bankruptcy with total outstanding debt of $17.2 billion.

Business journalist Bethany McLean reports similar findings. In an interview in *Fortune*, she clarified the financial failure of the shale revolution. As McLean explained:

> [The shale oil industry] as a whole, has yet to make money. There are a bunch of reasons, from low interest rates to a belief that returns lie ahead, why Wall Street has continued to throw capital at fracking companies. But you can't be sure that will continue forever. It's unclear how much oil and gas companies would produce if they could only reinvest their own cash flow, let alone if they had to produce a decent return for shareholders. (Gallagher 2018)

McLean (2018: 17) concurs with Thompson: "If it weren't for historically low interest rates, it's not clear there would even have been a fracking boom." To reinforce this view, McLean (2018: 54–55) cites the findings of investment consultant David Einhorn:

> Einhorn's firm had looked at the financial statements of the sixteen largest publicly traded frackers, which included companies like Pioneer and EOG. Einhorn found that from 2006 to 2014, the fracking firms had spent $80 billion more than they had received from selling oil and gas. Even when oil was at $100 a barrel, none of them generated excess cash flow—in fact, in 2014, when oil was at $100 for part of the year, the group burned through $20 billion.

McLean (2018: 89) concluded: "In its current financial form, the industry is still unsustainable."

Analysts Sanzillo and Williams-Derry (2018: 2, 12) found that after about 10 years of the fracking boom, petroleum producers were bleeding wealth:

> In financial terms, the oil and gas industry is weaker than it has been in decades. In the past several years, oil industry financial statements have revealed significant signs of strain: profits have dropped, cash flow is down, balance sheets are deteriorating and capital spending is falling. … The S&P 500 as a whole has dramatically outperformed the oil supermajors, as well as indices of smaller companies that produce and transport oil and gas in North America.

In short, the asset inflation that resulted in a post-2008 bull market did not extend to the stock of petroleum producers, who were pouring money into extraction ventures with a low EROI.

In sum, quantitative easing and zero-interest-rate policy made fracking possible, but cheap credit did not make fracking profitable. Sanzillo and Williams-Derry (2018: 23) suggest another mechanism that could be keeping the whole unprofitable game in motion.

> From a financial perspective, public policy designed to induce more drilling is really little more than publicly subsidized speculation, and can be challenged as such.

Subsidizing Losers

A 2014 study of subsidization of fossil fuels found that such subsidies recently rose substantially in two countries, China and the United States (Stefanski 2014: 15, 20–21). Since the 1990s, "fossil fuel subsidies [in North America] exploded, and the region became the second highest subsidizing region after East Asia." Subsidies to fossil fuels in the United States went "from almost nothing in 1991 to 170 billion dollars or 87% of all subsidies in the Americas in 2010."

Subsidies could play a crucial financial role in allowing the U.S. oil boom to continue. At the 2017 market price of US$50/barrel, "tax preferences and other subsidies push nearly half of new, yet-to-be-developed oil investments into profitability, potentially increasing U.S. oil production by 17 billion barrels over the next few decades" (Erickson et al. 2017: 891, 896). The projects that would be profitable only if current subsidies continue include roughly half of those in the largest shale oil areas and most of the deep-sea sites in the Gulf of Mexico.

If the shale-oil industry requires vast amounts of cheap credit at low interest, plus public subsidies, and still cannot turn a profit on a consistent basis without high oil prices, does it have much of a future? The U.S. Energy Information Administration (EIA) certainly thinks so. For the past few years, energy analyst J. David Hughes has published book-length studies of the EIA's annual forecast for the shale oil and gas industries. Hughes (2019: x) notes: "The EIA's reference case is widely used by industry and government as an authoritative forecast of what to expect for long-term energy supply." The EIA's reference case forecasts for U.S. oil production have risen each year since 2016, and the latest forecast shows daily production rising until 2031, remaining nearly stable for another 10 years, and then dropping gradually from 2040 to 2050, though it will still be higher than current production. (See Figure 2.)

Leaving aside the climate time bomb represented in this projection, is this economically plausible? Based on analysis of a data set that includes

Figure 2
U.S. EIA 2019 Reference Case Forecast of U.S. Oil Production by Source, 2012–2050

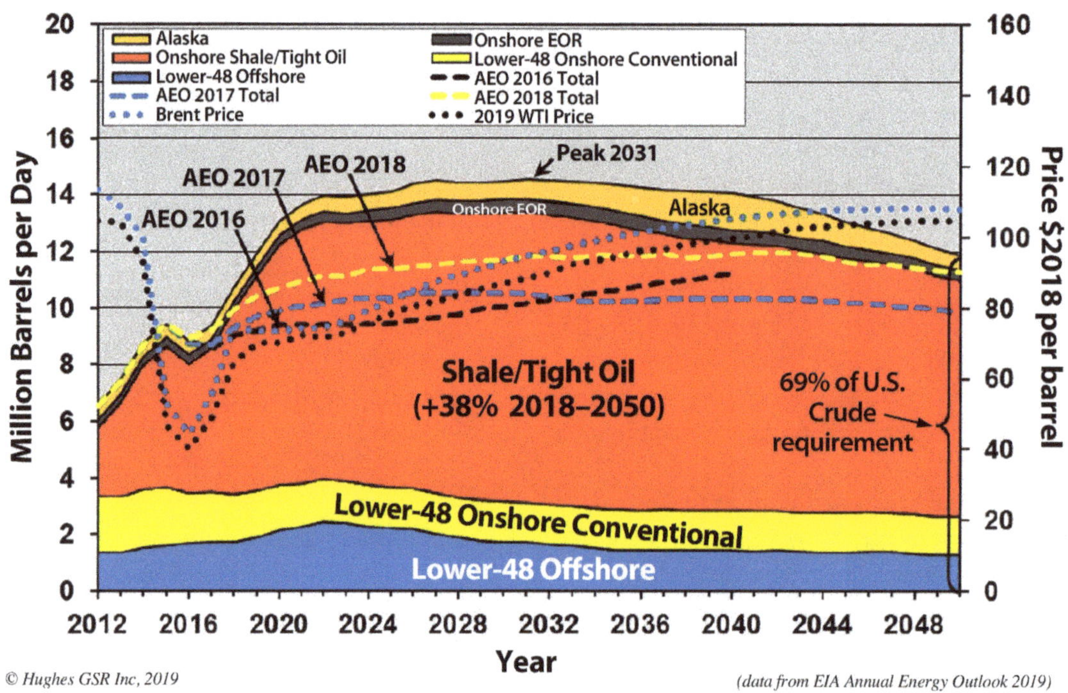

NOTE: AEO = Annual Energy Outlook (EIA estimate of future production). AEO 2016 to 2018 are earlier forecasts and projected prices (West Texas Intermediate and Brent in 2018 dollars per barrel).
SOURCE: Hughes (2019: 5); used with permission from J. David Hughes.

county-level drilling and production figures for the past several years for 13 shale plays in the United States, Hughes (2019: xi) finds that nine of the EIA's play-level projections are "extremely optimistic," three are "highly optimistic," and one is "moderately optimistic." The degree of optimism is clear:

> The EIA's reference case cannot deliver its forecast production requirement by 2050 if production from plays is limited to the EIA's estimated proven reserves plus unproven resources. The overall forecast falls short by nearly ten billion barrels of oil, or 10% of the required production volume. (Hughes 2019: xi)

In addition, the EIA forecast shows shale production continuing at a high level past 2050. This implies that the industry will recover 100 percent of the known oil that is currently technically and economically recoverable, plus 100 percent of the oil resources that are known or are thought likely to exist and that are thought to be technically recoverable even if not yet economically recoverable, plus much more.

What would be the cost of this project? Hughes (2019: xi) looks at several scenarios for meeting the EIA's figures for cumulative production by 2050, and the lowest-cost alternative would involve more than 1.1 million new wells in shale plays at a cost of $7.5 trillion. This cost averages to $220 billion every year from 2017 to 2050. Beyond the $7.5 trillion for shale, an additional $2 trillion would need to be invested in conventional wells, both onshore and offshore.

In spite of the high cost of the shale oil projects, the EIA projection indicates that two-thirds

Figure 3
U.S. EIA 2019 Reference Case Forecast of Cumulative Oil Production by Source, 2018–2050

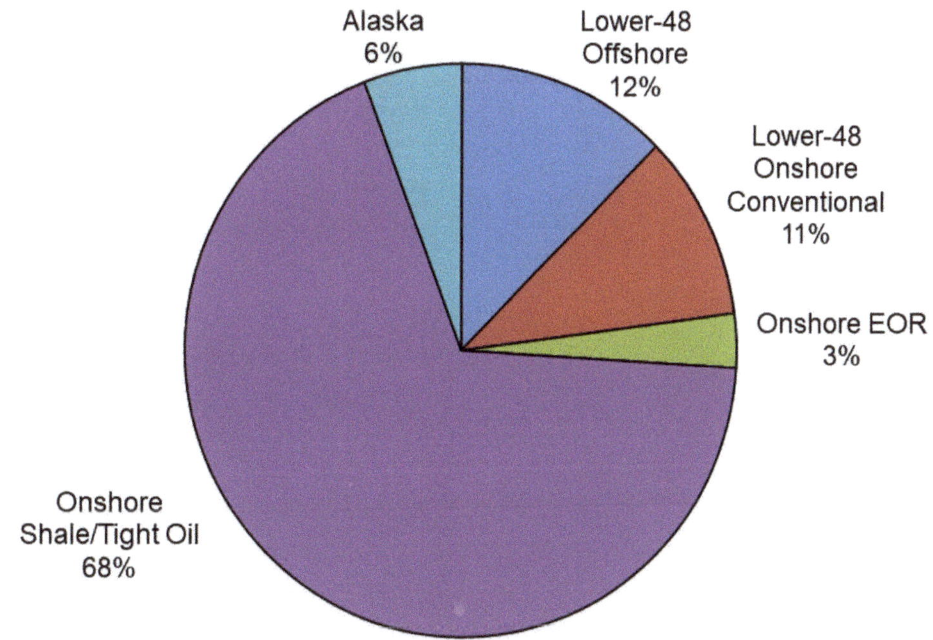

Source: Hughes (2019: 6); used with permission from J. David Hughes.

of cumulative U.S. oil production over the next three decades will be shale oil, as shown in Figure 3. Hughes portrays this as unlikely from the standpoint of geology and technical capabilities. If the boom did continue according to the EIA forecast, it would involve a massive and sustained program of well drilling and well servicing of a very different nature from the "drill once, collect oil and profits for decades" pattern of major conventional oil fields.

Would the EIA's sustained boom be *financially* viable, if oil prices rapidly rose to US$100/barrel and stayed that high or higher through the coming decades, as shown in Figure 2? Based on recent history, Helen Thompson (2017: 84) concludes:

> The evidence from what has happened between 2011 and 2016 is that there is now no possibility of an equilibrium price that would simultaneously keep large-scale shale production viable, allow sufficient market share for conventional oil producers, and allow Western and emerging market economies to grow at the rates to which their governments aspire.

That is the Catch-22 for a growth-dependent economic system in an era of high-cost, low-EROI fuels. Low market prices for energy allow consumers to buy lots of goods and services, and the economy can grow, except that unconventional oil producers lose money on every barrel, go bankrupt, and threaten the stability of the financial system.

High market prices for energy allow oil and gas companies to make profits on unconventional resources, meet interest payments, and possibly even

Figure 4
Global Oil Production, Conventional Oil Discoveries, and Development Expenses

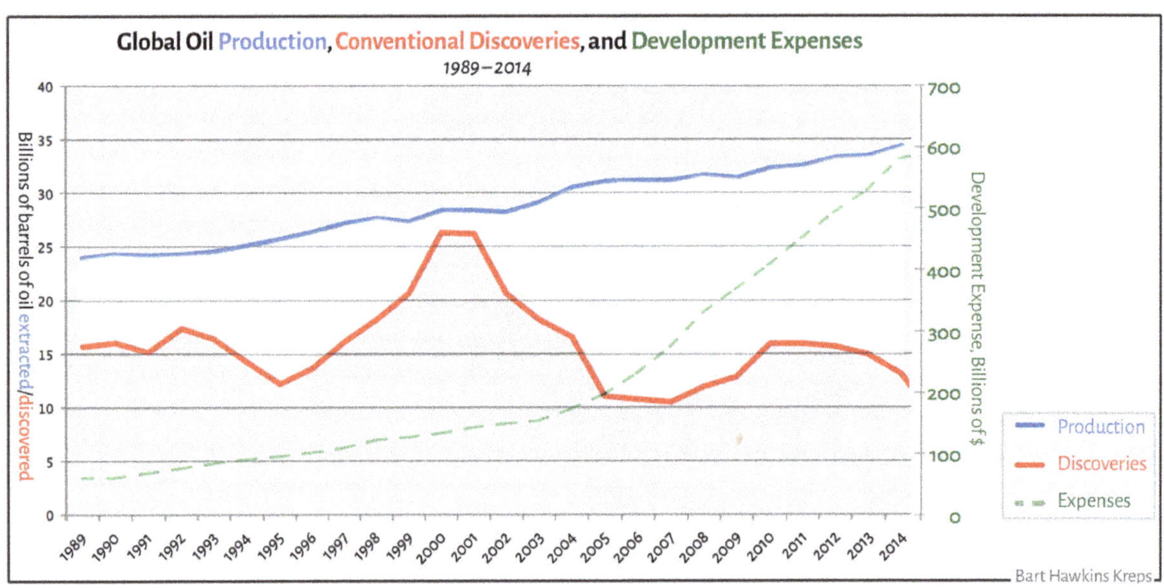

NOTE: Five-year running averages for global production of petroleum and other liquids.
SOURCE: Author's graphic. Data for production from U.S. Energy Information Administration (2020); for conventional oil discoveries from Holter (2016); for upstream capital expenditures from Barclays Global Survey (2016).

pay down some loans. But economic growth declines because reduced consumer spending on non-energy items translates into sluggish production.

In concluding this article, we will shift the focus from the United States back to the globe, looking at the rising costs of petroleum through another lens. Figure 4 shows the wide gap between global oil production and new discoveries over a 25-year period. The right axis shows the annual expenses for developing new extraction projects.

Figure 4 highlights the predicament faced by societies reliant on petroleum. It has been decades since we found as much new conventional oil in a year as we burned. Thus, the supplies of cheap oil are being steadily depleted. The trend has not been changed by the fracking boom in the United States, which involved unconventional oil resources that had been known for decades and that are costly to extract. Yet while natural capital in the form of conventional oil reserves is dwindling, the financial capital at play has risen steeply. In the 10-year period from 2005, upstream capital spending nearly tripled from $200 billion per year to almost $600 billion, while oil production climbed only about 15 percent, and there was no consistent growth in the discovery of new conventional oil.

For all the investment capital and labor it uses, the shale industry has yet to demonstrate that it can produce profits. The evidence from financial markets, then, is that "energy sprawl" is already evident as the world turns to fossil fuels with lower EROI: producing the amount of oil demanded by the world economy now takes much more effort and expense. Although the fracking boom has enabled the United States to top up otherwise declining oil output, this has come at a high cost. The expansion has required quantitative easing and a zero-interest-rate policy, which have distorted financial markets. In addition, a boost in public subsidies has left less budgetary room for other needs—which illustrates that even if market prices for biophysically costly fuels are kept artificially low through subsidies, low-EROI fuel sources nevertheless reduce the true surplus available for societal uses.

Conclusion

Much attention in recent years has been devoted to the challenges to society posed by the climate crisis, with very good reason. But while many people have focused on the urgent environmental need to wind down the fossil-fuel economy, relatively little notice has been paid to increasing inability of the fossil-fuel economy to sustain the economic growth that political leaders have taken for granted. As we have depleted conventional fossil fuels and turned to tight oil and other unconventional sources, the energy return on investment (EROI) has dropped, along with the net energy surplus that the fossil-fuel sector is able to provide for society as a whole. As I discuss in the following article (Chapter 4), it is implausible to expect that renewable energy sources will replace the vast and affordable energy surplus that was provided by coal, oil, and gas in the heyday of fossil fuels.

References

Ahmed, Nafeez Mosaddeq. (2017). *Failing States, Collapsing Systems: Biophysical Triggers of Political Violence.* Cham, Switzerland: Springer.

Barclays Global Survey. (2016). "Global Upstream Capital Spending, 1985– Present." *Energy Fuse* September 30. http://energyfuse.org/chart-of-the- week/. Also Barclays Equity Research (February 14, 2018: 128), source cited as Barclays Research, Barclays North America Oilfield Services & Equipment Team. https://bit.ly/3d5W4aM

Biophysical Economics Policy Center. (2017). *What Biophysical Economics Is Not.* https://biophyseco.org/biophysical-economics/what-biophysical-economics-is-not/

Erickson, Peter, Adrian Down, Michael Lazarus and Doug Koplow. (2017). "Effect of Subsidies to Fossil Fuel Companies on United States Crude Oil Production." *Nature Energy* 2: 891–898.

Gallagher, Leigh. (2018). "Why American Energy Independence Is Overhyped." *Fortune* September 12. https://fortune.com/2018/09/12/why-american-energy-independence-is-overhyped/

Hall, Charles A. S. and Kent Klitgaard. (2018). *Energy and the Wealth of Nations: An Introduction to Biophysical Economics,* 2nd ed. Cham, Switzerland: Springer.

Holter, Mikael. (2016). "Oil Discoveries at 70-Year Low Signal Supply Shortfall Ahead." *Bloomberg News* August 29. https://www.bloomberg.com/news/articles/2016-08-29/oil-discoveries-at-a-70-year-low-signal-a-supply-shortfall-ahead

Hughes, J. David. (2019). *Shale Reality Check 2019: Drilling into the U.S. Government's Optimistic Forecasts for Shale Gas and Tight Oil Production Through 2050.* Corvallis, OR: Post Carbon Institute.

Klitgaard, Kent. (2013). "Heterodox Political Economy and the Degrowth Perspective." *Sustainability* 5(1): 276–297.

McLean, Bethany. (2018). *Saudi America: The Truth About Fracking and How It's Changing the World.* New York: Columbia Global Reports.

Mearns, Euan. (2008). "The Global Energy Crisis and its Role in the Pending Collapse of the Global Economy." *Oil Drum: Europe.* http://theoildrum.com/node/4712

Mitchell, Timothy. (2013). *Carbon Democracy: Political Power in the Age of Oil.* London, New York: Verso.

Morgan, Tim. (2016). *Life After Growth: How the Global Economy Really Works—And Why 200 Years of Growth Are Over.* Hampshire, UK: Harriman House.

Oxfam International. (2019). *Public Good or Private Wealth?* https://www. oxfam.org/en/research/public-good-or-private-wealth?

Sanzillo, Tom, and Clark Williams-Derry. (2018). *Financial Stress in the Oil and Gas Industry: Strategic Implications for Climate Activism.* Seattle: Sightline Institute.

Staniford, Stewart. (2010). "The Net Energy of Pre-Industrial Agriculture." *Early Warning.* http://earlywarn.blogspot.com/2010/03/net-energy-of-pre-industrial.html

Stefanski, Radoslaw. (2014). *Into the Mire: A Closer Look at Fossil Fuel Subsidies.* SPP Research Papers #9. Calgary, Alberta: Calgary School of Public Policy. https://www.policyschool.ca/wp-content/uploads/2016/05/fossil-fuels-stefanski.pdf and Oxford, UK: Oxford Centre for the Analysis of Resource Rich Economies. https://www.economics.ox.ac.uk/images/Documents/OxCarre_Policy_Papers/OxCarrePP201420.pdf

Thompson, Helen. (2017). *Oil and the Western Economic Crisis.* Cham, Switzerland: Palgrave Macmillan.

U.S. Energy Information Administration (US EIA). (2020). *Annual Petroleum and Other Liquids Production.* Washington, DC: US EIA. https://www.eia.gov/international/data/world/petroleum-and-other-liquids/annual-petroleum-and-other-liquids-production

CHAPTER 4

Energy Sprawl in the Renewable-Energy Sector: Moving to Sufficiency in a Post-Growth Era

*Bart Hawkins Kreps**

Abstract. Renewable-energy technologies have exhibited rapid price drops in recent years, leading to hopes that such technologies will rapidly replace the entire fossil-fuel-energy sector. But renewable-energy systems have been manufactured in a fossil-fueled infrastructure. Renewable energy has been functioning as a relatively minor adjunct to the overall energy system rather than displacing fossil fuels. If we expect renewable energies to *replace* rather than merely *supplement* the fossil-fuel infrastructure, "energy sprawl" will be a major issue. The energy return on investment (EROI) of renewables is likely to be far lower than the EROI of fossil fuels in their heyday. If renewable sources were eventually to produce all required energy, the energy-provision sector would comprise a much larger share of the economy than at present and provide less net energy surplus to other economic sectors. This article examines key problems for wind- and solar-photovoltaic-energy industries, including: the dependence on fossil fuels to manufacture renewable-energy equipment; the need to move beyond renewable-energy "sweet spots"; the increasing need for new infrastructure, including storage and long-distance transmission; and the difficulty in providing the types of heat needed for many industrial processes. Because the era of abundant, affordable energy that has fueled economic growth is coming to an end, we will need to look beyond providing our existing services with greater *efficiency* and question which forms of these services are actually needed for *sufficiency*.

Introduction

Many energy commentators believe the solution to the twin crises of rising global temperatures and the depletion of fossil fuels is now within sight. Declining unit costs of energy from photovoltaic-solar panels and wind turbines have seemingly provided the technological answer to what had previously seemed a tragic situation. If renewable energy can simply replace the fossil fuels we are currently consuming, then we can proceed with business as usual, simultaneously allowing both economic growth and a healthy environment.

The twin crises cannot, however, be solved so easily. While costs of renewable-energy installations have dropped dramatically in recent years, there is no reason beyond wishful thinking to assume this trend will follow its current path for the next 30 years. Societies face enormous challenges in producing a sufficient net energy surplus to power civilization as we get deeper into the critically important task of shutting off fossil-carbon emissions.

The *net* energy surplus, rather than the *gross* amount of energy produced by our energy sector, is the key factor. Net energy is directly related to energy

*Worked as newspaper editor, and as financial controller and geographic information manager for the Gwich'in Tribal Council in the Canadian arctic. Four-season cyclist for 40 years. BA in philosophy from Calvin College, Michigan. Lives near Toronto. Email: bart@anoutsidechance.com

return on investment (EROI), a fundamental concept in biophysical economics (Hall and Klitgaard 2018). EROI is the ratio of the total energy output divided by the amount of energy investment required to get that energy output. Only the net energy—the total output minus the energy investment—is available for use by society as a whole. In order for net energy to be positive, the EROI must be higher than 1, and in order for the energy sector to support a much larger and complex economy, the EROI must be much higher than 1.

"Energy sprawl" refers to an energy sector that becomes a relatively larger proportion of the overall economy when its EROI is falling and the amount of net energy it can provide is dropping (Morgan 2016). Energy sprawl is occurring with fossil fuels as economies rely increasingly on difficult-to-extract deep offshore resources, fracked oil and gas, and heavy oils in tar sands (see Chapter 3). This article argues that energy sprawl will also be a major factor in the transition to renewable energy.

Our understanding of EROI in renewable-energy industries is aided when we extend such concepts as "mine mouth" and "point of use" EROI, originally used to discuss the fossil-fuel sector, to the renewable-energy sector. As the renewable-energy sector grows to the point where it might replace rather than merely supplement the fossil-fuel sector, the challenges of maintaining a high EROI will become more daunting. First, the sector will need to do without a "fossil-fuel subsidy"; most of the current basic manufacturing infrastructure is produced with fossil fuels. Renewable-energy sources are ill-suited for many industrial processes, and manufacturing of many products will be far more expensive without fossil fuels. Second, if renewables are expected to provide all our energy needs, these industries will need to move beyond "sweet spots" where the sun or wind is strongest or steadiest, and we will need expensive new storage and transmission systems. These factors will increase the relative size of the energy sector while lowering the overall EROI. Third, when we think beyond "energy return" (aggregate energy yield) to "power return" (annual energy yield), it is clear that we need to consider not only the *total amount* of net energy returned, but *how fast* that energy return happens. Because renewable-energy technologies typically require a large energy investment upfront, while returning energy gradually over two or three decades, a rapidly growing renewable-energy industry will go through a period of years where it acts as a net energy sink, or the "power return" will be only a small amount of energy per year.

Taken together, these critical issues mean that an energy system that relies entirely on renewables will not provide the high amounts of net energy each year that the fossil-fueled economy has depended on for growth. We must think beyond "energy efficiency" to "energy sufficiency," developing new ways to distribute wealth so that all people can prosper in a post-growth era.

Section One: Energy Sprawl in the Transition to Renewables

The most optimistic views on the future of renewable energy have backing from some compelling evidence. On the financial side, the cost per kilowatt-hour of solar- and wind-generated electricity and the cost per kilowatt of generating capacity have been dropping steeply in recent years. Some analysts project these price trends to continue well into the future. A 2019 study for the World Economic Forum says:

> It is accepted that solar electricity costs have been falling at over 15% a year since 2009, and that solar modules have enjoyed a learning rate of 28% for every doubling in capacity. Advocates argue that it therefore makes sense to look forward because of the speed of change and that costs are likely to continue to fall in line with the learning rate. (Bond et al. 2019: 14)

Bloomberg New Energy Finance (2019) projects rapid price drops in the costs of solar-photovoltaic (PV) modules, wind turbines, and batteries:

> [Solar PV modules] are down 89% since 2010 and we expect another 34% decline from today

> to 2030. … Turbine costs are down 40% since 2010 …. We expect the cost of wind energy to drop another 36% by 2030, and 48% by 2050. … Battery prices are already down 84% since 2010. We expect the build-out of battery manufacturing for electric vehicles to continue to drive down the price of batteries for stationary applications. These fall to $62/kWh by 2030, down some 64% from today.

At the same time, analysts are reporting a wide range of EROI values for wind- and solar-generated electricity. While many of the reported EROIs for renewables are low, the highest reported EROIs for renewables rival those of conventional fossil fuels.

Wind-generated electricity and solar photovoltaics are both relatively new technologies, so it is not surprising that their EROI ratios are not settled fact. In trying to make sense of the huge range in reported values, however, it will help to look more closely at how EROI can be calculated and how the figures might be used or misused.

Hall and Klitgaard introduce some important refinements to the basic concept of EROI—refinements that they discuss in reference to fossil fuels but that can be usefully extended to renewable energies. First, we can calculate EROI in the simplest way by analyzing the energy content of a product at the "mine mouth" or "well head"; they term this the $EROI_{mm}$. For petroleum, one could calculate the calories contained in a barrel of oil that comes out of a well, divided by the calories used in extracting that barrel, and the result would be the $EROI_{mm}$ (Hall and Klitgaard 2018: 394).

That barrel of oil is not yet truly useful. First, it must be trucked or piped to a refinery, refined into products such as diesel fuel, and then transported to a terminal where a truck, for example, will fill up its fuel tank. This is the "point of use," and the $EROI_{pou}$ takes into account the additional energy that has been expended in refining and transportation. Typically, for fossil fuels, the $EROI_{pou}$ is about 32 percent lower than $EROI_{mm}$ (Hall and Klitgaard 2018: 394–395).

To actually use that fuel in a truck, you first need to build the truck and you need to build roads to drive it on. Hall and Klitgaard (2018: 395, 396) cite an estimate of the energy cost of the transportation infrastructure in the United States as "about 38% of the energy used as fuel itself." These additional costs must be considered in estimating what they term "extended EROI" or $EROI_{ext}$, which they define as the "energy returned to society" divided by the "energy required to *get, deliver, and use* that energy" (emphasis in original).

In the simplified example of oil extracted, refined, and used in a transport truck on the highway, less than one-third of the energy in an average barrel of oil remains as energy for the truck to use, so an EROI of 20:1 at the wellhead is down to an EROI close to 6:1 by the time the fuel is used for trucking. This helps to explain why it takes fuels of very high EROI to sustain a society with the industrial, transportation, and commercial infrastructure that many of us take for granted.

The concepts of "mine mouth," "point of use," and "extended EROI" are equally useful in considering the prospects for renewable-energy transition. But the very different qualities of fuels make the comparisons less than straightforward.

Point of Use Costs for PV and Wind Electricity

Bhandari et al. (2015: 133) looked at EROI calculations for a wide range of solar-photovoltaic (PV) systems and found EROI values from 8.7 to 34. Their study helpfully spells out the energy cost of production of the components that are included in these calculations:

> A PV system consists of the PV module and the balance of system (BOS) components. The module encompasses the surface that harnesses the solar energy. The BOS components encompass all other supporting infrastructure and can include the wiring, switches (for connecting to the existing electric grid), support racks, and inverter (to convert direct current to alternating current). (Bhandari et al. 2015: 135)

Since this calculation is based on the costs for and amount of electrical energy "at source," one might say that this is comparable to $EROI_{mm}$. In the case of a solar-PV system mounted on a residential roof, the $EROI_{mm}$ would also be the same as the $EROI_{pou}$. The equivalence applies as long as the "point of use in space" is that very home, and the "point of use in time" is now.

If the electrical energy is to be used somewhere else or at a later time, there will be transportation and/or storage costs, with implications significantly different than those for fossil fuels. If solar-PV-generated electricity is sold into the grid, there are substantial costs associated with constructing and maintaining that grid. It is easy to overlook those costs as long as solar-PV generation remains a small factor in electricity supply and is distributed through an existing grid with little modification.

The different qualities of electricity and fossil fuels have other important implications for future energy trends. On the one hand, if coal, oil, or gas is converted to electricity, over half of the energy in the fuel is typically lost in the conversion. When, on the other hand, electricity is produced directly through renewable-energy technologies, there is no comparable conversion loss. As a World Economic Forum report states:

> The issue is how to count solar and wind electricity (a high-quality energy carrier) as a share of global energy supply. Because of thermodynamic losses, this is a real issue—*the introduction of 100 MWh of solar will replace primary energy supply of 200–300 MWh of coal.* (Bond et al. 2019: 12, emphasis added)

Applying an appropriate correction factor, "BP multiplies solar and wind electricity by 2.6 when converting them into Mtoe [megatons oil equivalent]" (Bond et al. 2019: 12). Using this correction factor also makes the current global share of solar and wind electricity 2.6 percent, instead of the 1 percent estimated by the International Energy Administration (Bond et al. 2019: 12). But there is a compensating factor that favors fossil fuels. Despite their relative inefficiency when converted to electricity, oil and natural gas are cheap to transport and store.

The varying characteristics of renewable technologies and fossil fuels fit well together today. Though the electricity from solar and PV is intermittent, coal-, oil-, or gas-powered generators can produce electricity when the sun is not shining and the wind is not blowing. Transitioning to net-zero carbon emissions by 2050 will necessitate extensive and expensive modifications to the electric grid. For renewable electricity, those changes will lower the point-of-use EROI and raise costs. Moriarty and Honnery (2016, 2019) note:

> The need for very large energy storage systems will progressively arise as grid penetration increases. … An important consideration is the low output per installed GW of these intermittent sources compared with fossil fuels (or even hydro). If wind and solar were to provide nearly all electricity, the installed capacity without major storage would need to be several times that of coal-fired power stations, further lowering their EROI.

One further alternative for a grid powered mostly by wind or solar PV is a big increase in regional, national, or international transmission. This is based on the common-sense theory that even if it is dark and calm in one location, it will be sunny or windy somewhere else. But major new connections will not only be expensive but time-consuming to implement. Moriarty and Honnery (2016) explain the limits of this option:

> Major grid expansion faces technical difficulties, and would take several decades, whereas constructing new solar or wind farms only takes a few years, imposing a limit on future RE [renewable energy] output growth rates. (Moriarty and Honnery 2016)

Taken together, these issues signal that renewable

energies could become more expensive as they scale up. Although the $EROI_{mm}$ of solar and wind power may appear high, the downstream costs of providing continuous power from intermittent, low-output sources will lower the $EROI_{pou}$ considerably. This constraint applies primarily to distributed uses of electricity through regional grids; it imposes far less of a limit to on-site, immediate use of renewable sources. In practice, this means that the energy transition imposed by declining EROI will entail decentralization of many types of production. Above all, it means modern, industrial economies cannot simply replace fossil-fuel sources with renewable-energy sources on a one-for-one basis in existing electric grids.

The Fossil-Fuel Subsidy to Renewable Energies

Another factor that must temper the optimism of those who envision a seamless transition to a future based on renewable energy is the large, indirect energy subsidy that wind power and solar power currently receive from fossil fuels.

> Reflect for a moment on what it takes for just a single large wind turbine to exist. The materials with which it is embodied were mined and processed with oil-dependent machinery; its components were transported by ships and heavy haulage vehicles; once erected it is held in place by massive—thousands of tonnes for the largest models—concrete foundations. These machines, the scale of which can inspire awe, might be viewed as amongst the pre-eminent and definitive expressions of carbon civilisation at its peak. (Alexander and Floyd 2018: 78–79)

Striking a similar note, energy historian Vaclav Smil (2016: 27) has described wind turbines as "pure embodiments of fossil fuels." He says that simply to produce the steel needed for wind turbines that could supply 25 percent of forecast global demand for electricity in 2030, we would need "fossil fuels equivalent to more than 600 million metric tons of coal."

Likewise, nearly all components of solar-PV systems are also manufactured and transported using fossil fuels. That will remain true in the short term because we do not yet have renewable-energy technologies with the scale and characteristics needed to power the construction of additional renewable-energy equipment. Therefore, the cost-effectiveness of wind and solar-PV generation will change as fossil-fuel prices change. On the one hand, if fossil fuels become more expensive, then renewable energies—assuming that their prices are stable or dropping—will be more attractive in the market. On the other hand, fossil-fuel inputs will cause the EROI of renewable energies to tend to drop as fossil-fuel EROI drops.

In the longer term, we need to question whether the roles played by fossil fuels in relevant industrial processes can be performed comparably well by electricity. If they cannot, or if the renewable-energy-powered replacement processes are considerably more expensive, that will make a complete transition to a renewable-energy economy much more difficult.

The Problem of Industrial Heat

As discussed above, there is a big conversion penalty to pay when converting chemical-energy sources, such as fossil fuels, to electricity: thermal generators lose around 60 percent of the fuels' energy content in producing electrical energy.

In other contexts, however, the conversion penalty works in the other direction. If you have a lot of electricity, but what you need is a lot of heat for an industrial process, then your industrial process may become very costly (Friedmann et al. 2019; Sandalow and Friedmann 2019). In processes reliant on heat sources with high temperature, high heat flux (rate of transfer of heat), or both, changing from current fossil-fueled production methods will cause costs to escalate (Friedmann et al. 2019: 12).

Burning hydrogen is a possible solution for some industrial processes, and the *combustion* would be carbon-free. Commonly used methods for the *production* of hydrogen, however, involve significant carbon emissions. Production of "green hydrogen" using low-carbon methods is much more expensive (Friedmann et al. 2019: 19, 20).

For example, the production of cement clinker is one of the most basic steps in our current built infrastructure. Coal is the primary fuel and heat represents at least half the production cost—the process requires temperatures of 1450°C. Replacing coal combustion with "green" hydrogen will entail a clinker price hike of between 50 percent and 200 percent, in most cases (Friedmann et al. 2019: 45, 46).

Likewise with steel production. Using "green" sources of heat would add significant costs (Friedmann et al. 2019: 46–47).

Many industrial processes would need to be substantially redesigned or, in some cases, rebuilt in different locations if different fuels were to be used. Processes that require unvarying high temperature and high heat flux 24 hours a day are a major challenge. Solar-thermal energy, harnessed through concentrated solar-power (CSP) plants can provide high enough temperatures for some, though not nearly all, industrial processes, and through the use of molten salt they can retain temperatures up to 560°C after the sun goes down. But suitable sites for CSP are very limited, and since heat cannot practically be transported away from the site, industries hoping to use the heat directly would need to be co-located with the CSP plant (Friedmann et al. 2019: 27–28).

One more difficult hurdle to note: chemical industries use an enormous range of processes that are dependent on high temperatures, and each process would have to be redesigned to use different fuels. At the same time, because many chemical plants "have tens to hundreds of small distributed heat sources," even applying carbon-capture processes "may prove unworkable" (Friedmann et al. 2019: 49).

Converting heat-dependent industries to low-carbon methods, then, is not likely to be quick or cheap. As the expensive changes are made, higher product prices will ripple through the economy. Because the expanding infrastructure for solar-PV and wind electricity will require steel, wiring, concrete, and many chemicals used in solar panel and battery production, the high costs of heat-dependent processes will be reflected in higher prices for this renewable-energy infrastructure.

This positive feedback loop (or self-reinforcing cycle) of rising costs mirrors what Robert Ayres terms a "double whammy" in costs of acquiring necessary materials for renewable energy as well as other infrastructure:

> The first whammy is that the [energy] requirements of separating desired materials from a mixed mineral mass rises without limit, as the concentration (grade) of the ore or resource falls. The second "whammy," as you have probably already guessed, is that the fuels and electric power needed for copper ore treatment are themselves produced from increasingly low-grade sources, and this applies not only to fossil fuels but also to renewables. It follows that essentially all extractive resources will be increasingly [energy]-intensive as time goes on. (Ayres 2016: 420)*

Though the number of factors at play here is large, we should, at the very least, question the predictions that recent cost-reduction trends for solar and wind will automatically continue through coming decades.

* To avoid confusion, I have substituted the word energy in the quote for what Ayres (2016: xi) calls "exergy": "that part of energy that can do work." In this article, we have been using the term "energy" to mean the same thing that Ayres refers to as "exergy," which is why the substitution in the quote is valid. In thermodynamics, however, the distinction between exergy and energy is fundamental: energy cannot be lost, but when we "use up" or consume exergy (useful energy), the exergy is turned into "anergy" (energy that does no work), and entropy increases.

Sweet Spots and Theoretical Potential

"Sweet spots" are sources that provide the easiest- and cheapest-to-extract fossil fuels. When they are tapped out, production moves to resources that are harder to extract and thus provide a lower EROI. This can happen on a broad geographic scale. For example, when large reservoirs of oil accessible from land-based wells are depleted, drilling might move to difficult wells in deep-water offshore areas. On a local scale, as reservoirs of fluids are depleted, drillers might turn to fracking specific layers of shale deep under the very same surfaces. Within a specific fracking play, drillers are likely to drill the most productive areas first, and then move to less productive locations around the perimeter of the play.

It is reasonable to expect that an analogous process will occur with renewable energies, including wind and solar PV. Average wind speeds are highly variable across continents and within regions. Known wind sweet spots—high ridges scattered throughout large areas of plains, for example—will attract wind-energy investors looking for a good return. In the early stages of the energy ramp-up there may be enough sweet spots to go around, but at some point the best areas will have been taken, and for the industry to continue to expand, development must then move into the less energy-productive locations.

In a survey asking whether sites in the European Union that are suitable for wind turbines or solar PV could yield sufficient energy to satisfy current demand, Dupont and Jeanmart (2019: 8, 10) conclude: "It does not seem possible to reach the 46.4 EJ [exajoules] of final energy consumption with wind and solar power only." Theoretically, wind and solar could meet most of that energy demand, but *only if EROI were no concern.* More specifically, wind and solar could theoretically provide up to 44 EJ/year, but only if developers accepted any EROI over 2. If developers worked only with locations where they could get EROI ratios of 6 or higher, the maximum output would be 32 EJ; if restricted to locations with EROI of 10 or higher, maximum output would be 19 EJ; and if restricted to locations with EROI of 12 or higher, maximum output would be about 10 EJ.

For solar power, even the most productive areas are likely to result in EROI ratios of only 6:1. These areas are in southern Europe, particularly in Spain and Portugal. Areas with significant wind-generation potential are more evenly distributed but nearly all of the areas with highest EROI—12:1 or better—are in northern Europe (Dupont and Jeanmart 2019: 12).

Taken together, these findings have significant implications for the potential to ameliorate the "intermittency" problem with renewables. During periods when solar-produced electricity is not abundant in the Iberian peninsula due to widespread clouds or nightfall, the potentially available electricity from wind will need to come from the northern reaches of the European Union. Conversely, when a widespread weather pattern reduces wind power in northern Europe, significant fill-in from solar PV will need to come from the southern areas of the European Union. This could only work with a very robust cross-continent distribution grid. Construction and maintenance costs for this grid, when properly accounted, would further reduce the EROI ratios of the renewable-energy system.

As Dupont and Jeanmart (2019) explain, the theoretical maxima shown by their model do not take into account any storage needs. If we take into account the need for extensive storage and transmission to deal with intermittency issues, then we can understand that installations with an EROI of 2 at the point of generation would make little or no net contribution in the overall system. So the theoretical maximum outputs would have little direct practical relevance. Conversely, an overall system where the weakest individual generating systems produce, for example, EROI of 10 or higher might produce significant net energy, even after overall systems costs including transmission and storage are factored in. But the maximum gross output would only equal about one-third of current E.U. energy usage.

This is another illustration of the energy sprawl inherent in using low-EROI energy sources. In spite of immense investments of labor and capital to build a new renewable-energy infrastructure, the system would produce a small energy surplus to share across the overall economy, compared with the large surplus produced by the fossil-fuel system we have known.

Energy Return and Power Return

In recent years, a variety of researchers have also focused on the issue of "power return on investment" (PROI) as a necessary complement to energy return on investment (EROI). In simple terms, the power return discussion asks: Over what period do we make the investment, and over what period do we get the return? Power return questions yield very different answers for wind and solar-PV projects than for fossil-fuel developments.

The "implications [of PROI] for large-scale transition in energy sources," Joshua Floyd (2013) writes, have "perhaps even greater significance than EROI."

Carbajales-Dale (2019) reviewed the commonly used formula "energy return on investment = energy output/energy investments." This does not refer to any time period, so it might be assumed that both the energy outputs and the energy investments mean the totals for a given facility over the life of that facility.

For an entire industry, however, Carbajales-Dale (2019) notes that it would be difficult, if not impossible, to acquire data on lifetime total outputs and total investments. Thus, in practice, researchers have tended to calculate industry-wide EROI based on outputs and inputs for a given year. This means "the numerator and denominator are *energy flow rates* (energy per year, i.e., power) in a year" (Carbajales-Dale 2019: 2, emphasis in original). To be precise, the equation then gives us "power return on investment" (PROI) rather than energy return on investment.

The distinction is not particularly important if both the energy outputs and the energy investments are steady over the period of years being examined. Otherwise, the distinction between EROI and PROI is *very* important:

> The solar and wind industries are growing rapidly, such that current investment is not matched by current output from the industry. Even mature industries, such as oil and gas, can see large shifts year-to-year in drilling activity, causing "EROI" (actually PROI) to bounce up and down. (Carbajales-Dale 2019: 2)

The difference between EROI and PROI is particularly pronounced for industries such as wind and solar generation, where nearly all the energy investment is upfront, while the energy outputs accrue steadily over 20 or more years. Carbajales-Dale (2019) illustrates with the simplified example of a renewable-energy industry with 100 percent of the input costs upfront, and a facility lifetime of 20 years. As long as the industry is growing steadily, the industry-wide PROI is much lower than each facility-level EROI.

This, too, has important implications for "energy sprawl." Given the need to ramp up renewable-energy production rapidly throughout coming decades, the surplus energy per year—power—will remain low as long as much of that power is being invested in new facility construction. Though many workers and a great deal of capital will be employed building these facilities, they will not be able to generate a high surplus of energy per year until the industry slows or stops growing.

The related concept of energy payback time (EPBT) is also the subject of much recent research (Dale and Benson 2013; Bhandari et al. 2015). With energy technologies such as solar PV and wind, in which nearly all the energy investment comes upfront while the energy output occurs gradually over decades, there is necessarily some period of time before a facility "pays back" as much energy as was invested. This payback period is directly correlated with energy return on investment, and with the lifetime of a facility over which the return on investment accrues.

The graphs in Figure 1 illustrate power return on investment (PROI) and cumulative net output. In the modeled industry, 100 percent of the energy investment is upfront—a simplification of solar-PV and wind generation, which have no fuel costs and very low ongoing maintenance costs. In the scenarios shown, the industry starts with an initial energy investment from a baseline of 0, and the investment

Figure 1
Power Return and Net Energy Output for a Growing Industry

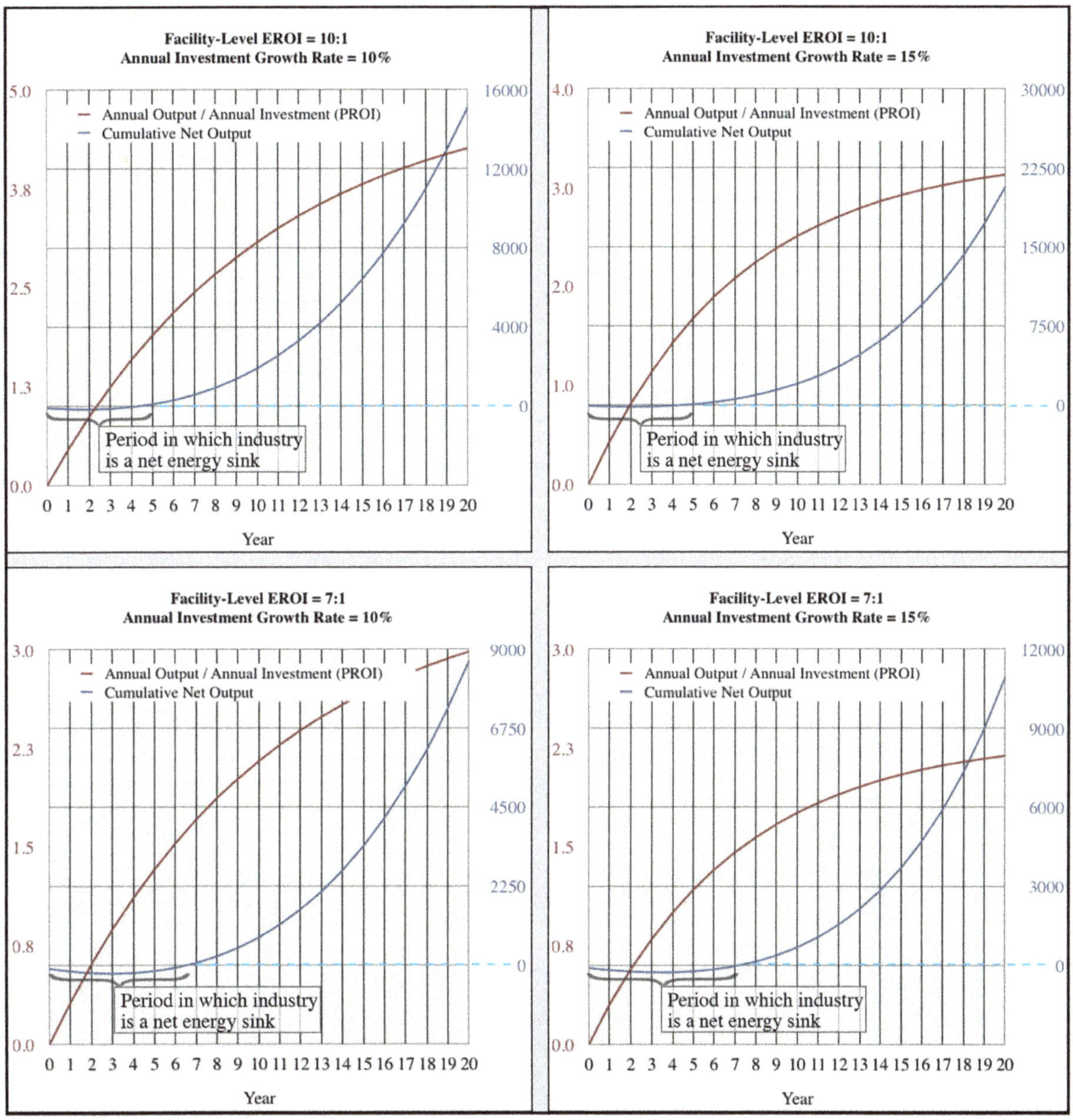

Source: Graphic by author, based on a spreadsheet by author. Note: These graphs illustrate annual power return on investment (PROI) on the left axes and cumulative net energy output on the right axes, for a simplified model of a growing renewable-energy industry. Each individual facility has an energy return on investment of either 10:1 or 7:1, 100 percent of the energy investment takes place upfront, and each facility operates for 20 years. The industry starts from investment and output of zero, with an initial investment of 100 energy units in year zero. As shown here, the industry's PROI grows rapidly but stays well below the lifetime EROI of each individual facility throughout this growth period. In each case, there is a period of some years before the cumulative net output of the industry surpasses zero.

grows at steady increments of 10 percent or 15 percent each year. The EROI of individual facilities is projected at 10:1 or 7:1, with individual facility lifetime of 20 years.

In these scenarios, there is a period of several years before the growing industry reaches a net cumulative energy output higher than 0. The industry's annual PROI grows rapidly but stays much lower than the facility-level EROI. Note also that whether the growth rate is 10 percent or 15 percent, there is a big difference—roughly 2 to 1—in net cumulative energy output, depending on whether EROI is 10:1 or 7:1.

These simplified scenarios are illustrative in four ways of the trade-offs that we will face as we transition from fossil fuels to renewable energy.

- First, with each year that the world economy continues to emit more carbon, the urgency of a rapid transition to renewable resources grows.
- Second, the higher our targets for renewable-resource energy consumption, the more we will need to go beyond renewable sweet spots, adding facilities in less windy or sunny areas that have lower EROI ratios and longer energy payback times.
- Third, the faster we ramp up renewable-energy production and the more we move beyond renewable-energy sweet spots, the longer the period in which we have negative cumulative net energy output and very low annual PROI ratios.
- Fourth, and equally important, the above scenarios consider only *facility-level* EROI, corresponding to mine-mouth or wellhead EROI for fossil fuels. As discussed earlier, as the proportion of renewable energy in the overall energy supply grows, there will be an increasing need for additional storage and transmission infrastructure. As the energy investment required for that infrastructure grows rapidly, that is an additional reason the annual PROI from renewables will remain low. The power surplus produced by the energy sector and shared with the overall economy will also remain low.

If there is an *energy payback time* for a new renewable-energy facility, and if the manufacturing of that facility is significantly dependent on fossil fuels, that also implies there will be a *carbon payback time* for that facility—the period before it has saved enough in avoided emissions through clean-power production to equal the emissions produced in the facility's creation. Researchers have calculated carbon payback times for specific technologies or installations. For our purposes here, the carbon payback concept represents an important and particular intertwining of ecological and economic imperatives. It is important to realize that both energy payback and carbon payback on an industry-wide scale will lengthen if that industry is growing rapidly and if that industry is determined to grow beyond "sweet spots" and into low-EROI areas.

A brief aside on nuclear energy is appropriate here. There are widely diverging estimates for the EROI for nuclear generation of electricity. Hall et al. (2014: 143) found a mean EROI of about 14:1 in a meta-review. Nuclear energy has one thing in common with renewable-energy technologies—most of the energy investment is upfront. However, the construction phase for a nuclear reactor lasts many years—a period in which there is a substantial energy investment with no energy return. This is particularly relevant when viewed through the lens of PROI. If societies were to decide on a rapid and sustained ramping up of nuclear generation, there would be a lengthy period in which usable energy would need to be diverted from other uses into the nuclear-generation project, and net energy available to the rest of the economy would drop accordingly.

The twin crises of global heating followed by dwindling cheap fossil-fuel supplies give us only about one generation to transform our economy. During that terribly abrupt transition, we have a choice. *We can have affordable energy or we can have abundant energy or we can have low-carbon energy. If we are lucky we might have two out of three—but not all three.*

Finally, it is worth taking a brief look at another large facet of the problem of energy supply in coming decades: the lasting environmental costs of hydrocarbons. Moriarty and Honnery (2019) illuminate the problem:

> Both the production of energy and its use—particularly combustion of fossil fuels—produce a variety of adverse environmental effects, which act to reduce the ecosystem services which are vital to the well-being of human and other species. … Energy producers are often reluctant to deal with—or even recognize—these problems, because production costs would be increased.

Many such environmental costs have been ignored and sloughed off to future generations. To take just one example, Nikiforuk (2019) writes that there are several hundred thousand oil and gas wells in the province of Alberta, Canada, but "more than 40 per cent of the oil and gas wells … are not pumping hydrocarbons or generating revenue. Many are leaking methane, CO_2, radon or hydrogen sulphide into the air, ground, or water table."

Depending on human population levels, future societies might make an awful choice to simply abandon some "sacrifice areas" of the globe. But there is no escape from the planetary problem of carbon emissions—both the emissions that continue to escape from abandoned hydrocarbon facilities and the excess emissions that are already in the atmosphere will continue to heat the global climate.

As White (2020) shows, some of the excess atmospheric carbon can be removed via regenerative agriculture, but the "negative-emissions technologies" that form a big part of the tenuous hope in IPCC climate scenarios are still to be developed at scale. This is deeply unfair, and Greta Thunberg was rightly angry when she addressed a U.N. assembly: negative-emissions technologies "rely on my and my children's generation sucking hundreds of billions of tons of your CO_2 out of the air with technologies that barely exist" (Thunberg 2019).

A "green EROI," Moriarty and Honnery (2019) say, will need to factor not only the current input costs, but also the energy costs of ecosystem maintenance, including greenhouse gas abatement costs, *"both for the current and past years."* One could question whether paying the deferred costs of past activities should be considered part of future EROI, or whether it is more correct to retrospectively recalculate the EROI of the fossil-fuel era and learn that this EROI was not as high as previously estimated. Either way, diverting some of their precious energy supply into paying the energy debts of earlier generations will reduce the power return and reduce the net energy available to future societies for as long as negative-emissions technologies remain necessary.

The End of Growth

In a society that is dependent on low-EROI energy sources, the energy sector will grow as a proportion of total economic activity, but the economy as a whole will grow slowly, if at all. That is the clear implication of research into the links between available energy and GDP growth. Brockway et al. (2019: 133–155) report:

> Very few countries have achieved *absolute* decoupling of primary energy consumption from GDP (i.e. GDP rising while energy consumption is falling) for more than short periods of time. Also, when absolute decoupling has been achieved (such as in the UK) it has partly been driven by the "outsourcing" of energy-intensive manufacturing to other regions.

Heun and Brockway analyzed the economies of two different nations—the United Kingdom and Ghana—to study the relationship of primary energy consumption with economic growth. They conclude that "absolute decoupling appears to be mission impossible" (Heun and Brockway 2019: 1).

The tight relationship between primary energy consumption and economic growth mirrors the relationship between carbon emissions and economic growth. For example, Ian Gough (2017) notes:

> There is no evidence yet of any absolute decoupling of carbon from output on a world scale.

> Indeed, there is scant evidence of any reversal of emissions growth, except in times of economic crisis.

Since fossil fuels have provided a dominant share of primary energy for the past century, it makes sense that economic growth has been correlated with *both* primary energy use and carbon emissions. As we move to low-carbon- or no-carbon-energy technologies, the correlation of growth with emissions could end—*if* it were also possible to break the correlation between growth and energy consumption. But faith in progress aside, there is no rational basis on which to conclude that growth will continue in spite of lower energy availability.

For those who accept current economic orthodoxy—including the faith that economic throughput can and must grow indefinitely—the above concepts may present an inconvenient Catch-22. For those who do not believe that infinite throughput is possible on a finite planet, on the other hand, the solution is simple in concept, even if it is difficult in practice: we will come to live with much lower per capita energy consumption. Being willing to adapt to that condition now is our best chance at a peaceable transformation.

Section Two: Human Well-Being in a Low-Energy World

Atmospheric scientist Peter Kalmus (2017: 22, 129, 143, 157) looked at the hard truths of climate change he faced every day at work, and he looked at his lifestyle. He had a thought: maybe I would be happier if my life were in accord with the urgent imperative to reduce carbon emissions. But where to start?

> Doing nothing is one extreme. Giving up fossil fuels cold turkey, if that were even possible, would be the other. I'm walking on a middle path.

After a few years, that "middle path" had the following results:

> So far, by making changes to my daily life, I've reduced my emissions by more than a factor of ten. I used to emit slightly more greenhouse gases than the average American. Now I emit less than the average human. However, I still emit nearly twice the average Bangladeshi.

As one might expect in a primarily fossil-fueled society, Kalmus's effort to reduce carbon emissions also resulted in an overall reduction in energy consumption. For example, he estimates that his household now has less than one-tenth the American average per capita electricity consumption. Far from being a penitence or a way of suffering, he has found his new lifestyle a joy:

> I think most people are afraid of a low-energy lifestyle because we equate quality of life with quantity of energy use. My experience has been the opposite: low-energy living is more fun and satisfying.

On a societal level, there is abundant evidence that the extraordinary explosion in per capita energy consumption in the last century has not been accompanied by a proportionate increase in human happiness or well-being—evidence we will return to shortly. Conversely, there is no reason to assume that a dramatic reduction in energy consumption must necessarily result in a reduction in well-being.

To Efficiency—And Beyond

Kalmus (2017: 269) notes that per capita energy use in the United States is about twice that in the United Kingdom, though standards of living and ways of living are very similar. He explains that if the United States were to cut its per capita energy use in half, the task of converting the electrical system to 100 percent carbon-free generation would be much less than half as big a task:

> In 2013, the U.S. generated 4,070 terawatt-hours (TWh) of electricity. Of this, 2,760 were from fossil fuels, and the rest from

> carbon-free sources. … With halved consumption, we'd need to replace only 725 TWh per year of fossil fuels with carbon-free generation, instead of 2,760 TWh. In other words, *we'd only need 1/4 of the carbon-free electricity infrastructure,* getting us to 100% carbon-free much more quickly. (emphasis in original)

Though he believes that much of the electricity, particularly in the residential sector, is simply wasted, he also says "increasing efficiency" is not enough. It is essential to look at "changing policies, norms, and behavior."

Shove and Walker (2014) note that people do not use energy in ways that can be adequately described simply in the language of joules, watts, or British thermal units. Rather, we use *energy services*, each of which is a specific conjunction of technologies and social practices.

Shove (2018: 782–783) argues that it is important not to fixate on ways to provide a given energy service more efficiently because it may be equally if not more important to question whether it is a good idea to provide that service, in its widespread form, at all. She adds that a focus on energy efficiency is conducive to a "business as usual" orientation:

> Programs of energy efficiency are politically uncontroversial precisely because they take current interpretations of "service" for granted. But in normalizing specific definitions of service, methods of evaluating efficiency carry normative assumptions about "need" forward, invisibly [em]bedding them into future programs of research and development.

A couple of examples are in order. Shove discusses the question of the "efficient" way to provide one particular energy service, having an adequate amount of heat to be comfortable:

> Wearing insulation close to the body is an exceptionally effective method of reducing heat loss, making better use of the body's own energy and thus requiring less additional input for the same "warm" service. So why is it that some technologies (insulation, heating systems) figure so prominently in evaluations of efficiency while others, including clothing, chairs, carpets, slippers and curtains, do not? Part of the answer has to do with the specification of service. In most cases, the focus is on room temperature, not on keeping warm.

Robert Ayres (2016: 342) provides another example of how to reframe the boundaries of an efficiency analysis. With the generations-long acceptance of the view that each adult should have personal use of an automobile, this configuration of an energy service is taken for granted and efficiency discussions are typically limited to the efficiency of the engine and power train:

> Conventional efficiency analysis draws the boundary around the vehicle itself, including the engine, drive-train, and tires. But the easiest way to improve the efficiency of automobile transport as a system (after weight reduction) would be to induce drivers to increase vehicle occupancy from the current average of 1.5–2.

We can take the line of questions much further. Should we rely on private cars to any significant extent to provide mobility, or should we rely far more on electric buses that can consume far less energy per passenger-mile? Should we assume that we need to provide the same level of *mobility* by any means—or could the focus be on providing maximum *accessibility* with only modest mobility through close-knit, integrated urban neighborhoods in which most trips are foot-powered? Could many of the rapidly climbing number of urban freight deliveries be done by pedal-power or electric-assist bicycles? Or should the focus be on reducing the number of deliveries by recognizing that much of the stuff is only destined for landfill within a year or two, and we would be better off if we simply buy less stuff?

These questions are sidestepped in a narrow

focus on efficiency, but as Shove (2018: 786) writes: "Contemporary assumptions embedded in efficiency policies are almost certainly not fostering and actively promoting ways of life that are compatible with radical carbon reduction."

In a crisply reasoned study, Kris De Decker (2018) argues that in significant ways, environmental goals would be better met by an "energy inefficiency" target than by improving efficiency:

> If we were to install 1960s internal combustion engines into modern SUVs, fuel use per kilometer driven would be much higher than it is today. Few people would be able or willing to afford to drive such cars, and they would have no other choice but to switch to a much lighter, smaller and less powerful vehicle, or to drive less.

De Decker argues, however, that an even better choice than simply abandoning efficiency as a value would be to incorporate *efficiency* as one component in an overall guiding policy of *sufficiency*.

Darby and Fawcett (2018: 8) define *sufficiency* as "an amount of something that is enough for a particular purpose." Zeroing in on energy, they add: "Energy sufficiency is a state in which people's basic needs for energy services are met equitably and ecological limits are respected."

A sufficiency strategy would be committed to reducing, not maintaining, current energy services wherever practical. For example, instead of selling every household a new clothes dryer that is marginally more efficient, we could focus on phasing out most clothes dryers in favor of clotheslines. We could dramatically reduce our overall energy consumption without hardship by employing *efficiency* and *sufficiency* approaches together "if we install an energy efficient engine in a much lighter vehicle, or if we combine an energy saving shower design with fewer and shorter showers" (De Decker 2018).

Would a general willingness to consume less present a challenge for our economic system? Yes, but it is also now clear that our current economic system is immediately threatening to the survival of ecosystems and to civilization, and thus of the economic system itself.

In trying to imagine what a sustainable economic system might look like, it will help to recognize clearly that our current system has been at war with both efficiency *and* sufficiency.

The Capitalization of Inefficiency

Is the U.S. auto industry an exemplar of efficiency? It depends on which side of the factory gates you stand. Within the factory, the assembly line has taken efficiency of movement in production to new lengths, with each task carefully analyzed and redesigned in order to wring maximum efficiency out of each operation.

But when the product rolls off the assembly line past the gates, the automobile represents the most energy-inefficient mode of mechanized transportation the world has ever known. Whitt and Wilson (1982: 186) calculate energy consumption per passenger-kilometer and find that an auto carrying one person uses about double the energy of a horse and rider, about five times the energy (per passenger) used by a passenger train, and about 20 times the energy used by a bicycle rider. An auto carrying five passengers is, however, about twice as energy-efficient as a horse carrying one rider. Air travel is not included in their table, but air travel was not a significant mode of transportation when the automobile came to prominence.

What is the source of the difference between the energy efficiency of auto production and the inefficiency of the transport system? The answer lies in different incentives. An auto company can increase profits by increasing production efficiency, but once the car is sold, the inefficiency of the transport system does not cost the company a thing.

Historian Timothy Mitchell (2013) takes the analysis a step further. The two biggest economic powers in the early 20th century were the auto industry and the oil industry, with the financial system tightly linked to both. The biggest problem for the oil companies at the time was that oil was so abundant that it threatened to be too cheap, which would have cut into profits.

The answer was a two-fold strategy of "capitalization of inefficiency" (Mitchell 2013: 40). Oil companies throttled production in some of the richest areas, particularly in the Middle East, by stalling extraction, building pipelines that were too small, and creating bottlenecks in transportation and refining. Without an excess of foreign competition, U.S. oil interests could earn high profits on their U.S. wells. For the first half of the century, this resulted in the United States quickly using up the better part of its considerable low-cost oil reserves at great profit to the oil companies. There was still plenty of accessible oil in the Middle East and other areas, much of it under Western control.

The second part of the price-boosting strategy "involved the rapid construction of lifestyles in the United States organized around the consumption of extraordinary quantities of energy" (Mitchell 2013: 41). A concerted push for "a car in every garage" was just the beginning of that high-energy lifestyle, followed by interstate and then intra-city highways, suburban zoning that promoted auto-dependence, coupled with a widespread shutdown or hollowing out of mass transit services. All of those changes were followed by the normalization of long-distance flying for purposes like spending a few days lying on a faraway beach.

These socio-technical developments helped capitalism to ward off an awful specter.

The Specter of Sufficiency

The very idea of *sufficiency* is an implicit critique of contemporary capitalism, which is driven by the need for people to always want and strive for more stuff so that the economy can grow forever.

As Aaron Karp (2020) argues, by the first few decades of the 20th century the traditional and widely respected virtue of frugality had become "a major problem for business, with the development of mass production, which for the first time led to a significant surplus of consumer goods beyond what citizens required to meet their basic needs. Business leaders feared a permanent crisis of overproduction."

The previously small advertising sector came to the rescue, growing 13-fold in the United States between 1900 and 1930. In the process, Karp argues, the core of "liberty" gradually changed to mean the unimpeded right to consume ever more. This redefinition also diverted popular energies away from fundamental challenges to capitalism—challenges backed by powerful political movements throughout industrial economies in the decades up to World War II (Karp 2020).

As part of his extensive work on what constitutes actual human need, Ian Gough has looked at the correlation between economic growth and measures such as life expectancy and reported levels of happiness. Gough (2017) says:

> While global GDP increased more than threefold between 1950 and 2003, global GPI [Genuine Progress Indicator] per capita among the major economies peaked in 1978. (Interestingly, this is around the same date that the global ecological footprint exceeded the Earth's biocapacity and that "life satisfaction" measures in most countries peaked.) Comparative research shows that GPI does not increase beyond a GDP of around $7,000 per capita.

Human *needs* are not infinite, but human *wants* can be—especially when urged on by an omnipresent advertising industry using sophisticated persuasion techniques honed over a century. Peter Kalmus (2017: 123) puts it this way: "Our industrial capitalist culture has elevated wanting into an end in itself, the purest of virtues."

During the flush of abundance of the high-energy culture, Mitchell (2013: 234) says: "Oil could be counted on *not to count.* It could be consumed as if there were no need to take account of the fact that its supply was not replenishable." It was during this era that what William Rees terms the "collective hallucination" of neoliberalism took a firm grip not only on economists, but politicians, the mass media, and much of the public.

Today, with the rapidly falling energy return on

investment, real energy surpluses are dwindling, even as advertisements urge people to keep their consumption growing. While real incomes shrink for most people and *under*consumption becomes a critical problem for increasingly large numbers of citizens, our world is still "in thrall to a mythic construct of perpetual material growth abetted by technological progress in which even 'exhaustible resources do not pose a fundamental problem'" (Rees 2020: 2).

Clinging to this mythic construct for as little as another decade may cause irreparable harm to the ecosystem that encloses all of us, pushing the climate system beyond crucial tipping points and thus pushing our species, along with most others, into probable collapse and quite possible extinction.

Conclusion: Toward an Age of Sufficiency

The economy we live in was based on an abundance of surplus energy, coupled with the belief that we can and must continue to use that energy at an ever more rapid pace. I have argued that, as we switch from the depletion of fossil fuels to the use of environmentally friendly, renewable-energy sources, it will be impossible to maintain the per capita energy consumption we have taken for granted. Our renewable-energy sector will be a larger part of the overall economy—we will see "energy sprawl"—but it will be unable to provide the high net-energy surplus our current ways of life require.

Yet it remains possible for us to create a future based on sufficiency. The preceding pages have argued that changes in attitudes were part of the problem in the 20th century and must be part of the solution in the 21st century—but fundamental structural change is equally important. We will need a determined economic-democracy movement because it is clear that investment bankers and oil company executives are not going to lead the way in creating the required changes. They will continue to seek subsidies to preserve high rates of energy consumption. But the EROI of most energy sources will fall so low that even the die-hard promoters of consumerism will be forced to recognize the impossibility of propping up a collapsing energy regime.

Rising labor productivity has been the result of the effective interaction of humans with embodied energy—to make roads, airplanes, cars, microwaves, and computers. Design improvements have been able to mask some of the decline in EROI, but as a society approaches the energy cliff, that will no longer be possible, as production costs rise and human labor increasingly substitutes for the work of machines.

Elites have found ways to claim for themselves most of the surplus created by rising productivity since the 1970s, and to claim larger shares of common wealth even as economic growth has stalled so far in the 21st century. We can expect they will strive to protect their own wealth as productivity declines. Aaron Karp (2020) writes:

> Growth is treated as the best (and only) way to improve the economic situation of working-class citizens—a substitute for equality—and every step towards a SSE [steady state economy] *would spotlight the need to redistribute wealth.* A non-growing economy requires clearly defined limits to economic inequality and calls into question the very existence of profit-maximizing institutions and the exorbitant private fortunes that exist today. To combat this threat to their financial interests and dominant social position, elites will vigorously oppose this transition. (emphasis added)

The conflict over how to divide a shrinking pie will occupy politics, and the rightward move of politics since 2015 around the world is an indicator of what could become the new normal. The right-wing populist strategy may succeed as long as a significant portion of the population can be distracted by pseudo-patriotism and racial or religious anxieties long enough for elites to restrict voting rights.

An awareness of this political battle is important because many people who hope for an economy based on local self-sufficiency are focused on developing communities with an agrarian focus. The success of that strategy in the face of declining productivity and an unwinding economy depends on conditions that will be set by national and local governments. If corporations own or control an increasing share of rural land and water, it will become more and more difficult to find a haven from the failing mainstream economy. Thus, an economy based on sufficiency can only be constructed if those who favor that option are also willing to work toward deep legal, political, and structural changes. A society based on sufficiency must also be a society based on economic democracy.

References

Alexander, Samuel, and Joshua Floyd. (2018). *Carbon Civilization and the Energy Descent Future: Life Beyond This Brief Anomaly.* Melbourne, Australia: Simplicity Institute.

Ayres, Robert. (2016). *Energy, Complexity and Wealth Maximization.* Cham, Switzerland: Springer.

Bhandari, Khagendra P., Jennifer M. Collier, Randy J. Ellingson, and Defne S. Apul. (2015). "Energy Payback Time (EPBT) and Energy Return on Energy Invested (EROI) of Solar Photovoltaic Systems: A Systematic Review and Meta-Analysis." *Renewable and Sustainable Energy Reviews* 47: 133–141.

Bloomberg New Energy Finance. (2019). *New Energy Outlook 2019.* https://about.bnef.com/new-energy-outlook/

Bond, Kingsmill, Angus McCrone, and Jules Kortenhorst. (2019). *The Speed of the Energy Transition: Gradual or Rapid Change?* Cologne and Geneva: World Economic Forum.

Brockway, Paul, Steve Sorrell, Tim Foxon, and Jack Miller. (2019). "Exergy Economics: New Insights into Energy Consumption and Economic Rowth." In *Transitions in Energy Efficiency and Demand: The Emergence, Diffusion and Impact of Low-Carbon Innovation.* Eds. Kirsten E. H. Jenkins and Debbie Hopkins, pp, 133–155. London and New York: Routledge.

Carbajales-Dale, Michael. (2019). "When Is EROI Not EROI?" *BioPhysical Economics and Resource Quality* 4(16): 1–4.

Dale, Michael, and Sally M. Benson. (2013). "Energy Balance of the Global Photovoltaic (PV) Industry—Is the PV Industry a Net Electricity Producer?" *Environmental Science & Technology* 47(7): 3482–3489.

Darby, Sarah, and Tina Fawcett. (2018). *Energy Sufficiency: An Introduction.* https://www.energysufficiency.org/libraryresources/library/items/energy-sufficiency-an-introduction/

De Decker, Kris. (2018). "Bedazzled by Energy Efficiency." *Low-Tech Magazine* January 9. https://www.lowtechmagazine.com/2018/01/bedazzled-by-energy-efficiency.html

Dupont, Elise, and Hervé Jeanmart. (2019). *Global Potential of Wind and Solar Energy with Physical and Energy Return on Investment (EROI) Constraints; Application at the European Level (EU 28 Countries).* Proceedings of ECOS 2019 Conference on Efficiency, Cost, Optimization, Simulation and Environmental Impact of Energy Systems. Wroclaw, Poland: ECOS 2019 Conference. https://www.researchgate.net/publication/336878796_Global_potential_of_wind_and_solar_energy_with_physical_and_energy_return_on_investment_EROI_constraints_application_at_the_European_level_EU_28_countries

Floyd, Joshua. (2013). "The Economic View of Systemic Efficiency: Energy Return on Energy Investment," *Beyond This Brief Anomaly* July 21. https://beyondthisbriefanomaly.org/2013/07/21/the-economic-view-of-systemic-efficiency-energy-return-on-energy-investment/#PROI

Friedmann, S. Julio, Zhiyuan Fan, and Ke Tang. (2019). *Low-Carbon Heat Solutions for Heavy Industry: Sources, Options, and Costs Today.* New York: Columbia Center on Global Energy Policy.

Gough, Ian. (2017). *Heat, Greed and Human Need: Climate Change, Capitalism and Sustainable Wellbeing.* Cheltenham, UK: Edward Elgar.

Hall, Charles A. S., and Kent Klitgaard. (2018). *Energy and the Wealth of Nations: An Introduction to Biophysical Economics,* 2nd ed. Cham, Switzerland: Springer.

Hall, Charles A. S., Jessica G. Lambert, and Stephen B. Balogh. (2014). "EROI of Different Fuels and the Implications for Society." *Energy Policy* 64: 141–152.

Heun, Matthew Kuperus, and Paul E. Brockway. (2019). "Meeting 2030 Primary Energy and Economic Growth Goals: Mission Impossible?" *Applied Energy* 251: 1.

Kalmus, Peter. (2017). *Being the Change: Live Well and Spark a Climate Revolution.* Gabriola Island, British Columbia: New Society Publishers.

Karp, Aaron. (2020). "Defending and Driving the Climate Movement by Redefining Freedom." In *Liberty and the Ecological Crisis: Freedom on a Finite Planet.* Eds. Katie Kish, Christopher Orr, and Bruce Jennings, Chapter 13. London: Routledge.

Mitchell, Timothy. (2013). *Carbon Democracy: Political Power in the Age of Oil.* London, New York: Verso.

Morgan, Tim. (2016). *Life After Growth: How the Global Economy Really Works—And Why 200 Years of Growth Are Over.* Hampshire, UK: Harriman House.

Moriarty, Patrick, and Damon Honnery. (2016). "Can Renewable Energy Power the Future?" *Energy Policy* 93: 3–7.

________. (2019). "Ecosystem Maintenance Energy and the Need for a Green EROI." *Energy Policy* 131: 229–234.

Nikiforuk, Andrew. (2019). "Crazy Days in Alberta: The Poison Wells File." *Tyee* December 16. https://thetyee.ca/Analysis/2019/12/16/Alberta-Poison-Wells-File/

Rees, William E.. (2020). "Ecological Economics for Humanity's Plague Phase." *Ecological Economics* 169: 1–9.

Sandalow, David, and S. Julio Friedmann. (2019). *ICEF Industrial Heat Decarbonization Roadmap.* New York: Columbia Center on Global Energy Policy.

Shove, Elizabeth. (2018). "What Is Wrong with Energy Efficiency?" *Building Research & Information* 46(7): 779–789.

Shove, Elizabeth, and Gordon Walker. (2014). "What Is Energy For? Social Practice and Energy Demand." *Theory, Culture & Society* 31(5): 41–58.

Smil, Vaclav. (2016). "What I See When I See a Wind Turbine." *IEEE Spectrum* 53(3): 27.

Thunberg, Greta. (2019). "If World Leaders Choose to Fail Us, My Generation Will Never Forgive Them" (address to the United Nations). *Guardian* September 23. https://www.theguardian.com/commentisfree/2019/sep/23/world-leaders-generation-climate-breakdown-greta-thunberg

White, Courtney. (2020). "Why Regenerative Agriculture?" *American Journal of Economics and Sociology* 79(3).

Whitt, Frank Rowland, and David Gordon Wilson. (1982). *Bicycling Science,* 2nd ed. Cambridge: Massachusetts Institute of Technology.

Part II:
How Will We Feed Ourselves?

CHAPTER 5

The Future Is Rural: Societal Adaptation to Energy Descent

*Jason C. Bradford**

Abstract. Our present era of high-energy modernity will likely end over the course of the 21st century, as fossil hydrocarbons wane and new energy technologies fail to compensate. Long-term trends of urbanization will reverse and a migration back to the countryside to regions of high biocapacity will ensue during the coming decades of energy descent. Food will become a central and organizing concern for de-industrializing populations, and key concepts and general methods to secure food supplies using less mechanization and with few outside inputs are presented. Given that high social complexity is institutionalized, with system identities locked-in, we should not expect a planned response to declining net energy. Instead, the so-called Great Simplification will unfold through a series of crises that force reorganization and alter belief systems. Resilience science suggests a role for promoting system transformability along more benign paths and into social forms that are more frugal.

"Make hay when the sun shines."
– old English proverb

"The whole problem with the world is that fools and fanatics are always so certain of themselves, and wiser people so full of doubts."
– *Bertrand Russell*

Introduction

As the Industrial Revolution unfolded, energy supplies extended far beyond contemporary sunlight and derivatives such as crops and wood for the first time in human history. Fossil hydrocarbons, namely, coal, oil, and natural gas, now comprise 81 percent of global energy consumption (IEA 2019). Over the course of several human generations, our now global civilization has used this energy glut to create a built environment of immense proportions. Even though people once made large monuments, such as stone pyramids, with the power of human bodies, human labor as a motive force is now an insignificant contribution to work in so-called advanced economies compared to the power wielded by machines. Construction of monuments such as modern skyscrapers and stadiums would have been impossible in earlier eras. Even more profound than an individual edifice is the scale of the built systems that comprise a megacity. But building something is not a one-time investment; like an elephant that has reached maturity, it still needs to eat each day. All infrastructure decays and needs to be replaced or decommissioned, in whole or by parts, eventually.

Our present time is an anomalous case of extreme energy use that we take for granted as we are "energy

*Research Fellow, Post Carbon Institute. Author: *The Future Is Rural: Food System Adaptations to the Great Simplification* (2019, Post Carbon Institute). Email: jcbradford4@gmail.com

blind," like fish who don't know they are in water. Anthropologists Love and Isenhour (2016) call our period "high-energy modernity" and urge their colleagues to "conceptualize what a now fragmented anthropology might offer a globalized world potentially on the brink of unprecedented power-down." "Power-down" is a good term for what we should be doing, that is, systematically curtailing energy consumption, like an animal entering hibernation, knowing that as the sun gets lower on the horizon the ecosystem will provide less food over the coming months. What Holmgren (2006) calls "energy descent" could be considered a normal part of the daily and seasonal rhythms to which life has adapted. But we are not yet planning the energy descent of our civilization as we rapidly oxidize fossil hydrocarbons and they become progressively rarer. In fact, our behavioral norms, institutionalized rules, and even myths, especially in the field of neoclassical economics, continue to push for expansion and conflate energy-demanding growth with notions of progress (Hagens 2020).

The size of the human economy is limited by well-understood dynamics between physical resources, environmental sinks, and system feedbacks (Meadows et al. 2004). While a precise estimate of when a rising metric such as gross world product (GWP) will stall and then fall is impossible, a biophysical lens on the economy anticipates that an unavoidable reduction in the flow of fossil hydrocarbons over the course of the 21st century will correlate with and contribute to a declining GWP. Economic contraction, in turn, will promote rural settlement patterns that may, over many decades, resemble pre-industrial conditions (Holmgren 2006, 2018).

The "future is rural" scenario is based on three lines of reasoning:

1. The degree of urbanization today could only have developed through the exploitation of fossil hydrocarbons, and to keep megacities functioning requires proportionally large and constant power supplies;
2. As flows of oil, natural gas, and coal inevitably wane, renewable energy sources and technologies will not be able to compensate to maintain the current scale of urbanization;
3. An adaptive social response to the loss of "high-energy modernity" is to live closer to the land, where basic needs can be met from local ecosystem provisioning and where episodic energy flows from the environment are available to harness.

Rural Depopulation

A key consequence of industrial expansion has been the steady loss of jobs in agriculture and an overall reduction in rural populations, either in absolute number or as a percentage (Mayumi 1991). The loss of agricultural employment is almost solely a consequence of mechanization, especially with progressively larger tractors commanding diesel fuel. Demographers have noted that, since the early years of the 21st century, more than half the world's population now lives in urban areas, where labor is predominantly relegated to services rather than productive sectors of the economy, as shown in Figure 1. Such a shift is seen as synonymous with development and the evolution of social complexity (Tainter 2000). Demographers also surmise this multi-decadal trend of greater urbanization will continue, which is rejected here as being naïve about the future supplies of energy and raw materials (Valero and Valero 2010; Capellán-Pérez et al. 2014).

As discussed further below, cities essentially lock in high energy and material consumption and are wholly dependent on the unique properties of fossil fuels (Rees 2012). Even if a major shift to an energy system based on contemporary solar flows, such as photovoltaics and wind turbines, were to happen, such a system would be woefully insufficient to power global civilization and urban settlements at the current scale (Lang 2018). During energy descent, decade by decade we will have less power available and will perform less work. As argued here, based on energy realities, a migration back to the countryside, reversing a trend that spans nearly two centuries, will be inevitable.

Economic depressions destabilize political systems, and with rival nations holding nuclear arsenals we live with high existential risk. If we manage to avoid nuclear war, societies will need to cope with decades of economic contraction and migration to regions of biocapacity. Perhaps we can learn from studies on so-called climigration that model which regions will lose and gain population as an adaptation to climate change (Malo 2019) but extend and incorporate energy descent into the analyses. Day and Hall (2016), for example, integrate energy, climate, land productivity, and fresh-water-supply projections and suggest major cities will shrink and migrants will go to where prime farmland is abundant and population density is low. Rees (2019) offers policy prescriptions to foster the inevitable shift to place-based food systems. This article reviews why this future scenario is likely and offers some thoughts on how elements of society can prepare and adapt.

Cities and Endothermic Basal Metabolisms

In biology, the basal metabolic rate is the power required for an organism at rest. Mammals and birds are endothermic vertebrates, meaning they have physiological mechanisms to maintain a nearly constant internal temperature. Other vertebrates, such as fish, amphibians, and reptiles, are exothermic, which means they lack internal temperature regulation. Having a set internal temperature may give mammals and birds a competitive advantage and open up more ecological niches compared to other vertebrates because they can be physically active under a wide range of environmental conditions, such as foraging for food at night or during cold times of day.

Figure 1
Global Population: Rural vs. Urban

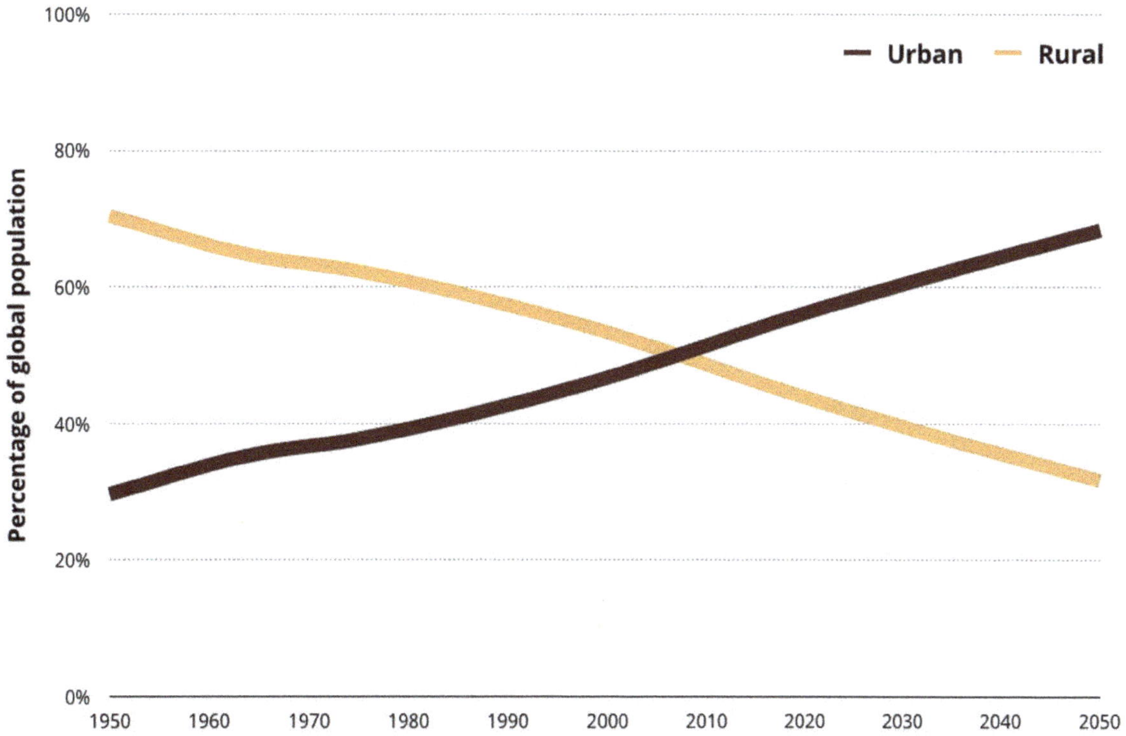

Source: United Nations (2018).
Note: Percent of global population in rural vs. urban settings from 1950 to 2017, with U.N. projections to 2050.

However, endothermy has a high energetic cost. For a given body size, endotherms require much more power than ectotherms (White et al. 2006). A small lizard or snake, for example, may only need to feed every week or month, whereas a mouse is constantly foraging and burns around an order of magnitude more calories than a similar-sized reptile, as shown in Figure 2.

Mass urbanization has been made possible by the prodigious exploitation of fossil fuels, and not only because machines have replaced people in agriculture. Cities have always been wholly reliant on the capacity of rural areas to produce basic goods, most importantly food. But due to the concentrated energy in oil, with its ability to power heavy equipment and transport goods over long distances, cities have been able to achieve the scale they do today by drawing support from a theoretical land base often several hundred times their own area with materials from any part of the globe (Folke et al. 1997; Rees 2020).

Prior to the Industrial Revolution, the population of the largest cities was on the order of 100,000 to 1,000,000 (Modelski 2003; Morris 2013). With rivers, canals, clay pipes, and cobblestone roads as

Figure 2
Endotherms (Birds, Mammals) Need About 10 Times the Energy Required by Exotherms (Fish, Reptiles)

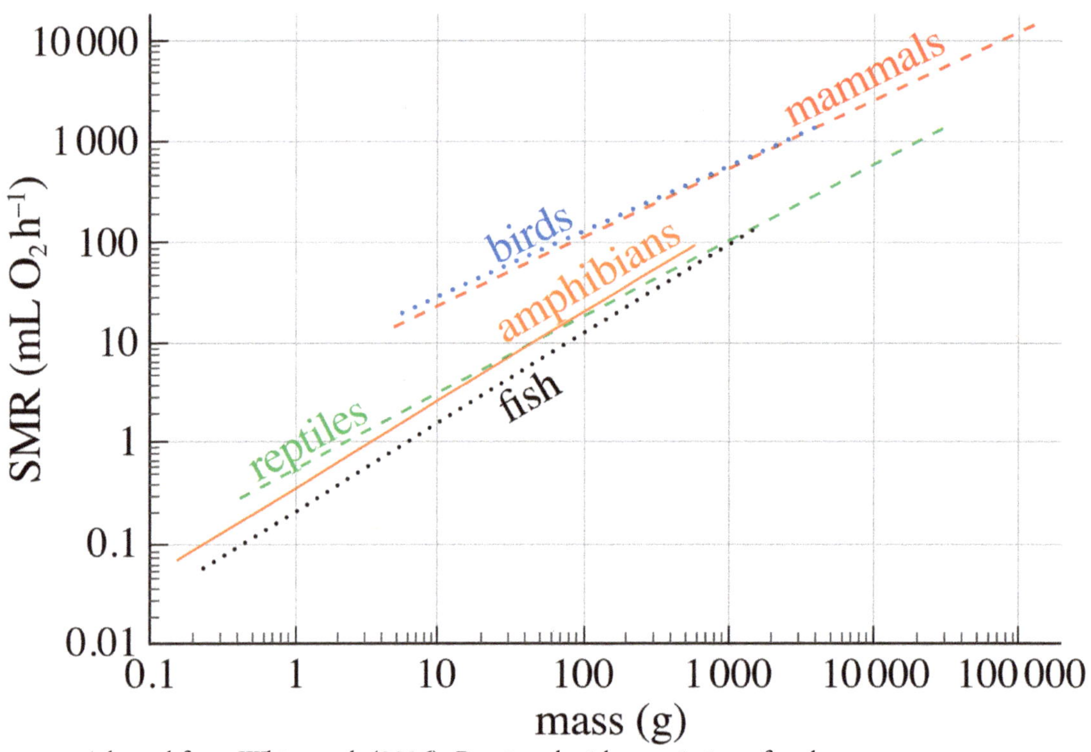

Source: Adapted from White et al. (2006). Reprinted with permission of author.

Note: Standard metabolic rate (SMR), in units of oxygen consumption per hour, is shown as a function of body mass (grams) in vertebrates. For a given body size, the metabolic rate of endotherms (birds and mammals) is about an order of magnitude higher than that of ectotherms (amphibians, fish and reptiles). For example, a 10,000 gram reptile has the same metabolic rate as a 1,000 gram mammal.

the conduits for moving people and goods, cities could grow only so big. Most people (typically more than 90 percent) lived in the countryside, where they could access food and dispose of their waste directly in the environment. The modest surplus from those living in the countryside supplied cities with needed resources (Pimentel and Pimentel 2007).

As of 2019, the world has over 1,000 urban areas (which may include multiple city jurisdictions) with over 500,000 people at an average (median) density of 5,600 per square kilometer (or 14,500 per square mile). There are 38 urban areas with over 10 million inhabitants and 87 have over 5 million (Cox 2019).

To understand why cities are the size they are, it is useful to consider models of urban systems, which are akin to biological models of metabolism (Kennedy 2012). Infrastructure serves as a city's giant circulatory system, with steel pipes, electric wires, concrete roads, railroad tracks, and canals moving fluids, solids, and energy into and out of the city. The circulatory system of a modern city is very active, and it requires high energy inputs to keep the city-dwellers fed and prevent the buildup of wastes. This infrastructure locks in high energy demand compared to locations with simpler systems to manage basic needs. In highly urbanized nations, this high-energy lock-in applies to the countryside as well. The rural residents in places like the United States are living with a depauperate associative economy, characterized by the lack of nearby services. They often make their living driving around the countryside managing expansive tracts of land with big machines. Their lives are not ones of frugality and self-sufficiency, but instead are tied into the global economy where *cheap*, *concentrated*, and *prodigious use* of energy, or what together I will refer to as extreme energy, is taken for granted.

Insect biology provides another insight into city size. A widely accepted explanation for why insects are not larger is their lack of an active respiratory system that exchanges air with a circulatory system. In contrast to animals with lungs, insects rely on diffusion of air through their tracheas. Although diffusion limits the size of insects, it has the advantage of not requiring metabolic energy to function. To complete the analogy, prior to the fossil fuel era, cities could only be "insect-sized," whereas with fossil fuels they have grown "as large as dinosaurs."

As seen in Figure 2, the slope of the regression between metabolic rate and mass is less than one, meaning that larger animals are more energy efficient than smaller ones. The same scaling effect is found between cities, making per capita infrastructure requirements and use of some resources lower in larger cities (Bettencourt et al. 2007). Owen (2009) and others have used this finding to argue that to conserve resources we should encourage even larger cities. This reasoning is flawed by focusing on too narrow a boundary of analysis. Comparisons are made between cities of different sizes within nations that have fully adopted industrial-scale infrastructure and energy consumption. Within this context the scaling laws that show larger as being more efficient may be true, but are beside the point. The consequence of modern development patterns is to set a high basal metabolism, akin to endotherms, with cities of *all* sizes locked in to extreme and continuous power usage. To complete the analogy, what we should be asking is not how to be a more efficient mammal, but how to live more like a reptile and greatly reduce our power demand. *A compact, rural village probably has a much lower per capita resource consumption pattern than an apartment building in a large city.*

For examples we can look to places, both contemporary and historic, where ways of life are energetically and materially frugal. Potential study locations are shown in Figure 3, where the percent rural population in a nation is plotted versus per capita energy use. Prior to the Industrial Revolution nearly all countries would have been plotted in the upper left corner of Figure 3.

In 2008, there were only 24 countries, with a combined population of about 332 million people, that were over 75 percent rural. In these countries, energy consumption averages less than one barrel of oil equivalent (BOE) per capita each year, which is about 1/50th of U.S. levels. These are the places with the lowest basal metabolic rates. Urbanization would transform them from ectotherms into endotherms by thrusting them into the consumer economy and into places where food, water, energy, and waste are actively transported. Over half the world's population, about 4 billion, lives in countries that are 50 to 75 percent rural, with average per capita BOE of 5.6. It first appears that only a modest addition of energy to an economy allows for substantial urbanization.

In energetic terms, we can compare the work of oil with human labor by translating both into kilowatt hours (kWh). Using estimates by factory owners around 1900 of how much work could be performed in one day by a laborer, Johnson (2006) estimates that a barrel of oil represents around 10 years of work output by a human body.

> 1 hour labor = 68 watts = 0.068 kWh. Thus 1,000 hrs labor = 68 kWh. ** 1 barrel of oil = 1,700 kWh. So, (1700/68) * 1,000 = 25,000 hours labor. Assume 2,500 work hours/year (50 hours/week × 50 weeks/year). 1 barrel of oil ≈ 10 years of *intense* human labor. (**Johnson [2006] estimates 75 watt-hours for

Figure 3
Urbanization and Energy Consumption

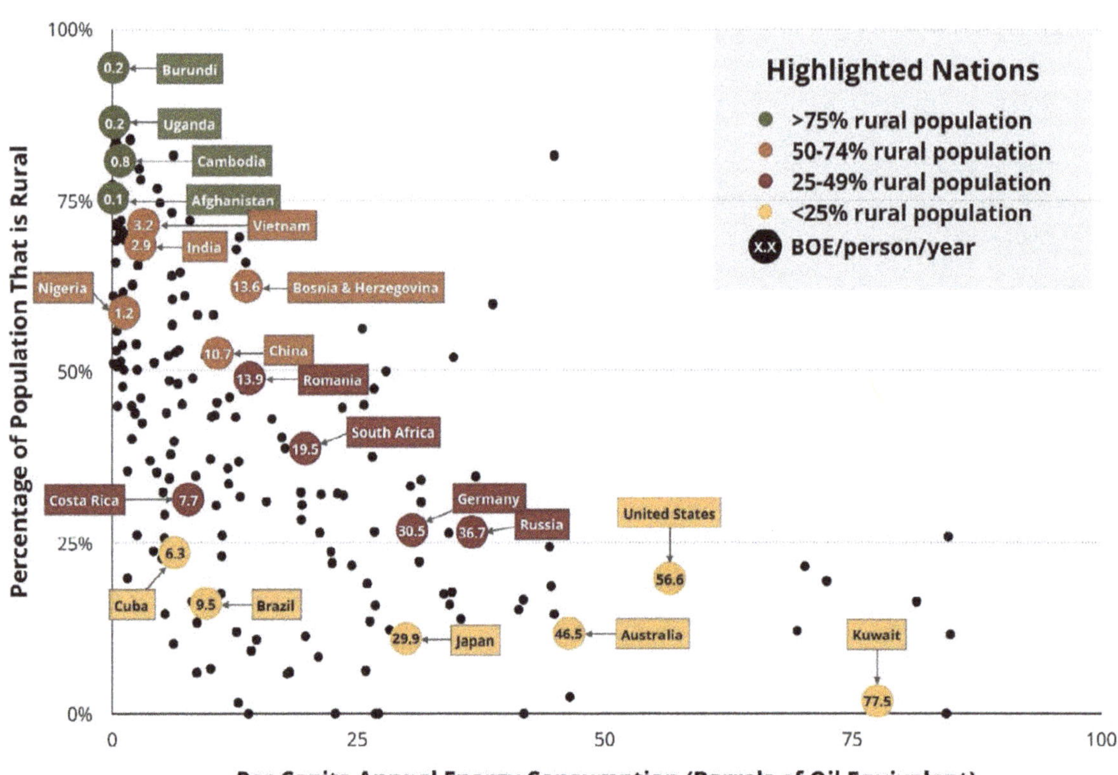

Source: U.S. Energy Information Agency (2018): energy; United Nations (2018): population. Data sets harmonized by author.

Note: Per capita energy consumption and rural population by country for 2008. The percentage of population that is rural is plotted with respect to per capita energy consumption and shows that, in general, countries with high energy use tend to be more urbanized. Some of the largest countries are highlighted, and outliers tend to be small island nations.

a 35 year-old healthy man. My estimate of 68 is 10 percent less to include women and older men.)

So in countries with the seemingly modest consumption of five BOE per capita per year, on average everyone is leveraging the energy equivalent of 50 people working for them full-time.

Among countries ranked by percent of population living in rural areas, the second quartile (25–50 percent) and the first quartile (0–25 percent) use 18.6 and 32.2 BOE per capita per year, respectively. Looked at inversely, the countries in the first quartile, which are the ones with the highest levels of urbanization, use almost twice as much energy per capita as the next quartile. The range of values by country is large, and likely reflects differences in latitude (tropical nations do not need to heat buildings), special circumstances (large petroleum exporters often have massive domestic consumption), variation in land use policies and transportation (such as the ability to live in the countryside but drive into the city for work), and, in the era of globalization, the ability to specialize in service industries, such as finance and tourism, and import most basic goods, as Singapore does.

The social metabolism of countries has been profiled formally using the MuSIASEM (Multi-Scale Integrated Analysis of Social Metabolism) model (Andreoni 2017; Giampietro et al. 2006, 2009). This articulates how the net energy of economies relates to types and productivity of labor and investment in infrastructure and why "it is possible to observe that all the countries in the world that have a GDP per capita higher than 15,000 US$ per capita per year, have a fraction of the work force in agriculture which is below the level of 5%." (Giampietro 1997).

We can also ask what happens to cities when they lose access to the capital needed for maintenance? This is occurring in many places even today, for example the U.S. Rust Belt, where cities have been depopulated and the residents who remain establish urban farms on abandoned blocks (Masi et al. 2014). In another example across the Atlantic Ocean, the Greek government took on massive debts as it integrated into the E.U. economy. Following the 2008 financial crisis, a period of forced austerity led to an economic depression. Many people left Athens and returned to small villages where they had family, citing very practical concerns:

> When someone loses their job in a city and has no hope of finding another, they come here as a last resort. We will be the last to starve because when you have a field or a garden, you can produce food for yourself and make sure you survive. (Babington and Papadimas 2012)

As energy descent unfolds, we will likely see growing unemployment and infrastructure decay in urban areas. It will not make sense (and may no longer be possible) to maintain energy-demanding roads, sewage treatment, and electric systems with declining tax revenues and more costly energy and materials (Rees 2020). Instead, we may want to explore how to transform our society into one that is less reliant on extreme energy.

Renewables and the Problem of Scale

Some surmise on technical grounds that a low-cost, all-renewable energy economy can keep high-energy modernity going (Jacobson et al. 2015). Others have argued that such optimism is derived from flawed assumptions buried in complex models (Clack et al. 2017). The purpose of this section is not to get lost in the technical details of energy systems, but to review basic energy literacy that reinforces the notion that energy descent is highly likely. For an example of sophisticated modeling that incorporates the principles discussed below, see Capellán-Pérez et al. (2019) and the MEDEAS-World project.

If society will have to get by on less energy and will have to use energy very differently, these changes will have profound ripple effects on the economy, politics, and culture. Heinberg and Fridley (2016) provide a thorough explanation of the matter, beginning with an introduction that frames the discussion under the heading "Why a Renewable World Will Be Different":

> Solar, wind, hydro, and geothermal generators produce electricity, and we already have an abundance of technologies that rely on electricity. So why should we need to change the ways we use energy? Presumably all that's necessary is to unplug coal power plants, plug in solar panels and wind turbines, and continue living as we do currently. This is a misleading way of imagining the energy transition for six important reasons.

Their six reasons why renewables will not scale to compensate for fossil hydrocarbon decline can be summarized as follows:

1. **Intermittency**. The electric grid has been designed to match supply and demand at any time of day, year-round by using reliably available stores of energy such as coal as a baseload and natural gas for reacting to fluctuating demand. The electrical system is not designed to cope with the variable supplies from solar and wind. Compensating for intermittency through overcapacity, long-distance transmission, and energy storage is costly, complex, and difficult to scale. We will need to find ways to shift from an on-demand system to making use of what is available when it is temporarily abundant, and to reduce our overall demand.
2. **The liquid-fuels problem**. Our single largest source of energy is oil, which fuels nearly all transportation and heavy equipment, as well as many industrial processes. Replacements for oil, such as biofuels, are not chemically identical to petroleum and so require expensive retrofits, compete with other land uses such as growing food, and, when highly processed, are barely net-energy positive. Only portions of our transport infrastructure, such as light passenger vehicles, lend themselves easily to electrification since batteries are not nearly as energy dense as liquid hydrocarbons. Figure 4 shows why we should expect a future of less mobility.
3. **Other uses of fossil fuels.** Fossil fuels are essential in high temperature manufacturing processes, such as making steel, cement, rubber, ceramics, and glass. Hydrocarbons are also feedstocks for many materials, such as plastics, chemicals, and pharmaceuticals. Renewable electricity has very little to offer as an energy substitute as it contributes effectively to kinetic but not thermal work. Crop-based replacements for raw materials, such as natural rubber, cannot match the current scale of demand. The availability of many core industrial products will decline.
4. **Area density of energy collection activities.** Capturing diffuse, ambient sources of energy, such as with solar farms or biofuel crops, requires an infrastructure that is spread out across the landscape. As explained by Vaclav Smil (2003), cities have high power consumption per unit area (high power density requirements) that cannot be matched by diffuse sources of ambient-energy capture and distribution (low power density supplies). Furthermore, the more we scale renewable infrastructure, the more we will run into competing uses and nontrivial environmental impacts, such as the waste products of a biofuel plant.
5. **Location**. Sunlight, wind, hydropower, and biomass are more readily available in some places than others, and long-distance transmission and transport entails significant costs and energy losses. Energy systems will shift from large, centralized processing and distribution centers, such as a 500,000 barrel per day crude oil refinery, to distributed and smaller-scale facilities, such as a biofuel factory within a defined collection zone or "shed," since the same amount of "feedstock" cannot be concentrated in one place.
6. **Energy quantity**. Our global energy system provides for over 500 exajoules of annual consumption. It has been built over the course of many decades, and it is over 80 percent reliant on combustion of fossil fuels, while also using as much biomass as ever. Mature technologies, such as hydroelectric, are nearly fully deployed already. A massive build-out of newer technologies like solar and wind during the next few decades would rapidly consume fossil fuel reserves and, even if done

at a heroic scale, would not replace the gross, let alone net, quantity of energy currently provided by fossil fuels. We will need to get by on less energy.

Humans are adept at deriving useful work from energy sources outside of their bodies, which is known as exosomatic metabolism. To grasp what 500 exajoules of annual energy consumption is, first divide that number by the global human population of 7.8 billion to yield about 64 billion joules per capita. Then convert joules per capita to kilocalories

Figure 4

Low-Density Fuels and Storage Systems: Heavier or More Voluminous Than Gasoline or Coal

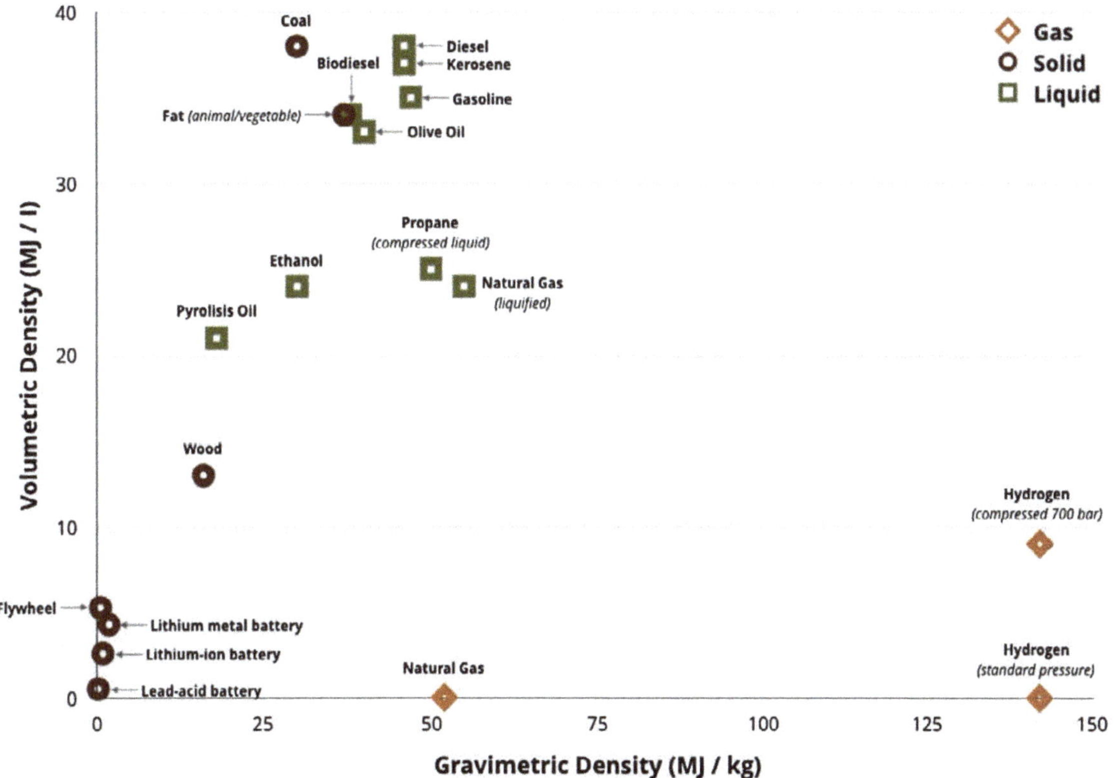

Source: Created by author from data in: Engineering Tool Box (2008) and from Wikipedia articles that compile data: https://en.wikipedia.org/wiki/Energy_density, and https://en.wikipedia.org/wiki/Energy_content_of_biofuel.

Note: Energy density (gross heating value) of various storage forms is plotted by weight (MJ/kg) and volume (MJ/l). An ideal energy storage source has both high gravimetric and volumetric density (upper right corner of graph). Alternatives to fossil fuels tend to be of lower density, making them more burdensome and costlier to use in general. Work performed will be less than gross heating value due to conversion inefficiencies, and efficiency can vary by the kind of work and how well the storage system is suited to it. For example, electric batteries to electric motors is a more efficient conversion (about 90 percent) than gasoline to internal combustion engines (about 30 percent). Batteries and other potential storage technologies can improve, but even at theoretical limits they would be many times less energy dense than fossil fuels (Zenz House 2009).

per capita, a familiar unit we use for food. This yields 15 million kilocalories per capita. A person may reasonably consume food containing around 1 million kilocalories per year, which implies the exosomatic metabolism, on a global average, is around 15 times larger than the endosomatic metabolism. As shown in Figure 3, a person in a highly industrialized country would consume several times more than this average (Andreoni 2017). Relating this back to energy and body size allometry in Figure 2, the exosomatic energy use of the average U.S. person is equivalent to the endosomatic metabolism of a 40-ton sperm whale (Odum 1998).

Lang (2018) gives an overview of how energy descent may play out from an urban perspective, surmising that cities will depopulate, and that food will be a key societal concern. It is natural to wonder about the scale and pace of change, but of course addressing these questions for dynamic, complex systems is fraught with uncertainty. One could imagine that economic decline is as rapid as ascent, perhaps 2–3 percent a year, which would mean gross world production (GWP) halves every 25–30 years. Since energy is so tightly coupled to economic activity, this suggests a society with power use by the end of the 21st century that is roughly 10–15 percent of today's use. While this is a rapid and large drop in energy consumption, it is about half the pace suggested by carbon budgets that aim to keep global warming limited to 1.5 degrees Celsius above pre-industrial levels (Masson-Delmotte et al. 2018). A steady decline in gross energy is also an overly simplistic way to think about energy systems since decline rates could be higher during a prolonged period of economic and political distress. What allows for high levels of labor productivity, wages, and household consumption is the degree to which energy supply is *not needed to procure more energy supply* (Giampietro et al. 2006). During energy descent the allocation of energy within the energy sector will rise, leading to concerns of an eventual "net-energy cliff" (Lambert et al. 2014).

If we expect high-energy modernity to unravel during the rest of this century, then we need scenario planning and education to address it. The rest of this article will do so by asking what mostly urban populations need to understand about the related subjects of energy, food systems, and agriculture.

Energy Descent and Food System Vulnerabilities

A key driver for rural resettlement will be to secure basic needs. The formal economy will leave more and more people behind, and concepts such as commodity and consumer will become less relevant (Fleming and Chamberlin 2016). A full-fledged reinvention of social life that places food at the center again is in store, but it will be a food system completely transformed from what passes as normal today.

Heinberg and Fridley's (2016) six reasons why renewable energy systems will not seamlessly power a highly industrialized, global society can easily be applied to the food system, which, in places like the United States, is just as fossil-fuel dependent as any other economic sector. The food system is also globalized, with regional hyper-specialization in crop production that has made local communities reliant on distant trade for basic food, a situation that has only recently developed and that cannot be maintained indefinitely.

The industrial food system has been steadily replacing human and animal labor and local markets with mechanization and globally traded commodities. Figure 5 shows that just about every step in the industrial food system is so energy-demanding that, by now, someone eating a meal in the United States is ingesting only one kilocalorie of food for about every 10 kilocalories spent getting that food to their plate. Metrics for other highly industrialized countries are expected to be roughly similar. How that excessive energy budget breaks down by activity is informative. The Center for Sustainable Systems (2017) has compiled relevant data for the United States:

- Farm activities and the embedded energy of inputs such as fertilizers account for about 14 percent of the total.
- Processing and packaging, which gives us such

convenience and allows food to be shipped globally, is another 25 percent.

- The energy spent by warehouses, grocery stores, cafeterias, and restaurants is about 29 percent.
- The remainder, a whopping 28 percent, is used by households to go shopping, keep food in refrigerators, and cook.
- Transportation is only about 4 percent of the total, but consider that much of the energy used in the food system, such as processing and warehousing, allows for transportation efficiency.

Analyses of the U.S. food system show trends of greater consumption of highly processed foods and reliance on appliances rather than manual labor, both of which tend to increase energy consumption (Canning et al. 2010).

We can provide here only a cursory overview of the complexities involved with dependence on petroleum, natural gas, and electricity and with the difficulties in making substitutions in the food system. For the sake of brevity, and to give a sense of the depth and scale of the challenge, a focus on

Figure 5
Energy Input and Output in the U.S. Food System

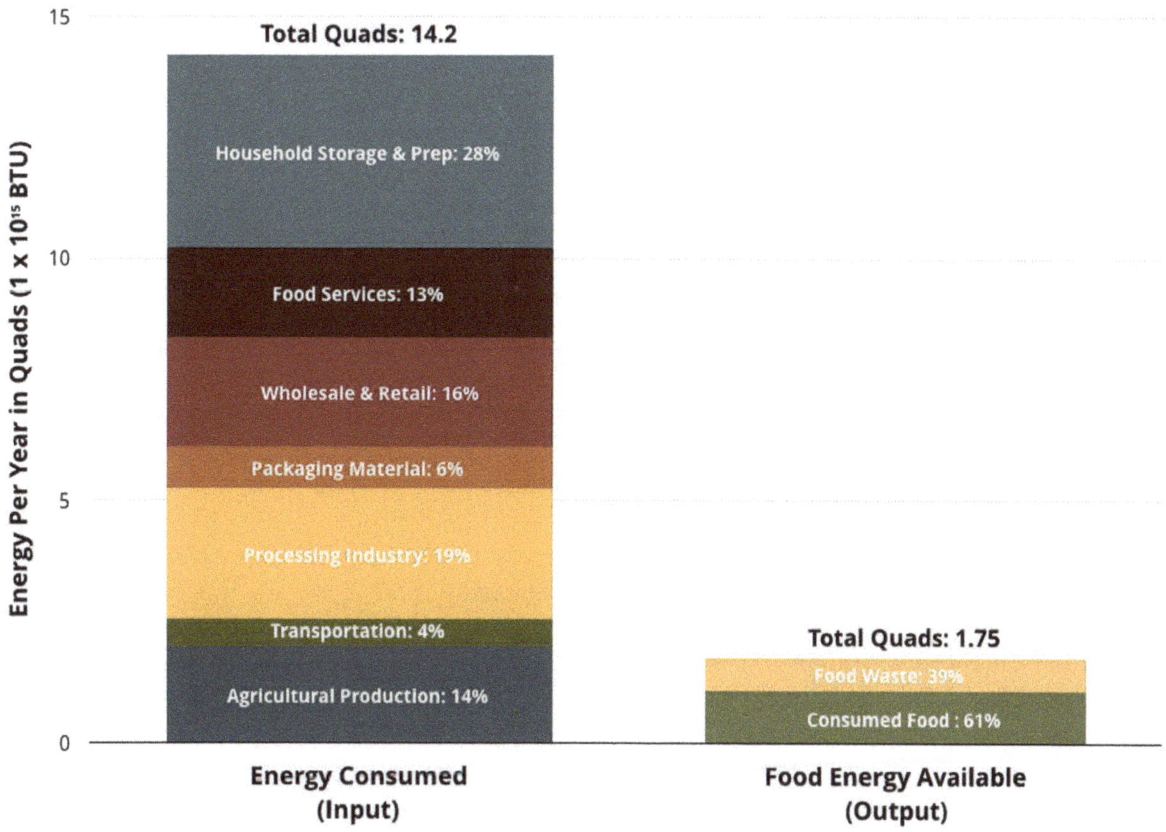

Source: Author, using data from Center for Sustainable Systems (2017).
Note: Whereas food that is grown, harvested, and distributed locally by hand or livestock produces positive net energy relative to the energy of human labor, industrialized food systems consume 5–10 times more energy than they produce. High energy use reduces farm labor via processing and packaging, allows for expanded trade, and makes it convenient to store and prepare food.

one segment of the food system—agricultural production—is given in the context of the six limiting factors discussed by Heinberg and Fridley (2016).

Let us begin with *intermittency*. Farmers tend to wait for ideal weather conditions and then, as quickly as possible, prepare soil, plant seeds, and harvest crops. What they rely on today is liquid fuels (specifically, diesel and gasoline), delivered to on-farm storage tanks that fill large fuel tanks on tractors and harvesters. Farms cannot afford to wait for the sun to shine or the wind to blow and hope that such an event corresponds to the right weather conditions for field activities. Although the intermittency problem could conceivably be solved by battery storage, this is not likely to work for many farm operations because of the low energy density of batteries.

Hence, we have *the liquid-fuels problem*. Although farms could theoretically be operated with electric-powered equipment, no technology known or likely to become available has the combination of transportability, storability, and high energy density that hydrocarbon liquid fuels offer. People often believe that because cars can successfully run on electricity, with battery packs allowing hundreds of miles between recharge, this same technology can apply to tractors. However, unlike cars running on smooth roads, typically at steady speeds, tractors are literally dragging steel through rough ground much of the time. Farm equipment tends to operate near its horsepower capacity, whereas a car might only work near capacity when accelerating into traffic now and then. Hydrocarbon liquid fuels are the only known substances with enough energy density that can be carried easily onboard a tractor under typical working conditions of temperature variability and rough terrain and enable work to be performed continuously for many hours. (See Figure 4.)

Other uses of fossil fuels include the feedstock for many products used on farms, such as pesticides and fertilizer. Plastics are becoming more abundant on farms as well, including irrigation pipes, weed suppression cloth, and roofing for greenhouses. While there may be ways to replace fossil-fuel-based supplies with renewable ones, such as crop-based feedstocks to make bioplastics and biofuels, these substitutes require using land that could otherwise be used to grow food.

Using land to yield renewable energy supplies also reveals the problem of *area density of energy collection activities*. In some parts of the country it is common to see an oil well in the middle of a farm field. The oil well may occupy an area the size of a typical home to tap into a sizable underground reservoir. By contrast, if a farm needs to grow biofuel crops to power equipment, the area required to do so is going to be many times larger than the oil well.

Just as fossil fuel deposits are not evenly distributed around the Earth, renewable energy potential varies by *location*. Furthermore, renewable energy sources are best used near their place of capture and storage. Farms tend to be located where soil and climate conditions are ideal. Some farms will be fortunately situated where great soils and rainfall patterns coincide with optimum solar radiation, consistent winds, or hydroelectric potential. But we have already reviewed why electricity will have a limited role in powering farms, even if it happens to be convenient to produce. The more certain renewable energy source on farms will be biomass. Farms of the future will need to make do with wood, straw, other crop residues, and extracted sugars or oils. They will also become far more dependent on human and animal labor, as they were in the past.

The *energy quantity* available to our society when powered by biomass plus renewable electricity will be far less than what we are accustomed to now. Societies may ration energy supplies using non-price mechanisms (Cox 2013). They will then be able preferentially to provide farms with fuels and other inputs to maintain production, but, even in that scenario, agriculture will be under tremendous pressure to reduce energy use.

The story we tell ourselves about modern farming and the food system—that it is incredibly efficient—may only be true through the lens of human labor. Seen through other perspectives, such as resource use and pollution, astonishing inefficiencies and atrocities abound (TEEB 2018). Agricultural economist

Michael Perelman (1972) wrote:

> If we are facing an energy crisis, then we might do well to measure efficiency in terms of output per unit of energy instead of output per unit of labor, not only in agriculture but elsewhere in our economy.
>
> If we should decide to measure efficiency in terms of the conservation of energy, then American agriculture comes out very poorly. Harris estimated that Chinese wet rice agriculture could produce 53.5 BTU of energy for each BTU of human energy expended in farming it. For each unit of energy the wet rice farmer expends he gets more than 50 in return; for each unit of fossil fuel energy we expend we get about one-fifth in return. On the basis of these two ratios, Chinese wet rice agriculture is far more efficient than our own system.

During energy descent, as the cost of energy goes up and economies stumble, wages will most likely go down (King 2020). This scenario will 1) make it more difficult to live in high-cost, urban settings, 2) drive migration to rural areas, 3) spur development of non-monetary exchange systems, and 4) reestablish labor as a competitive and essential factor of production in farming. The food system will eventually shift from energy-demanding activities so that it becomes an energy source, not an energy sink.

Principles and Practices of an Energy-Positive Food System

Humans survived to create a food system that is an energy sink only by previously managing an energy-positive one (Pimentel and Pimentel 2007). Given so few of us make a living as farmers, however, we will need to learn how to build the food system in ways that reflect energy, soil, and climate realities. We may seek opportunities to recover elements of past cultures that inhabited the Earth with grace, learn from the mistakes of our ancestors so we can avoid them, study and adopt the lifestyles of remaining rural people, and also take advantage of the wealth of knowledge accumulated from modern scientific advances, technologies, and tools, if appropriate.

This section will review some key knowledge areas and concepts that can help those living with high-energy modernity reimagine the future. Energy savings will need to occur throughout the food system and society in general, but here I will focus on the agricultural production sector of the food system:

- How local geography affects crop and livestock selection;
- Variation in adoption of industrial agriculture and urbanization;
- Appreciating the multi-functional aspects of crops and livestock;
- Soil structure and processes;
- Nutrients and soil fertility management;
- Erosion control and soil conservation;
- The risks of intensification;
- Ecosystem services on farmland;
- Agroecology and functional diversity;
- Modern schools of thought.

Geography and Crop/Livestock Selection

If we follow the reasoning of permaculturalist David Holmgren (2006, 2018) that adaptations to energy descent will reflect preindustrial human settlement patterns, then it is worth understanding how our ancestors evolved food systems as they spread around the planet and encountered diverse biomes. Ancient human cultures found ways to live within their local environments using only solar energy flows, so they knew some things that will be useful to us.

Agriculture characterized by extensive crop fields is a relatively recent invention. For at least 90 percent of our species' time on Earth, people ate wild animals and plants. Horticulture developed not more than 10,000 years ago, at the end of the Pleistocene, as favored plants were brought into or adjacent to human camps and settlements. Mixed systems of gardening and hunting were common in tropical, subtropical, and relatively benign temperate climates. But not all places are suited to cultivating plants. In especially dry or cold environments, hunting and livestock husbandry dominated. Animals are especially important in higher latitudes for the storage of fat, ability to move with the seasons in nomadic cultures, and for byproducts such as leather and fur to keep people warm. Migratory marine fish and mammals are especially important for bringing energy from low to high latitudes. Settled farming cultures revolve around domesticated seeds, mainly grasses, including wheat, rice, and maize. The grasses are typically paired with the seeds of legumes, such as lentils, pinto beans, and mung beans, which tend to have lower yields but are higher in protein than grains. Grains and legumes have some key properties that make them suitable foods for the rise of cities. Seeds typically have a high caloric density and dry on their own when ripe, which makes them rot-resistant in storage and easy to transport. For example, a pound of wheat contains about 1,500 kilocalories, whereas a pound of potatoes has only about 350. Getting high yields of grains requires fertile soil, which is why river valleys, where floods deposit deep, nutrient-rich soils, were the first locations of largely grain-based civilizations in eastern China, the Indo-Gangetic plain, Mesopotamia, the Nile, and Meso-America.

Certain animals were often kept close to dwellings to be fed leftovers. Pigs and chickens, for example, are monogastrics like us and have similar dietary needs. They are not picky eaters and can live off discarded kitchen scraps and the harvested crops that are not quite good enough for making bread. The modern-day practice of growing grains for the "feed market" is a recent invention. Animals were domesticated to be our partners in managing our spoilage, to eat what we considered low-quality, and to consume the occasional bumper harvest to avoid a rat population explosion.

Even more dietary flexibility is exhibited by ruminants, such as cattle and sheep. Symbiotic populations of bacteria living in the guts of these livestock allow them to digest plant fiber and turn it into milk, meat, fat, bones, skin, and fur. Very little of the rural landscape is composed of things humans can readily eat, such as simple sugars, starches, fats, and protein, and most of what grows naturally is made of cellulose and lignin. Domesticated ruminants are how people found a way to turn the indigestible into the sweet and savory.

Prior to the Industrial Revolution, much kinetic work was performed by people and their animals. Animals pulled tillage equipment and carts and helped with assorted tasks like grinding grain on mill stones or dragging lumber. Perhaps more important than this obvious kind of work, though, was the harnessing of livestock to improve field fertility.

Our primary crops are annual plants, meaning they are sown by seed and die within a year. To successfully grow these crops, at least the surface of the soil must be cleared of competing plants, traditionally through tillage, and sufficient soil nutrients must be available. Animals were often employed to shift and concentrate fertility. For example, livestock would graze extensively on hillsides or pasture fields during the day and then be moved into a field at night where they urinate and defecate. If nighttime stocking is done for several weeks on the same field, it will become clear of competing vegetation, requiring little tillage prior to planting, and it will be loaded with nutrients from all the urine and manure. This is one way to grow a nutrient-demanding annual crop without mechanically applying synthetic fertilizer or hauling and spreading manure out of a barn. Farmers can manage the movement and concentration of fertility without livestock, but with livestock strenuous labor is avoided.

Successful human settlement of an area without significant trade requires not only producing sufficient food on average but being able to supply food security during lean seasons and years. Domesticated species of crops and livestock have been introduced around the world, and cultures have incorporated them to suit their needs. People have adapted their production techniques and achieved food security in a variety of places with gradients of land fertility and climate. A local food culture therefore evolves, and so do the genetics of human populations in response. Modern debates about what "should" be eaten usually fail to appreciate deep historical and environmental factors.

In the most benign tropical to subtropical environments, there is relatively little seasonality, and the growing season lasts almost all year. The need to store surplus food between seasons is low, so plants dominate the food supply, with perhaps a few chickens or pigs around to eat any food excess or waste. Certain tropical plants, such as palms, can provide dietary fat. A local near-vegetarian diet makes sense, given the type of agriculture in this climate.

In areas with plenty of tillable land, but more extreme seasonality, such as harsh winters or prolonged dry periods, storage of seasonal grain surplus is more critical. In addition to large granaries, more livestock are generally required than in tropical climates. To cope with harvest yield uncertainty, grains are over-sown, and any excess is shunted to livestock to act as a "feed buffer." If harvests are short, the livestock go hungry (and can be culled) before the people do. Animals convert grains into fat, which has 3,500 kilocalories per pound, more than double the caloric density of grains, and so is prized by people who perform physical labor. Dietary fat from livestock, which can store food without refrigeration, move on their own, and protect themselves from rodents and insects, is often more important than protein in these environments.

Most parts of Earth are not so-called breadbaskets with expansive, contiguous areas of deep topsoil and plentiful rainfall with which to grow crops. The landscape may only have pockets of good soil, which could be used to grow high-value tubers, vegetables, fruits, and some grains. But because of limited tillable area, livestock, especially dairy producers, may be an even more significant means of subsistence. And in the most extreme environments, including deserts and polar regions, nomadic herders, hunters, and foragers prevail.

Variable Food System Industrialization

Today, the degree of adoption of industrial agricultural practices and participation in the global food system varies significantly around the world (Pellegrini and Fernández 2018). The most dedicated industrial systems are in countries with high per capita energy use and, perhaps consequently, relatively small rural populations, as fossil fuels are needed both to industrialize food systems and to support urban infrastructure (Figure 3).

Many people employ a mix of traditional and modern practices. For example, farmers who spread synthetic fertilizer by hand exhibit a minor turn toward industrialization. Substituting human and animal labor with more mechanization not only leads to decreases in rural population, but also comes with other consequences. Using more fuel and machines may increase labor productivity, but often comes with a decline in resource efficiency and an increase in pollution.

For those working in international development or on national agricultural policy, following recent paths of modernization and globalization are counterproductive. Food systems that have not yet modernized need to be preserved and societies that are hyper-industrialized may have the most difficult time adapting. Those in very high consumption countries can take solace in the fact that most of their consumption is probably wasted, and they could live on a fraction of what they do now, as most of the world still does. In the United States, for example, GDP per capita in 1950, hardly a time of material deprivation, was about a third of today's (Mulbrandon 2011).

Multi-Functional Crops and Livestock

One of the key lessons from a study of traditional agrarian systems is that crop and livestock choices are multifaceted. An unusual feature of today's food system, and an obvious consequence of extreme surplus, is that grains are grown specifically to feed livestock in amounts that exceed any historic norm. In peasant societies, livestock numbers were kept to what is termed "default" levels, where livestock were used for labor, to manage fertility, as clean-up artists, as feed buffers, and to harvest roughage (Fairlie 2011). The preponderance of beef cattle, for example, is a modern invention. In the past, beef was a byproduct of old cows, male dairy calves, and retired oxen. Chicken meat was also the byproduct of old laying hens and young roosters. Historically, we see that animals served multiple functions to a greater extent than today.

Beef cattle and meat chickens are one example of a general rule. Specialization in agriculture has been taken to extremes in all kinds of crops and livestock. Dwarf wheat, for example, has very high seed yields, but is lacking in straw. If you are a specialized grain farmer and can buy fertilizer, the low straw yield may not seem important. For a diversified farmer using livestock and lacking cheap fertilizers, the old wheat variety may look better to you. That is because the abundant straw, when gathered, provides bedding for the barn and will turn into compost, and when left on the field, provides a welcome soil mulch that suppresses weeds and benefits the soil biology.

Interest in so-called heritage breeds of crops and livestock is not just nostalgic. Some realize they have not had their multi-functional nature bred out of them and that such traits will be important again someday. Breeding programs for a wide array of crops and livestock that combine modern techniques with the needs of farming systems that function without fossil fuels would be very welcome.

Soil Structure and Processes

The creation of soil from rock and minerals is both a physical and biological process, called weathering, and soil itself is a mixture of inert minerals, pore space for air and water to move, living organisms, and dead parts of plants, animals, fungi, and bacteria in various states of decay. Soil minerals consist of particles that range in size—large in sand and very small in clay, with silt in between. Soils with high sand content don't store water and nutrients well but tend to have easy movement of air and water. Soils with high clay content are full of nutrients and can store a lot of water, but the clay holds onto water and nutrients tightly and doesn't allow for air movement, so plant roots don't grow well. Silt is more ideal for plant growth, and the very best farming soils, called loams, have a balance of silt, sand, and clay (Figure 6).

The dead organic debris that becomes stabilized, similar to finished compost, is called soil organic matter (SOM) and makes up about 5 percent of high-quality farm topsoil (DuPont 2012). Soils have recognizable layers, called horizons, resulting from the environmental gradient between the air and bedrock. (See Figure 7.) SOM is concentrated in the upper, or A, horizon. Even though organic matter makes up a small percentage of topsoil, it has an outsized influence on soil function.

The presence of SOM enhances crop yield potential, while reducing farming costs and risk, by helping build and maintain relationships among air, water, and nutrients. Roots and many other living things in soil need to breathe. Organic matter has sponge-like properties, creating pockets for air and water movement that can help the soil resist compaction. Soils high in SOM allow water to infiltrate the soil profile more quickly, store water well, and release it slowly between rain and irrigation episodes. Crops are therefore less likely to be drought-stressed when SOM levels are high. Soil humus carries negative charges that keep positively charged minerals from leaching out during heavy rains and irrigation, while still allowing those minerals to be absorbed by plants. Organic matter also acts as a buffer to keep soils from becoming too acidic or alkaline, and a more neutral pH fosters nutrient uptake by plants. Extracellular polymeric substances produced by bacteria and filamentous strands of fungi with glue-like molecules, such as glomalin, allow SOM to hold soil together, so it is less likely to erode.

The main agricultural soil is called mollisol, derived from the Latin word *mollis*, which means soft. Mollisols come from grasslands, where biological and climatic conditions are just right for rich soil formation. Prairie grasses send copious, long, and dense roots deep below ground to create pore space, promote soil aggregation, and build structure. Roots also create vertical channels for the movement of water and nutrients. Over time, as more and more root material builds up, grasslands yield large influxes of soil organic matter, which turns the soil dark brown.

History is riddled with examples of civilizations

that progressively degraded soils to the point of food system collapse (Montgomery 2012; Diamond 2011). Perhaps we can forgive people for not understanding what they were doing, although plenty of documents suggest that many living at the time did. But we should not give ourselves a pass for what is happening today as geology, archeology, soil science, and agronomy have progressed to the point where anyone can understand our predicament and the reasons for the sad state of most agricultural soils around the world. Only with the use of fossil fuels have we been able to temporarily postpone the reckoning by supplying the means to import lost nutrients and add synthetic nitrogen, and those will not

Figure 6
USDA Soil Texture Pyramid

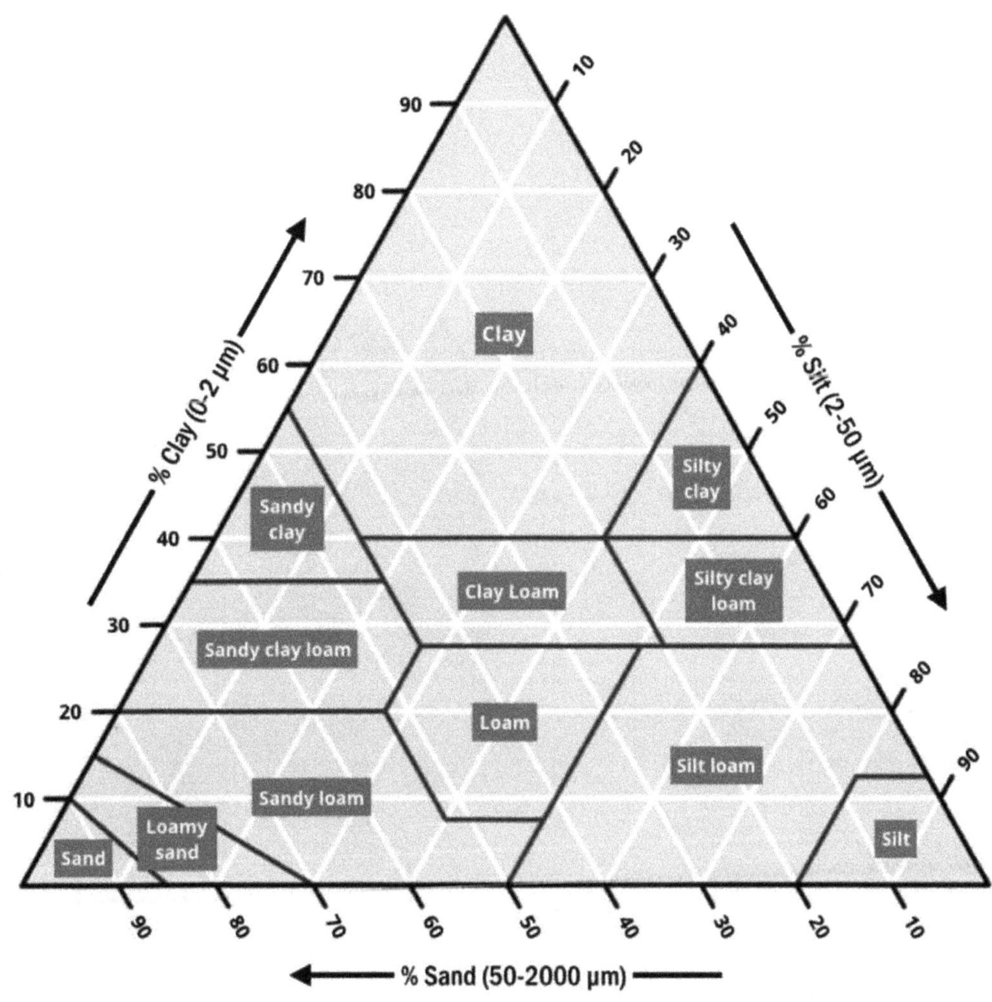

Source: Bradford (2019).
Note: The soil texture pyramid shows the ratio of particles within the soil. The middle of loam is 40 percent silt, 40 percent sand, and 20 percent clay. Jelinski (2014) provides a description of the development of the soil texture pyramid.

last forever. Perhaps resource management would improve if people recognized that someday the ability of their families to eat will depend on the presence of healthy soils.

Fertility and Nutrient Management

When farmers till prairie grasslands for the first time, they unlock a store of nutrients held in SOM that translates into fantastic crop yields. As the disc blades chop and churn sod, SOM is more fully exposed to air and warmth, leading to its decomposition. The breakdown of SOM is akin to what happens in a compost pile or a pile of lawn clippings. Bacteria feed off the material and release heat, carbon dioxide, nitrogen, and minerals. Having been broken down into simple chemical forms, these minerals are available for root uptake, enabling crops to thrive. The great stores of organic matter in mollisols are the original fertilizer and the catalyst for the expansion of agrarian societies that have profited from exploitation of ecological wealth built over centuries, akin to a great forest felled, but below ground and thus largely invisible to us (Jackson 2010a, 2010b).

Most farms are losing soil organic matter through oxidation. Repeated tillage, crop residue removal, and some ways of applying synthetic fertilizers cause soil bacteria to decompose SOM faster than crops can rebuild it. In the United States, it is estimated that about half of SOM on cropland has been lost over the past several decades (Burke et al. 1989).

The harvest of crops removes some of the minerals that were originally in the soil. In natural scenarios,

Figure 7
Soil Horizons

O horizon: Organic/humus layer. Mostly organic matter like decaying leaves.

A horizon: Topsoil. Mostly minerals from parent material with some organic matter; good material for organisms and plants to live in.

B horizon: Subsoil. Rich in minerals that leached from A horizon and accumulated in this layer.

C horizon: Parent materials. The deposit at Earth's surface from which the soil developed.

R horizon: Bedrock (below C horizon/not pictured). A mass of rock (granite, basalt, quartzite, limestone, or sandstone that forms the parent material for some soils if the bedrock is close enough to the surface to weather. This is not considered soil.

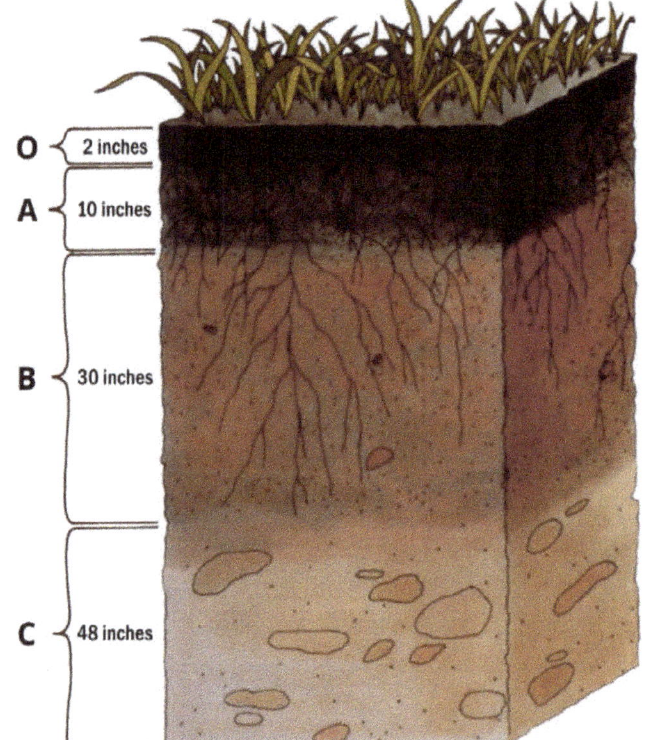

Source: USNRCS (nd-a).
Image Source: https://commons.wikimedia.org/wiki/File:Soil_profile.jpg. Public domain.

such as bison grazing on a prairie, the animals eat plants that have ingested minerals from the soil to build their leaves. The bison extract these minerals, plus energy, from the leaves to construct their bones, muscles, and other tissues. They also urinate and defecate, processes that directly return most of the nutrients prairie plants need to regrow. And eventually even the elements temporarily trapped in the bodies of the bison are returned to the soil after death.

Agronomists are aware of nutrient removal by crops, and the U.S. Department of Agriculture maintains a searchable database that allows a farmer to model losses from the field with each harvest (USNRCS nd-b). One purpose of nutrient removal tables is to recommend fertilizer rates, both to compensate for what the previous crop removed and to anticipate the needs of the next crop. In industrial agricultural systems, there tend to be no qualms about purchasing mineral inputs to replace exports, although this practice is clearly unsustainable.

Most fertilizers used today are products of mining and other energy-intensive manufacturing processes. Natural gas is the chief precursor to synthesized nitrogen fertilizer. Phosphate rock is mined from a few key locations around the planet and subjected to grinding and energy-demanding chemical transformations to yield superphosphate fertilizers. Deposits from ancient sea beds are mined to yield potassium salts. Limestone, dolomite, and gypsum rocks are excavated from quarries, ground into powder and spread over acidic fields to raise soil pH toward neutral and add minerals such as calcium, magnesium, and sulfur. Other minerals may be required now and then, but those are the most common ones.

If human societies were spatially organized more like a herd of bison, fertility management would not be so complicated and energy demanding. People could eat, deposit their wastes, and keep their animals within the plant communities that the whole system relies on. Instead we have dissociated ourselves from productive landscapes. We pay to take care of the resulting pollution in cities and feedlots. (Cities are functionally analogous to feedlots for people [Rees 2012].) We pay again to mine, manufacture, transport, and spread replacement minerals back to the land. This replacement of a cyclical process of continuous nutrient recovery with a linear process of use, discard, and replace from afar is called progress.

It would be wise to sort out how to return to land what we take from it and dispense with energy-demanding mining and processing. Returning all human waste to fields is entirely possible and was the method by which Chinese and Japanese farmers persisted for centuries (King 2004; Jenkins 1996). In the late stages of energy descent, long-distance transport of food to cities and long-distance transport of wastes back to farms will be very costly. As an illustrative example, the daily volume of biosolids from New York City and how it is dealt with is a fascinating topic (NYC-DEP 2020; Danner 2018; Marchetti 2013).

Erosion Control and Soil Conservation

Farms are usually situated on the most productive soils, which means they are the quickest to develop, the deepest, and most resilient to disturbance. But "quick" in geologic time may be slow on a human scale. For example, it takes the actions of plant roots and earthworms about 100 to 500 years to produce one inch of fresh topsoil (Arsenault 2014; Lisetskii 2019; U.S. NRCS 2003). Under the cover of a forest or native grassland, erosion is similarly slow, so soils maintain a characteristic depth over long periods. However, once vegetation is cleared to plant crops, rates of soil erosion on most farms exceed soil development, typically by an order of magnitude (Nearing et al. 2017). This is how agrarian societies have repeatedly failed, by farming in a manner that leads to shallower soils, which eventually causes crop yields to plummet. Temples get buried by forests and some hundreds of year, later, once the soil has been restored, the cycle may begin again.

We know how to reduce rates of erosion to nearly natural levels and thereby protect agricultural soils so they can last a very long time. Soil erodes most quickly when it loses SOM and is laid bare by tillage and subject to the forces of wind and water without protective plant cover. Limiting tillage and keeping soil covered by living plants and plant residues as much as possible decreases erosion. And to protect hillsides from erosion requires maintaining perennial cover, such a pasture, or using contour tillage and terracing techniques.

The Risks of Intensification

Those rightfully concerned about the expansion of agriculture into forests and other shrinking habitats are promoting the notion of "sustainable intensification" (Pretty and Bharucha 2014). The laudable goal is to intensify by increasing output per unit of land, while achieving sustainable management by recognizing the negative externalities of most current practices and limiting them. Some proponents of sustainable intensification want to deliver a greener package of industrial farming technologies, such as modern seed varieties, precision fertilizer applications, and expansion of irrigation systems. Others insist on a more ecologically minded, biologically intensive approach, hoping to sidestep the industrial farming model and find a symbiotic relationship between agroecosystems and natural ecosystems. Some are critical of the notion that global agricultural output needs to increase at all. Far more food is grown than can be consumed already, but it is poorly distributed. Models of demand for future food assume large increases in global consumer spending on meat and other luxury foods. But that assumption begs crucial questions: Why not improve diets? Will real incomes actually be higher in the future?

Proponents of sustainable intensification hope to avoid the errors of past agrarian societies, where population growth led to cultivation on marginal lands, which is the kind of extensive growth that has led to massive crop failure and the collapse of civilizations in the past. The world cannot afford to make that mistake again. Modern society can learn from cultures that farmed successfully *in the same places* for thousands of years, accomplished by returning removed nutrients back to the land and keeping soil covered. Still, most societies have failed to adequately protect their soil over the long run, and intensification can backfire if not done properly.

Let's unpack that last sentence, as we want to prevent an unfortunate repeat of history. The factors of production in agrarian societies are the land base, human labor, fuel, and the various tools available, which may include farm equipment, beasts of burden, and granaries. Food calories per land area are maximized by growing the seeds of domesticated grasses, such as wheat and corn, or starchy tubers, such as potatoes. As population rises, pressure mounts to intensify by increasing the yield of calories for a given area. The other option is extensive development by clearing more land to grow food.

Let's imagine a scenario where expansion onto new land is impossible, so farmers must eke out more food from the same area. There are two general ways to intensify: 1) increase the yield of the crops being grown, or 2) shift the mix of crops and preferentially grow the ones with higher yields. Animals do not yield as many calories per acre, so if the second form of intensification is adopted, livestock numbers would decrease as less land is allocated to feed them. Their role as a feed buffer would shrink, making the community under-insured against a poor grain harvest. As farming intensifies, farmers can harvest more calories because a greater area has come under cultivation for grains or potatoes. Some additional discussion on soil, plant, and animal biology is useful to appreciate why such intensification can be the beginning of a downward spiral.

Soil quality varies across a landscape—there are outstanding, mediocre, and inferior areas for farming. On the best soils, farmers can get high yields with modest efforts, so that is usually where farming begins. Farmers avoid tilling and planting on lower-quality soils unless absolutely necessary because their efforts produce low returns with high risk of crop failure. Lower-quality soils tend to have shallow topsoil and are more vulnerable to erosion, so they do not have the same resilience as the best soils. A heavy rain at an inopportune time can wash away newly planted crops and the thin topsoil and make the area even less productive going forward.

Raising livestock on land of marginal quality is less risky than trying to grow a crop on it because the plants that dominate pastures are not the annual crops grown for grains but perennials, which means they live for many years once established. Perennials keep the soil covered year-round, which helps to prevent erosion. Their roots have years to grow into deep soil layers and so have access to larger stores of water and nutrients than annuals. Grazing pressure often encourages the development of a biologically diverse field where no single plant species dominates. As a result, clovers, with their beneficial nitrogen-fixing bacteria, can become established. Like the bison on the prairie, grazing livestock redeposit most of the minerals they eat in a form that fosters pasture regrowth, and deep roots with mycorrhizal fungi can move minerals from deep soil horizons to the surface. The overall effect is an increase in SOM and enrichment of the topsoil, and farmers without synthetic fertilizers can take advantage of this effect by tilling the pasture and getting a high, albeit short-lived, boost in crop yields.

The crop-versus-livestock question for a field is not an either-or proposition, however. It may be reasonable to keep marginal-quality land in pasture most of the time and occasionally rotate the field into a crop that might do all right. For example, oats do not need soils that are as fertile or well-drained as wheat, so a field that will never yield a good wheat harvest may be fine for oats every few years. Typically, intensification leads to an increase in the proportion of fields dedicated to annual crops instead of livestock grazing, which ends up reducing soil quality across the landscape.

The example of intensification and soil decline provided above is indicative of an integrated crop and livestock system, akin to European mixed farming. However, similar dynamics apply elsewhere, even when domesticated ruminants are not included. Swidden systems (cleared using a slash-and-burn method) of sweet potatoes and taro that rotate gardens with wet tropical forests fail if forests are not allowed enough time to regrow. Growing potatoes on Andean slopes leads to enormous soil losses if fields are not kept small and rotated across the landscape to allow native vegetation to regrow.

The key points here are that soils vary in quality, and all soils need to be managed to optimize mineral composition, organic matter, and structure if they are expected to yield indefinitely. Ruminant livestock on perennial pastures can be excellent for soil health but will not return as many calories per area as grains or potatoes. Can yields be increased while protecting the soil? Achieving sustainable intensification is therefore complex, needing cropping systems to support soil health. It can work only if it is adopted by a culture that understands the challenge.

Ecosystem Services on Farmland

We have been fortunate to take ecosystem services for granted until now. It is uncomfortable to worry about whether there are enough insectivorous birds and bats around to keep pest outbreaks in check. Nobody likes wondering if wetlands can buffer rivers from heavy rainfall events enough to prevent their town from flooding. Who wants to lose sleep over the question of the size of pollinator populations and whether we will have the fruits and vegetables we expect? We all can hope forests and fields will thrive, overcome the stresses of heat and disease, and can continue to drive the hydrological cycle effectively to yield enough rainfall.

As more people live close to the land, it will become more difficult to compensate for a local lack of ecosystem services, such as the provisioning of resources like food and the regulation of processes like water storage and release. To prepare for the decline of imported services and to avoid the burdensome costs of substitution with energy and technology, we can start planning to take care of ourselves by restoring ecosystem services.

Healthy agricultural landscapes can provide a wide range of ecosystem services, and we know how to foster these. A focus on soil health will improve watershed functions, such as water infiltration, storage, and quality. We can also view farms as parts of complex, diverse landscapes instead of just places to produce things we need. Landscapes tend to have various habitats related to underlying soil and geographic features. Wetlands, rocky outcrops, and river corridors, for example, can be protected and enhanced. These areas provide homes for wildlife, such as birds, bees, and bats, that are crucial partners in crop production.

Agroecology and Functional Diversity

The word agroecology is a fusion of agronomy and ecology. The idea is to apply ecological concepts to agricultural design and practice (Altieri and Farrell 2018). An ecologist views the world through flows of energy and materials. On Earth, the energy flow starts with the sun. Plants generate material flows through photosynthesis by capturing this energy and producing biomass that animals can consume. Dead biomass and manure decompose in the soil—a living ecosystem itself—where plants can recapture nutrients and initiate another cycle of growth. With agriculture, humans are structuring an ecosystem around their own needs.

Ecologists have observed rules about what makes ecosystems function well, and these can be applied in agricultural settings, too. If we state a desired goal, we can ask what ecological design or structure could work best. Farmers want high yields relative to inputs, as well as minimal risk of crop failures. Ecologists know that to achieve these goals, the agroecosystem needs diversity.

Diversity is a critical component of agriculture at multiple scales. A pasture can have many species of forage and a variety of animals that graze on those species. A farm may have many different crops among fields. The landscape that contains the farm may have natural areas managed to promote pollination or predation services. Over time, as fields rotate in and out of crops and pasture, diversity can migrate across space.

Diversity means not simply a high number of species, but also a wide range of ecological functions. For example, perennial plants function differently than annual plants by growing over years, not just seasons, and building extensive root structures that change soil conditions. Livestock also add functional diversity on farms by increasing plant productivity and soil fertility and by affecting plant population dynamics.

How does more diversity create these desired functions? Primarily by adding to the "skill set" on the farm. Having more organisms on the farm broadens the array of skills being used. For example, grasses tend to have shallow, fibrous roots that capture near-surface moisture quickly and effectively, as shown in Figure 8. Other plants, such as white clover, have tap roots that give them access to deeper soil moisture during dry spells. Together, a grass and white clover field will be more productive than either would be alone. Episodic environmental stresses, such as drought or disease outbreak, are less likely to wipe out a diverse ecosystem because some members of the ecosystem have traits that allow them to rebound from the stress.

Natural ecosystems have evolved to optimize energy payback. The most energy- and resource-efficient land ecosystems are diverse, perennial plant communities with a healthy set of herbivores and predators. This explains why pasture helps build soil organic matter, which in turn makes it possible to grow annual crops with fewer external inputs. Many of the lessons from agroecology are practiced in organic and related systems of farming.

Modern Schools of Thought

Many contemporary innovators have applied key concepts from soil science, ecology, sustainability, and resilience thinking to the question of what kind of agriculture can conserve soil, succeed without extravagant energy use, and protect the natural environment, including the climate and other species that live with us on Earth. Prominent examples include organic, biodynamic, holistic livestock management, natural systems agriculture (perennial polycultures), Grow-Biointensive, and permaculture. Recently, the term "regenerative agriculture" has come into use and is often focused on managing for soil health (Montgomery 2017).

While each has a unique emphasis, all aim to reduce external inputs and align human activities with ecological processes. For example, the USDA National Organic Standards Board defined organic agriculture in 1995 as follows (Gold 2007):

> Organic agriculture is an ecological production management system that promotes and enhances biodiversity, biological cycles, and soil biological activity. It is based on minimal use of off-farm inputs and on management practices that restore, maintain, and enhance ecological harmony.

Much could be done to spread the core concepts and practices of these schools of thought and research. Breeding and other services could improve applications. There is no lack of basic understanding on how to manage agroecosystems wisely and productively. Because these systems purchase fewer outside inputs, require more labor, and add management complexity, widespread adoption has been hindered by lack of associated business interest, near-term financial constraints, and practical uncertainties about how to change farming systems.

Conclusion

Even institutional environmental organizations have largely stopped promoting frugality as a virtue, drifting instead towards "ecomodernism" with happy promises of technological innovation, efficiency, and emphasis on social justice concerns to manage a "just transition" to an all-renewable economy that does not question growth and complexity (Nijhuis 2015). Perhaps it was naïve to hope for a planned energy descent, such as *A Prosperous Way Down* (Odum and Odum 2001) or the "simpler way" proposed by Ted Trainer (Alexander 2012). Instead, we are left

Figure 8
Two Types of Root Systems

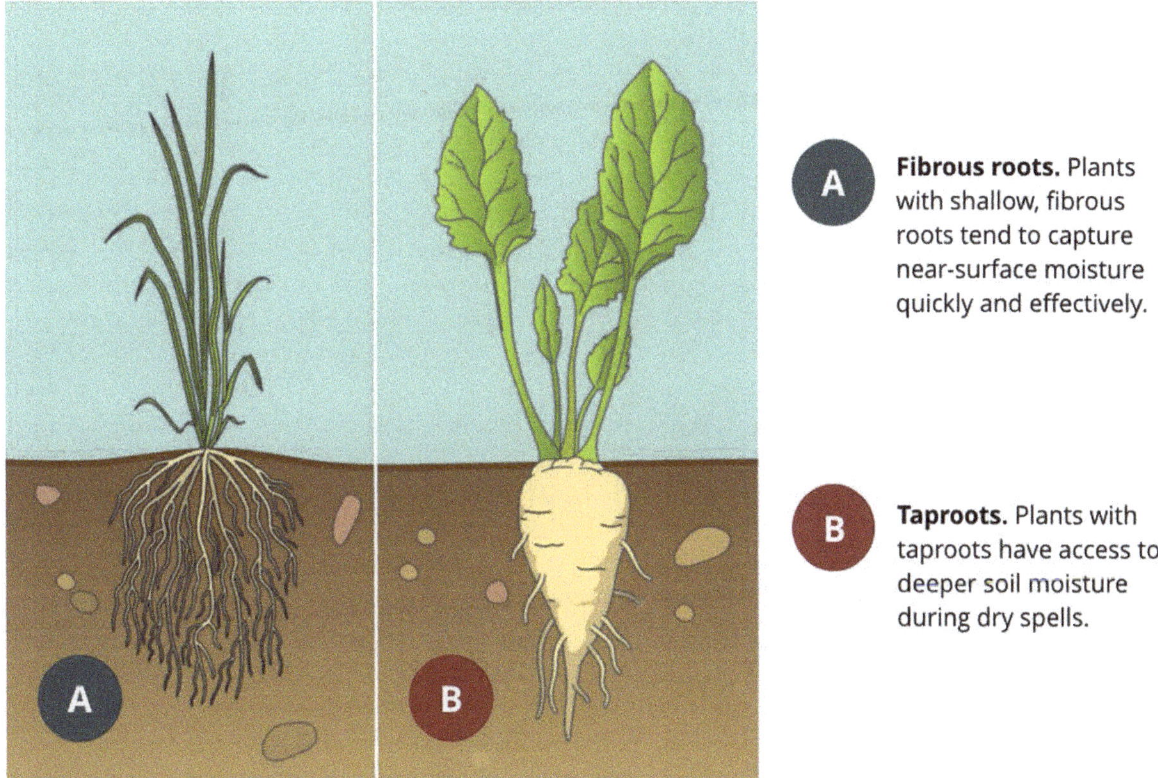

Source: Bradford (2019).
Note: Image of a plant with fibrous roots (left) and a plant with a taproot (right).

to wonder, citing a neo-Malthusian rhetorical question, "Are humans smarter than yeast?" In describing the human predicament, Hagens (2020) articulates "how a social species self-organizing around surplus has metabolically morphed into a single, mindless, energy-hungry 'Superorganism.'" If this is a true expression of our predicament, then instead of expecting a transition to a sustainable economy that maintains a semblance of high-energy modernity, we should expect growth until collapse. Not all collapses are equal, however, and at this point we can still advocate for a more graceful fall, or what Hagens (2020) calls a *bend* instead of a *break*.

Tainter (2000) reviews the history of problem solving by institutions to avoid or cope with collapse and argues that there are three basic historical models, which he calls the Roman, the Byzantine, and the European. The Romans held on to their highly complex social structure as long as possible but were eventually overwhelmed by diminishing returns to problem solving via complexity and suffered a *deep* collapse. The Byzantines simplified their social structure, navigating a *shallow* collapse, and persisted as a political entity, though in a different form. The European model is the ongoing story of ever-increasing access to resources, such as overseas colonies and fossil fuels, and the timely development of advanced technologies allowing for the increasingly complex and globally integrated society we live in today.

Centuries of fossil-fueled growth following the European model have now placed the human species into global overshoot for the first time in history (Catton 1980). Now the question is whether we will be able to continue along this path or transition to the Roman or the Byzantine one. We know many would prefer to keep on expanding. For example, we can watch tech-billionaires on YouTube explicitly propose to avoid an inevitable collapse of the present course we are following on Earth by colonizing space and other planets (Robson 2019; McFall-Johnsen and Mosher 2020). The choice presented is binary: colonize space or crash on Earth.

This is a false dichotomy. A less risky path would be to simplify, something advocated by ecologists and permaculturalists. As Tainter (2000) explains:

> The Byzantine Empire responded with one of history's only examples of a complex society simplifying. Much of the structure of ranks and honors, based on urban life, disappeared. Civil administration simplified and merged in the countryside with the military. Governmental transaction costs were reduced. The economy contracted and there were fewer artisans and merchants. Elite social life focused on the capitol and the emperor, rather than on the cities that no longer existed. Literacy, writing, and education declined. Barter and feudal social relations replaced the millennium old monetary economy.

While some may respond with dread and fatalism to our predicament, Bradford (2019) offers resilience science, as presented by Walker and Salt (2017), as a frame for our situation that encourages engagement and promotes a sense of agency. Perhaps concerned and knowledgeable people might prepare to hasten reorganization of society into simpler forms, anticipating the future that Hagens (2020) calls "The Great Simplification." In resilience terms, we would be promoting system *transformability* by creating awareness of the need for system change and options to facilitate it. The needed changes may involve activities regarded as 1) uneconomic, such as choosing human labor over mechanization, 2) on too small a scale, such as a community garden, or 3) on the fringe, such as horse farming. Those sorts of activities should be pursued now with an eye towards how they will be valued during energy descent.

The development of the social system known as high-energy modernity is analogous to the metabolic system known as the endotherm, which thrives in an ecological niche of high-power throughput. There are other, less power-consuming ways to live in the world, but it is perhaps too much to expect an endotherm to willfully change into an ectotherm, which would constitute a fundamentally different system identity (Sorman and Giampietro 2013).

Although human volition may not prevent 21st-century energy descent and subsequent crises, human initiative may lead to more benign paths of reorganization once material conditions force a shift in mass psychology. Perhaps in a collective state of mind that is more humble and less individualistic, societies will be able to face, rather than avoid, reality (Ophuls 1977; Quilley 2013).

References

Alexander, Samuel. (2012). "Ted Trainer and the Simpler Way." *Simplicity Institute Report 12d.* Melbourne, NSW: Simplicity Institute. https://doi. org/10.2139/ssrn.2060196

Altieri, Miguel A., and John G. Farrell. (2018). *Agroecology: The Science of Sustainable Agriculture*, 2nd ed. Boca Raton, FL: CRC Press.

Andreoni, Valeria. (2017). "Energy Metabolism of 28 World Countries: A Multi- Scale Integrated Analysis." *Ecological Economics* 142(C): 56–69.

Arsenault, Chris. (2014). "Only 60 Years of Farming Left If Soil Degradation Continues." *Scientific American* December 5. https://www.scientificamerican.com/article/only-60-years-of-farming-left-if-soil-degradation-continues/

Babington, Deepa, and Lefteris Papadimas. (2012). "In Greece, a Painful Return to Country Roots." *Reuters* June 7. https://www.reuters.com/article/us-greece-countryside-idUSBRE85708920120608

Bettencourt, Luis M. A., José Lobo, Dirk Helbing, Christian Kühnert, and Geoffrey B. West. (2007). "Growth, Innovation, Scaling, and the Pace of Life in Cities." *Proceedings of the National Academy of Sciences of the United States of America* 104(17): 7301–7306.

Bradford, Jason. (2019). *The Future Is Rural: Food System Adaptations to the Great Simplification.* Corvallis, OR: Post Carbon Institute.

Burke, Ingrid C., Caroline M. Yonker, William J. Parton, C. Vernon Cole, Klaus Flach, and David S. Schimel. (1989). "Texture, Climate, and Cultivation Effects on Soil Organic Matter Content in US Grassland Soils." *Soil Science Society of America Journal* 53(3): 800–805. https://doi.org/10.2136/sssaj 1989.03615995005300030029x

Canning, Patrick, Ainsley Charles, Sonya Huang, Karen R. Polenske, and Arnold Waters. (2010). *Energy Use in the U.S. Food System.* Economic Research Report Number 94, Washington, DC: U.S. Department of Agriculture, Economic Research Service.

Capellán-Pérez, Iñigo, Carlos de Castro, and Luis Javier Miguel González. (2019). "Dynamic Energy Return on Energy Investment (EROI) and Material Requirements in Scenarios of Global Transition to Renewable Energies." *Energy Strategy Reviews* 26: 1–26.

Capellán-Pérez, Iñigo, Margarita Mediavilla, Carlos de Castro, Oscar Carpintero, and Luis Javier Miguel. (2014). "Fossil Fuel Depletion and Socio-Economic Scenarios: An Integrated Approach." *Energy* 77: 641–666.

Catton, William R., Jr. (1980). *Overshoot: The Ecological Basis of Revolutionary Change.* University of Illinois Press.

Center for Sustainable Systems. (2017). *U.S. Food System Factsheet.* Pub. No. CSS01-06. Ann Arbor: School for Environment and Sustainability, University of Michigan. http://css.umich.edu/factsheets/us-food-system-factsheet or Food System_CSS01-06_e2019.pdf

Clack, Christopher T. M., Staffan A. Qvist, Jay Apt, Morgan Bazilian, Adam R. Brandt, Ken Caldeira, Steven J. Davis, Victor Diakov, Mark A. Handschy, Paul D. H. Hines, Paulina Jaramillo, Daniel M. Kammen, C. S. Jane, M. Granger Long, Adam Reed Morgan, Varun Sivaram, James Sweeney, George R. Tynan, David G. Victor, John P. Weyant, and Jay F. Whitacre. (2017). "Evaluation of 100% Wind, Water, and Solar Power." *Proceedings of the National Academy of Sciences of the United States of America* 114(26): 6722–6727.

Cox, Stan. (2013). *Any Way You Slice It: The Past, Present, and Future of Rationing.* New York: New Press.

Cox, Wendell. (2019). *Demographia World Urban Areas,* 15th annual ed. Belleville, IL: Demographia. http://www.demographia.com/db-worldua.pdf

Danner, Chas. (2018). "Alabamians Are Sick of New York City's Crap." *New York Intelligencer* March 11. http://nymag.com/intelligencer/2018/03/alabamians-are-sick-of-new-yorks-crap.html

Day, John W., and Charles Hall. (2016). *America's Most Sustainable Cities and Regions: Surviving the 21st Century Megatrends.* New York: Springer.

Diamond, Jared. (2011). *Collapse: How Societies Choose to Fail or Succeed,* 2nd ed. New York: Penguin Books.

DuPont, S. Tianna. (2012). *Soil Quality Information.* Penn State Extension, August 28. University Park, PA: Pennsylvania State University. https://extension.psu.edu/soil-quality-information

Engineering Tool Box. (2008). *Fossil and Alternative Fuels—Energy Content.* https://www.engineeringtoolbox.com/fossil-fuels-energy-content-d_1298.html

Fairlie, Simon. (2011). *Meat: A Benign Extravagance.* East Meon, Hampshire, UK: Permanent Publications.

Fleming, David, and Shaun Chamberlin. (2016). *Surviving the Future: Culture, Carnival and Capital in the Aftermath of the Market Economy.* White River Junction, VT: Chelsea Green.

Folke, Carl, Asa Jansson, Jonas Larsson, and Robert Costanza. (1997). "Ecosystem Appropriation by Cities." *Ambio* 26(3): 167–172.

Giampietro, Mario. (1997). "The Link Between Resources, Technology and Standard of Living: A Theoretical Model." In *Advances in Human Ecology* 6. Ed. L. Freese, pp. 73–128. Greenwich: JAI Press.

Giampietro, Mario, Kozo Mayumi, and Jesus Ramos-Martin. (2006). "Can Biofuels Replace Fossil Energy Fuels? A Multi-Scale Integrated Analysis Based on the Concept of Societal and Ecosystem Metabolism: Part 1." *International Journal of Transdisciplinary Research* 1(1): 51–87.

________. (2009). "Multi-Scale Integrated Analysis of Societal and Ecosystem Metabolism (MuSIASEM): Theoretical Concepts and Basic Rationale." *Energy* 34(3): 313–322.

Gold, Mary. (2007). *Organic Production/Organic Food: Information Access Tools.* Washington, DC: U.S. Department of Agriculture, National Agricultural Library. https://www.nal.usda.gov/afsic/organic-productionorganic-food-information-access-tools

Hagens, Nathan J. (2020). "Economics for the Future—Beyond the Superorganism." *Ecological Economics* 169: 1–16.

Heinberg, Richard, and David Fridley. (2016). *Our Renewable Future: Laying the Path for 100% Clean Energy.* Washington, DC: Island Press. http://ourrenewablefuture.org/

Holmgren, David. (2006). *Permaculture: Solutions for the Energy Descent.* Presentation at Urban Sustainable Living Expo Warrnambool. Hepburn, Victoria, Australia: Holmgren Design Services. https://holmgren.com.au/wp-content/uploads/2013/02/PermSolutionsWarn.pdf

________. (2018). *Retrosuburbia: The Downshifter's Guide to a Resilient Future.* Hepburn, Victoria, Australia: Melliodora Publishing. https://melliodora.com/product-tag/melliodora-publishing/

International Energy Agency (IEA). (2019). *Global Energy & CO_2 Status Report 2019.* Paris: IEA. https://www.iea.org/reports/global-energy-and-co2-status-report-2019

Jackson, Wes. (2010a). *Consulting the Genius of the Place: An Ecological Approach to a New Agriculture.* Counterpoint Press.

________. (2010b). "Tackling the Oldest Environmental Problem: Agriculture and its Impact on Soil." In *The Post Carbon Reader: Managing the 21st Century's Sustainability Crisis.* Eds. Richard Heinberg and Daniel Lerch. Santa Rosa, CA: Post Carbon Institute. https://www.postcarbon.org/publications/post-carbon-reader/

Jacobson, Mark Z., Mark A. Delucchi, Mary A. Cameron, and Bethany A. Frew. (2015). "Low-Cost Solution to the Grid Reliability Problem with 100% Penetration of Intermittent Wind, Water, and Solar for All Purposes." *Proceedings of the National Academy of Sciences of the United States of America* 112(49): 15060–15065.

Jelinski, Nic. (2014). *The Historical Development of the USDA Textural Triangle.* Minneapolis: University of Minnesota Soil Judging Team. http://umnsoilsteam.blogspot.com/2014/09/the-historical-development-of-usda.html

Jenkins, Joseph C. (1996). *The Humanure Handbook.* Grove City, PA: Joseph Jenkins Inc.

Johnson, C. (2006). "Human Being—Thermal Efficiency." *Public Encyclopedia.* http://mb-soft.com/public2/humaneff.html

Kennedy, Christopher. (2012). "A Mathematical Description of Urban Metabolism." In *Sustainability Science: The Emerging Paradigm and the Urban Environment.* Eds. M. P. Weinstein and R. E. Turner, pp. 275–291. New York: Springer.

King, Casey W. (2020). "An Integrated Biophysical and Economic Modeling Framework for Long-Term Sustainability Analysis: The HARMONEY Model." *Ecological Economics* 169: 106464. ISSN 0921–8009, https://doi. org/10.1016/j.ecolecon.2019.106464

King, Franklin H. (2004). *Farmers of Forty Centuries: Organic Farming in China, Korea, and Japan.* Mineola, NY: Dover Publications.

Lambert, Jessica, Charles Hall, Stephen Balogh, Ajay Gupta, and Michelle Arnold. (2014). "Energy, EROI and Quality of Life." *Energy Policy* 64: 153–167.

Lang, Graeme. (2018). "Urban Energy Futures: A Comparative Analysis." *European Journal of Futures Research* 6: 19. https://eujournalfuturesresearch.springeropen.com/track/pdf/10.1186/s40309-018-0146-8

Lisetskii, Fedor. (2019). "Estimates of Soil Renewal Rates: Applications for Anti-Erosion Arrangement of the Agricultural Landscape." *Geosciences* 9(6): 266. https://www.mdpi.com/2076-3263/9/6/266/htm

Love, Thomas, and Cindy Isenhour. (2016). "Energy and Economy: Recognizing High-Energy Modernity as a Historical Period." *Economic Anthropology* 3: 6–16.

Malo, Sebastien. (2019). "Cool U.S. Cities Prepare as Future 'Havens' for Climate Migrants." *Reuters.* https://www.reuters.com/article/us-usa-climatechange-migration-cool-u-s-cities-prepare-as-future-havens-for-climate-migrants

Marchetti, Damiano. (2013). "The Sludge at the Bottom of the Sea." WNYC (public radio). https://www.wnycstudios.org/podcasts/radiolab/articles/sludge-bottom-sea and https://www.wnycstudios.org/story/poop-train

Masi, Brad, Janet Fiskio, and Rumi Shammin. (2014). "Urban Agriculture in Rust Belt Cities." *Solutions* 5(1): 44–53.

Masson-Delmotte, Valerie, Panmao Zhai, Hans-Otto Pörtner, Debra Roberts, Jim Skea, Priyadarshi R. Shukla, Anna Pirani, Wilfran Moufouma-Okia, Clotilde Péan, Roz Pidcock, Sarah Connors, J. B. Robin Matthews, Yang Chen, Xiao Zhou, Melissa I. Gomis, Elisabeth Lonnoy, Tom Maycock, Melinda Tignor, and Tim Waterfield, eds. (2018). *Global Warming of 1.5°C. An IPCC Special Report on the Impacts of Global Warming of 1.5°C Above Pre-Industrial Levels and Related Global Greenhouse Gas Emission Pathways, in the Context of Strengthening the Global Response to the Threat of Climate Change, Sustainable Development, and Efforts to Eradicate Poverty.* Geneva, Switzerland: Intergovernmental Panel on Climate Change. https://www.ipcc.ch/site/assets/uploads/sites/2/2019/06/SR15_Full_Report_High_Res.pdf

Mayumi, Kozo. (1991). "Temporary Emancipation from Land: From the Industrial Revolution to the Present Time." *Ecological Economics* 4: 35–56.

McFall-Johnsen, Morgan, and Dave Mosher. (2020). "Elon Musk Says He Plans to Send 1 Million People to Mars by 2050 by Launching 3 Starship Rockets Every Day and Creating 'A Lot of Jobs' on the Red Planet." *Business Insider* January 17. https://www.businessinsider.com/elon-musk-plans-1-million-people-to-mars-by-2050-2020-1

Meadows, Donella, Jorgen Randers, and Dennis Meadows. (2004). *Limits to Growth: The 30-Year Update.* Chelsea: Green.

Modelski, George. (2003). *World Cities: –3000 to 2000.* Washington, DC: Faros 2000.

Montgomery, David R. (2012). *Dirt: The Erosion of Civilizations.* Berkeley, CA: University of California Press.

________. (2017). *Growing a Revolution: Bringing Our Soil Back to Life.* New York: W. W. Norton.

Morris, Ian. (2013). *The Measure of Civilization: How Social Development Decides the Fate of Nations.* Princeton, NJ: Princeton University Press.

Mulbrandon, Catherine. (2011). "Long-Term Real Growth in US GDP per Capita 1871–2009." *Visualizing Economics* March 8. http://visualizingeconomics.com/blog/2011/03/08/long-term-real-growth-in-us-gdp-per-capita-1871-2009

Nearing, Mark A., Yun Xie, Baoyuan Liu, and Yu Ye. (2017). "Natural and Anthropogenic Rates of Soil Erosion." *International Soil and Water Conservation Research* 5(2): 77–84. https://doi.org/10.1016/j.iswcr.2017.04.001

New York City, Department of Environmental Protection (NYC-DEP). (2020). *Wastewater Treatment System.* New York: DEP. https://www1.nyc.gov/site/dep/water/wastewater-treatment-system.page, http://www.nyc.gov/html/dep/html/wastewater/biohome.shtml

Nijhuis, Michelle (2015). "Is the 'Ecomodernist Manifesto' the Future of Environmentalism?" *New Yorker* June 2. https://www.newyorker.com/tech/annals-of-technology-is-the-ecomodernist-manifesto-the-future-of-environmentalism

Odum, Eugene. (1998). *Ecological Vignettes: Ecological Approaches to Dealing with Human Predicaments.* Amsterdam, Netherlands: Harwood Academic Publishers.

Odum, Howard T., and Elisabeth C. Odum. (2001). *A Prosperous Way Down: Principles and Policies.* Boulder: University Press of Colorado.

Ophuls, William. (1977). *Ecology and the Politics of Scarcity.* San Francisco: W. H. Freeman and Company.

Owen, David. (2009). *Green Metropolis: Why Living Smaller, Living Closer, and Driving Less Are the Keys to Sustainability.* New York: Riverhead Books.

Pellegrini, Pedro, and Roberto J. Fernández. (2018). "Crop Energy Use and the Green Revolution." *Proceedings of the National Academy of Sciences* 115(10): 2335–2340. https://doi.org/10.1073/pnas.1717072115

Perelman, Michael J. (1972). "Farming with Petroleum." *Environment* 14(8): 8–13.

Pimentel, David, and Marcia H. Pimentel. (2007). *Food, Energy, and Society,* 3rd ed. Boca Raton, FL: CRC Press.

Pretty, Jules, and Zareen Pervez Bharucha. (2014). "Sustainable Intensification in Agricultural Systems." *Annals of Botany* 114(8): 1571–1596. https://doi. org/10.1093/aob/mcu205

Quilley, Stephen. (2013). "De-Growth Is Not a Liberal Agenda: Relocalisation and the Limits to Low-Energy Cosmopolitanism." *Environmental Values* 22: 261–285.

Rees, William E. (2012). "Cities as Dissipative Structures: Global Change and the Vulnerability of Urban Civilization." In *Sustainability Science: The Emerging Paradigm and the Urban Environment.* Eds. M. P. Weinstein and R. E. Turner, pp. 247–274. New York: Springer.

________. (2019). "Why Place-Based Food Systems? Food Security in a Chaotic World." *Journal of Agriculture, Food Systems, and Community Development* 9(A): 5–13.

________. (2020). "MegaCities at Risk: The Climate-Energy Conundrum." In *The International Handbook on Megacities and Megacity Regions.* Eds. A. Sorensen and D. Labbe. Cheltenham, UK: Edward Elgar.

Robson, Elisabeth. (2019). "The Horrific Human Supremacy of Jeff Bezos." *Medium.com.* https://medium.com/@elisabethrobson/the-horrific-human-supremacy-of-jeff-bezos-8ce1fbb116aa

Smil, Vaclav. (2003). *Energy at the Crossroads.* MIT Press.

Sorman, Alevgul H., and Mario Giampietro (2013). "The Energetic Metabolism of Societies and the Degrowth Paradigm: Analyzing Biophysical Constraints and Realities." *Journal of Cleaner Production* 38: 80–93.

Tainter, Joseph A. (2000). "Problem Solving: Complexity, History, Sustainability." *Population and Environment: A Journal of Interdisciplinary Studies* 22(1): 3–41.

The Economics of Ecosystems and Biodiversity (TEEB). (2018). *Measuring What Matters in Agriculture and Food Systems: A Synthesis of the Results and Recommendations of TEEB for Agriculture and Food's Scientific and Economic Foundations Report.* Geneva, Switzerland: U.N. Environment Program. http://www.teebweb.org/agrifood/measuring-what-matters-in-agriculture-and-food-systems/

United Nations. (2018). *World Urbanization Prospects 2018.* New York: U.N. Department of Economics and Social Affairs. https://esa.un.org/unpd/wup/

U.S. Energy Information Administration (USEIA). (2018). *Primary Energy* [data set for total energy consumption by country]. Washington, DC: USEIA. https://www.eia.gov/international/data/world/total-energy/total-energy-consumption

U.S. Natural Resources Conservation Service (USNRCS). (2003). *What on Earth Is Soil?* [factsheet]. Washington, DC: U.S. Department of Agriculture, Natural Resource Conservation Service. https://www.nrcs.usda.gov/Internet/FSE_DOCUMENTS/nrcs144p2_002430.pdf

________. (no date nd-a). *Soil Education.* Washington, DC: U.S. Department of Agriculture, Natural Resource Conservation Service. https://www.nrcs.usda.gov/wps/portal/nrcs/main/soils/edu/

________. (no date nd-b). *Nutrient Content of Crops* (calculator). Washington, DC: U.S. Department of Agriculture, Natural Resource Conservation Service. https://plants.usda.gov/npk/main

Valero, Alicia, and Antonio Valero (2010). "Physical Geonomics: Combining the Exergy and Hubbert Peak Analysis for Predicting Mineral Resources Depletion." *Resources, Conservation and Recycling* 54: 1074–1083.

Walker, Brian, and David Salt. (2017). "A Crash Course in the Science of Resilience." In *The Community Resilience Reader: Essential Resources for an Era of Upheaval.* Ed. Daniel Lerch, pp. 163–178. Washington, DC: Island Press.

White, Craig R., Nichole F. Phillips, and Roger S. Seymour. (2006). "The Scaling and Temperature Dependence of Vertebrate Metabolism." *Biological Letters* 2: 125–127.

Zenz House, Kurt. (2009). "The Limits of Energy Storage Technology." *Bulletin of the Atomic Scientists.* https://thebulletin.org/2009/01/the-limits-of-energy-storage-technology

CHAPTER 6

Why Regenerative Agriculture?

*Courtney White**

Abstract. Regenerative agriculture is both an attitude and a suite of practices that restores and maintains soil health and fertility, supports biodiversity, protects watersheds, and improves ecological and economic resilience. It focuses on creating the conditions for life above and below ground and takes its cues from nature, which has a very long track record of successfully growing things. By re-carbonizing soils via photosynthesis and biology, particularly on degraded land, regenerative agriculture can also sequester increasing quantities of atmospheric carbon (CO_2) underground, making it a low-cost "shovel-ready" solution to climate change. Its multiple co-benefits, including the production of healthy, nutritious food, means it will be a critical component of our response to rising climate instability.

"One of the buzzwords today is 'sustainable.' Everybody wants to be sustainable. My question is why in the world would we want to sustain a degraded resource? We need to work on regenerating our soils, not sustaining them."
– *Gabe Brown, farmer and regenerative agriculture pioneer*

Introduction

Is topsoil a renewable or nonrenewable resource? This question came to mind some years ago after reading *Dirt: the Erosion of Civilizations* by David Montgomery (2012), a professor of geology at the University of Washington. Although ostensibly a history of dirt, it is actually a book about the failure of societies to avoid repeating mistakes that hastened the demise of past civilizations. Dirt is created by the weathering of solid rock over time, usually accumulating at the rate of about *one inch per thousand years.* The top layer becomes biologically active with the presence of green plants and soil microbes. Unfortunately, we are eroding our topsoil at the alarming rate of an *inch per decade*, wrote Montgomery (2012), mostly as a consequence of poor agricultural practices. This imbalance has created a crisis for a simple reason: there is no substitute for dirt. Oil and natural gas can be replaced by other energy sources, preferably renewable ones, but nothing else can do what dirt does. In addition to being the medium in which our food grows, dirt stores drinking water, recycles dead material into new life, circulates essential nutrients, and stores carbon. Montgomery (2012) called it our most underappreciated and yet essential natural resource. If we wash it away, we pay the consequences.

*Cofounded Quivira Coalition, nonprofit dedicated to improving resilience in western working landscapes. Author: *Revolution on the Range*; *Grass, Soil, Hope*; *The Age of Consequences*; *2% Solutions for the Planet*, and *The Working Wilderness* in Wendell Berry's collection *The Way of Ignorance*. Co-author with Rebecca Burgess: *Fibersheds: a New Textile Economy*. Also author: *The Sun*, mystery novel set on cattle ranch in northern New Mexico. He lives in Santa Fe. Email: courtney@jcourtneywhite.com

This is not a new phenomenon, of course. As the Sumerians, Greeks, Romans, Mayans, Chinese, and early settlers in America could tell you, dirt matters. Time and again over the course of human history, social and political conflicts are exacerbated when there are more people to feed than can be supported by the land. Civilizations do not disappear overnight and they do not choose to fail. More often, they falter and then decline as their soil washes away over generations. Rome did not so much collapse as it crumbled, wrote Montgomery (2012), wearing away as erosion sapped its food-growing capacity.

Erosion is not just ancient history. In America today, millions of tons of topsoil are eroded annually from farm fields in the Mississippi River basin into the Gulf of Mexico. America's farms lose enough soil every year to fill a pickup truck for every family in the country. Worldwide today, an estimated 36 billion tons of soil are lost annually as a result of various land-degrading practices, a rate that has increased by 2.5 percent between 2000 and 2012, mainly due to clearing forests for agriculture (Borrelli et al. 2017). Until the last decades of the 20th century, clearing new land compensated for loss of productive agricultural land to erosion. According to the Global Land Assessment of Degradation published by the U.N. Food and Agricultural Organization (FAO), nearly 2 billion hectares worldwide (4.8 billion acres) have been degraded since the 1950s, representing nearly 25 percent of the world's, cropland, pastures, and woodlands (Future Directions International 2011). Meanwhile, the world's population is expected to increase by 2 billion people by 2050, from 7.7 billion today to 9.7 billion (UN DESA 2019). This will place increasing stress on our arable land to provide sufficient food.

Land is critical to other ecosystem services, including the maintenance of biodiversity. IPBES (2019a) is a landmark report compiled by 145 experts from 50 nations, based on 15,000 scientific and governmental sources. It concluded that 1 million animal and plant species are now threatened with extinction and that biodiversity is declining around the world at accelerating rates unprecedented in human history. As noted by Sir Robert Watson, Chairperson of the Intergovernmental Science-Policy Platform on Biodiversity and Ecosystem Services, upon issuing the report:

> The health of ecosystems on which we and all other species depend is deteriorating more rapidly than ever. We are eroding the very foundations of our economies, livelihoods, food security, health, and quality of life worldwide. (IPBES 2019b)

Since agriculture is one of the primary activities that is reducing biodiversity, a summary of the IPBES (2019b) report concludes:

- More than a third of the world's land surface and nearly 75 percent of freshwater resources are now devoted to crop or livestock production.
- The value of crop production has increased by about 300 percent since 1970; raw timber harvest rose by 45 percent; and 60 billion tons of renewable and nonrenewable resources are now extracted globally every year, nearly double since 1980.
- Land degradation has reduced the productivity of nearly 25 percent of the global land surface; global crops are at significant risk from pollinator loss; and 100–300 million people are at increased risk of floods and hurricanes because of loss of coastal habitats.

Technology will not save us. It cannot create more dirt, only nature can. This is the big lesson of dirt, Montgomery (2012) observed: when you depend on a resource that is difficult to renew quickly, eventually you wind up in serious trouble. Modern society fosters the notion that technology will provide solutions to almost any problem, but no matter how fervently we believe in its power to improve our lives, technology simply cannot solve the problem of consuming a natural resource faster than we regenerate it.

> A common lesson of the ancient empires of the Old and New Worlds is that even innovative adaptations cannot make up for a lack of fertile soil to sustain increased productivity. As long as people take care of their land, the land can sustain them. (Montgomery 2012)

Creation

What if dirt—or more accurately soil—could be created quickly and by natural means? In fact, it is already happening and that is where regenerative agriculture comes in.

First, I want to take a quick detour to Charles Darwin. In his last book, published shortly before his death in 1882, Darwin focused on the lowly earthworm and the role it played in the mystery of soil formation. Conducting experiments in the backyard of his house over many years, Darwin discovered that topsoil can be expanded (deepened) in only a matter of years, largely as a result of the digestive work of earthworms. His thesis that soil was biologically alive with creatures transforming inert subsoil into rich topsoil by eating and excreting was rather revolutionary for its day, though his book was largely overlooked. Nearly a century would pass before we began to truly appreciate nature's innate capacity to create topsoil biologically.

Worms are important, but the real key to building topsoil is carbon. The process by which atmospheric carbon dioxide (CO_2) gets converted into soil carbon has been going on for at least a billion years and all it requires is sunlight, green plants, water, nutrients, and soil microbes. One of the first researchers to recognize the significance of this equation for its regenerative implications was Dr. Christine Jones, an independent soil scientist in Australia. According to Jones (2007), there are four basic steps:

- Photosynthesis: This is the process by which energy in sunlight is transformed into biochemical energy in the form of a simple sugar called glucose via green plants—which use CO2 from the air and water from the soil, releasing oxygen as a byproduct. The chemical reaction: CO2 + H2O + energy = CH2O + O2.
- *Resynthesis*: Through a complex sequence of chemical reactions, glucose is resynthesized into a wide variety of carbon compounds, including carbohydrates (such as cellulose and starch), proteins, organic acids, waxes, and oils (including hydrocarbons), all of which serve as "fuel" for life on Earth.
- *Exudation*: Carbon compounds can be exuded directly into soil by plant roots to nurture microbes and other organisms. This process is essential to the creation of soil from the lifeless mineral dirt. The amount of increase in organic carbon is governed by the volume of plant roots per unit of soil and their rate of growth. More active green leaves mean more roots, which mean more carbon exuded.
- *Humification*: This refers to the creation of humus, a chemically stable type of organic matter composed of large, complex molecules made up of carbon, nitrogen, minerals, and soil particles. Visually, humus is the dark, rich layer of topsoil that people generally associate with stable wetlands, healthy rangelands, and productive farmland. Once carbon is safely stored as humus it has a high resistance to decomposition and therefore can remain intact and stable for hundreds or thousands of years.

The key to creating humus is a class of microbes called mycorrhizal fungi, which get their energy in liquid form as soluble carbon directly from actively growing plant roots. In turn, these fungi facilitate the transport of essential nutrients, such as phosphorus, zinc, and nitrogen, into plant roots in exchange for carbon. When mycorrhizal fungi are functioning properly, a great deal of the carbon that enters the leaves of plants can be channeled directly into soil as soluble carbon—which is why people get excited about the prospect of storing excess CO_2 in the soil as one remedy for global warming. Not only is it possible on a practical level, all it requires are the processes that create life—and creating life is something that the Earth does very well.

Healthy soils have a 6–8 percent fraction of carbon in them, typically. If undisturbed or restored to health, soils not only continue to hold their carbon but can "soak up" even more from the atmosphere, which is very good news for fighting global warming. Soil is one of the great carbon pools on the planet, along with the atmosphere, oceans, and vegetation. Thanks to the miracle of photosynthesis, carbon can be safely stored underground in plant roots and as part of the natural, biological soil-building process (Cho 2018).

An important co-benefit of increasing the carbon content of soils is its improved capacity to hold water. It is estimated that a 1 percent increase in organic matter can add as much as 16,000 gallons of water storage capacity per acre [about 144,000 liters per hectare] (Sullivan 2002). This is accomplished by increasing the porosity of the soil through improved soil structure as humus is formed. Carbon, in the form of a sticky protein called *glomalin*, attaches to loose minerals and can bind them together into aggregates, creating micro-pockets that fill with moisture that has infiltrated from the ground surface. Over time, these soil aggregates bind to other aggregates and if undisturbed can form underground "reservoirs" of water. This is very useful for surviving drought and will be increasingly important in many arid and semi-arid regions as dry times become the norm under climate change.

Improved soil structure also mitigates floods—another significant element of climate instability. The experience of Gabe Brown (2018) is illustrative. An innovative farmer in North Dakota, Brown transformed his family's conventionally managed, eroded, worn-out land into a biologically rich, healthy, and productive operation by turning *dirt into soil* with regenerative agriculture.

> When we purchased the farm in 1991, the infiltration rate on our cropland was only ½-inch per hour. That meant when a big storm came along, dumping two or three inches of rain, most of the water left the farm in a hurry usually taking a bunch of topsoil with it.

After raising the carbon fraction of his soil from 2 percent to 5 with regenerative practices, including year-round cover crops, this situation changed dramatically.

> By 2009, the infiltration rate had risen to more than *ten inches* per hour thanks to well-aggregated soils due to mycorrhizal fungi and soil biology.

As Brown discovered, there is an important requirement for successfully regenerating topsoil: *we must not till.* Turning over the ground with a plow every year exposes soil to wind and water erosion and releases large amounts of carbon dioxide into the atmosphere that was previously stored safely. Tilling breaks up (pulverizes) soil aggregates, destroys critical fungal networks, and can result in bare or compacted soil that creates a hostile environment for microbes, earthworms, and other forms of life. When life departs, erosion soon follows.

Transition

Dirt is *chemistry*—individual particles, minerals, and other elements, including calcium, phosphorus, and potassium. Soil is *biology*—bacteria, fungi, protozoa, nematodes, earthworms, reproduction, growth, life. Getting plants to grow in dirt is chiefly a matter of getting the chemistry right and applying it mechanically according to a calculated prescription. Getting plants to grow in soil, by contrast, is a matter of getting the biology right. If the ground is devoid of micro-organisms, for instance, you need to foster the conditions for their return.

There is where regenerative agriculture comes in. Perhaps the best way to explain its potential for building topsoil is to walk through the transition of a farm from industrial production to a regenerative one, as Brown did. The vast majority of farmers in the United States grow just a few crops, such as corn and soybeans, in an annual rotation using lots of killing chemicals—herbicides, insecticides, and fungicides—and artificial fertilizers. They usually leave their fields bare for six months between the harvest and spring planting (when they are likely to use GMO seed, but that is another story).

The first step in the regenerative transition is to stop using the synthetic chemicals, which are also killing beneficial insects and important soil microbes and fungi. This step is the essence of certified *organic* agriculture. Life returns quickly to the land. Gabe Brown likes to joke that he could never go fishing because there were no earthworms on his farm under conventional management. When he stopped using chemicals, however, earthworms appeared! It was a sign the land had begun the healing process.

The next step in the transition is a big one: stop using the plow. Stop killing life in the soil by turning it over every spring. Go "no-till." This is a difficult step for many farmers because plowing the land is an almost religious belief. Most organic farms continue to till, for example. The mental leap required to go no-till is much harder than the physical one. The next step is to keep fields covered with plants year-round, which boosts the biology underground. It can be cover crops or winter crops—whatever it takes to help plant roots and soil microbes collaborate as nature intended.

The next step is to diversify a farm's crops as much as possible, mimicking what happens in the natural world. There is a reason why nature *loves* polycultures—everything is working symbiotically. The next step is to stop artificial fertilizer use. The return of life and health to the soil via the previous steps means natural fertility will return as well. The last step is also a big one—integrate livestock into the operation by rotating cattle, pigs, and chickens through the crop fields and pastures. Grazing keeps the weeds under control and animal manure adds natural fertilizer to the soil. This transition can happen *anywhere*. Brown (2018) wrote:

> I follow five principles that were developed by nature, over eons of time. They are the same anyplace in the world where the sun shines and plants grow. Gardeners, farmers, and ranchers around the world are using these principles to grow nutrient-rich, deep topsoil with healthy watersheds.

Here are Brown's "five principles" for creating topsoil:

1. **Limit disturbance.** Limit mechanical, chemical, and physical disturbance of the soil. Tillage destroys soil structure. It is constantly tearing apart the "house" that nature builds to protect the living organisms in the soil that create natural soil fertility.
2. **Armor.** Keep the soil covered at all times. Bare soil is an anomaly—nature always works to cover the soil. Providing a natural "coat of armor" protects the soil from wind and water erosion while providing food and habitat for macro- and micro organisms.
3. **Diversity.** Strive for diversity of both plant and animal species. Grasses, forbs, legumes, and shrubs all live and thrive in harmony with each other. Some have shallow roots, some deep, some fibrous, some tap. Some are high-carbon, some are low-carbon, some are legumes. Each of them plays a role in maintaining soil health.
4. **Living roots.** Maintain a living root in the soil as long as possible throughout the year. When you see green growing plants any time of year it is a sign of living roots. Those living roots are feeding soil biology by providing its basic food source: carbon. This biology, in turn, fuels the nutrient cycle that feeds plants.
5. **Integrate animals.** Nature does not function without animals. The grazing of plants stimulates the plants to pump more carbon into the soil. This drives nutrient cycling by feeding biology. If you want a healthy functioning ecosystem on your farm or ranch, you must provide a home and habitat for not only farm animals but pollinators, predator insects, earthworms, and all of the microbiology that drive ecosystem function.

Brown's last point is critical and generally misunderstood by farmers and consumers alike. The role of animals in regenerative agriculture is essential to building topsoil. Consider the symbiotic relationships between herds of bison and native plants that existed for millennia on the Great Plains. The vast herds traveled across the land in annual migrations, never lingering in one place for long. They took what they needed from the plant community and kept going, leaving behind natural fertilizer in the form of manure and urine. The removal of plant foliage by grazing stimulates root activity, which, in turn, stimulates carbon exchange with soil microbes as the plants seek additional nutrients. The disturbance caused by thousands of hooves to the soil surface facilitates seed-to-soil contact and creates mini-water-collecting divots. All of this makes a significant contribution to soil formation. This process occurs everywhere, not just the Great Plains—the grass-grazer relationship is a natural one that can be found worldwide (Frank et al. 1998).

Regenerative ranchers and farmers mimic the behavior of wild herbivores by grouping their livestock—cattle, sheep, or goats—into a single herd and carefully controlling the timing, intensity, and frequency of the herd's impact on the land (usually with solar-powered electric fencing). "Timing" refers not only to the season of the year but how many days the herd spends in a specific pasture or paddock (often only seven-to-ten days per year). "Intensity" indicates the size of the herd for that period of time. "Frequency" measures how long the paddock is rested from grazing before the herd returns. This style of management is called adaptive multi-paddock (AMP), though it goes by other names as well: planned, short-duration, management-intensive, pulse, and cell grazing. All of them are based on the ideas of biologist Allan Savory, who developed his innovative model after years of observing migrating wildlife in southern Africa.

In a study led by a rangeland ecologist at Texas A&M University that compared AMP grazed plots to those grazed under conventional management, Dr. Richard Teague et al. (2016) concluded that AMP grazing test plots sequestered 2.7 metric tons *more* carbon per hectare than plots that were continuously grazed.

> Incorporating forages and ruminants into regeneratively managed agroecosystems can elevate soil organic [carbon], improve soil ecological function by minimizing the damage of tillage and inorganic fertilizers and biocides, and enhance biodiversity and wildlife habitat.

(The sequestered 2.7 metric tons from one hectare are equivalent to one-sixth of a U.S. individual's annual greenhouse gas contribution.)

The role of animal agriculture in climate change has been highly politicized recently with many well-meaning people advocating meatless diets as a way to reduce or eliminate the contribution of livestock to greenhouse gas emissions. However, this viewpoint does not take into account the larger picture of how ecosystems function. *It is simply not possible to sequester the necessary amounts of carbon dioxide in the soil to slow global warming without utilizing grazing animals, particularly since grasslands are one of the largest terrestrial biomes on the planet.* Cattle are not the problem—our management of them is. In fact, as Gabe Brown (2018) puts it, livestock are part of the solution:

> I thoroughly enjoy debating with vegetarians and vegans as to the importance of animals on the landscape. My contention is that if they are truly concerned about the health of ecosystems, they have to recognize the benefits that grazing ruminants provide, even if they choose not to partake of eating meat.

Food

One of the significant co-benefits of increasing topsoil via regenerative agriculture is the production of healthy, nutrient-dense food, including the potential for intensification—a useful prospect for a world trying to feed billions of people under the stress of climate change and resource depletion.

This potential hit home for me during a visit to Singing Frogs Farm (singingfrogsfarm.com), owned and operated by Paul and Elizabeth Kaiser and located on seven acres near Sebastopol, in northern California. I went to the farm because I was intrigued by the Kaisers' success at pioneering an innovative practice called *year-round farming*. I knew the operation was organic, no-till, and pollinator-friendly (they planted lots of hedgerows). I knew they sold their crops through a community-supported agriculture model, which meant they were local. I knew the farm was very profitable too. Paul was on record saying they grossed over $100,000 per crop-acre per year. In comparison, a typical organic farm in California grosses between $12,000 and $20,000 per crop-acre.

I also knew that the Kaisers considered themselves to be *carbon farmers,* having successfully elevated the carbon content of their soil from 2 to 6 percent (measured at a depth of 12 inches). They do it primarily via their composting and no-till practices. The key is the microbial population in the soil, which tripled under the Kaisers' stewardship. Everything flowed from this vibrant underground world they had fostered—crops, profits, and a high quality of life for themselves and their children.

What I did not know much about was year-round farming itself. In the Kaisers' model, vegetable seeds are sown in a greenhouse and then the seedlings are nurtured to a transplantable age. When a crop is harvested in the field, a young plant takes its place, often within hours. This way, the farm never stops producing food—and does so without growing weeds or using cover crops and commercial fertilizers. Instead, the Kaisers produce a great deal of compost on-farm and spread it along each row of crops on the top of the ground, rather than mix it with soil as is normally done. It is all done by hand by the Kaisers and their four full-time year-round employees.

To say this approach to farming is paradigm-busting is a huge understatement. When the Kaisers began farming in 2007, they followed the conventional model of growing one or two crops each year and then let the land idle until the following spring. However, two developments changed their mind during the first year on Singing Frogs: first, lots of mechanical things kept breaking down, which frustrated them immensely, and second, closing down the farm at the end of the growing season and reopening it again in the spring required an immense amount of time, energy, and more heavy machinery. The Kaisers decided there had to be a better way. The answer was to become a "knowledge-intensive" farm and work smarter, not harder. This led to two radical changes during the second growing season: (1) replace the machines with people; and (2) never stop farming.

Conclusion

Building topsoil quickly and producing lots of healthy food is not a pipe dream. It is a practicality, thanks to regenerative agriculture. It is possible because it is based on the same biological components that create and maintain life on the planet: photosynthesis, carbon, plant roots, water, and microbes. By building topsoil naturally we create the potential to put many hopeful, proactive solutions into operation, including the restoration of land health, intensified production of local food, expansion of watershed-based collaboratives, and the exploration of regenerative economic strategies. Perhaps the wise king of the province of Brobdingnag, as imagined by Jonathan Swift ([1726] 1918: 198–199), put it best:

> Whoever could make two ears of corn, or two blades of grass, to grow upon a spot of ground where only one grew before, would deserve better of mankind, and do more essential service to his country, than the whole race of politicians put together.

References

Borrelli, Pasquale, David A. Robinson, Larissa R. Fleischer, Emanuele Lugato, Cristiano Ballabio, K. Christine Alewell, Sirio Modugno Meusberger, Brigitta Schutt, Vito Ferro, Vincenzo Bagarello, Kristof Van Oost, Luca Montanarella, and Panos Panagos. (2017). "An Assessment of the Global Impact of 21st Century Land Use Change on Soil Erosion." *Nature Communications* 8(1). https://doi.org/10.1038/s41467-017-02142-7

Brown, Gabe. (2018). *Dirt to Soil: One Family's Journey into Regenerative Agriculture.* White River Junction, VT: Chelsea Green Publishing.

Cho, Renee. (2018). *Can Soil Help Combat Climate Change?* New York: Columbia University Earth Institute State of the Planet. https://blogs.ei.columbia.edu/2018/02/21/can-soil-help-combat-climate-change/

Frank, Douglas, Samuel McNaughton, and Benjamin Tracy. (1998). "The Ecology of the Earth's Grazing Ecosystems." *BioScience* 48(7): 513–521. https://www.jstor.org/stable/1313313?seq=1#page_scan_tab_contents

Future Directions International. (2011). *The Future Prospects for Global Arable Land.* http://www.futuredirections.org.au/publication/the-future-prospects-for-global-arable-land/

Intergovernmental Science-Policy Platform on Biodiversity and Ecosystem Services (IPBES). (2019a). *Global Assessment Report on Biodiversity and Ecosystem Services.* Bonn, Germany: IPBES. https://ipbes.net/global-assessment

________. (2019b). *Nature's Dangerous Decline "Unprecedented" Species Extinction Rates "Accelerating"* [press release]. Bonn, Germany: IPBES.

Jones, Christine. (2007). "Building Soil Carbon with Yearlong Green Farming." *Evergreen Farming* September. https://www.amazingcarbon.com/PDF/Jones-EvergreenFarming(Sept07).pdf

Montgomery, David. (2012). *Dirt: the Erosion of Civilizations,* 2nd ed. Berkeley, CA: University of California Press.

Sullivan, Preston. (2002). *Drought Resistant Soil.* Fayetteville, AR: National Center for Appropriate Techtnology. http://agwaterstewards.org/wp-content/uploads/2016/08/Drought_Resistant_Soils_ATTRA.pdf

Swift, Jonathan. ([1726] 1918). *Gulliver's Travels.* London: Lippincott. https://archive.org/details/gulliverstravels1918swif/page/198/mode/2up/search/grass

Teague, W. Richard, Steven Irwin Apfelbaum, Rattan Lal, Urs P. Kreuter, Jason E. Rowntree, C. A. Davies, Russ Conser, Mark A. Rasmussen, Jerry Hatfield, Tong Wang, F. Wang, and P. Byck. (2016). "The Role of Ruminants in Reducing Agriculture's Carbon Footprint in North America." *Journal of Soil and Water Conservation* 71(2): 156–164. http://www.jswconline.org/content/71/2/156.abstract

U.N. Department of Economic and Social Affairs (UN DESA). (2019). *Growing at a Slower Pace, World Population Is Expected to Reach 9.7 Billion in 2050 and Could Peak at Nearly 11 Billion Around 2100.* New York: United Nations. https://www.un.org/development/desa/en/news/population/world-population-prospects-2019.html

CHAPTER 7

Differing Visions of Agriculture: Industrial-Chemical vs. Small Farm and Urban Organic Production

Heather Gray and K. Rashid Nuri†*

Abstract. Seed diversity and soil preservation are the foundations of healthy agriculture. Over many generations, farmers have developed varieties of wheat, rice, corn, and other crops that are adapted to local growing conditions. Industrial-chemical agriculture has abandoned that local knowledge, replacing seed diversity with genetically uniform crops that require large doses of fertilizers and chemical poisons to survive. One way the United States exerted control over Iraq, starting in 2003, was to enable agribusiness to disrupt thousands of years of tradition by imposing industrial methods on the country where evidence of the earliest mass production of food was discovered. Thus, it seems that conquest of people goes hand in hand with conquest of soil. There is resistance to agribusiness around the world. In the United States, small farms and urban agriculture are not only providing healthy food but also reconnecting people who grow up in cities with the life of the soil.

Introduction

There is no culture without agriculture. It is essential to have knowledge of the history of agriculture to understand the contemporary world of agriculture and the increasing interest in small farms and urban organic agriculture. Rarely is this history taught in schools or shared within the general population. Food is essential for all human beings. Yet the origin and integrity of this most important aspect of our lives is often marginalized.

This article begins with a focus on the origins of agriculture. It will then trace the degradation of agricultural production that has led to a food system that lacks social integrity. Finally, the discussion will examine the contemporary practice of small farms and urban organic food production, which has the potential to reclaim food sovereignty and the integrity of our food system, while simultaneously creating a healthier world for us all.

The Origin of Agriculture and its Degradation

There is evidence that the first mass production of food was approximately 13,000 years ago in the Fertile Crescent of Mesopotamia—in the area now

*Journalist, commentator, and community activist. For 23 years, Director of Communications for the Federation of Southern Cooperatives/Land Assistance Fund, the primary organization in the United States working with Black farmers across the South. Email: hmcgray@earthlink.net

†Founder of the Truly Living Well Center for Natural Agriculture in Atlanta, Georgia. Worked in 36 countries, observing local food economies in Asia, Africa, and Europe. Leader in development of small farms and urban organic production in the United States. Author of *Growing Out Loud: Journey of a Food Revolutionary.* Email: rashid@thenurigroup.com; Website: thenurigroup.com

called Iraq. This is where the Tigris and the Euphrates Rivers intersect. The Iraqi ancestral farmers growing on this fertile land brought us major crops such as wheat, barley, dates, and pulses. The area is hugely important in world history. For thousands of years, the contributions of the Iraqi farmers to the world's agricultural production system have been unquestionably profound (Diamond 2005).

Humans as Hunters and Gatherers and the Initiation of Agriculture

Prior to the compilation and mass production of major crops, humans were hunters and gatherers, largely in Africa, for close to 300,000 years. As hunters and gatherers, men were hunting animals and women were gathering a wide variety of nuts, fruits, vegetables, and roots for their community's food needs. It is estimated that women gathered from 75–80 percent of the food for our human groups.

> Archeologists estimate that, in ordinary circumstances, the activity of gathering in temperate and tropical areas provides 75 to 80% of the total calories consumed, with hunting providing the balance. In existing hunting and gathering cultures, women usually do most of the gathering, while the men specialize in hunting. Other than this kind of gender specialization—and it is by no means universal—there is little specialization of roles within the group. Hunter-gatherers tend to accumulate a large and intimate knowledge of their range and the food sources, dangers, and opportunities which exist within it. And this knowledge is largely communal; it is shared by the group. (Law 1996)

Women as the Initiators of Agriculture

In many ways, women were the initiators of agriculture. Women were the gatherers in hunting-and-gathering pre-agricultural societies. Women gathered fruits, nuts, and roots for their communities and were the observers of plants, seeds, and their growth patterns. This is why the majority of the small farmers throughout the world, historically and today, are women:

> The exact data on women in agriculture is difficult to pin down. There are variations between countries and agriculture data is challenging to collect. What is clear, however, is that most small-scale farmers are women, and more women in developing countries are joining the labor force in the agricultural sector. Women make up *60–80 percent of farmers* in non-industrialized countries. The FAO (Food and Agriculture Organization of the UN) estimates that between *43 percent [and] 70 percent* of agricultural labor in some countries comes from women. (Werft 2016)

The Primary Focus of Family Farmers: The Two S's—Soil and Seed—and the Diversity of Crops

No history of agriculture could be complete without understanding the importance of both soil and seed. Throughout our history, protection of soil and seed has been the family farmer's preoccupation.

Soil is not monolithic. It is amazingly diverse. Its components and minerals differ everywhere. Farmers have always adjusted to this through crop rotations. Farmers will also let the soil rest and lay fallow for specified periods of time. Traditional farmers also used natural nutrients like compost and manure to replenish the soil. In this way, the soil remains alive with organic nutrients, earthworms, and the like. Seeds and plants are also selected for the specific type of soil. Farmers have performed this selection process since the beginning of agriculture, and they still perform it (Singh and Singh 2017).

Seeds are also not monolithic, even within the same plant family. The diversity of seeds is our lifeblood. Like humans, plants are vulnerable to disease. The more diverse our plants, the less vulnerable they are to diseases that can wipe out a crop within days or hours. The diversity of plants also protects and maintains the viability of the soil. Without diversity, there is virtually no resistance to disease. The Irish potato famine in 1845 resulted from the production of genetically uniform potatoes that had no resistance to the potato blight.

> The "Great Potato Famine" or the "Irish Famine" occurred in 1845–49 when the potato crop failed in successive years. The crop failures were caused by blight that destroyed the potato plant. It was the worst famine to occur in Europe in the 19th century. By the early 1840s, almost one-half of the Irish population—but primarily the rural poor—had come to depend almost exclusively on the potato for their diet, and the rest of the population also consumed it in large quantities. A heavy reliance on just one or two high-yielding varieties of potato greatly reduced the genetic variety that ordinarily prevents the decimation of an entire crop by disease, and thus made the Irish vulnerable. In 1845 a fungus arrived accidentally from North America, and that same year Ireland had unusually cool, moist weather, in which the blight thrived. About 1.1 million people died from starvation or typhus and other famine-related diseases. Many emigrated, and by 1921 the population was barely half of what it had been in the early 1840s. (Strassman 2001)

Farmers have preserved crop diversity. They protect the food supply by maintaining the fertility of soil in their area and selecting and saving the seeds of successful plantings. This is a very local process. For thousands of years, farmers have maintained the diversity and quality of our food chain (Teitel and Wilson 1999).

Farmers have historically saved seeds for the next year's crop. Most farmers in the world do not go to the supply store to buy seeds. The seeds are preserved on the farm. Grandparents, great-grandparents, and great-great-grandparents likely grew versions of the same seed stock.

In the southern part of the United States, cotton remains "king." In the late 1800s, however, this monocrop destroyed the soil, making it vulnerable to the boll weevil and other diseases. George Washington Carver then came to the Tuskegee Institute in Alabama in 1896 as Director of Agricultural Research. Carver focused primarily on what he could do to help southern farmers. He saved southern agriculture in the early 1900s by encouraging farmers to rotate the cotton crop with legumes and sweet potatoes that revitalized the soil. Today, a standard catechism of agriculture is to rotate crops. George Washington Carver introduced crop rotation to southern agriculture. The rotation model has been used worldwide.

Growing Food Close to Home: The Historical Model

The mission of farmers has always been to grow food for family and community sustenance, and not in competition with each other—a mission that is much to the ire of Western capitalists. Invariably, farmers will also share their seeds with neighboring farmers. This collective and cooperative spirit of the farming community is legendary (Wynberg 2012).

Vandana Shiva (1988) refers to the importance of local agricultural production in a sustainable environment and to the threat of removing it from local control. She notes that the "feminine principle" is associated with diversity and sharing. Homogenization and privatization can lead to the destruction of both diversity and the community. She also notes that a "sustenance" economy requires a creative and organic nature that is based on local knowledge associated with the needs of the community.

Small farmers everywhere are the best stewards and sustainers of the land. They know what it takes to feed it and care for it. Many of us working with farmers have seen them lift soil in their hands and know exactly what is needed in the soil. In this sense, small family farmers are also the most efficient farmers in terms of crop yields, as virtually every part of that farm is known to them. Millions of farm families—women, men, and children—are sophisticated homegrown agronomists who work the fields.

Survival has depended on that sort of detailed local knowledge that has been held by farmers for millennia. One can see a glow in farmers' eyes as they talk about being involved in one of the most sacred of all professions—the practice of nurturing and witnessing the flowering of crops from small seeds. Consequently, they sustain all of us through the production of food.

Tradition vs. Modernization: The Ongoing Battle in Agriculture

In the past century, new forms of agriculture have emerged that ignored traditional methods. Instead of adapting seeds to local soil conditions, modern farmers have been taught to treat every plot of land as empty space that can be transformed into productive fields with machinery and chemicals. Instead of seed variety, farmers now plant millions of hectares with a single variety of wheat or corn or rice. Instead of nurturing the soil with organic material, modern farmers apply fertilizers derived from fossil fuels as well as chemical insecticides and herbicides. Without habitat provided for them, natural predators largely disappear. In short, modern agriculture transfers the principles of assembly-line manufacturing from the factory to the field. The modern farmer is nothing more than a cog in an elaborate machine that is designed to extract a limited range of nutrients without concern for soil or seeds.

Europe and the United States have overwhelmingly adopted this modern model of industrial agriculture. It is also making rapid inroads in the rest of the world. Since modern agriculture is bad for the soil and bad for the farmers who intimately know the soil, it is imperative that we act now to help the farmers resist chemical agriculture and all it entails. To assist their efforts, we need to understand how major corporations, working with the U.S. government, are attempting to force farmers in other countries to adopt industrial methods.

Corporate Control of Food Production: From World War II to Iraq

One consistent feature of the industrial model of agriculture is that corporate entities have wanted to control the market for food in every part of the world, whenever possible. Corporate agribusiness has disrupted the powerful soil-seed mantra and eroded the independence of family farmers. In the last century, chemicals were employed that have polluted and poisoned the soil, which destroys the diversity of organisms within it. Seed patents have proliferated, including hybrid seeds that farmers could not replant the next season, forcing them to buy seeds rather than maintain their own supply. These changes were coupled with the development of genetically modified organisms (GMOs). Corporations have attempted to make farmers dependent on all of these interventions.

After World War II, there were vast amounts of nitrogen left over from making bombs. Major companies, such as Dow, Shell, and Dupont, decided they could sell the nitrogen to farmers as fertilizer for a profit. The now infamous Green Revolution emerged from these obscure military origins, leading to huge amounts of chemical poisons in agriculture. The U.S. Department of Agriculture was also complicit in instigating the Green Revolution. Because the hybrid seeds promoted by this transformation of agriculture could only grow with massive inputs of fertilizer and chemical poisons, farmers became dependent on the chemical industry. The soil was poisoned. The chemical and poison additives in soil have made it easier for farmers dependent on corporate supplies to disregard the organic condition of their once-fertile soil. That dependence paved the way for reliance on hybrid seed stocks that were planted as monoculture crops (Krebs 1992).

For those who seek to break away from dependence on chemical inputs, the good news is that it is possible to regain freedom from corporate control. Black farmers across the South, who are attempting to veer away from dependency on chemicals, have described their soil as "dead." They have discovered that it can come alive again, but only after a few years of more traditional methods that restore the organic component to the soil.

The Potential Damage from Hybrids and GMOs

Hybrid crops were introduced into modern agriculture on a large scale beginning in the 1940s. Henry Wallace, as the U.S. Secretary of Agriculture, and Norman Borlaug, as a government plant geneticist, developed varieties of wheat, corn, and rice that produced large yields and enhanced both resistance to disease and the ability to withstand chemicals. Evidence has shown, however, that the quality of the food has suffered.

> Hybridization is the process of crossing two genetically different individuals to result in a third genotype with a different, often preferred, set of traits. Plants of the same species cross easily in the field and produce fertile progeny. Such plants are referred to as cross-pollinated plants. Seed companies create hybridized seeds such as corn, soy, wheat and rice in laboratories. It is not possible to replant these synthetically hybridized seeds. The problem with hybridization is that the seeds cannot be put back in the ground. Rather than saving seed for next year's crop, as farmers have always done, farmers must return to the seed companies to purchase the seeds for the new crop. In the 20th century this represented a major power shift, from the individual farmer's control over production, to corporate control. (Nuri 2019: 77)

GMOs are seeds that incorporate DNA from an altogether different species. Historically, plants are bred from within the same plant family. Combining genes from different organisms is known as recombinant DNA technology and the resulting organism is said to be a genetically modified organism or GMO. As Bawa and Amilakumar (2013) note:

> The biggest threat caused by GM foods is that they can have harmful effects on the human body. It is believed that consumption of these genetically engineered foods can cause the development of diseases which are immune to antibiotics.

Teitel and Wilson (1999) add another concern about GMOs—the effects of genetic uniformity on the crops themselves. The use of GMOs leads to an irreversible erosion of genetic diversity and encourages monoculture.

Companies patent GMO seeds and encourage farmers to grow them. Once seeds are purchased, farmers are required to sign contracts specifying what they cannot do with these seeds, such as save them or share them. To further complicate matters, companies, citing legal priorities due to patent rights, will prosecute farmers who save seeds rather than purchase the seeds from the seed company the next year. Companies will even sue if a farmer's non-GMO crops have been polluted by GMO pollen and are planted without permission (Kimbrell and Mendelson 2005). The major GMO crops grown since GMO soy was first commercialized in 1996 are corn, soy, cotton, and canola. According to the Center for Food Safety, the Monsanto Corporation, headquartered in Missouri and now owned by Bayer, provided 90 percent of seed technology for genetically engineered crops in the world (Kimbrell and Mendelson 2005).

Simply put, corporate agribusiness is attempting to take away the independence of farmers with these practices.

Iraq as Lab Rat for Agribusiness

The Gulf War, which took place in Iraq and Kuwait in 1991, created a new opportunity to impose industrial agriculture in a country where farmers had preserved seeds and soil for thousands of years. This important history attracted corporate agribusiness companies, such as Cargill, to intervene and control Iraq's agriculture.

Henry Kissinger noted that if you "control the food, you control the people" (Engdahl 2007). Along this line of thought, corporate agribusiness welcomed the opportunity to "control" the Iraqi agricultural system as a corporate model for farmers worldwide. It would be a significant symbol for the corporate agribusiness desire for ongoing control of the world's agricultural system.

When the United States occupied Iraq in April 2003, President George W. Bush's Secretary of Agriculture Ann Veneman appointed Daniel Amstutz, formerly an executive of the Cargill Corporation, to oversee the "rehabilitation" of agriculture in Iraq. This is an extreme example of how the U.S. government has assisted corporate giants to gain control of agriculture worldwide by turning the local farmers into unwilling consumers of equipment, chemicals, and seeds.

When considering this appointment of Amstutz to Iraq, it is also relevant to understand the degree to which Ann Veneman was herself associated with corporate agribusiness. Mattera (2004) provides a brief description of how the process worked:

> The extent to which agribusiness has packed USDA with its people is apparent when looking at the biographies of the top officials of the Department, up to and including Secretary Ann Veneman. In addition to her time as a public official, Veneman served on the board of biotech company Calgene (later taken over by Monsanto). Many of Veneman's key aides and the heads of various USDA agencies are political appointees who spent much of their career working for agribusiness companies and trade associations. For example, Veneman's chief of staff Dale Moore was executive director for legislative affairs of the National Cattlemen's Beef Association (NCBA), a trade association heavily supported by and aligned with the interests of the big meatpacking companies, such as Tyson and Cargill. Deputy Secretary James Moseley was a co-owner of a large factory farm in Indiana. Floyd Gaibler, a Deputy Under Secretary, used to be executive director of the dairy industry's National Cheese Institute. Assistant Secretary for Congressional Relations Mary Waters was a senior director and legislative counsel for ConAgra Foods, one of the country's largest food processors.

Cargill is the largest private company in the United States (Murphy 2019). As an agribusiness company, Cargill is involved in virtually every aspect of agriculture, including the promotion of genetically modified crops:

> Cargill has played a significant role in introducing genetically modified crops and promoting genetically modified food to a skeptical public. Generally, grain elevators choose which types of crops they will purchase and contract with farmers to grow certain specialty varieties, including products like high oil corn. High oil corn is made from genetically modified corn and other specialty corn hybrids. In 2007, Cargill's Renessen, a joint venture with Monsanto, released Extrax, a patented technology that processes high oil corn into biodiesel and animal feed. This joint venture also developed a genetically modified crop for use in animal feed. Contracts for specialty grains such as high oil corn are limiting, specifying the volume and timing of the delivery as well as production and handling practices. As one of the dominant buyers in the grain market, Cargill's support of genetically modified crops effectively encourages farmers to grow these crops. (Food and Water Watch 2009)

This process, in effect, undermines small farmers, helps to destroy local food production systems, and forces dependence of small farmers and local rural economies on corporate agribusiness.

Amstutz's career reveals how corporate power works hand in glove with government power: the same people work on both sides of the divide. Before working for Cargill, Amstutz gained diplomatic experience under President Reagan as an undersecretary in the U.S. Department of Agriculture and chief negotiator for agriculture during trade talks. He also held the post of president of the North American Grain Export Association. None of these qualifications were encouraging for the well-being of the small family farmers in Iraq. Amstutz was one of the most powerful proponents of industrial agriculture in the world. Kevin Watkins, Oxfam's policy director at that time, said:

> Putting Dan Amstutz in charge of agriculture reconstruction in Iraq is like putting Saddam Hussein in the chair of a human rights commission.

> This guy is uniquely well placed to advance the commercial interests of American grain companies and bust open the Iraqi market, but singularly ill equipped to lead a reconstruction effort in a developing country. (Stewart 2003)

The deep and bitter irony of making Iraq's Fertile Crescent into one of the major areas for GMO production was entirely lost on Amstutz and his colleagues. All they could see was the potential profits for corporate agribusiness companies like Cargill and Monsanto. Amstutz had input into the disastrous "transfer of sovereignty" policies developed by L. Paul Bremer III, the administrator of the Coalition Provisional Authority (CPA) in Iraq. Of the 100 orders left by Bremer, one was Order 81 on "Patent, Industrial Design, Undisclosed Information, Integrated Circuits and Plant Variety." It was essentially a declaration of war against the Iraqi farmers (Grain and Focus on the Global South 2004).

It is significant that seeds are the entry point for forcing farmers to shift from forms of agriculture based on inherent soil fertility to forms that mimic industrial production. By imposing uniformity on seeds, they indirectly draw farmers into a system that depends on chemical inputs:

> For generations, small farmers in Iraq operated in an essentially unregulated, informal seed supply system. This is now history. The CPA has made it illegal for Iraqi farmers to re-use seeds harvested from new varieties registered under the law. Iraqis may continue to use and save from their traditional seed stocks or what is left of them after the years of war and drought, but that is not the agenda for reconstruction embedded in the ruling. The purpose of the law is to facilitate the establishment of a new seed market in Iraq, modified or not, which farmers would have to purchase afresh every single cropping season. Eliminating competition from farmers is a prerequisite for these companies (i.e. major international corporate seed traders such as Monsanto, Syngenta, Bayer and Dow Chemical). The new patent law also explicitly promotes the commercialization of genetically modified seeds in Iraq. (Grain and Focus on the Global South 2004)

In other contexts, the interest groups that have force-fed their industrial form of agriculture on the farmers of Iraq would rhapsodically extol the virtues of the free market. But in this case, the market was not sufficient to compel farmers to adopt the model of agriculture promoted by corporate agribusiness. They had to use the political muscle of an occupying army to require the farmers of Iraq to give up their traditional practices. This behavior clearly demonstrates that industrial agriculture is not driven by market forces but by an ideology that seeks profits in place of market freedom.

The Impact of Corporate Agribusiness in America

> Almost every step of America's food supply chain has grown more concentrated in the past few decades. From manufacturers of agricultural inputs, such as pesticides and equipment, to commodity buyers and meat processors, growing corporate power has left relatively small farms and ranches vulnerable to exploitation at the hands of the oligopolies with which they do business. Recent mergers and acquisitions continue the relentless trend toward increasing corporate concentration across many agricultural markets. (Willingham and Green 2019)

Many farmers and agriculture specialists in the United States have been troubled by genetically modified organisms (GMOs). GMO seed varieties are engineered and grown under the monoculture conditions of industrial agriculture utilizing oil-based chemical inputs.

A primary model of the devastating impact of GMO crops was the "Round-up Ready® soy" GMO that was introduced to farmers in the 1990s by the Monsanto Corporation. This included soybean seeds that were resistant to Round-up® weed killer. As it turned out, nature was smarter than the Monsanto scientists, as nature itself developed hardy weeds that were resistant to the Round-up® herbicide. This meant that farmers had to use even more and/or stronger herbicides.

> In the history of agriculture, no technology has been adopted so quickly and completely as genetically engineered crops. Particularly useful crops are ones that have an engineered resistance to herbicides. These crops have alluring benefits: reduced crop damage when herbicides are sprayed, easier weed management, and even the potential for environmental benefits. So, what's the problem? Herbicide-resistant weeds. The benefits gleaned from these crops begin to disappear as these superweeds gain prominence on farmlands across world. (Wilkerson 2015)

Under President Donald Trump, the U.S. Department of Agriculture has been remiss in adhering to appointments and policies in order to promote healthy food. According to the Union of Concerned Scientists (2018):

> The USDA is responsible for applying science to ensure the US food system serves the public interest. This mission includes setting standards to maintain food safety, protect food system workers from job-related illness and injury, improve child nutrition, and alleviate hunger. In each of these areas, [USDA] Secretary Perdue has initiated policy decisions that appear to override evidence, and disregard the public interest, in favor of agribusiness. (Union of Concerned Scientists 2018)

Trump's appointment of Sonny Perdue as Secretary of Agriculture did not bode well for those concerned about the impact of corporate agribusiness. Perdue has made liberal use of the revolving door to fill USDA leadership posts, appointing former business associates, agribusiness executives, and lobbyists to senior-level agency positions.

> Betrayal at the USDA offers several examples of such questionable appointments. In one, Kailee Tkacz, a former lobbyist for the Corn Refiners Association and Snack Food Association, was appointed to advise the USDA on federal dietary guidelines—a job for which she needed (and got) a White House waiver to sidestep ethics rules. Tkacz has no training in science, public health, or nutrition. (Union of Concerned Scientists 2018)

Many farmers have been interested in finding ways to disconnect from the system of dependence on corporate GMO-seed companies and chemical companies. One of the critical problems has been that advisors sent out by the U.S. Department of Agriculture to assist farmers are often tied into the agribusiness corporate network. The small farmers are often forced to fend for themselves.

> According to data compiled by the University of Missouri-Columbia in 2012, in the agriculture and food sector, the four largest companies in agriculture and food controlled 82 percent of the beef packing industry, 85 percent of soybean processing, 63 percent of pork packing and 53 percent of broiler chicken processing. These national concentration measurements can conceal even higher levels of concentration at the regional or local level. (Food and Water Watch 2012)

Another Model for Agriculture: Small Farm and Urban Organic Production

> Urban agriculture has become a worldwide phenomenon over the last sixty years. There are great varieties of forms, both between and within countries, including the ways in which agricultural activities are organized and how they respond to market needs. (Bryant et al. 2016)

> Urban and peri-urban farms already supply food to about 700 million city dwellers—one-quarter of the world's urban population—and nearly all of the world's population growth between now

> and 2030 will be concentrated in urban areas in developing countries, so that by then almost 60% of people in developing countries will live in cities. Urban agriculture involves using small plots such as vacant lots, gardens or roof tops in the city for growing crops and even for raising small livestock or milk cows. It can take many forms, from small "micro-gardens" to larger operations. (FAO 2005)

In recent years, there has been a shift in many parts of the world toward the more traditional practice of growing healthy food. This is counter to the fact that in the United States, in much of Europe, and in many other parts of the world, the industrial model of agriculture has been dominant for several generations. As a result, the problems of that model have become increasingly apparent. Treating the land as a machine has harmed the quality of food, the people who grow it, many who eat it, and the many forms of life that have aided humans in agriculture for over 10,000 years. On virtually every continent, a movement is growing that demands both healthy food and a healthy environment. The effort to spread industrial agriculture throughout the world as a predominant agricultural system is not working as effectively as it has in the past.

Many farmers who grow chemically based commodity crops on their land generally also have traditional "organic" gardens on their property for the benefit of family and community. This has been customary for Black farmers in the rural South. They often provide their local communities and neighbors, as much as possible, with healthy food.

When talking with Black farmers about their traditional organic vegetable gardens on small plots of land, you will often witness a gleam in their eyes. It is seemingly an expression of spirituality that comes from being both witness and practitioner of their time-honored traditions in growing food in the United States. Their traditions enable them to continue growing healthy food in many rural areas in America.

One of the most surprising features of the backlash against industrial farming is that non-GMO, organic farming has taken root in cities in America and elsewhere. The United States is an urban country with 82 percent of the people living in metropolitan areas. Throughout most of human history people lived within walking distance of where their food was grown. Regarding this important history, many cities in the country are now in the process of helping humans return to their ancestral past of being close to where their food is grown.

> Why urban agriculture? Because, we need to reclaim our food sovereignty. It's as simple as that and as profound as that. Plus, most of us are now living in cities. If that's where we are, we need to be growing our own food and feeding our own families and communities. (Gray and Nuri 2010)

We are witnessing changes across the United States regarding both interest in and implementation of organic urban agriculture. This includes an increase in urban farmers' markets, farmer-to-consumer direct marketing, and urban agricultural education for adults and children. The Truly Living Well Center for Natural Urban Agriculture, created in Atlanta by Rashid Nuri in 2006, is a prime example of this model. Here is information about its work and mission:

> Since its beginning in 2006, Truly Living Well Center for Natural Urban Agriculture (TLW) has used its expertise to demonstrate how food can be a bridge across diverse cultures, backgrounds, and experiences. Our goal is to use food production as the plate on which we create a culture of health and wellness in our community. Our programs and activities provide agriculture training, nutrition, education, and job creation. By regularly harvesting healthy produce throughout the year, TLW provides our community with a dependable, consistent source of fresh produce, much of which can be earmarked specifically for those who cannot afford to purchase it otherwise. Truly Living Well grows better communities by

> connecting people with the land through education, training, and demonstration of economic success in natural urban agriculture. We demonstrate sustainable and economically viable solutions for helping people to eat and live better. (Truly Living Well 2020)

The Truly Living Well Center for Natural Urban Agriculture is an excellent example of what can be witnessed all over the United States. In Georgia and the Atlanta area, in the past 20 years, we also have had many other urban organic farms and organizations, such as Georgia Organics, Atlanta Local Food Initiative, and the Food Well Alliance. Another unique development is that the City of Atlanta has created a Department of Urban Agriculture, which has also led to the creation of similar urban agriculture departments in Boston, MA, and Washington, DC.

The Food Well Alliance is another community organization that is an outgrowth of the collective work done around the mission of urban agriculture in Atlanta. It is a collaborative network of local leaders working to build thriving farms and gardens that enhance the health, vitality, and resilience of communities across Metro Atlanta.

One of its significant contributions is its *2017 Baseline Report*, which quantified the size and impact of the local food economy (Food Well Alliance 2017). The report outlined an incredible amount of growth and participation.

- 52 urban farms
- 300 community gardens
- 110 locally produced food products
- 5 commercial shared kitchens
- 2 locally sourced food hubs
- 63 farmers' markets
- 40 food hubs launched
- 524 farm-to-school programs
- 4 locally owned food waste recovery companies

As an assessment of what "small farm and urban organic farmers" are doing, Grain (2014) lists six major concerns:

1. The vast majority of farms in the world today are small and getting smaller.
2. Small farms are currently squeezed onto less than a quarter of the world's farmland.
3. We are fast losing farms and farmers in many places, while big farms are getting bigger.
4. Small farms continue to be the major food producers in the world.
5. Small farms are overall more productive than big farms.
6. Most small farmers are women.

Finally, Nuri (2020) observes that the change involved in creating a new culture based on urban farming has the potential to change the world:

> The new world order envisions food justice, exemplified by universal access to wholesome foods, close to where people—ALL PEOPLE—live. A new food economy is an imperative of our time. We have to choose what order will lie on the other side of the COVID-19 pandemic. The time to choose is now. Grow your own food and grow your community.

Summary: Reclaiming Our Healthy Food History and Experiences

Small farms and urban organic food production take us back to an earlier agricultural history and model. More people are growing healthy food for our communities. Food is growing closer to where people are living. This is what has been done throughout most of human history. We are witnessing the re-creation of local food economies through small farm and local urban agricultural production. This will hopefully lead to heathier communities.

What can be seen in the United States is a transformative pedagogy. Small farms and urban organic food production represent a definitive paradigm shift from control by big agriculture. Local control of thriving local food systems is offering people nutritious, healthy food, food self-sufficiency, and food sovereignty.

References

Bawa, A. S., and K. R. Anilakunar. (2013). "Genetically Modified Foods: Safety, Risks and Public Concerns—A Review." *Journal of Food Science Technology* 50(6): 1035–1046. https://www.ncbi.nlm.nih.gov/pmc/articles/PMC3791249/

Bryant, Christopher R., Jorge Peña Díaz, Bernard Keraita, Frank Lohrberg, and Makoto Yokohari. (2016). "Urban Agriculture from a Global Perspective." In *Urban Agriculture Europe*. Eds. Frank Lohrberg and Axel Timpe, pp. 30–37. Berlin: Jovis.

Diamond, Jared. (2005). *Guns, Germs, and Steel: The Fates of Human Societies*. New York: W.W. Norton.

Engdahl, William. (2007). *Seeds of Destruction: The Hidden Agenda of Genetic Manipulation*. Montreal, Canada: Global Research.

Food and Agriculture Organization of the United Nations (FAO). (2005). *Farming in Urban Areas Can Boost Food Security*. Rome, Italy: FAO. http://www.fao.org/newsroom/en/news/2005/102877/index.html

Food and Water Watch. (2009). *Cargill: A Threat to Food and Farming*. Washington, DC: Food and Water Watch. https://www.foodandwaterwatch.org/sites/default/files/cargill_a_threat_to_food_and_farming.pdf

________. (2012). *The Economic Cost of the Food Monopolies*. Washington, DC: Food and Water Watch. https://www.foodandwaterwatch.org/sites/default/files/Food%20Monopolies%20Report%20Nov%202012.pdf

Food Well Alliance. (2017). *2017 Baseline Report*. Atlanta, GA: Food Well Alliance. https://static1.squarespace.com/static/543c2e74e4b0a10347055c4d/t/59d66bbdd7bdceaa9c93ba63/1507224523326/FoodWellAlliance_LocalFoodBaselineReport2017_Final.pdf

Grain. (2014). *Hungry for Land: Small Farmers Feed the World with Less Than a Quarter of All Farm Land*. Barcelona: Grain. https://www.grain.org/ article/entries/4929-hungry-for-land-small-farmers-feed-the-world-with-less-than-a-quarter-of-all-farmland

Grain and Focus on the Global South. (2004). *Iraq's New Patent Law: A Declaration of War Against Farmers*. Barcelona: Grain. https://www. grain.org/article/entries/150-iraq-s-new-patent-law-a-declaration-of-war-against-farmers

Gray, Heather, and Rashid Nuri. (2010). "Grow Your Own." *Counterpunch* February 17. https://www.counterpunch.org/2010/02/17/grow-your-own/

Kimbrell, Andrew, and Joseph Mendelson. (2005). *Monsanto vs. U.S. Farmers*. Washington, DC: Center for Food Safety. https://www.centerforfoodsafety.org/files/cfsmonsantovsfarmerreport11305.pdf

Krebs, Al. (1992). *Corporate Reapers: The Book of Agribusiness*. Washington, DC: Essential Books. http://www.essential-book.org

Law, Richard. (1996). *The Agricultural Revolution*. Pullman: Washington State University. https://old-www.wsu.edu/gened/learn-modules/top_agrev/3-Hunting-and-Gathering/hunt-gathering2.html

Mattera, Philip. (2004). *USDA INC.: How Agribusiness Has Hijacked Regulatory Policy at the U.S. Department Of Agriculture*. Washington, DC: Corporate Research Project of Good Jobs First. https://www.iatp.org/sites/default/ files/451_2_36882.pdf

Murphy, Andrea. (2019). "Largest Private Companies 2019." *Forbes* December 17. https://www.forbes.com/sites/andreamurphy/2019/12/17/americas-largest-private-companies-2019/#940ec75261fa

Nuri, Rashid. (2019). *Growing Out Loud: Journey of a Food Revolutionary.* Atlanta, Georgia: Nuri Group.

________. (2020). "Homegrown Crisis Response: Who Grows Your Food?" *Counterpunch* April 3. https://www.counterpunch.org/2020/04/03/homegrown-crisis-response-who-grows-your-food/

Shiva, Vandana. (1988). *Staying Alive: Women, Ecology and Development.* Berkeley, CA: North Atlantic Books.

Singh, Rinku, and G. S. Singh. (2017). "Traditional Agriculture: A Climate-Smart Approach for Sustainable Food Production." *Energy, Ecology and Environment* 2: 296–316. https://doi.org/10.1007/s40974-017-0074-7

Stewart, Heather. (2003). "Fury at Agriculture Post for US Businessman." *Guardian* (U.S. Edition) April 28. https://www.theguardian.com/world/2003/apr/28/iraq.usa

Strassman, Paul. (2001). *The Pernicious Characteristics of Monocultures.* Boston: Frontline (PBS), WGBH. https://www.pbs.org/wgbh/pages/front line/shows/hackers/blame/threat.html

Teitel, Martin, and Kimberly A. Wilson. (1999). *Genetically Engineered Food: Changing the Nature of Nature: What You Need to Know to Protect Yourself, Your Family, and Our Planet.* South Paris, ME: Park Street Press.

Truly Living Well. (2020). *About Us.* Atlanta, GA: Truly Living Well Center for Natural Urban Agriculture. https://www.trulylivingwell.com/about-us

Union of Concerned Scientists (UCS). (2018). *Betrayal at the USDA: How the Trump Administration is Sidelining Science and Favoring Industry Over Farmers and the Public.* Cambridge, MA: UCS. https://www.ucsusa.org/resources/betrayal-usda

Werft, Meghan. (2016). *Surprise! Most Small Farms in the World Are Run by Women.* New York, London, Toronto, Melbourne, and Johannesburg: Global Citizen. https://www.globalcitizen.org/en/content/small-farmers-are-not-who-you-think-how-female-far/

Wilkerson, Jordan. (2015). "Why Roundup Ready Crops Have Lost Their Allure." *Science in the News.* Cambridge, MA: Harvard University. http://sitn.hms.harvard.edu/flash/2015/roundup-ready-crops/

Willingham, Zoe, and Andy Green. (2019). *A Fair Deal for Farmers: Raising Earnings and Rebalancing Power in Rural America.* Washington, DC: Center for American Progress. https://www.americanprogress.org/issues/economy/reports/2019/05/07/469385/fair-deal-farmers/

Wynberg, Rachel. (2012). *Policy Brief: Securing Farmers' Rights and Seed Sovereignty in South Africa.* Durban: Biowatch South Africa. https://www.researchgate.net/publication/284514077_Policy_Brief_Securing_Farmers%27_Rights_and_Seed_Sovereignty_in_South_Africa

CHAPTER 8

Consumer Food Co-ops in the Age of Grocery Giants

*Jon Steinman**

Abstract. As the primary purveyors of food within most neighborhoods, food retailers—particularly grocery stores—are key determinants of health. Grocery stores are also an important venue for food producers to access their customers. Over the previous 100 years—and more rapidly over the previous 40 years—ownership among grocery retailers has become concentrated in fewer firms. As a consequence, grocery stores have emerged as food system "gatekeepers." On one side of the gate are consumers, who depend on these firms to access the food supply. On the other side are the food producers: farmers, ranchers, fishers, processors, and manufacturers. As concentration in the grocery retail sector increases, so too have the grocery giants' practices enabled them to assume much stronger positions in the buyer-supplier relationship. With a focus on the United States and Canada, this article examines the history and rise to dominance of the largest grocery retailers and the impacts this dominance has had on the food system. Whereas most food retailers are structured under private or publicly traded models of ownership, the cooperative business model—specifically, the consumer-cooperative model—is presented as an important alternative. Cooperatives are a democratic form of ownership that enable the people who most depend on the grocery store (shoppers) to become equal owners in the business along with thousands of others in their community. The importance of consumer-food cooperatives (food co-ops) is examined, including specific case studies of small and large urban centers where food co-ops are providing substantial benefits to the communities they operate in.

Introduction

Grocery stores are deeply embedded within the social, cultural, and economic fabric of the West. In contrast to the other businesses that consumers frequent, however, the grocery store is considerably different as it retails a product that no human can do without—food.

For better or worse, despite its tremendous importance to human life, the evolution of modern grocery retailing over the previous century has produced a socioeconomic relationship to food that is almost entirely influenced and determined by the same market forces that influence the most nonessential of products. This trajectory remains curious. In much of the West, there has been historical and continued interest to place some of the most essential

*Author of *Grocery Story: The Promise of Food Co-ops in the Age of Grocery Giants* (New Society 2019). Producer and host of internationally syndicated radio show and podcast *Deconstructing Dinner*. Writer and host of *Deconstructing Dinner: Reconstructing Our Food System*—a television and web series. Elected director, 2006–2016, Kootenay Co-op in Nelson, British Columbia; Board President from 2014–2016. Degree in Hotel and Food Administration, University of Guelph. Email: jon@deconstructingdinner.com

products and services to people and communities in the hands of publicly controlled and/or publicly regulated entities: first-responders, drinking water, libraries, transit, and roads are but some examples. Food, however, despite it being a product or service no human can do without, has been treated markedly different than these other "essentials."

In addition, many people today recognize that major changes are needed in our food production systems. There is widespread interest in farming methods that use less or no fossil energy, and methods that might restore health to soil and to ecosystems more widely. Many people believe that a revival of local and regional food production is an appropriate response to both rising energy costs and the imperative to reduce carbon emissions. Yet individuals who want to take steps towards local food reliance are often thwarted by dominant grocery chains that act as gatekeepers and give strong preference to large-scale monocultural food producers. Thus we need major changes not only in the way farming is done but in the way food retailing is done.

Grocery Stores and Community Well-Being

Despite the impact grocery retailers have on health, the environment, the local economy, and the food system, this industry has received comparatively little scrutiny from the media, from food system reformers, or from health professionals. Meanwhile, those watchdogs have investigated other aspects of the supply chain for food, including primary producers (farms, ranches, and fishing operations), food processors (including storage, transportation, and packaging), and consumption (including meat consumption and specific consumer food choices). The grocery retail sector is an apparent blind spot.

All sectors of the food system are being hollowed out, leaving fewer and fewer companies dominating each link in the supply chain. The largest grocery retailers—the grocery giants—have emerged as the dominant players in the system. These retailers have reduced farmers' power in the marketplace, just as they have diminished the market power of all food producers, processors, wholesalers, and transporters. To simplify the language used to describe the myriad links in the supply chain, we will narrow it down to three groups: producers, retailers, and consumers. The term "producers" encompasses every entity involved prior to the point at which a food item appears on the shelf of a grocery store. Producers are being squeezed by the largest food retailers, who use trade fees, long-term contracts, delayed payments, and the acquisition of smaller regional and alternative chains to consolidate their power. Consumers are left with fewer options and higher grocery prices (Volpe 2011).

Some local governments have acknowledged the need for more public oversight. They are reimagining the role they play. After the one grocer closed in Baldwin, Florida (population 1,600) in 2018, the Town of Baldwin opened its own grocery store. All employees were put on the municipal payroll. In this case, the interest in applying public oversight or ownership originated from a need for food access. How might a sense of urgency emerge in response to the hollowing out of local food systems? The barriers to entry for food producers are high at the chain grocers and the long-term reliability of regional, privately owned stores is precarious. There is a strong need for local food producers to have stable, supportive, long-term customers.

In this article, I make a case for assigning grocery stores with greater responsibility in keeping with their influence. I also make a case for a consumer-cooperative model as a way to demand public accountability from grocery stores. Through the presence of food co-ops in the United States and Canada, a future of diverse, place-based food systems is possible.

Four Social Impacts of Grocery Stores

Grocery stores play a much larger role in social well-being than is generally recognized. We can see the hidden role of retail grocers in four different domains: health, food systems, economy, and the environment.

As Determinants of Health. The connections between food and health are now well understood. The common cold (Rennard et al. 2000), diabetes (de

Munter et al. 2007), and heart disease (Stampfer et al. 2000) can be prevented, curtailed, or managed through the foods we eat. Food is medicine. As the sole purveyor of food in most neighborhoods, grocery retailers are engaged in a trade that is crucial to health. What responsibilities or requirements should be placed upon grocery retailers that are proportional to the health services they are providing? What efforts are being carried out to ensure that all people, regardless of income, race, or geography, are provided access to healthy, wholesome, and risk-free food at the grocery stores in their neighborhoods? To date, there have been few such efforts. Grocery stores are free to operate as they choose. One of the most impactful decisions a grocer can make, one that does not receive any public oversight, is the decision to close a store. No community consultations are required despite the significant impacts closures can have on human health. Fiechtner et al. (2016) report that easier access to grocery stores is associated with greater fruit and vegetable intake and lower body mass index.

As the Primary Influence Shaping Food Systems. The food system is effectively a series of bottlenecks that food must pass through, with each bottleneck being controlled by a handful of companies that have consolidated within each sector. Commodity traders, processors, manufacturers, distributors, and retailers are all highly concentrated. Among retailers, grocers maintain a considerable influence in setting the food system agenda through their role as gatekeeper between the food system and consumers. In this position, grocers are determining which foods make it to market and which do not. This, in turn, has the power to dictate how each upstream sector of the food system evolves.

Within Local Economies. The money consumers spend on food is mostly handed over to a shrinking number of grocery giants that extract the wealth of communities. Grocers have the capacity to choose between local suppliers and distant national and global suppliers. This, too, has an influence on local economies. Through this position as gatekeeper, grocers retain the capacity to either cultivate or hollow out the infrastructure and capacity of local food systems.

Influence on Environment. The Intergovernmental Panel on Climate Change (IPCC) reported upwards of 37 percent of the planet's greenhouse gas emissions are caused by food systems (IPCC 2020). As gatekeepers standing between the upstream food system and consumers, the product decisions made by food retailers result in substantial environmental ripple effects on climate and on aquatic and terrestrial ecosystems.

The Damaging Effects of Market Concentration

In the past 100 years since the birth of the modern grocery store, market power in grocery retail has become concentrated in fewer hands. The top 15 global supermarket companies account for more than 30 percent of world supermarket sales (USDA-ERS 2017). When the geographic focus narrows, the concentration of power in food retail widens. In the United States, the five largest food retailers account for over 66 percent of national retail food sales. In Canada, over 80 percent of retail food purchases end up in the hands of the five largest. (See Table 1.)

National concentration figures, however, are not a completely accurate picture of the dominance retailers maintain at the regional and local levels. In the entire south of Texas (San Antonio, Austin, Corpus Christi), 60 percent of retail food purchases are made at H-E-B stores. H-E-B and Walmart together command 87 percent of consumers' grocery dollars in that part of the state (Karst 2018). Rural markets are the most concentrated of any, with usually one, maybe two grocers serving the area. In urban markets, market concentration can also be quite high. In the Denver, Colorado, metro area, five companies receive 82 percent of consumers' grocery dollars (Baker 2016). In Cincinnati, Ohio, Kroger holds 60 percent of the market (Watkins 2015). In Miami, Florida, Publix receives 46.3 percent of the grocery dollars; the top three companies receive 75.2 percent (F&D Reports 2017: 5). The U.S. Justice Department defines markets as "highly concentrated" when one company commands more than 50 percent of a market. "Walmart's market share meets or exceeds this measure in 43 metropolitan areas and 160 smaller markets around the United States" (Mitchell 2019). This localized perspective provides the most accurate picture of the power of the grocery giants and their impacts on health, food systems, and local economies. A food producer in Miami, for example, looking to get its product into the homes of Miami consumers, is confronted with a single company that commands nearly half of the Miami grocery retail market. (See Table 2.)

Regulating Market Power

Antitrust enforcement today is a faint whisper of what it was in the mid-20th century. Throughout the formative years of the emerging chain grocers, a number of mechanisms were put in place that sought to restrain the capacity of the chains to gain excessive market power. Taxes on chain stores are one example. By the late 1930s, 29 states had implemented chain-store taxes. Levinson (2013) reports annual chain-store taxes from 1933 to 1935 in a few states (with the price in 2020 dollars in parentheses) as follows:

> Minnesota: $155/store for chains with more than 50 stores ($2,957/store)
>
> Michigan: $250/store for chains with more than 25 stores ($4,770/store)
>
> Florida: $400/store for chains above 15 stores (plus 5 percent gross receipts tax) ($7,632/store)
>
> Pennsylvania: $500/store for chains with more than 500 stores ($9,539/ store)
>
> Louisiana: $550 for each store above 500 stores *nationwide* (even if the chain only had one store in the state) ($10,493/store)

In the 1930s, the impacts the chains were having on small business in America and the resulting sentiments of restraint resided at the highest levels of government. In a message to Congress on curbing monopolies, President Franklin D. Roosevelt (1938) made an appeal to his colleagues to consider the limits that had been placed upon the American entrepreneurial spirit:

> Men will dare to compete against men but not against giants. ... If you believe with me in private initiative, you must acknowledge the right of well-managed small business to expect to make reasonable profits. You must admit that

Table 1
Top Five U.S. and Canadian Grocers

Top 5 U.S. Grocers		**Top 5 Canadian Grocers**	
Share of Grocery Retail Sales 2016 (%)		Share of Grocery 2016 (%) Retail Sales	
Walmart	24.7	Loblaw	29.8
Kroger	15.2	Sobeys	21.5
Costco	11.1	Metro	11.5
Albertsons	9.2	Costco	10.5
Ahold-Delhaize	6.6	Walmart	7.2
C5*	66.8	C5*	80.5

*Market concentration of top five firms.
SOURCES: Chain Store Guide (2018), USDA-ERS (2019b), Mangino and Arbulu (2018).

> the destruction of this opportunity follows concentration of control of any given industry into a small number of dominating corporations.

Ellickson (2011) describes the merger laws of the 1960s as "by far the most stringent in the world." In one of the most cited cases of the lengths anti-trust enforcement would go to protect competition and small business in America, the Supreme Court blocked the merger of two supermarket chains in Los Angeles. Had they been allowed to merge, the chains would have controlled only 7.5 percent of the local market (*United States v. Vons* 1966). As a result of this restraint, market concentration in grocery retail remained flat for 28 years (Marion 1986). (See Table 3.)

Table 2
Urban Market Concentration in Select Cities: Share of Grocery Retail Sales 2017 (%)

Miami, FL		Houston, TX	
Publix	46.3	H-E-B	28
Walmart	18.4	Walmart	25
Southeastern Grocers	10.5	Kroger	23
Whole Foods (Amazon)	3.6	C3*	76
ALDI	2.7		
C3*	75.2		
C5*	81.5		

Nashville, TN		Charlotte, NC	
Kroger	40.2	Walmart	26.2
Walmart	27.2	Kroger	25.4
Publix	14.7	Ahold Delhaize	20.1
ALDI	2.3	Southeastern Grocers	7.1
Ahold Delhaize	1.9	Publix	6.1
C3*	82.1	C3*	71.7
C5*	86.3	C5*	84.9

*Market concentration of top three or five firms. Sources: F&D Reports (2017), Green (2017).

Table 3
The Effects of Restraint on Retailer Market Concentration: Market Share (%) of National Grocery Retail (U.S.)

	1954	1958	1963	1967	1972	1977	1982
4 largest firms	20.9	21.7	20.0	19.0	17.5	17.4	17.8
8 largest firms	25.4	27.5	26.6	25.7	24.4	24.4	25.1
20 largest firms	29.9	34.1	34.0	34.0	34.8	34.5	35.6

Source: Marion (1986).

The Evisceration of Antitrust Enforcement

Commencing in the early 1980s, the Reagan administration decisively "eviscerated America's century-long tradition of antitrust enforcement" (Lynn 2006). In 1982, antitrust prosecutions came under new guidelines. Considerations of social cost, regional equity, or local control were no longer relevant to decisions on mergers and acquisitions. In this new regime, antitrust enforcement became a tool for combating only the most egregious anti-competitive practices—collusion or anything that would blatantly gouge consumers (Longman 2015). This unleashed an initial wave of leveraged buyouts in the 1980s followed by another wave of mergers and acquisitions in the 1990s. Whereas market concentration of the top four grocery chains was at 17 percent in 1982, by 1999 the top four commanded 28 percent of the market (Martens 2008).

Walmart's entry into groceries in 1988 through its Supercenter format also accelerated market concentration in the United States (Martens 2008). Ellickson (2011) describes Walmart's arrival into food as the "largest change in market structure since the rise and fall of A&P." Only 14 years after entry, Walmart became the top grocer in the country. In that same time, 29 chains filed for bankruptcy. Walmart is said to be responsible for 25 of them (Basker and Noel 2009).

There were few resources and little political will to curb the concentration of market power that began in the final decade of the 20th century. As Commissioner Andrew J. Strenio Jr. of the Federal Trade Commission (FTC) said:

> The FTC is a gaunt and bloodied agency. Since fiscal year 1980, there has been a drop of more than forty percent in the work years allocated to antitrust enforcement. In the same period, merger filings skyrocketed to more than three-hundred-twenty percent of their 1980 level. (quoted in Behr 1988)

Walmart's disrupting of the grocery retail sector spurred some notable mergers in grocery retail in

Figure 1
National Retail Grocery Market Share of Top Four Retailers

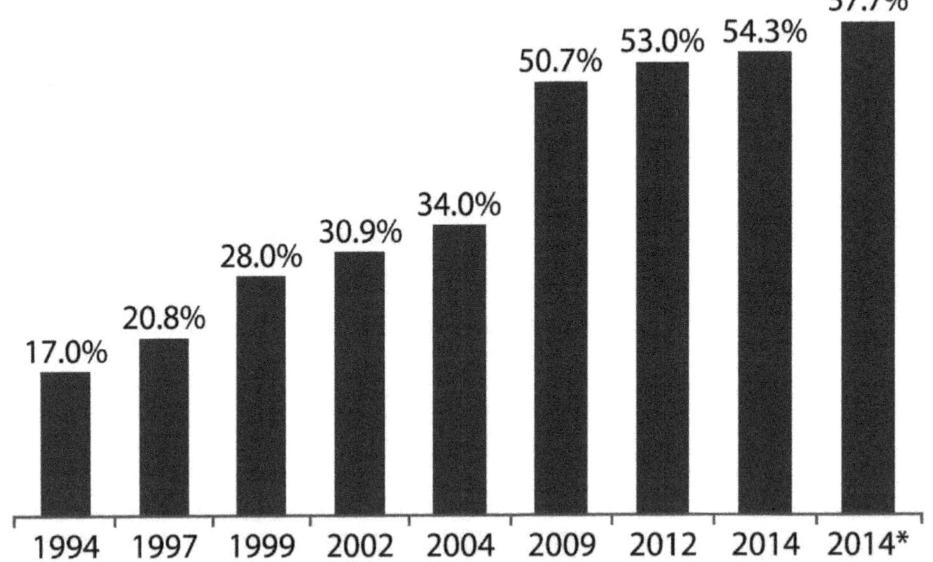

Source: Food & Water Watch (2014). *Post Albertsons-Safeway merger.

1998. First was Kroger's acquisition of Fred Meyer—the largest and fifth-largest grocery chains in the country. Next was Albertsons' acquisition of American Stores—the second- and fourth-largest firms. (See Figure 1.)

Impacts of Market Concentration on Food Producers

The farm income crisis has been connected to the growing market power of firms in all sectors of the food system. Canada's farm income crisis parallels that of the United States. Between 1942 and 1982, realized net income (RNI) per farm in Canada remained steady between $10,000 and $20,000. In 1985, RNI dropped to zero. With the exception of a mid-1990s rise, it remained near zero for the rest of the 1980s and 1990s. Then the crisis worsened. In 2000, RNI plummeted into the negative, dropping as low as negative $20,000 (National Farmers Union 2005). Despite modest increases since then, RNI remains below zero. In the United States, it has declined 50 percent since 2013, with median farm income for 2018 being negative $1,735 (USDA-ERS 2019a).

The capacity among farmers to confront these declines has also eroded. An easily understood measure of farmer power in the marketplace is the "farm share"—the portion farmers receive of the food dollars that consumers spend at restaurants, fast-food outlets, convenience stores, and the grocery checkout. It is the total cost to produce the food before it leaves the farm gate, as a percentage of the cost to the consumer. Schnepf (2013) defines the relevant terms. The "farm share of the market price" is the portion of the food dollar ending up at the farm, which includes all costs of producing the food, including what ends up in a farmer's pocket. By contrast, the "marketing share" consists of every additional cost it takes to get food from farm to plate.

According to Schnepf (2013: 2), these non-farm costs include

> labor expenses for handling, sorting, cleaning, and packaging the product, transportation charges to move the product along at each stage, and fees for processing, storing, insuring, financing, and retailing the product.

These figures have been calculated annually in the United States since 1946. For every dollar spent on food, the portion that ends up at the farm (the farm share) is at its lowest point in history: 14.6 cents (USDA-ERS 2020). In 1950, by comparison, farmers received considerably more of that dollar: 41 cents (Schnepf 2013). The farm share and marketing share help us begin to understand where power in the food system resides—particularly the power to set prices. The plummeting farm share of the food dollar since 1950 has left farmers with less power to determine their future. (See Figure 2.)

What if consumers paid more for food? Surely farmers would receive more income if food prices rose? Maybe so at a farmers' market but not necessarily at grocery stores, where many companies influence and handle the product from farm to plate—each extracting its own portion of that dollar. As food prices increase, farmers may not benefit correspondingly. The farm-to-retail price spreads that have been estimated by the U.S. Department of Agriculture (USDA) demonstrate how increases in food prices over time do not necessarily transmit into farm value—the portion farmers keep for themselves *after* expenses. See Figures 3 and 4.

When former antitrust attorney for the U.S. Department of Justice Peter Carstensen was asked about price spreads in the beef sector, he refused to agree that "cost-increasing elements" are the sole cause of widening price spreads. "I'm very skeptical that unit costs have gone up as substantially as the spreads have gone up. Most data suggest wages have gone down in [meat] packing plants—and many plants are increasingly mechanized in ways that are intended to lower costs, not increase costs." He believes the widening price spreads indicate a failure of the marketing system to reflect back to the producer the revenue potential of the livestock (Peck 2003). The late distinguished agricultural economist Wayne Purcell pointed the finger at the grocery giants:

Figure 2
Farm Share of U.S. Food Expenditures Has Declined Since 1950

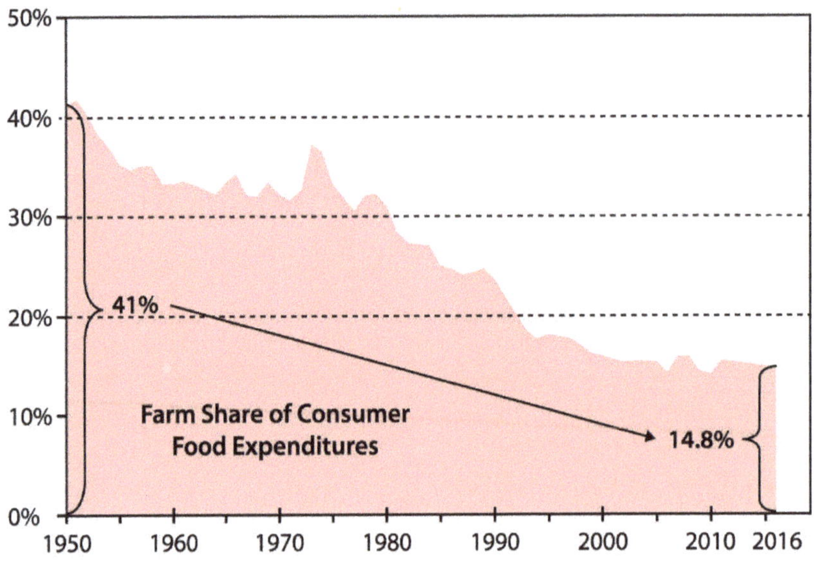

Source: Schnepf (2013), and USDA-ERS (2020).

Figure 3
Bread, Farm Value vs. Retail Price, 1999–2014

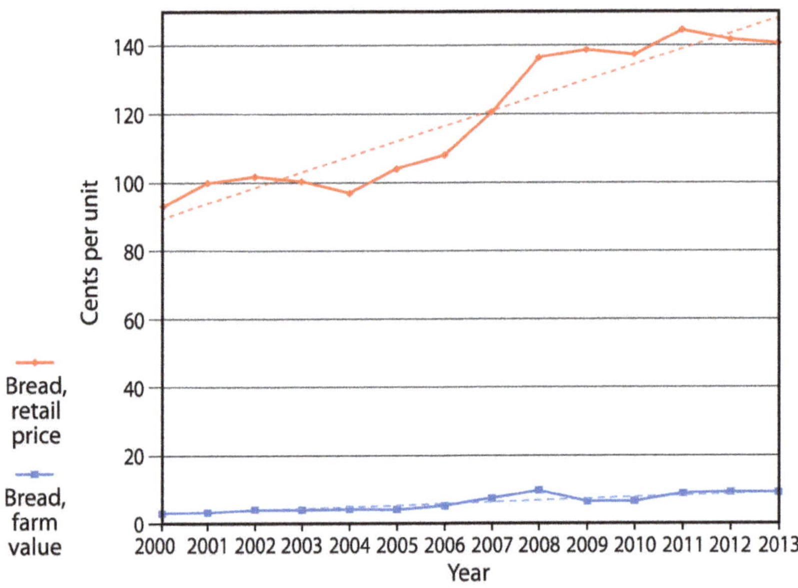

Source: Schnepf (2013), and USDA-ERS (2020).

> Retailers ... are increasingly telling [meat] packers what to do .... Retailers mandate to packers how they want meat cut, packaged, labeled and bar-coded. They stipulate assurances on safety and, to top it off, they want packers to maintain and manage their inventory. If retailers are pulling $500–$600/head out of a $1,200/head retail value—as it appears they are—I wonder why it is that they need so much of the share? Of all the players along the beef supply chain, the retailers do the least to add value to the product. (Peck 2003)

Impacts of Market Concentration on Consumers

From PricewaterhouseCoopers (2007) to the FTC (Hosken, Olson, and Smith 2018) to the U.S. Department of Agriculture, the overwhelming consensus is that "supermarkets set prices less competitively as concentration increases" (Volpe 2011).

At the local level, high concentration among retailers enables competitors to *tacitly* coordinate pricing strategies—an indirect form of price-fixing. Two of Seattle's largest retailers were found to be matching each other's milk prices, leaving consumers to pay more for milk than in other parts of the country (Chidmi and Murova 2011). As the theory of oligopoly power proposes, in markets with only a few dominant firms, companies are less likely to adopt aggressive strategies that might accelerate competition and jeopardize their chances of larger profits.

In another analysis of the localized impacts of market concentration, the grocery price index (GPI) went up in the most highly concentrated markets when the number of grocery chains either increased or decreased by adding or losing chains. The GPI increased three times more in "highly concentrated" markets than in "moderately concentrated" markets. In unconcentrated markets with many grocers, the GPI decreased, particularly as more chains were added to the market. The rising prices on the shelves in the more concentrated areas outpaced overall inflation (Food & Water Watch 2014). See Figure 5.

In 2017, Loblaw, Canada's largest grocer, admitted to fixing the price of bread from 2001 to 2015 with four other grocers: Sobeys, Metro, Walmart, and Giant Tiger. These five companies together hold

Figure 4
Broccoli, Farm Value vs. Retail Price, 1999–2014

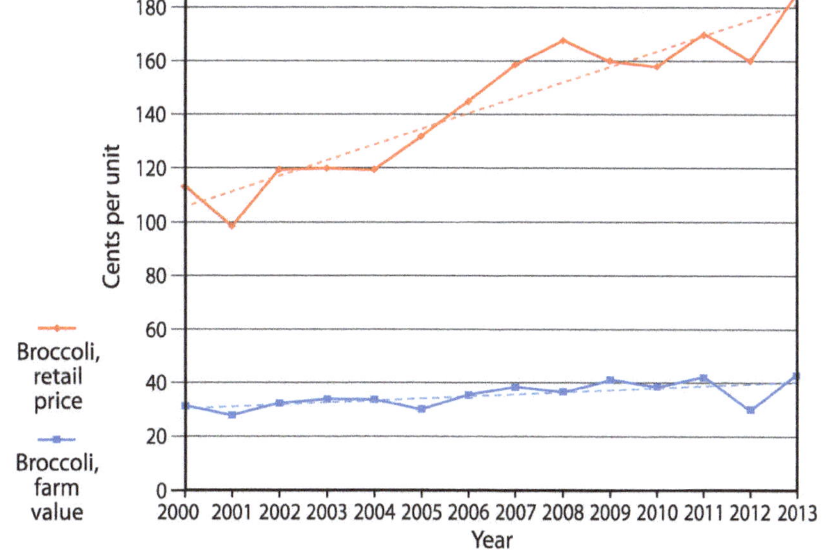

Source: Schnepf (2013), and USDA-ERS (2020).

over 70 percent of the Canadian grocery market. Their price manipulation cost a family purchasing two loaves of bread per week an additional $104 per year (Markusoff 2018). The capacity to coordinate such schemes is only possible and viable in highly concentrated industries.

The Power of Grocers Over Their Suppliers

As grocery store ownership reduces into the hands of fewer companies, food producers are left with fewer choices to move their product into the market. Thus, retailers are afforded the lucrative position to more freely dictate terms and conditions to suppliers. Furthermore, small and mid-size food producers compete with the largest suppliers for access to shelf space in grocery stores. The largest grocers take advantage of their position by installing numerous hurdles and barriers for their suppliers, such as trade spend, slotting fees, contract allowances, promotional allowances, category management, long-term contracts, and delayed payments.

Trade Spend (Vendor Allowances). The revenues of grocery giants are not derived solely from selling products to consumers. Most chains require fees from suppliers before agreeing to carry their products. Safeway recorded $2.5 billion in vendor allowances in 2015 (US-SEC 2015), and Kroger recorded $8.5 billion in 2017 (US-SEC 2018).

Slotting Fees. The initial payments for placing new product on the shelf are called "slotting fees." The retailer is under no obligation to keep it on the shelf. Often, they are nonrefundable. Regulators have not known what to do about slotting fees. When the U.S. Senate Committee on Small Business & Entrepreneurship held a hearing on the subject in 1999, anyone willing to testify hid behind a screen and spoke through a voice-altering machine. "[Slotting fees are] nothing but a device to exploit money from manufacturers and squeeze all the independent and smaller processors off the shelves and out of business," said one food manufacturer (Jennings 2015). When the FTC was then tasked to investigate slotting fees, no one from the grocery industry was willing to come forward. No regulatory action was ever taken.

Figure 5
Change in Grocery Price Index by Change in Number of Grocery Chains and Market Concentration Level, 2004–2011

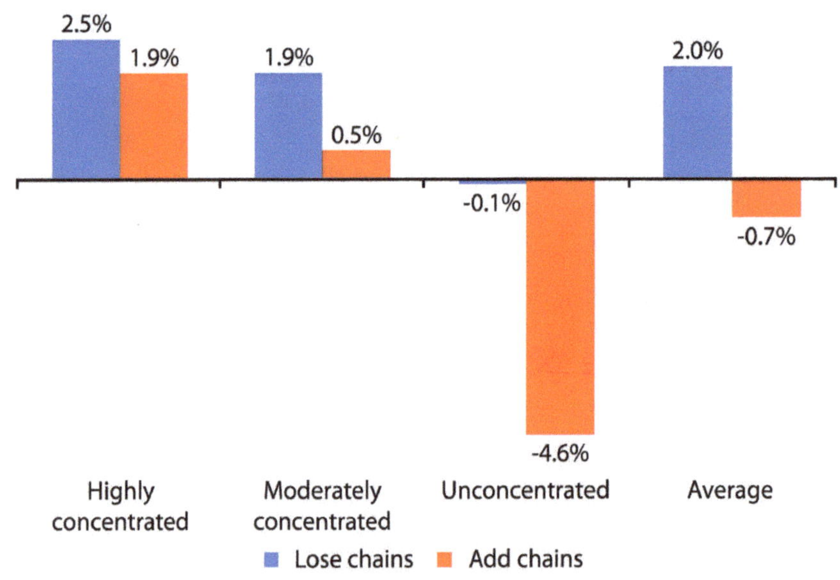

Source: Food & Water Watch (2014).

Contract Allowances. A fee called a "contract allowance" is charged for keeping a product on the shelf either for a minimum period of time or until a volume threshold is achieved.

Promotional Allowances. Suppliers pay retailers promotional allowances to feature their products in advertising or in-store placement. The promotion may be any combination of a temporary price reduction, a feature in print ads, a feature in a flyer, or a preferred location in the store.

Category Management. Most antitrust scholars and authorities are still trying to figure out what to make of category management (CM). A retailer will appoint a single manufacturer as a "category captain" and relinquish exclusive control of that category. The captain will often be an industry leader like Nestlé. In one example, Nestlé has been the captain for frozen desserts in 22 of the country's 25 largest chains (Rivlin 2016). A "category" of products comprises more than just the products of the appointed manufacturer. This leaves the captain with the responsibility to manage the placement of *all* brands, including those the manufacturer directly competes with. "As an antitrust matter, it seems rather strange that you'd have one company advising a store on how to handle the product of its competitors," said former FTC Commissioner Thomas Leary. "Some aspects of category management present high antitrust risks" (FTC 2005). As Carameli (2004) observes: "Category captaincies can result in an exclusive vertical relationship between a retail chain and a single manufacturer. By its very nature, this exclusive arrangement reduces or eliminates competition." Carameli projects that CM practices may, however, pass "unchallenged or even recognized" except for the most heinous of abuses.

Long-Term Contracts. When a retailer enters into long-term contracts with large well-established suppliers, smaller suppliers can easily be excluded from the market, further contributing to consolidation in the supply chain and increasing the market power of retailers in their position as buyers (Sexton 2010).

Delayed Payments. With so few retailers to sell to, delayed payments to suppliers have become an industry standard. In 2015, the U.K.'s largest grocer, Tesco, was found guilty of deliberately and "unreasonably" holding back payments to its suppliers. Some of the practices were made public by the U.K.'s new grocery watchdog. In one instance, Tesco took "two years [to] repay a supplier who was owed a multimillion-pound sum." In another case, "a supplier waited for more than a year for a £2m repayment due because of duplicate invoicing." In another, "Tesco deliberately delayed payments at key financial reporting periods to bolster its bottom line, even if suppliers requested payments." The investigator emphasized how "widespread" Tesco's behavior was. "Every supplier I spoke to had evidence of delays in payments" (Butler 2016).

Alternatives to Grocery Giants

There are alternatives that permit food producers to bypass the grocery giants. This is particularly true for food producers looking to serve regional markets. Each of these alternatives, however, carries its own similar and unique challenges.

Direct Marketing. Farmers' markets, box programs of community-supported agriculture (CSAs), and farmstands offer important retail alternatives for small- and mid-scale food producers. Whereas many food producers are happy integrating these sales channels into their businesses, many turn to these alternatives out of necessity. Whether they have difficulties accessing the shelves of their local grocers or have less-than-favorable buyer-supplier relationships, many food producers are reluctant participants in direct-marketing venues. These alternatives require considerable time, energy, and financial outlays to operate within these channels. Marketing costs add to the considerable investments they have already made producing food. For many food producers, if retailers were interested in their product and offered fair prices and conditions, food producers would not need to market their products directly to consumers or manage CSA programs. Food producers would instead rely on less time-consuming and more efficient distribution through food retailers. When direct marketing is the most accessible channel to reach consumers, the growth of a local food system is restrained. Many food producers and consumers cannot afford the time and effort required to participate in the alternative distribution methods.

Natural Foods Retailers. Privately owned natural foods retailers have evolved considerably since they first began appearing in the 1970s. Today, many natural foods retailers are formidable chains. Some of the most notable are Whole Foods, Natural Grocers, Sprouts Farmers Markets, Earth Fare (pre-2020), Lucky's Market (pre-2020), and New Seasons Market. Many of these alternative grocers have provided shelf space to regional products. Whereas some of these natural foods retailers have remained regional, others have been pursuing national expansion strategies. A more regional focus of operations may not, however, translate into a commitment to regional food producers. Earth Fare, for example, was founded in 1975 and has grown to 53 locations in 10 states with 50 more locations planned over the next five years. At one of the company's hometown stores in Asheville, North Carolina, only a handful of local products are found in the store despite the region being a hotbed of food production. ("Local" here is defined as coming from within a 100-mile [160 km] radius.)

The rising demand in natural and organic foods has also left many of these alternative grocers as attractive targets for acquisition. Here is a list of recent acquisitions:

2013—New Seasons Market acquires New Leaf Community Markets
2016—Kroger invests in Lucky's Market
2017—Amazon acquires Whole Foods
2019—Ahold Delhaize acquires Wild by Nature
2019—Stripes Group (private-equity) invests in Erewhon Market
2019—Emart acquires New Seasons Market

In Canada, some of the most successful natural foods chains have also recently been acquired by some of the largest ones: Capers Markets (acquired by Amazon via Whole Foods and Wild Oats), Choices Markets (by Jim Pattison Group), Nature's Fare Markets (by Jim Pattison Group), and Farm Boy (by Sobeys).

The shifting sands of grocery-retailer ownership make for a less certain future for food producers, many of whom require strong, long-term relationships with retailers in order to mitigate the financial risk of a food-based business. When a grocery chain is acquired, there is a risk that the parent company might erode the acquired retailer's relationship with suppliers. After Whole Foods was acquired by Amazon, a new culture emerged. Whereas Whole Foods once permitted direct relations between suppliers and regional offices, suppliers are now required to work with Connecticut-based Daymon Worldwide—a global brand consultant serving more than 15,000 retail locations and 16,000 suppliers and manufacturers across 19 countries. Whole Foods put Daymon in charge of inventory management, display creation, and in-store tastings. Following the change, four-hour in-store tastings were charged to suppliers and any food producers selling more than $300k of product annually were required to discount their products by 3 percent (Bhattarai 2018). Post-acquisition changes in the buyer-supplier culture are occurring across the continent and affecting food producers of all sizes.

Acquisitions of or investments in alternative grocers can also severely disrupt local food markets. In 2016, Lucky's Market of Colorado received a hefty investment from Kroger to help the small company expand further east into new markets. Lucky's went from 17 locations pre-Kroger to 39 stores by December 2019. In theory, the expansion of alternative grocers should support food producers in these locations by easing access to the market for food producers. Lucky's, however, did not maintain this commitment to local food producers when opening in new markets. Instead, Lucky's entry into new areas severely stressed already-established locally owned grocers who *were* committed to local food producers. Both Oryana Community Food Co-op (c.1973) in Traverse City, Michigan, and Mountain Avenue Market (c.1972) in Fort Collins, Colorado, immediately felt the arrival of Lucky's on their bottom lines.

Many independent grocers that supported local food systems have closed their doors because of the arrival of alternative national grocers like Lucky's.

If the demise of the locally oriented independent grocers because of competition from a national or regional chain were the end of the story, that could be counted as a demonstration of the inefficiency of local supply chains. But the ending turns that "moral lesson" on its head. In December 2019—less than three years following Kroger's investment—Kroger announced it was divesting itself of Lucky's. In January 2020, Lucky's announced it would be closing most of its 39 stores. These results clearly indicate the relative financial strength of the independent grocers compared to the alternative food channels that grow rapidly through aggressive pricing and overcapitalization. The independent grocers who bought from local suppliers were more sustainable in a competitive market than the heavily capitalized outsiders who mistook size for efficiency. Nevertheless, the tactics of national chains that seek to grow rapidly at the cost of local supply chains threaten the livelihoods of local producers and the opportunities for consumers to buy their products.

Regional/Local Independents. Small regional and local chains are owned and managed by people living nearby. This has often meant stronger relationships with local food producers and easier access for food producers to the retailers' shelves. As a privately owned business, however, the future of those stores is dependent on the decisions of a single individual, family, or company. The sale of the store or stores to another company does not require any consultations with the community—namely, consumers and the regional food producers who may depend on those relationships. Retirement among independent grocers is also a risk to those who depend on them. This is of particular concern in rural communities where aging ownership and lack of transfer opportunities among grocery stores is high. Of 280 independent rural Minnesota grocery stores surveyed in 2016, 63 percent were not planning on owning their store in 10 years' time and few had developed succession plans (Draeger et al. 2016).

Deceptive Use of Labels "Local" and "Organic". Food producers looking to establish themselves within place-based food systems and benefit from the value consumers place on "local" are impacted by the deceptive use by chains of signs indicating local production. Safeway Canada (Sobeys) and the Jim Pattison Group actively market foods as "local" in their stores in western Canada if the product originated anywhere in western Canada. In some instances, products are marketed as "local" if they are produced inside the nation. At a Safeway (Albertsons) store in Cle Elum, Washington, and a Lucky's Market in Winter Park, Florida, "local" signs hang above produce that originates in California. At a Whole Foods in Hadley, Massachusetts, a sign above the cheese department reads: "We carry a variety of local products made less than 100 miles from here." Not one cheese in the entire store fit this description.

At Walmart stores across the country, "organic" signs are placed directly in the center of the store's largest produce cooler. The central location of the signs is highly suggestive that the entire display is filled with organic products when, in many instances, very few organic products can be found. At the Walmart in Dickinson, North Dakota, only one organic product could be found on display in the cooler below the "organic" sign. At Lucky's Market stores, the slogan "Organic 99%" is used on roadside signs and in other branding. The slogan leaves consumers believing the store carries 99% organic products; however, for anyone taking the time to look much closer—microscopically closer—a text in a much smaller font is found vertically alongside the two words. The slogan actually reads "Organic *for the 99%.*" However, the middle two words are imperceptible to people in passing vehicles.

When retailers use "local" and "organic" terminology as marketing tools rather than as a means to genuinely support alternative and/or place-based food systems, they undermine the distinctive contribution made by place-based businesses that supply locally produced food.

The Benefits of Food Co-ops

Consumer cooperatives are businesses owned by their customers. Most of the consumer food co-ops in North America are owned by 1,000–20,000 of their shoppers. All but a handful of these stores do not require ownership (membership) in order to shop at the store. Food co-ops are open to anyone to shop at. The most successful food co-ops today were founded in the 1970s. A small number have histories dating back to the post-Depression era, and a new wave of food co-op formation began strongly in 2008.

Food co-ops are democratic. Members (shareholders) annually elect from among the membership their co-op's board of directors.

The sustainability of this model to the communities they serve is evidenced by the complete absence of any chain grocer having ever successfully acquired a food co-op. Whereas consumers and food producers have no input into changes in ownership of privately owned or publicly traded retailers, food co-ops, on the other hand, cannot be sold to other interests without the approval of the co-op's shareholders (their member-owners). Never before has there been an instance of a co-op's thousands of owners voting to sell their community-owned grocery store to a grocery giant. As the model also only permits one voting share per member, no one shareholder has any more voting power than the next. Built into the business model itself is a level of security to a community. The only factor that could cause their grocery store to no longer serve the interests of members is business failure.

Food co-ops also enable public accountability in the relationship between consumers and grocery stores. Consumers can hold their grocery store accountable in the most important areas of influence—health, food system, local economy, and environment. With the cooperative model, shoppers have a powerful voice in determining the future of their grocery store and how it conducts itself in their communities. After all, they own it.

As food producers may also be consumer-owners of the food co-op, they too carry a heightened level of influence over these grocery stores upon which they rely. Co-ops of all kinds are also held to a set of globally accepted cooperative principles that guide their decisions. As one of these principles is "concern for community," food co-ops are effectively mandated through their business model to be venues for the sale of local foods. Food co-ops are thereby a grocery-retail model that embeds place-based food systems directly into their purpose.

Food Co-ops Today

In the United States, there are currently 230 consumer food co-ops with over 300 locations among them. Another 90 are in various stages of development. In Canada, 15 food co-ops comprise those that are of a similar model to those operating in the United States.*

There is no particular size or geographic location that is specific to food co-ops. Food co-ops can be found in the middle of large urban centers, in small towns, and at the crossroads of rural country roads. They are found from Fairbanks, Alaska, to San Diego, California, from Florida to Maine, and from British Columbia to Nova Scotia. They are located within historic schoolhouses, suburban malls, and multi-story condominiums. They range in size from less than 1,000 square feet to well over 20,000, and from single-store locations to entire multi-store chains. Geographically, there are some areas of higher-than-usual food co-op concentration: the American Midwest and New England are the most concentrated of any. The metropolitan area of Minneapolis– St. Paul is one of the most concentrated with food co-ops—with 10 co-ops comprising 17 locations. In the Seattle metro area, there are two single-store food co-ops alongside the largest food

* Canada is also home to two networks of food co-op federations and a large multi-store co-op of 23 stores that comprise about 345 food stores among them. However, for this research, these co-ops were not included, as their relationship to local food systems is different than the one examined in this work.

co-op in the United States—PCC Community Markets, with its 13 stores and another four planned. The physical size of a cooperative grocery store pales in comparison to the modern supermarket's average size of 45,000 square feet.* According to annual reports, annual sales at food co-ops range from as low as $1 million at a single store to as high as $288 million at PCC's 12 locations. Many single-store food co-ops generate impressive sales relative to their size. City Market's (Onion River Co-op) downtown location in Burlington, Vermont, moves $42 million of product out of a 12,000-square-foot retail space. The Flatbush Food Co-op in Brooklyn, New York, sells $17.5 million in only 4,500 square feet. At the nearby Park Slope Food Co-op, also in Brooklyn, sales volume is $56 million in only 6,000 square feet.

Contributions to Local Economies

The 35 member co-ops of the Neighboring Food Co-op Association (NFCA) purchase more than $60 million worth of product from local businesses in the northeastern United States. They employ more than 2,000 people and pay wages of over $49 million. In the metro area of Minnesota's Twin Cities with a population of 3.4 million, 15 co-ops with 17 stores (2014) serve 91,000 owners and another 50,000 shoppers. Sales of local products at those co-ops amount to $54 million—of which $30 million passes through the farm gate (Stockinger and Gutknecht 2014). The local economic and social impact of food co-ops begins with their interest and capacity to support small-scale farmers. The contribution of small farms to the social fabric of communities was well understood as early as 1946. In Goldschmidt (1949)—commissioned by the U.S. Senate—two California farming communities that were "similar in population, shared value systems, and social customs" were compared. Where the two communities differed was in the size of farms. One community was made up of small farms, the other large. The study set out to determine whether or not "other aspects of society, economy and culture" were affected by this. Noticeable differences were observed. The "large industrialized farming communities lacked solidarity, leadership, prosperity, permanent settlement, adequate educational facilities, and in general, a life of their own." These characteristics were reversed in the community with smaller farms (Bennett 1949). Many regions across the country are also topographically constrained. Hilly, rocky, and mountainous characteristics can constrain farm size and limit the type of production. By providing easier access to the marketplace for small-scale farms, food co-ops can ensure viability of farming in these geographically diverse areas.

Easier Access to Eaters

Food co-ops are providing food producers a level of access to eaters that is often unavailable through the large chains. Small-scale food producers are often unable to supply the volumes necessary for the national distribution the chains require or favor, and many are unable to meet the long list of fees. Food co-ops, on the other hand, are often happy to accept direct deliveries at their loading docks—and slotting fees are not part of food co-op culture.

Local Food at Food Co-ops

Of all grocery categories, the local foods sold most often through food co-ops are meat, eggs, fresh produce, and dairy. The average co-op carries a range of 15 to 42 percent local product. For small-scale food producers, food co-ops are a critical market that helps ensure their survival. Among local producers selling into co-ops in the Twin Cities, food co-ops represent between 25 and 90 percent of their customer base (Stockinger and Gutknecht 2014). Great Basin Community Food Co-op in Reno, Nevada, works with 101 local suppliers, selling 10,327 pounds of local meat, 3,904 pounds of local honey, and 4,444 pounds of local tomatoes each year. At City Market in Vermont, of the co-op's $52.1 million in sales, 41

* Revenue figures, supplier numbers, and other quantities pertaining to specific food co-ops come from the author's own research, except where otherwise noted.

percent of sales were local products made in Vermont ($21.8M). See Table 4.

Defining Local

When Canadian regulators set out in 2013 to redefine the marketing of "local" from its previous requirement of 50 kilometers (31 miles) from point of origin, they chose to expand the definition to apply to products originating from anywhere within the entire province (or from 50 kilometers across provincial borders). Whereas in New Hampshire, "local" is defined as coming from an area no bigger than 9,349 square miles, the geographic range of "local" in British Columbia is over 40 times that. A jar of honey from Victoria can be sold in a store in Sparwood—a 14-hour drive along 660 miles of highway—and legally be marketed as "local."

Food co-ops have responded to the widening of the "local" definition by actively reminding their shoppers of what "local" means at their co-op. Examples of "local" definitions at food co-ops are Kootenay Co-op (Nelson, BC)—100-mile radius; Ashland Food Co-op (Ashland, OR)—200-mile radius; Medford Food Co-op (Medford, OR)—100-mile radius; Port Townsend Food Co-op (Port Townsend, WA)—"Local 5" = five counties / "Local WA" = Washington State; Placerville Food Co-op (Placerville, CA)—100-mile radius; San Juan Island Food Co-op (Friday Harbor, WA)—San Juan Islands.

Economic Impact

When the River Valley Co-op opened in Northampton, Massachusetts, at the height of the financial crisis in 2008, one dairy farmer told the store that they likely would have lost their farm had the co-op not opened and featured their brand. In their first year, River Valley's purchases of local product exceeded $1 million. Ten years later, local purchases had tripled.

The contributions of local food purchases to a local economy through the multiplier effect are substantial. At Weaver Street Market Co-op in North Carolina, the co-op recorded annual sales of 1.44 million local eggs, 29,050 containers of local berries, and 212,643 loaves of local organic bread. Resulting from these purchases of local product, Weaver Street tracks an extra $10 million of additional spending in their local economy compared to the same dollars spent at chain stores. Civic Economics (2017: 5) calculated that for every dollar spent at a conventional store, 23 cents was recirculated locally. At the average co-op nationally—36 cents. At Central Co-op in Seattle—52 cents.

Table 4
Local Suppliers at Food Co-ops

	Number of Local Suppliers	Annual Sales of Local Products
Brattleboro Food Co-op (VT)	450	$4M
Co-op Food Stores (NH/VT)	300	$13M
Hunger Mountain Co-op (VT)	500	$8.7M
Middlebury Natural Foods Co-op (VT)	300	$4.7M
Monadnock Food Co-op (NH)	374	$3.7M
River Valley Co-op (MA)	403	$6M
Viroqua Food Co-op (WI)	200	$2.5M

SOURCE: Interviews conducted by author.

Local Food System Stimulation

Food co-ops actively stimulate the development of local food systems beyond the purchase of local products. Vermont's Putney Food Co-op hosts farmers' markets directly on site. Other co-ops have positioned themselves as pickup locations for community-supported-agriculture (CSA) box programs like Eastside Food Co-op (Minnesota) and Mississippi Market (Minnesota). The Merc Co-op (Kansas) has been a pickup location for 300 members of the Rolling Prairie CSA since 1994. Mississippi Market is a pickup location for a community-supported bakery. Seward Co-op (Minnesota) hosts an annual CSA Fair—linking consumers with CSA farms. In 2018, 27 farms participated. By supporting these alternative channels, co-ops are supporting the continued existence of their suppliers and cultivating "food-system ecosystems."

Micro lending to suppliers is another initiative food co-ops engage in. At Chequamegon Food Co-op (Wisconsin), a micro-lending program provides loans to local food producers looking to expand their businesses. Loans have supported a drinkable yogurt product from a local dairy, the acquisition of a grain mill, and a poultry processing trailer. The co-op caps loans at $5,000 with three-year terms. At City Market (Vermont), a $40,000, five-year, no-interest loan helped support the Vermont Tortilla Company, a corn chip manufacturer that uses 90 percent Vermont corn. Since 2000, Community Food Co-op (Washington) has dedicated a portion of its budget to food and farm projects. With the support of other local funding agencies and credit unions, the fund has financed 50 projects to the tune of $245,000. Following the recession of 2007–2008, North Coast Co-op (California) partnered with Tofu Shop Specialty Foods by lending it the money to purchase organic soy beans in bulk. Tofu Shop applied a credit to its invoices to pay back the investment. Monadnock Food Co-op (New Hampshire) launched a Farm Fund in 2017 in partnership with its regional municipality. The fund has awarded grants to local farms producing dairy, pork, beef, and root crops. At the Kootenay Co-op (British Columbia), 3 percent of sales is donated once per month to a local nonprofit. The Kootenay Organic Growers Society (KOGS) represents 25 local farmers, and, each year, KOGS is a donation-day recipient. The single-day contribution has come to represent 25 percent of KOGS' annual budget.

Planning the Co-op Shelves with Local Producers

A clear example of food co-ops' commitments to their suppliers are the seasonal planning meetings some co-ops host with local farmers. Whereas the dominant food system leaves one supplier pitted against another—both vying for the same shelf space—some food co-ops actively bring farmers together in a more collaborative approach. Each winter at the North Coast Co-op, farmers meet directly with co-op staff to plan out the season. The planning process allows farmers to understand the co-op's needs for the coming year and avoid under- or over-planting. North Coast Co-op periodically asks its more than 200 local suppliers: "Did we pay promptly, did we pay a fair price, and did we represent your product in the best light?" At Hanover Co-op (New Hampshire/Vermont), crop-planning meetings date back to 1998. When General Manager Terry Appleby first arrived at the co-op in 1992, he was shocked at the glut of local pumpkins on display and yet there was not one head of locally grown broccoli to be found. Hanover's grower meetings enable greater on-farm efficiencies. Farmers discuss their capacities for the season and determine who is in the best position to grow what and by when. By planning out the season with each other, the grower meetings help curb the inefficiencies of a poorly coordinated local food market. "Before the growers' meetings, you'd practically be throwing seeds in the ground and hope you have a market for it in the summer," says one of Hanover's farmers. "The model of working together takes care of 90 percent of the certainty of profit—the other 10 percent is the weather." Hanover is successfully bringing stability and predictability to small-scale farming.

Anchors for Place-Based Food Systems: Case Study 1—Kootenay Co-op

In its 2019 fiscal year, the Kootenay Co-op in Nelson, British Columbia, paid \$2.96 million to 151 suppliers within its "true local" region (generally a 60-mile radius), representing 18 percent of its total payments. (See Table 5.) The co-op's "true local" program employs two staff who work directly with local suppliers to support them in growing their businesses. The co-op is an incubator of the local food system. In a city with a population of only 10,664 and a regional population near 80,000, the impacts of a grocery store like this on a rural, place-based food system are considerable.

Table 5
Sales of True Local Products at Kootenay Co-op, 2019

Organic milk & cream	84,000 liters
Bread	38,100 loaves
Organic eggs	607,200
Organic potatoes	23,600 pounds
Organic carrots	62,900 pounds
Meat	65,800 pounds

Source: Author's working knowledge.

Nelson's grocery store landscape is not so dissimilar to that of any town or large urban center. Nelson is home to three grocery giants: Safeway (Sobeys), Save-On-Foods (Jim Pattison Group), and Wholesale Club (Loblaw). A small selection of groceries is also found at Shoppers Drug Mart (Loblaw) and at Walmart (not a Supercenter).

In the shadows of Nelson's grocery giants is a vibrant local food economy. The Kootenay Co-op has played a pivotal role as a hub for its development. See Table 6.

Farmers' markets happen weekly in almost all West Kootenay communities. Nelson alone hosts two of them each week, with one shutting down an entire block of the city's downtown. A century-old heritage warehouse in the city is home to the Nelson Brewing Company, one of Canada's first certified organic breweries; Oso Negro, a fair-trade organic coffee roaster; Kutenai Chai, supplying restaurants, coffee shops, and retailers with chai tea; Silverking Soya Foods, organic tofu; and the Nelson Flour Milling Co-op, a cooperatively owned flour mill where shareholders mill organic grains grown in the nearby Creston Valley. Outside the city exists an unusually large number of organic farmers. In the nearby Creston Valley, a locally grown grain economy has emerged,

Table 6
Kootenay Co-op—By the Numbers

Total sales (2019)	\$23.6M
Retail sq. ft.	20,000
Member-owners	14,000+
Payments to businesses in local region	\$4.2M (25% of payments)
Payments to suppliers in local region	\$2.96M
Payments within British Columbia	\$9.54M (83% of total payments)
Employees	180
Full time	110
Wages and benefits	\$5.4M
Community donations	\$145,332
Community groups supported	169

Source: Author's working knowledge.

bolstered by the formation in 2008 of Canada's first CSA program for grain. In its second year, the Kootenay Grain CSA was delivering 100-pound shares of organically grown heritage wheats, oats, lentils, and dry peas to 450 families and a dozen businesses. With the West Kootenay region once famous for its fruit orchards, the West Kootenay Permaculture Co-op Association (WKPCA) supports the orchardists of today by coordinating a mobile juice press to travel between communities. The WKPCA also organizes annual conferences with sector-specific themes like "livestock and meat processing" or "herbs and plant medicines." It coordinates monthly educational activities, like local root cellar tours, and it operates a mobile classroom. Once a year, more than 40 local food businesses sponsor a multi-day food documentary film festival centered in Nelson and hosted in other West Kootenay communities. The festival curates films to inspire residents to be more active in the region's food culture and economy.

As with any thriving local food economy like this, a hub is necessary to help incubate, communicate, and centralize activity. The Kootenay Co-op serves this role. Formed in 1975 as a buying club, the co-op is today owned by more than 14,000 people and generated $23.6 million in 2019. By either incubating them, purchasing from them, or donating food or financial resources to them, the co-op has, in one way or another, partnered with all of the businesses and organizations discussed here. No other food organization in the region has been so integrated into all aspects of the region's food economy. Whereas other local food economies may require sector-wide support through a nonprofit, charity, or a food council of volunteers (all of whose futures depend on the precarious nature of government funding, grants, and donations), the West Kootenay's food system is reinforced by the most important link in the chain—a grocery store.

Incubating Food Producers

By not requiring prohibitive fees to access their shelves, food co-ops allow products to be brought to market at far less cost, which allows local entrepreneurs to innovate and take risks. When Lana and Brad Braun purchased Hummingbird Farm in the Slocan Valley of British Columbia, they constructed a commercial kitchen. The kitchen would enable them to process product from the farm into higher-value foods like tomatillo and tomato salsas. When the Brauns walked into the Kootenay Co-op and described their vision, without hesitation the co-op agreed to take whatever they could produce. The commitment provided the Brauns the security they needed to make investments, and they began to experiment with small batches of products. The co-op effectively became a research and development testing ground for their start-up business. One successful product was their pickled beets, delivered in bulk for the co-op's self-serve tapas bar. During one of the Braun's deliveries, a co-op manager pointed out other items in the tapas bar that were being imported from Europe but that could easily be made locally. This led Hummingbird to begin producing sweet pickled peppers and pickled beans. The local food system was evolving right on the floor of the retail space. Spontaneous purchases of local product are common at food co-ops—quite different than the average 6 to 12 months required to bring new products to market at chain retailers. When Hummingbird had grown an oversupply of tomatoes, it transformed the surplus into sundried tomatoes and the co-op took the product without question. To help ensure Hummingbird's products sell, the co-op provides prime shelf space. At other retailers, Hummingbird must first convince them that they should sell the product, and, if it is not successful in two weeks, the product is discontinued. At the co-op, when a product is not selling, co-op staff work with Hummingbird to reevaluate the approach to product quality and labeling.

These types of supportive buyer-supplier relationships within local food systems are common at all food co-ops. Financially, the Kootenay Co-op wants local suppliers to succeed. When the co-op puts local products on special, the price the co-op pays the supplier does not change. Other retailers will often require local suppliers to absorb the discount.

Local Economy and the Multiplier Effect

A portion of every local food dollar spent at a grocery store ends up in the hands of the people who produce the food. They, in turn, go out and spend that portion in myriad ways—some of it for expenses incurred by the business itself, the rest for personal expenditures. Of the portion spent on the business, the more local the supplier is, the greater the chance that those expenditures will recirculate back into the local economy and support other local businesses. Website design, legal services, financial consultants, label printing, advertising in local community newspapers—this is the local multiplier effect of food dollars when they are used to purchase local foods.

Two other local food producers who have been supported in their ventures by the Kootenay Co-op are Uphill Bakery and Valerie's Fermented Foods. Beringer bakes baguettes and sourdough breads for the bakery. Partner Sanderson prepares sauerkraut and soups for the fermented food business. Their combined sales of $108,000 are small, but they are comfortable operating at that scale. The sauerkraut business exists only as a result of sustained support by the Kootenay Co-op, which packaged her product for the first five years and helped to print off her product labels. The co-op's marketing department also helped Beringer with the redesign of his Uphill Bakery labels.

For every dollar spent on Sanderson's sauerkrauts and soups, a portion ends up in the pockets of other local farmers: one who provides cabbage, another who grows carrots, potatoes, and beets, a third who supplies parsnips and zucchini, and a fourth who grows onions. Another portion of the food dollar ends up at various independent businesses that sell labels, office supplies, and computers. The same principle applies to personal expenditures: shoes, bicycles, beer, skis, sushi, coffee, movies, and professional services. At the center of this local economy is the Kootenay Co-op, which has fostered a thriving community of local businesses that recirculate a portion of every food dollar in Nelson to other local businesses.

These examples demonstrate a powerful lesson. The survival of community depends on the ability of a local economy to sustain itself. That, in turn, requires the development of local businesses that can produce goods for local consumption that were formerly imported from other regions or nations. Some leakage from the local economy will always occur, as residents buy goods from other places, but if the leakage is so high that investment in the local economy is determined by distant financial centers, then the economic basis of community disappears. Co-ops are one anchor of local communities, as we have seen. Credit unions are another anchor because they prevent investment capital being siphoned away from small towns into regional and national banking centers.

Anchors for Place-Based Food Systems: Case Study 2—Viroqua Food Co-op

As the county seat of a rural agricultural community, Viroqua, Wisconsin's population of 4,400 has used a place-based economy built around a food co-op to stave off the decimation of the farm economy and the hollowing out of the town's businesses and employers. Many towns of this size in the United States have simply vanished as small, integrated farms were bought by larger monoculture operators, labor was displaced by machines, and the young adults emigrated to the city in search of work. The explanation for the success of this town is rooted in food culture. The region surrounding Viroqua is home to more organic farms per capita than anywhere in the country.

Viroqua is home to three full-service grocers—a Walmart Supercenter, a store that is part of a small regional grocery chain, and a food co-op. The Viroqua Food Co-op (VFC) is an important hub helping to incubate the local food economy. Founded in 1995 in a 700 sq. ft. space, the co-op has grown steadily and is owned by more than 4,000 members (equal to the town's population), and generates $7.96 million in sales (2019) out of its newer 9,200 sq. ft. store completed in 2018. Using the multiplier effect, VFC projects its $7.96 million in sales generates $12.7 millon in total economic activity. Of its sales revenue, $2.1 million was from the sale of local products—defined as originating from within a 100-mile radius. See Table 7.

Food Enterprise Center

The Viroqua Food Co-op (VFC) has served as a testing ground for the many food producers operating out of Viroqua's Food Enterprise Center (FEC). In 2019, VFC sold $223,000 of product made by local food producers operating in the FEC. In 2009, when tech giant NCR shuttered its Viroqua factory, 80 jobs disappeared. When the Chamber of Commerce failed to attract new owners to the facility, the Vernon Economic Development Association acquired the property and turned the 100,000 square foot factory into a Food Enterprise Center. The center is home to 23 food-based businesses with dedicated and shared space for food processing, distribution, and storage. Tenants include Wisco-Pop—organic craft-brewed soda; B&E's Trees—bourbon-barrel-aged maple syrup; Plovgh—agricultural coordinator connecting the region's farmers and food producers; and Fifth Season Cooperative (FSC)—a multi-stakeholder distribution cooperative for local food producers. FSC aggregates and coordinates delivery for its local food-producer members to restaurants, institutions, and co-op grocery stores in Madison, Milwaukee, Chicago, and Minneapolis-St. Paul. FSC is owned by 62 small farms, six farmer/producer groups, 25 processors, four distributors, and thousands of buyers. Buyer members include institutions like Gundersen Health System, Mayo Clinic Health System, Reedsburg Area Medical Center, University of Wisconsin, and area school districts. VFC's general manager was a founding advisory council member for FSC.

Micro Lending

VFC incubates local food producers beyond the shelves by annually awarding one zero-interest loan to local food producers. In 2017, for example, VFC loaned $3,500 to Deep Rooted, a local certified organic farm that supplies $18,775 worth of tomatoes to the co-op between May and October. The loan helped the farm construct a walk-in cooler on the farm to expand its production into greens, vegetables, and cut flowers and to extend the shelf life of its produce.

In 2018, a zero-interest loan for $3,500 went to local certified organic maple-syrup producer B&E's Trees. B&E's produces certified organic bourbon-barrel-aged maple syrup, using repurposed bourbon barrels to age the syrup. When the syrup is mature, B&E's sends the maple-soaked barrels to Central Waters Brewing in Amherst, Wisconsin, which then uses them to age its maple-barrel stout. The micro loan helped B&E's turn a space at the

Table 7
Viroqua Food Co-ops – By the Numbers

Total sales (2019)	$7.96M
Retail sq ft	9,500
Member-owners	4,000+
Sales of local products (from within 100-miles)	$2.1M (27% of total sales)
Portion of total sales that are certified organic	46%
Portion of fresh produce sales that are certified organic	99%
Local organic farms as suppliers	68
Local food producers as suppliers	200+
Employees	69
Full time	58

Source: Author's working knowledge.

Food Enterprise Center into a maple-syrup-aging rickhouse—a traditional facility where whiskey is aged in barrels. The project allowed B&E's to increase its maple-syrup-aging capacity.

Anchors for Place-Based Food Systems: Case Study 3—Minneapolis/St. Paul Co-ops

The concentration of food co-ops in the Minneapolis–St. Paul metro area is one of the highest of any urban center in North America. There are 10 independent co-ops, operating in 17 locations. (See Table 8.) Stockinger and Gutknecht (2014) present the most recent analysis of the collective impact of these food co-ops on local food producers:

> A multi-level cooperative system built over a period of 40 years, this local food value chain comprises well over 300 producers, a cooperatively owned distributor of organic product, and 15 consumer cooperatives operating 17 retail food stores, backed by 91,000 co-op member-owners and an additional 50,000 shoppers. In the year leading up to this study, total retail sales through this cooperative system were $179 [million], with local product accounting for 30 percent of sales, or around $54 [million]. Local farm gate income (income flowing to producers) after distributor and retail margins is estimated to be over half of those local sales, or $30 [million].

At the time of the study, food producers directly delivered 60 percent of local purchases by food co-ops. Another 20 percent was delivered by privately owned distributors. The remaining 20 percent was through Co-op Partners Warehouse (CPW). CPW is a certified organic regional distributor founded in 1999 and owned by one of the more successful Minneapolis food co-ops—Wedge Community Co-op. CPW is the last distributor of its kind in the United States and plays an integral role in the Twin Cities local food economy—serving food co-ops,

Table 8
2012–2013 Retail Co-op Local Sales and Purchases by Grocery Category in the Twin Cities (MN)

Category	% of Total Sales	Category (millions)	Local Sales %	Local Sales (millions)	Farm Gate Payments* (millions)
Meats	9%	$15.9	72%	$11.4	$7.4
Produce	20%	$35.2	25%	$9.0	$5.3
Refrigerated (incl. dairy)	11%	$19.2	45%	$8.7	$5.7
Packaged	21%	$37.4	8%	$2.9	$1.7
Deli (incl. cheese)	13%	$23.6	51%	$11.9	$5.0
Health & beauty care	10%	$18.5	8%	$1.6	$0.8
Frozen	4%	$7.5	8%	$0.6	$0.4
Bulk	9%	$15.3	30%	$4.6	$2.6
Bread	2%	$4.3	60%	$2.6	$1.7
Other	1%	$1.6	42%	$0.7	$0.2
Total all metro stores	100%	$178.6	30%	$53.9	$30.9

Source: Stockinger and Gutknecht (2014).
*Farm gate is the income that is paid to farmers. Farm gate income is calculated here as retail sales minus retail and distributor margins.

independent retailers, foodservice businesses, and buying clubs in six states. One of the unique services it offers to food producers is cross-docking. Whereas CPW purchases most of its products direct from the supplier, there are 33 local food producers (mostly farmers) who use CPW for logistics only, by paying a fee to CPW to distribute their products to food co-ops for them. Rather than a food producer distributing their products to multiple food co-ops in the metro area, or losing margin by selling through a distributor, these food producers are able to make a single trip to CPW's warehouse in St. Paul. CPW puts the products on trucks that are already frequenting the food co-ops. This model enables food producers to only pay for CPW's delivery of the product, thereby avoiding the added costs of warehousing, distributor marketing, and the loss of margin. CPW is a unique example of the potential for retail food co-ops to incubate strong local food economies.

Conclusion

The grocery retail sector plays a crucial role in the health of individuals, the social health of communities, and the economic viability of food producers. The corporate chain-store model, dedicated, above all, to increasing profits for corporate shareholders, is not suited to safeguarding the best interests of consumers, food producers, or communities. The need for greater community control over food is becoming more apparent as grocery stores disappear from urban and rural neighborhoods alike, or are acquired by larger chains.

For much of the previous century, the dangers of corporate concentration in retail were well understood and many legislated provisions were used to protect consumers, businesses, and local economies. But in recent decades the restrictions on chain stores have been almost entirely removed, and market concentration in grocery retail has grown rapidly. This tremendous liberalizing of the market has dealt significant harm to food producers, especially small- and mid-scale food producers.

Consumer-owned grocery stores (food co-ops), though still a small part of the food-retail business, have been providing an extremely important alternative for consumers and food producers alike. There are strong examples of how new and existing food co-ops are growing and expanding their businesses and growing place-based food systems. Their successes can be found in communities of all sizes and locations and are enabling consumers to exert greater control over the food available in their communities. For consumers seeking to support their local food systems and economies, food co-ops are a highly accessible venue to do so—open seven days a week, 365 days a year.

Glossary

Food Co-op

The term "food co-op" is most often used in reference to cooperatively owned retail grocery stores. The term is sometimes used to describe unincorporated food buying clubs or agricultural cooperatives. Its use in this article specifically refers to consumer-owned retail grocery stores that are formally incorporated as cooperatives.

Food Producer

This term is used to describe any supplier of a food or beverage product that is supplied to a retailer. A food producer, for example, could be a farmer, fisher, rancher, coffee roaster, ice-cream maker, baker, or juice manufacturer.

References

Baker, Mike. (2016). "Kroger Market Share Across the Country." *Chain Store Guide* April 25. http://newsroom.chainstoreguide.com/2016/04/kroger-market-share-across-the-country/

Basker, Emek, and Michael Noel. (2009). "The Evolving Food Chain: Competitive Effects of Wal-Mart's Entry into the Supermarket Industry." *Journal of Economics & Management Strategy* 18(4): 977–1009. https://doi.org/10.1111/j.1530-9134.2009.00235.x

Behr, Peter. (1988). "Wave of Mergers, Takeovers is a Part of Reagan Legacy." *Washington Post* October 30. https://www.washingtonpost.com/archive/business/1988/10/30/wave-of-mergers-takeovers-is-a-part-of-reagan-legacy/e90598c2-628d-40fe-b9c6-a621e298671d/

Bennett, John W. (1949). "Reviewed Works: *As You Sow: Small Business and the Community: A Study in Central Valley of California on Effects of Scale of Farm Operations* by Walter R. Goldschmidt." *American Anthropologist* 51(1): 118–123.

Bhattarai, Abha. (2018). "Whole Foods Places New Limits on Suppliers, Upsetting Some Small Vendors." *Washington Post* January 5.

Butler, Sarah. (2016). "Tesco Delayed Payments to Suppliers to Boost Profits, Watchdog Finds." *Guardian* January 26.

Carameli, Leo S. Jr. (2004). "The Anti-Competitive Effects and Antitrust Implications of Category Management and Category Captains of Consumer Products." *Chicago-Kent Law Review* 79: 1313–1356.

Chain Store Guide. (2018). *Directory of Supermarket, Grocery & Convenience Store Chains.* Tampa, FL: Chain Store Guide.

Chidmi, Benaissa, and Olga Murova. (2011). "Measuring Market Power in the Supermarket Industry: The Case of the Seattle-Tacoma Fluid Milk Market." *Agribusiness* 27(4): 435–449. https://doi.org/10.1002/agr.20276

Civic Economics. (2017). *Central Co-op: Feeding the Washington Economy.* Seattle, WA: Central Co-op. https://www.centralcoop.coop/docs/Feeding_the_Washington_Economy_2017.pdf

de Munter, Jeroen S. L., Frank B. Hu, Donna Spiegelman, Mary Franz, and Rob M. van Dam. (2007). "Whole Grain, Bran, and Germ Intake and Risk of Type 2 Diabetes: A Prospective Cohort Study and Systematic Review." *PLoS Medicine* 4(8): e261. https://doi.org/10.1371/journal.pmed.0040261

Draeger, Kathryn, Karen Lanthier, Caryn Mohr, and Nich Tremper. (2016). *The Future of Rural Grocery Stores.* St. Paul, MN: University of Minnesota Extension. https://extension.umn.edu/vital-connections/future-rural-grocery-stores

Ellickson, Paul. (2011). "The Evolution of the Supermarket Industry: From A&P to Wal-Mart." In *Handbook on the Economics of Retail and Distribution.* Ed. Emek Basker, pp. 368–391. Northampton, MA: Edward Elgar. https://doi.org/10.2139/ssrn.1814166

F&D Reports. (2017). "Publix Super Markets, Inc." *Strategic Sales Insights.* Great Neck, NY: F&D Reports. https://www.fdreports.com/reports/29824.pdf

Fiechtner, Lauren, Ken Kleinman, Steven J. Melly, Mona Sharifi, Richard Marshall, Jason Block, Erika R. Cheng, and Elsie M. Taveras. (2016). "Effects of Proximity to Supermarkets on a Randomized Trial

Studying Interventions for Obesity." *American Journal of Public Health* 106(3): 557–562. https://doi.org/10.2105/AJPH.2015.302986

Food & Water Watch. (2014). *In re: Proposed Albertsons-Safeway Supermarket Merger* [letter to Federal Trade Commission]. April 7. Washington, DC: Food & Water Watch. https://www.foodandwaterwatch.org/sites/default/files/albertsons_safeway_merger_comment.pdf

Goldschmidt, Walter. (1949). *Small Business and the Community: A Study in Central Valley of California on Effects of Scale of Farm Operations.* Report of the Special Committee to Study Problems of American Small Business, U.S. Senate, Seventy-Ninth Congress, Second Session, Pursuant to S. Res. 28 (Extending S. Res. 298–76th Congress), a Resolution to Appoint a Special Committee to Study and Survey Problems of American Small Business Enterprises, December 23. Washington: U.S. Government Printing Office. https://books.google.com/books?id=BDNDAQAAMAAJ

Green, Jeff. (2017). *Grocery Wars Intensify in Texas.* Phoenix, AZ: Jeff Green Partners. https://www.jeffgreen-partners.com/grocery-wars-intensify-in-texas/

Hosken, Daniel S., Luke M. Olson, and Loren K. Smith. (2018). "Do Retail Mergers Affect Competition? Evidence from Grocery Retailing." *Journal of Economics & Management Strategy* 27(1): 3–22. https://doi.org/10.1111/jems.12218

Intergovernmental Panel on Climate Change (IPCC). (2020). *Climate Change and Land.* Geneva, Switzerland: IPCC. https://www.ipcc.ch/site/assets/uploads/sites/4/2020/02/SPM_Updated-Jan20.pdf

Jennings, Marianne. (2015). *Business Ethics: Case Studies and Selected Readings*, 8th ed. Stamford, CT: Cengage Learning.

Karst, Tom. (2018). "H-E-B Controls South Texas Market Share." *Packer* January 22. https://www.thepacker.com/article/h-e-b-controls-south-texas-market-share

Levinson, Marc. (2013). *The Great A&P and the Struggle for Small Business in America.* New York: Farrar, Straus and Giroux.

Longman, Phillip. (2015). "Why the Economic Fates of America's Cities Diverged." *Atlantic* November 28. https://www.theatlantic.com/business/archive/2015/11/cities-economic-fates-diverge/417372/

Lynn, Barry C. (2006). "The Antitrust Case Against Wal-Mart." *Chesterton Review* 32(3): 538–542. https://doi.org/10.5840/chesterton2006323/443

Mangino, Evan, and Maria Arbulu. (2018). *Canada Retail Foods: Retail Sector Overview—2018.* Global Agricultural Information Network (GAIN) Report: CA18039. Washington, DC: U.S. Department of Agriculture, Foreign Agricultural Service. https://apps.fas.usda.gov/newgainapi/api/report/downloadreportbyfilename?filename=Retail%20Foods_Ottawa_Canada_6-26-2018.pdf

Marion, Bruce W. (1986). *The Organization and Performance of the U.S. Food System.* Lexington, MA: Lexington: Books.

Markusoff, Jason. (2018). "Loblaws' Price-Fixing May Have Cost You at Least $400." *Macleans.ca* January 11. https://www.macleans.ca/economy/economicanalysis/14-years-of-loblaws-bread-price-fixing-may-have-cost-you-at-least-400/

Martens, Bobby J. (2008). "The Effect of Entry by Wal-Mart Supercenters on Retail Grocery Concentration." *Journal of Food Distribution Research* 39(3): 1–16.

Mitchell, Stacy. (2019). *Walmart's Monopolization of Local Grocery Markets.* Washington, DC: Institute for Local Self-Reliance. June 26. https://ilsr.org/walmarts-monopolization-of-local-grocery-markets/

National Farmers Union [of Canada] (NFU). (2005). *The Farm Crisis: Its Causes and Solutions: The National Farmers Union's Submission to the Ministers of Agriculture Meeting.* Kananakis, Alberta: NFU. https://www.nfu.ca/wp-content/uploads/2018/05/2005-07-05-Ministers_of_Ag_brief_FOUR. pdf

Peck, Clint. (2003). "The Price Spread Debate." *Beef Magazine* January 1.

PricewaterhouseCoopers. (2007). "The Economic Contribution of Small to Medium-Sized Grocery Retailers to the Australian Economy, with a Particular Focus on Western Australia." Submitted to Australian Competition & Consumer Commission. Hurstville, New South Wales: National Association of Retail Grocers of Australia. https://www.accc.gov.au/system/files/014%20-%20National%20Association%20 of%20Retail%20 Grocers%20of%20Australia%20%2859%20pages%29.pdf

Rennard, Barbara O., Ronald F. Ertl, Gail L. Gossman, Richard A. Robbins, and Stephen I. Rennard. (2000). "Chicken Soup Inhibits Neutrophil Chemotaxis In Vitro." *Chest* 118(4): 1150–1157. https://doi.org/10.1378/chest.118.4.1150

Rivlin, Gary. (2016). *Rigged: Supermarket Shelves for Sale.* Washington, DC: Center for Science in the Public Interest. https://cspinet.org/sites/default/files/attachment/CSPI_Rigged_4_small.pdf

Roosevelt, Franklin D. (1938). *Message to Congress on Curbing Monopolies.* Santa Barbara, CA: University of California at Santa Barbara, American Presidency Project. http://www.presidency.ucsb.edu/ws/?pid=15637

Schnepf, Randy. (2013). *Farm-to-Food Price Dynamics.* CRS Report for Congress: R40621. Washington, DC: Congressional Research Service. https://fas.org/sgp/crs/misc/R40621.pdf

Sexton, Richard J. (2010). "Grocery Retailers' Dominant Role in Evolving World Food Markets." *Choices: The Magazine of Food, Farm, and Resource Issues, Agricultural and Applied Economics Association* 25(2): 1–13. https://doi.org/10.22004/ag.econ.94763

Stampfer, Meir J., Frank B. Hu, Jo Ann E. Manson, Eric B. Rimm, and Walter C. Willett. (2000). "Primary Prevention of Coronary Heart Disease in Women Through Diet and Lifestyle." *New England Journal of Medicine* 343(1): 16–22. https://doi.org/10.1056/NEJM200007063430103

Stockinger, Joan, and Dave Gutknecht. (2014). *The Twin Cities Cooperative Local Food System: A Case Study and Commentary.* St. Paul, MN: Cooperative Development Services (CDS). https://www.crcworks.org/tccoops.pdf

U.S. Department of Agriculture, Economic Research Service (USDA-ERS). (2017). *Global Food Industry.* Washington, DC: USDA-ERS. https://web.archive.org/web/20170821183913/http://www.ers.usda.gov/topics/international-markets-trade/global-food-markets/global-food-industry.aspx

________. (2019a). *Farm Household Income Forecast.* Washington, DC: U.S. Department of Agriculture. https://www.ers.usda.gov/topics/farm-economy/farm-household-well-being/farm-household-income-forecast/

________. (2019b). *Retail Trends.* Washington, DC: U.S. Department of Agriculture. https://www.ers.usda.gov/topics/food-markets-prices/retailing-wholesaling/retail-trends/

________. (2020). *Food Dollar Series.* Washington, DC: U.S. Department of Agriculture. https://www.ers.usda.gov/data-products/food-dollar-series/

U.S. Federal Trade Commission (US-FTC). (2005). *Category Management: An Interview with FTC Commissioner Thomas B. Leary.* Washington, DC: US- FTC. https://www.ftc.gov/public-statements/2005/03/category-management-interview-ftc-commissioner-thomas-b-leary

U.S. Securities and Exchange Commission (US-SEC). (2015). *Safeway Inc.: Form 10-K for Fiscal Year Ended January 3, 2015.* March 4. Washington, DC: US-SEC. https://www.sec.gov/Archives/edgar/data/86144/000008614415000004/swy-1315x10k.htm

________. (2018). *The Kroger Co., Form 10-K for Fiscal Year Ended February 3, 2018.* April 3, 2018. Washington, DC: US-SEC. https://www.sec.gov/Archives/edgar/data/56873/000155837018002753/kr-20180203x10k.htm

United States v. Von's Grocery Co. (1966). 384 U.S. 270. https://supreme.justia.com/cases/federal/us/384/270/

Volpe, Richard. (2011). *The Relationship Between National Brand and Private Label Food Products: Prices, Promotions, Recessions, and Recoveries.* Economic Research Report 129. Washington, DC: U.S. Department of Agriculture, Economic Research Service. https://pdfs.semanticscholar. org/986a/993df7bdf0aa5504241c66accdb63e6ebfa0.pdf?_ga=2.198954223.1169034986.1586029959-760066268.1575783597

Watkins, Steve. (2015). "Kroger Discloses Cincinnati Market Share: 'We Use it as a Benchmark'." *Cincinnati Business Courier* October 29.

Part III
Generation, Transportation and Education

CHAPTER 9

Reorienting the Economy to the Rhythms of Nature: Learning to Live with Intermittent Energy Supply

*Kris De Decker**

Abstract. In much current thinking about the necessary and rapid transition to a carbon-emissions-free energy system, there is implicit acceptance of the high-tech, high-energy nature of the current economy. But by asking deeper questions about this economy, we reveal new opportunities as well as new challenges. First, throughout most of history, both production and consumption were dramatically influenced by the weather, and activities were undertaken or curtailed according to varying availability of energy. In the future, if we again adjust energy demand to such intermittent supplies wherever and whenever possible, we can nevertheless benefit from many scientific and technological advantages that our ancestors did not have centuries ago. Second, in the pursuit of highly energy-efficient machines that might become new sources of highly concentrated energy, we have begun to rely on "clean energy" machinery made in significant part from non-recyclable materials. With our current generation of wind turbines, for example, we have sacrificed sustainability in the pursuit of a supposedly renewable-energy system. By contrast, if we reduce our need for always-on energy sources by adjusting energy demand to intermittent energy supply, we can greatly reduce the overall energy infrastructure needed, and we will face less pressure to sacrifice sustainability.

Introduction

There are two assumptions that have become so basic to the current high-tech and high-energy economic system that they are seldom even thought about. First, we assume that natural environmental rhythms should not and cannot limit our activities. We expect to be able to count on the same amount of light at night as in daytime, to keep our houses the same temperature in winter as in summer, or to travel or perform work to the same extent regardless of season or weather. Second, efficiency is a supreme value, as long as "efficiency" is calculated according to the short-term criteria that ignore social and environmental consequences.

If we question both of these assumptions, we see new opportunities as well as new challenges. For example, we might think about how to run the economy by adjusting to the weather rather than ignoring it. If we adjusted expectations to allow variable work and travel schedules that are more weather- and season-dependent, we could dramatically reduce the need for energy-storage infrastructure. We could still provide some essential services 24 hours a day, 365 days a year. But if we do not assume that *all* goods and services must be available at all times, then the task of building a 100 percent renewable-energy economy is much less daunting.

However, if we question the short time-horizon

*Publisher and writer of *Low-Tech Magazine,* online since 2007 and now available in print as well. He lives in Barcelona, Spain. Email: kris@lowtechmagazine.com

of today's energy corporations—and not just the fossil-fuel interests—we can see that major components of the renewable-energy complex are achieving high "efficiency" by handing major problems off to future generations. The current wind-power "revolution," for example, claims both high energy efficiency and high economic returns. But the blades in a 5 MW wind turbine contain more than 50 tons of unrecyclable plastic—a major waste disposal issue for the next generation, especially if we build vast numbers of these turbines today. Old-fashioned windmills were not as thermodynamically efficient, but they also did not result in mountains of non-biodegradable garbage. So we should be asking how to make wind power sustainable again.

How to Run the Economy Based on the Weather

Throughout history until the Industrial Revolution, people adjusted their energy demand to a variable energy supply. Our global trade and transport system—which relied on sailboats—operated only when the wind blew, as did the mills that supplied our food and powered many manufacturing processes. The same approach could be very useful today, especially when improved by modern technology. In particular, factories and cargo transportation—such as ships and even trains—could be operated only when renewable energy is available. Adjusting energy demand to supply would make switching to renewable energy much more realistic than it is today.

Before the Industrial Revolution, both industry and transportation were largely dependent on intermittent renewable-energy sources. Water mills, windmills, and sailing boats have been in use since antiquity, but the Europeans brought these technologies to full development from the 1400s onwards. At their peak, right before the Industrial Revolution took off, there were an estimated 200,000 wind-powered mills and 500,000 water-powered mills in Europe (Heymann 1995: 20; Cech 2010: 18; De Decker 2009).

Initially, watermills and windmills were mainly used for grinding grain, a laborious task that had been done by hand for many centuries, first with the aid of stones and later with a rotary hand mill. However, soon water- and wind-powered mills were adapted to industrial processes like sawing wood, polishing glass, making paper, boring pipes, cutting marble, slitting metal, sharpening knives, crushing chalk, grinding mortar, making gunpowder, minting coins, and so on (Lucas 2006; Reynolds 2002; Hills 1996). Wind- and watermills also processed a host of agricultural products—pressing olives, hulling barley and rice, grinding spices and tobacco, and crushing linseed, rapeseed, and hempseed for cooking and lighting. So-called industrial watermills had been used in antiquity and were widely adopted in Europe by the 15th century, but "industrial windmills" appeared only in the 1600s in the Netherlands, a country that took wind power to the extreme. The Dutch even applied wind power to reclaim land from the sea, and the whole country was kept dry by intermittently operating windmills until 1850.

Even though it relied on intermittent wind sources, international trade was crucial to many European economies before the Industrial Revolution. The use of wind power for transportation—in the form of the sailboat—boomed from the 1500s onwards, when Europeans "discovered" new lands. Wind-powered transportation supported a robust, diverse, and ever-expanding international trading system in both bulk goods (such as grain, wine, wood, metals, ceramics, and preserved fish), luxury items (such as precious metals, furs, spices, ivory, silks, and medicine), and human slaves (Paine 2014).

The Dutch shipbuilding industry, which was centered around some 450 wind-powered sawmills, imported virtually all its naval stores from the Baltic: wood, tar, iron, hemp, and flax. Even the food supply could depend on wind-powered transportation. Towards the end of the 1500s, the Dutch imported 2,000 shiploads of grain per year from Gdansk (Paine 2014). Sailboats were also important for fishing.

Industrial Production on Intermittent Power

Although variable renewable-energy sources were critical to European society for 500 years before fossil fuels took over, there were no chemical batteries, no electric transmission lines, and no balancing capacity of fossil-fuel power plants to deal with the variable energy output of wind and water power. So, how did our ancestors deal with the large variability of renewable-power sources? To some extent, they were counting on technological solutions to match energy supply to energy demand, just as we do today. The water level in a river depends on the weather and the seasons. Boat mills and bridge mills were among the earliest technological fixes to this problem. They went up and down with the water level, which allowed them to maintain a more predictable operating regime (Lucas 2006; Reynolds 2002).

However, water power could also be stored for later use. Starting in the Middle Ages, dams were built to create mill ponds, a form of energy storage that is similar to today's hydropower reservoirs. The storage reservoirs evened out the flow of streams and ensured that water was available when it was needed (Reynolds 2002). One of the earliest large hydropower dams was the Cento dam in Italy (1450), which was 71 meters long and almost 6 meters high. By the 18th century, the largest dams were up to 260 meters long and 25 meters high, with power canals leading to dozens of waterwheels (Reynolds 2002).

But rivers could still dry out or freeze over for prolonged periods, rendering dams and adjustable water wheels useless. Furthermore, when one counted on windmills, no such technological fixes were available (Hills 1996). Although windmills had all kinds of internal mechanisms to adapt to sudden changes in wind speed and wind direction, wind power had no counterpart for the dam in water power. This explains why windmills became especially important in regions with dry climates, in flat countries, or in very cold areas, where water power was not available. In countries with good water resources, windmills only appeared when the increased demand for power created a crisis because the best water-power sites were already occupied.

A technological solution to the intermittency of both water and wind power was the "beast mill" or "horse mill." In contrast to wind and water power, horses, donkeys, or oxen could be counted on to supply power whenever it was required. However, beast mills were expensive and energy inefficient to operate: feeding a horse required land area capable of feeding eight humans (Sieferle and Osman 2001). Consequently, the use of animal power in large-scale manufacturing processes was rare. Beast mills were mostly used for the milling of grain or as a power source in small workshop settings, using draft animals (Lucas 2006).

Intermittent Wind Power and Historic Ocean Sailing

Obviously, beast mills were not a viable backup power source for sailing ships either. In principle, sailing boats could revert to human power when wind was not available. However, a sufficiently large rowing crew needed extra water and food, which would have limited the range of the ship, or its cargo capacity. Therefore, rowing was mainly restricted to battleships and smaller boats.

Because of their limited technological options for dealing with the variability of renewable-energy sources, our ancestors mainly resorted to a strategy that we have largely forgotten about: they adapted their energy demand to the variable energy supply. In other words, they accepted that renewable energy was not always available and acted accordingly. For example, windmills and sailboats were simply not operated when there was no wind. In industrial windmills, work was done whenever the wind blew, even if that meant that the miller had to work night and day, taking only short naps. For example, a document reveals that at the Union Mill in Cranbrook, England, the miller once had only three hours' sleep during a windy period lasting 60 hours (Hills 1996).

Freese (1957), in an account partly based on interviews with the last surviving millers, reveals the urgency of using wind when it was available:

> Often enough when the wind blew in autumn, the miller would work from Sunday midnight to Tuesday evening, Wednesday morning to Thursday night, and Friday morning to Saturday midnight, taking only a few snatches of

> sleep; and a good windmiller always woke up in bed when the wind rose, getting up in the middle of the night to set the mill going, because the wind was his taskmaster and must be taken advantage of whenever it blew. Many a village has at times gone short of wheaten bread because the local mill was becalmed in a waterless district before the invention of the steam engine; and barley-meal bread or even potato bread had to suffice in the crisis of a windless autumn.

In earlier, more conservative times, the miller was punished for working on Sunday, but he did not always care. When a protest against Sunday work was made to Mr. Wade of Wicklewood towermill, Norfolk, he retorted: "If the Lord is good enough to send me wind on a Sunday, I'm going to use it" (Wailes 1954). On the other hand, when there was no wind, millers did other work, like maintaining their machinery, or took time off. Noah Edwards, the last miller of Arkley tower mill, Hertfordshire, would "sit on the fan stage of a fine evening and play his fiddle" (Wailes 1954).

A similar approach existed for overseas travel using sailboats. When there was no wind, sailors stayed ashore, maintained and repaired their ships, or did other things. They planned their trips according to the seasons, making use of favorable seasonal winds and currents.

Winds at sea are not only much stronger than those over land but also more predictable. The lower atmosphere of the planet is encircled by six major wind belts, three in each hemisphere. From Equator to poles these "prevailing winds" are the trade winds, the westerlies, and the easterlies. The six wind belts move north in the northern summer and south in the northern winter. Five major sea current gyres are correlated with the dominant wind flows. Gradually, European sailors deciphered the global pattern of winds and currents and took full advantage of them to establish new sea routes all over the world.

By the 1500s, Christopher Columbus had

Figure 1
Schooner *Thomas W. Lawson* Sailing Ship Carrying Cargo, Early 20th Century

Source: Painting in 1907 by Thomas Willis, oil on canvas with silk embroidery. Courtesy: Vallejo Gallery, Costa Mesa, CA. Image in public domain.
Note: This schooner, built in 1902, was the largest sailing vessel ever built without an auxiliary engine.

figured out that the combination of trade winds and westerlies enabled a round-trip route for sailing ships crossing the Atlantic Ocean. The trade winds reach their northernmost latitude at or after the end of the northern summer, bringing them in reach of Spain and Portugal. These summer trade winds made it easy to sail from southern Europe to the Caribbean and South America because the wind was blowing in that direction along the route. Taking the same route back would be nearly impossible. However, Iberian sailors first sailed north to catch the westerlies, which reach their southernmost location at or after the end of winter and carried the sailors straight back to southern Europe. In the 1560s, Basque explorer Andrés de Urdaneta discovered a similar round-trip route in the Pacific Ocean.

Figure 1 shows the *Thomas W. Lawson,* a seven-masted, steel-hulled schooner built in 1902 for the Pacific trade. It had a crew of 18. Her three desks running her entire length, accessed through six cargo hatches, allowed for a 7,500-ton capacity. She was the largest sailing vessel without an auxiliary engine ever built.

The global wind pattern is complemented by regional wind patterns, such as land and sea breezes. The Northern Indian Ocean has semi-annually reversing monsoon winds. These blow from the southwest from June to November, and from the northeast from December to May. Maritime trade in the Indian Ocean started earlier than in other seas, and the established trade routes were entirely dependent on the season.

The use of favorable winds made the travel times of sailboats relatively predictable. Jenkins (1973) mentions that typical passage times from New York to the English Channel for a mid-19th to early-20th century sailing vessel were 25 to 30 days. From 1818 to 1832, the fastest crossing was 21 days, the slowest 29 days. The journey from the English Channel to New York took 35–40 days in winter and 40–50 days in summer. To Cape Town, Melbourne, and Calcutta, trips took 50–60 days, 80–90 days, and 100–120 days, respectively. These travel times are double to triple those of today's container ships, which vary their speed based on oil prices and economic demand.

Fitting Demand to Supply Today

As a strategy to deal with variable energy sources, adjusting energy demand to renewable-energy supply is just as valuable a solution today as it was in pre-industrial times. However, this does not mean returning to pre-industrial methods. We have better technology available, which makes it much easier to synchronize the economic demands with the vagaries of the weather. In the following paragraphs, I investigate in more detail how industry and transportation could be operated on variable energy sources alone, and demonstrate how new technologies open new possibilities. I then conclude by analyzing the effects on consumers, workers, and economic growth.

On a global scale, industrial manufacturing accounts for nearly half of all energy end use. Many mechanical processes that were run by windmills are still important today, such as sawing, cutting, boring, drilling, crushing, hammering, sharpening, polishing, milling, turning, and so on. All these production processes can be run with an intermittent power supply. Figure 2 shows a small printing press that was operated at a public exhibition using only solar power.

The same goes for food production processes (mincing, grinding, or hulling grains, pressing olives and seeds), mining and excavation (picking and shoveling, rock and ore crushing), or textile production (fulling cloth, preparing fibers, knitting, and weaving). In all these examples, intermittent energy input does not affect the quality of the production process, only the production speed. Running these processes on variable power sources has become a lot easier than it was in earlier times. For one thing, wind-power plants are now completely automated, while the traditional windmill required constant attention. Windmillers had to be alert to keep the gap between the stones constant, however choppy the wind, and before the days of the centrifugal governor this was done by hand. The miller had to watch the power of the wind, to judge how much sail cloth to spread, and to be prepared to stop the mill under sail and either take in or let out more cloth, for there were no patent sails.

However, not only are wind turbines (and water turbines) more practical and powerful than in earlier times, we can now make use of kinetic wind energy to produce electricity. Likewise, we can use solar photovoltaic (PV) panels to convert sunlight into electricity. Consequently, a factory that requires mechanical energy can be run on a combination of wind and solar power, which increases the chances that there is sufficient energy to run its machinery. The ability to harvest solar energy is important because it is by far the most widely available renewable-power source. (Most of the potential capacity for water power is already taken.) Apart from electricity, the Industrial Revolution also brought us compressed air, water under pressure, and improved mechanical power transmission, which can all be valuable alternatives for electricity in certain applications.

Another crucial difference with pre-industrial times is that we can apply the same strategy to basic industrial processes that require thermal energy instead of mechanical energy. Heat dominates industrial energy use, for instance, in the making of chemicals or microchips, or in the smelting of metals. In pre-industrial times, manufacturing processes that required thermal energy were powered

Figure 2
Solar Printing Press, 1882

Le tirage d'un journal opéré par la chaleur solaire. Expérience executée par M. Abel Pifre dans le Jardin des Tuileries, à Paris, le 6 août 1882, lors de la fête de l'*Union française de la Jeunesse*.

Source: Tissandier (1882: 193) Public domain. Made available courtesy of Conservatoire numerique des Arts et Métiers, http://cnum.cnam.fr Inscription: Le tirage d'un journal opéré par la chaleur solaire. Expérience executée par M. Able Pifre dans le Jardin des Tuileries à Paris, le 6 août 1882, lors de la fête de l'Union française de la Jeunesse. (Printing a magazine with solar power (heat). Production carried out by Able Pifre in the Tuileries Garden in Paris on August 6, 1882 as part of a celebration of the French Youth Union.)

by the burning of biomass, peat, and/or coal. The use of these energy sources caused grave problems, such as large-scale deforestation, loss of land, and air pollution.

Although solar energy was used in earlier times, for instance, to evaporate salt along seashores, to dry crops for preservation, or to sunbake clay bricks, its use was limited to processes that required relatively low temperatures. Today, renewable energy other than biomass can be used to produce thermal energy in two ways. First, we can use wind turbines, water turbines, or solar PV panels to produce electricity, which can then be used to produce heat by electrical resistance. This was not possible in pre-industrial times because there was no electricity. Second, we can apply solar heat directly, using water-based flat plate collectors or evacuated tube collectors, which collect solar radiation from all directions and can reach temperatures of 120 degrees Celsius. We also have solar concentrator collectors, which track the sun, concentrate its radiation, and can generate temperatures high enough to melt metals or produce microchips and solar cells. These solar technologies only became available in the late 19th century, following advances in the manufacturing of glass and mirrors.

Running factories on variable power sources does not exclude the use of energy storage or a backup of dispatchable power plants. Adjusting demand to supply should take priority, but other strategies can play a supportive role.

First, energy storage or backup power-generation capacity could be useful for critical production processes that cannot be halted for prolonged periods, such as food processing.

Second, short-term energy storage is also useful to run production processes that are disadvantaged by an intermittent power supply. A similar distinction was made in the old days. For example, when spinning cloth, a constant speed was required to avoid gearwheels hunting and causing the machines to deliver thick and thin parts in rovings or yarns (Hills 1996). That is why spinning was only mechanized using water power, which could be stored to guarantee a more regular power supply. Wind power was too irregular. Wind power was also unsuited for processes like papermaking, mine haulage, or operating blast furnace bellows in ironworks.

Third, short-term energy storage is crucial for computer-controlled manufacturing processes, allowing these to continue operating during short interruptions in the power supply, and to shut down safely in case of longer power cuts. Very short-term energy storage is required for many mechanical production processes running on variable power sources in order to smooth out small and sudden variations in energy supply. Such mechanical systems were already used in pre-industrial windmills.

Compared to pre-industrial times, we now have a wide range of energy storage options available. For example, we can use biomass as a backup power source for mechanical energy production, something pre-industrial millers could not do. Before the arrival of the steam engine, there was no way of converting biomass into mechanical energy. We also have chemical batteries, and we have low-tech systems like flywheels, compressed air storage, hydraulic accumulators, and pumped storage plants. Heat energy can be stored in well-insulated water reservoirs (up to 100 degrees) or in salt, oil, or ceramics (for much higher temperatures). All these storage solutions would fail if they were tasked with storing a large share of renewable-energy production, but they can be very useful on a smaller scale in support of demand adjustment.

Cargo transportation is another candidate for using renewable power when it is available. This is most obvious for shipping. Ships still carry about 90 percent of the world's trade, and although shipping is the most energy-efficient way of transportation per ton-kilometer, total energy use is high, and today's oil-powered vessels are extremely polluting. A common high-tech idea is to install wind turbines offshore, convert the electricity they generate into hydrogen, and then use that hydrogen to power seagoing vessels. However, it is much more practical and energy efficient to use wind to power ships directly, as we have done for thousands of years. Furthermore, oil-powered cargo ships often float idle for days or even weeks before they can enter a port or leave it, which makes the relative unpredictability of sailboats comparatively less problematic.

As with industrial manufacturing, we now have much better technology and knowledge available to base a worldwide shipping industry on wind power alone. We have new materials to build better and longer-lasting ships and sails; we have more accurate navigation and communication instruments; we have more predictable weather forecasts; we can make use of solar panels for backup engine power; and we have more detailed knowledge about winds and currents.

Wind- and Solar-Powered Trains

We could follow a similar approach for land-based transportation, in the form of wind- and solar-powered trains. Like sailing boats, trains could be running whenever there is renewable energy available. Not by putting sails on trains, of course, but by running them on electricity made by solar PV panels or wind turbines along the tracks. This would be an entirely new application of a centuries-old strategy to deal with variable energy sources, only made possible by the invention of electricity. Running cargo trains on renewable energy is a great use of intermittent wind power because they are usually operated at night, when wind power is often at its best and energy demand is at its lowest. Furthermore, just like cargo ships, cargo trains already have unreliable schedules because they often sit stationary in train-yards for days, waiting to become fully loaded. Even the speed of the trains could be regulated by the amount of renewable energy that is available, just as the wind speed determines the speed of a sailing ship. A similar approach could also work with other electrical transportation systems, such as trolleytrucks, trolleyboats, or aerial ropeways.

Combining solar- and wind-powered cargo trains with solar- and wind-powered factories creates extra possibilities. For example, at first sight, solar- or wind-powered passenger trains appear to be impossible because people are less flexible than goods. If a solar-powered train is not running or is running too slow, an appointment may have to be rescheduled at the last minute. Likewise, on cloudy days, few people would make it to the office. However, this could be solved by using the same renewable-power sources for factories and passenger trains. Solar panels along the railway lines could be sized for cloudy days, and thus guarantee a minimum level of energy for a minimum service of passenger trains (but no industrial production). During sunny days, the extra solar power could be used to run the factories along the railway line or to run extra passenger (or cargo) trains.

Consequences for Society: Consumption and Production

As we have seen, if industrial production and cargo transportation became dependent on the availability of renewable energy, we would still be able to produce a diverse range of consumer goods and transport them all over the globe. However, not all products would be available all the time. If I want to buy new shoes, I might have to wait for the right season to get them manufactured and delivered. Production and consumption would depend on the weather and the seasons. Solar-powered factories would have higher production rates in the summer months, while wind-powered factories would have higher production rates in the winter months. Sailing seasons also need to be taken into account.

Running an economy on the rhythms of the weather does not *necessarily* mean that production and consumption rates would go down. If factories and cargo transportation adjust their energy use to the weather, they can use the full annual power production of wind turbines and solar panels. Manufacturers could counter seasonal production shortages by producing items "in season" and then stocking them close to consumers for sale during low-energy periods. In fact, the products themselves would become "energy storage" in this scenario. Instead of storing energy to manufacture products in the future, we would manufacture products whenever there is energy available, and store the products for later sale instead.

However, seasonal production may well lead to

lower production and consumption rates. Overproducing in high-energy times requires large production facilities and warehouses, which would be underused for the rest of the year. To produce cost-efficiently, manufacturers will need to make compromises. From time to time, these compromises will lead to product shortages, which in turn could encourage people to consider other solutions, such as repair and reuse of existing products, crafted products, do-it-yourself, or the exchange and sharing of goods.

Adjusting energy demand to energy supply also implies that the workforce adapts to the weather. If a factory runs on solar power, then the availability of power corresponds very well with human rhythms. The only downside is that workers would be free from work especially in winter and on cloudy days. However, if a factory or a cargo train runs on wind power, then people will also have to work during the night, which is considered unhealthy. The upside is that they would have holidays in summer and on good-weather days. If a factory or a transportation system is operated by wind or solar energy alone, workers would also have to deal with uncertainty about their work schedules. Although we have much better weather forecasts than in pre-industrial times, it remains difficult to make accurate predictions more than a few days ahead.

Finally, we could also limit the main share of industrial manufacturing and railway transportation to normal working hours, and curtail the oversupply during the night. In this scenario, we would simply have fewer material goods and more holidays. On the other hand, there would be an increased need for other types of jobs, like craftsmanship and sailing.

In conclusion, industrial manufacturing and cargo transportation—both over land and over sea—could be run almost entirely on variable renewable-power sources, with little need for energy storage, transmission networks, balancing capacity, or overbuilding renewable-power plants. In contrast, the modern high-tech approach of matching energy supply to energy demand at all times requires a lot of extra infrastructure that makes renewable-power production a complex, slow, expensive, and unsustainable undertaking. Adjusting energy demand to supply would make switching to renewable energy much more realistic than it is today. There would be no curtailment of energy, and no storage and transmission losses. All the energy produced by solar panels and wind turbines would be used on the spot and nothing would go to waste.

Admittedly, adjusting energy demand to energy supply can be less straightforward in sectors other than shipping and manufacturing. Although the Internet could be entirely operated on variable power sources—using asynchronous networks and delay-tolerant software—many newer Internet applications would then disappear. At home, we probably cannot expect people to sit in the dark or not to cook meals when there is no renewable energy. Likewise, people will not come to hospitals only on sunny days. In such instances, there is a larger need for energy storage or other measures to counter an intermittent power supply.

Transitioning the economy so that it will again "run based on the weather" will require more flexible thinking than we have become accustomed to during this brief historical period in which all goods and services have been available at all times. One of the big advantages of a flexible approach to energy demand and supply is that we would no longer "need" to produce energy in the staggering quantities that fossil-fuel sources have provided for the past century.

If we take a similarly flexible approach to thinking about energy efficiency, we can also move beyond a short-term focus on maximizing energy output to also consider the long-term impact of our consumption of non-recyclable materials. The wind-turbine industry is a good case study of a "renewable-energy industry" that is, in its current form, less than sustainable.

How to Make Wind Power Sustainable Again

For more than 2,000 years, windmills were built from recyclable or reusable materials: wood, stone, brick, canvas, metal. When electricity-producing wind turbines appeared in the 1880s, the materials did not change. It is only since the arrival of plastic composite blades in the 1980s that wind power has become the source of a toxic waste product that ends up in landfills. New wood-production technology and design makes it possible to build larger wind turbines almost entirely out of wood again—not just the blades, but also the rest of the structure. This would solve the waste issue and make the manufacturing of wind turbines largely independent of fossil fuels and mined materials. A forest planted in between the wind turbines could provide the wood for the next generation of wind turbines.

Wind turbines are considered to be a clean and sustainable source of power. However, while they can indeed generate electricity with lower CO_2 emissions than fossil-fuel power plants, they also produce a lot of waste. This is easily overlooked because roughly 90 percent of the mass of a large wind turbine is steel, mainly concentrated in the tower. Steel is commonly recycled, and this explains why wind turbines have very short energy-payback times—the recycled steel can be used to produce new wind turbine parts, which greatly lowers the energy required during the manufacturing process. However, wind-turbine blades are made from light-weight, plastic-composite materials, which are voluminous and impossible to recycle. Although the mass of the blades is limited compared to the total mass of a wind turbine, it is not negligible. For example, one 60-meter-long fiberglass blade weighs 17 tons, meaning that a 5 megawatt (MW) wind turbine produces more than 50 tons of plastic-composite waste from the blades alone. A windmill blade typically consists of a combination of epoxy—a petroleum product—with fiberglass reinforcements. The blades also contain sandwiched core materials, such as polyvinyl-chloride foam, polyethylene-terephtalate foam, balsa wood (intertwined in fibers and epoxy), and polyurethane coatings (Ramirez-Tejeda, Turcotte, and Pike 2017; Wilburn 2011; Jensen 2019; Martínez et al. 2009).

Unlike the steel in the tower, the plastic in blades cannot be recycled to make new plastic blades. The material can only be "downcycled," for instance, by shredding it, which damages the fibers and makes them useless for anything but a filler reinforcement in cement or asphalt production. Other methods are being investigated, but they all run into the same problem: nobody wants the "recycled" material. Some architects have reused windmill blades, for example, to build benches or playgrounds. But we cannot build everything out of wind-turbine blades. Because of the limited options for recycling and reuse, windmill blades are usually landfilled (in the United States) or incinerated (in Europe). The latter approach is not less unsustainable because incinerating the blades only partially reduces the amount of material to be landfilled (60 percent of the scrap remains as ash) and converts the rest into air pollution. Furthermore, given that fiberglass is incombustible, the caloric value of the blades is so limited that little or no power can be produced (Ramirez-Tejeda, Turcotte and Pike 2017; Wilburn 2011; Jensen 2019; Martínez et al. 2009).

Dealing with Waste—25 Years Later

Most of the roughly 250,000 wind turbines now in operation worldwide were installed less than 25 years ago, which is their estimated life expectancy. However, the rapid growth of wind power over the last two decades will soon be reflected in a delayed, but ever-increasing and never-ending, supply of waste materials. For example, in Europe, the share of installed wind turbines older than 15 years increases from 12 percent in 2016 to 28 percent in 2020. In Germany, Spain, and Denmark, their share increases to 41–57 percent. In 2020 alone, these countries will each have to dispose of 6,000 to 12,000 wind-turbine blades (Ziegler et al. 2018). Discarded blades will not only become more numerous but also larger, reflecting a continuous trend towards ever larger rotor diameters. Wind turbines built 25 years ago had blade lengths of around 15–20 meters, while today's blades reach lengths of 75–80 meters or more (Jensen 2019). Estimates based on current growth figures for wind power have suggested that composite materials from blades worldwide will amount to 330,000 tons of waste per year by 2028, and to 418,000 tons per year by 2040 (Ramirez-Tejeda, Turcotte, and

Pike 2017). These are conservative estimates because numerous blade failures have been reported and because constant development of more efficient blades with higher power-generating capacity is resulting in blade replacement well before their estimated lifespan (Ramirez-Tejeda, Turcotte, and Pike 2017; Lefeuvre et al. 2017). Furthermore, this amount of waste results from wind turbines installed between 2005 and 2015, when wind power only supplied a maximum of 4 percent of global power demand. If wind would supply a more desirable 40 percent of (current) power demand, there would be 3 to 4 million tons of waste per year.

Windmill Blades Through History

Yet a look at the history of wind power shows that plastic is not an essential material. The use of wind for mechanical power production dates back to antiquity. The first electricity-generating windmills—now called wind turbines—were built in the 1880s. However, fiberglass blades only took off in the 1980s. For 2000 years, windmills were entirely recyclable. Old-fashioned windmills had towers built of wood, stone, or brick. Their "blades" or "sails" were usually made of a wood framework covered with canvas or wood boards. (See Figure 3.) In later centuries, parts were increasingly made from iron, also a recyclable material. When new types of sails were invented in the 18th and 19th centuries (such as spring, patent, and rolling-reefer sails), as well as in the 20th century (Dekkerized and Bilau sails), the design changed but the materials remained the same (eventually including aluminum) (De Decker 2009).

Furthermore, unlike modern wind turbines that need to be replaced regularly and in their entirety, old-fashioned windmills could last for many decades or even centuries through regular repair and maintenance. The first wind turbine in the United States, built by Charles F. Brush, had a 17-meter diameter annular sail with 144 thin blades made of cedar wood. The first wind turbine in Europe, built by Paul La Cour in Denmark, had four traditional slatted wooden sails with a rotor diameter of 22.8 meters. La Cour's design was copied by local enterprises in Denmark, resulting in thousands of wind turbines operating on Danish farms between 1900 and 1920. Dozens of experimental wind turbines were built during the first half of the 20th century, including some with steel blades, such as the 1939 Smith-Putnam wind turbine in the United States (Maegaard, Krenz, and Palz 2013). In 1957, Johannes Juul—a student of Paul La Cour—built the three-bladed Gedser wind turbine. It had a rotor diameter of 24 meters and relied on an air frame superstructure of steel wires for rotor and blade stiffening. The blades

Figure 3
A Windmill Blade of Cloth and Wood

Photographer: Rasbak. Image source: https://nl.wikipedia.org/wiki/Gevlucht. https://commons.wikimedia.org/wiki/File:Molen_Zuidhollandse_molen,_Hank,_wiek.jpg. License: GFDL & Creative Commons Attribution-Share Alike 3.0 (CC BY-SA 3.0).

Note: The blade is on a mill in South Holland in the Netherlands.

were built from steel spars, with aluminum shells supported by wooden ribs. The Gedser turbine remained the most successful wind turbine until the mid-1980s. It ran for 11 years without maintenance, generating up to 360,000 kWh per year, but was not repaired when a bearing failed. When the turbine was refurbished and tested in the late 1970s, it performed better than the first wind turbines with fiberglass blades (Maegaard, Krenz, and Palz 2013; Lundsager, Frandsen, and Christensen 1980).

The first wind turbine with fiberglass blades was installed in 1978 in Denmark, where it powered a school. With its 54-meter diameter rotor, the Tvind turbine was at the time the largest wind turbine ever built. After 1980, fiberglass blades became standard in Denmark and the "Danish design" was later copied all over the world. The plastic blade, so it seems, is what defines the modern wind turbine. This presents us with a dilemma. The switch to fiberglass blades was mainly driven by the desire to build larger wind turbines. Larger wind turbines lower the cost per kilowatt-hour of generated electricity, for two reasons: the wind increases with height, and the doubling of the rotor radius increases power output four times. The desire to build larger wind turbines has driven the wind industry ever since. Rotor diameters increased from around 50 meters in the 1990s to 120 meters in the 2000s. Today's largest offshore wind turbines have rotor diameters of more than 160 meters, and a 12 MW turbine with a 220 meter rotor diameter is being constructed in the Netherlands (Jensen 2019; Lefeuvre et al. 2017; Gupta 2015).

However, with increasing size, the mass of the rotor blade also increases, which requires lighter materials. At the same time, larger blades deflect more, so that their structural stiffness is of increasing importance to maintain optimal aerodynamic performance and to avoid the blade hitting the tower. In short, larger wind turbines with longer blades place ever higher demands on the materials used, and these exceed the capacities of recyclable materials (Brøndsted, Lilholt, and Lystrup 2005; Koh 2017). Wind turbines have become more efficient, but also less sustainable. Right now, this trend is illustrated by the increasing use of carbon-fiber-reinforced plastic, which is even stronger, stiffer, and lighter than fiberglass-reinforced plastic (Brøndsted, Lilholt, and Lystrup 2005). The use of carbon fibers—which further complicates potential recycling—has become standard in the largest wind-turbine blades, mainly in highly stressed locations such as the blade root or the spar caps. Consequently, we have entered a new era in which blades are now so large that they cannot be made out of fiberglass-reinforced composites alone anymore.

Reinventing the Windmill Blade

An industry that calls itself sustainable and renewable cannot send millions of tons of plastic waste to landfills each year. Consequently, could we revert to building wind-turbine blades from recyclable materials alone? And how large could we build them? To what extent can efficiency and sustainability be reconciled? Most research into the design of more sustainable wind-turbine blades sticks with plastic as the main material. Thermoplastics can be melted and reused, making it possible to recycle the blades into new wind-turbine blades, even on-site. However, due to the material's lower strength and stiffness, these blades have not been built larger than 9 meters for now (Ramirez-Tejeda, Turcotte, and Pike 2017; Murray et al. 2017). Another area of development is the substitution of glass fibers for wood or flax fibers. These blades can be larger, but they have only small sustainability advantages over fiberglass-epoxy blades. (Borrmann 2016; Spera 2009). The petroleum-based epoxy is more harmful than the glass fiber, and natural-fiber-based composite materials absorb more of it (Corona et al. 2015; Gougeon and Zuteck 1979; Koh 2017).

Some engineers and scientists follow different paths and revert to more traditional wood construction. For small wind turbines, blades can be carved out of solid wood. For larger wind turbines, the blades can be composed of a hollow aerodynamic shell and an internal framework of ribs and stringers, supported by a beam called the spar—all built from laminated veneer wood boards, beams, and panels.

Laminated veneer lumber—in which the wood is peeled off the tree and then glued back together in thin layers—is a wood product that appeared in the 1980s and that has an important advantage in relation to solid wood components. The consistency of wood can vary within a single tree. Therefore, the length of the wood spars used in pre-industrial windmills was limited by the availability of large tree trunks of consistent quality. The largest traditional windmill ever built—the 1900 Murphy mill in San Francisco—had a rotor diameter of 35 meters. In contrast, the process of veneering spreads out defects such as knots, giving better and more predictable stiffness properties. This allows the building of larger wooden blades. Wood laminates offer substantial cost and weight reductions as compared to fiberglass. Although the strength and stiffness are lower, much of the load that the blade must support is a consequence of its own weight, so a wood blade does not need to be as strong as a fiberglass blade (Koh 2017). Nevertheless, the low stiffness of wood makes it difficult to limit the elastic deflections for very large rotor blades.

In a 2017 study of a 5 MW wind turbine with 61.5-meter blades, conducted at the University of Massachusetts, Amherst (USA), it was calculated that in order to be stiff enough and withstand the forces that it is exposed to, a blade made of laminated wood veneer panels would be 2.8 times heavier than a plastic blade (48 versus 17 tons) and have a laminate over 50 centimeters thick (Koh 2017). Although this suggests that it is technically possible to build a wooden blade more than 60 meters long, it is not very practical. With heavier blades the wind turbine needs to be built much stronger, which increases the costs and the use of resources. There are two ways to solve this problem. The first is to design a blade largely made from laminated veneer lumber, but reinforced with carbon composite spars and covered with an outer layer of fiberglass composite. In the above-mentioned study, it was found that such a wood-carbon hybrid blade is stiff enough to reach a length of 61.5 meters of a 5 MW turbine, and can be built 3 tons lighter than a fiberglass blade (Koh 2017). Another study of a wood-carbon blade of the same length comes to a similar conclusion, although in this case the wood-carbon blade is slightly heavier than the plastic blade (Borrmann 2016). Wood-carbon blades contain less plastic composite material, and the plastic is not intertwined with wood throughout the blade but clearly separated from it, making blade reuse, recycling, or incineration more attractive. However, according to the studies mentioned above, a wood-carbon blade still contains 2.5 tons to 6.2 tons of plastic composites (Borrmann 2016; Koh 2017). Thus, a three-bladed 5 MW wind turbine would produce 7.5 to 18.4 tons of unrecyclable waste—compared to 50 tons for a conventional blade. The environmental damage of the carbon-epoxy spars can be viewed as acceptable, if compared to the larger damage done by conventional wind-turbine blades. However, the waste problem is not solved, and further growth in wind power would still result in ever larger waste streams.

Alternatively, we could define sustainability in more ambitious terms and build wind-turbine blades completely out of wood again—even if this means that we have to build them smaller.

There is an extra reason to question our focus on efficiency: the decrease in sustainability is evident not only in the blades. Other parts of wind turbines are also increasingly made from plastic composites—most notably the nose cone and the nacelle cover (the housing that protects the drivetrain and the auxiliary equipment from the elements) (Ramirez-Tejeda, Turcotte, and Pike 2017; Wilburn 2011; Jensen 2019; Martínez et al. 2009). Other trends are the increased use of electronics, which are not suited for recycling, and of permanent magnet generators based on rare earth materials, which save costs compared to a mechanical gearbox but only at the expense of more destructive mining. Larger wind turbines also kill more birds and bats (Loss, Will, and Marra 2013).

By sacrificing some efficiency we could gain a lot in sustainability. Wind-power advocates may not like this because it would make wind power less competitive with fossil fuels. However, more expensive wind power can always be counteracted by higher prices for fossil fuels. What is really problematic is our choice of cheap fossil fuels as a benchmark to determine the viability of wind power. It is by aiming to compete with fossil fuels—and thus by aiming to provide the energy for a lifestyle built on fossil fuels—that wind turbines have become increasingly damaging to the environment. If we would reduce energy demand, smaller and less efficient wind turbines would not be a problem.

How large could we build practical wind-turbine blades from laminated veneer lumber alone? Nobody seems to know. I asked Rachel Koh, the scientist who calculated the requirements for the 61.5-meter wood-only blade, but she could not help me. Koh (2019) explained:

> I only ran the model for the blades of a 5 MW turbine. It would be hypothetically possible to run another study to answer your question, but it's not a small undertaking.

She also notes that it is possible to further improve the stiffness of wood laminates with manufacturing innovations.

Whether we opt for large wood-carbon blades or smaller wood-only blades, in both cases we could also build the tower and the nacelle cover from laminated wood products. In 2012, the German company TimberTower built a laminated wood tower 100 meters tall for a 1.5 MW wind turbine. A wooden tower seems to be beside the point because it replaces part of a wind turbine that is already perfectly recyclable. However, a wind turbine of which the structure is almost completely built out of wood offers extra benefits. Wood could make the production of wind turbines entirely independent of mined materials and of fossil fuels, except for the gearwork and the electric components (but further gains can be achieved, whenever possible, by using wind power for direct mechanical or direct heat production) (De Decker 2019). Furthermore, wooden wind turbines could become a carbon sink—sequestering CO_2 from the atmosphere in their wood components. Finally, the space between wind turbines on a wind farm, which is not suited as a residential area, could be used to grow a forest that would provide the wood for the next generation of wind turbines. The lumber could be sawed, processed, and assembled onsite, which eliminates the energy use associated with the transport of wind-turbine parts. The energy required for manufacturing the laminates and for constructing the turbines could come from the windmills, as well as from forest biomass. Especially if blades are made of wood only, the wind turbine could become a textbook example of the circular economy.

References

Borrmann, Rasmus. (2016). *Structural Design of a Wood-CFRP Wind Turbine Blade Model.* Flensburg, Netherlands: Flensburg University of Applied Sciences.

Brøndsted, Povl, Hans Lilholt, and Aage Lystrup. (2005). "Composite Materials for Wind Power Turbine Blades." *Annual Review of Materials Research* 35: 505–538.

Cech, T. V. (2010). *Principles of Water Resources: History, Development, Management, and Policy.* Hoboken, NJ: Wiley.

Corona, Andrea, Christen Malte Markussen, Morten Birkved, and Bo Madsen. (2015). "Comparative Environmental Sustainability Assessment of Bio- Based Fibre Reinforcement Materials for Wind Turbine Blades." *Wind Engineering* 39(1): 53–63.

De Decker, Kris. (2009). *Wind Powered Factories: History (and Future) of Industrial Windmills.* Barcelona: Low-Tech Magazine. https://www.lowtechmagazine.com/2009/10/history-of-industrial-windmills.html

________. (2019). *Heat Your House with a Mechanical Windmill.* Barcelona: Low-Tech Magazine. https://www.lowtechmagazine.com/2019/02/heat-your-house-with-a-water-brake-windmill.html

Freese, Stanley. (1957). *Windmills and Millwrighting.* Cambridge, UK: Cambridge University Press.

Gougeon, Meade, and Mike Zuteck. (1979). "The Use of Wood for Wind Turbine Construction". In *Large Wind Turbine Design Characteristics and R&D Requirements.* Ed. Seymour Lieblein, pp. 293-308. Cleveland, OH: NASA Lewis Research Center. https://ntrs.nasa.gov/archive/nasa/casi.ntrs.nasa.gov/19800008214.pdf

Gupta, Ashwani K. (2015). "Efficient Wind Energy Conversion: Evolution to Modern Design." *Journal of Energy Resources Technology* 137(5): 051201.

Heymann, Mattias. (1995). *Die Geschichte der Windenergiegenutzung, 1890–1990.* Frankfurt am Main: Campus.

Hills, Richard Leslie. (1996). *Power from Wind: A History of Windmill Technology.* Cambridge University Press.

Jenkins, H. L. C. (1973). *Ocean Passages for the World.* Somerset: Royal Navy.

Jensen, Jonas Pagh. (2019). "Evaluating the Environmental Impacts of Recycling Wind Turbines." *Wind Energy* 22(2): 316–326.

Koh, Rachel. (2017). "Bio-Based Wind Turbine Blades: Renewable Energy Meets Sustainable Materials for Clean, Green Power." (2017). PhD dissertation, mechanical engineering. Amherst: University of Massachusett. https://scholarworks.umass.edu/dissertations_2/1102/

________. (2019). Conversation with author. May 27.

Lefeuvre, Anaële, Sebastien Garnier, Leslie Jacquemin, Baptiste Pillain, and Guido Sonnemann. (2017). "Anticipating In-Use Stocks of Carbon Fiber Reinforced Polymers and Related Waste Flows Generated by the Commercial Aeronautical Sector until 2050." *Resources, Conservation and Recycling* 125: 264–272.

Loss, Scott R., Tom Will, and Peter P. Marra. (2013). "Estimates of Bird Collision Mortality at Wind Facilities in the Contiguous United States." *Biological Conservation* 168: 201–209.

Lucas, Adam. (2006). *Wind, Water, Work: Ancient and Medieval Milling Technology*. Vol. 8. Leiden, Netherlands: Brill.

Lundsager, P., Sten Tronæs Frandsen, and Carl Jørgen Christensen. (1980). *Analysis of Data from the Gedser Wind Turbine 1977–1979.* Roskilde, Denmark: Risø National Laboratory.

Maegaard, Preben, Anna Krenz, and Wolfgang Palz. (2013). *Wind Power for the World: The Rise of Modern Wind Energy.* New York: CRC Press.

Martínez, Eduardo, Félix Sanz, Stefano Pelligrini, Emilio Jiménez, and Julio Blanco. (2009). "Life Cycle Assessment of a Multi-Megawatt Wind Turbine." *Renewable Energy* 34(3): 667–673.

Murray, Robynne, Dana Swan, David Snowberg, Derek Berry, Ryan Beach, and Sam Rooney. (2017). *Manufacturing a 9-Meter Thermoplastic Composite Wind Turbine Blade.* No. NREL/CP-5000-68615. Golden, CO: National Renewable Energy Lab (NREL).

Paine, Lincoln. (2014). *The Sea and Civilization: A Maritime History of the World.* Atlantic Books Ltd.

Ramirez-Tejeda, Katerin, David A. Turcotte, and Sarah Pike. (2017). "Unsustainable Wind Turbine Blade Disposal Practices in the United States: A Case for Policy Intervention and Technological Innovation." *New Solutions: A Journal of Environmental and Occupational Health Policy* 26(4): 581–598.

Reynolds, Terry S. (2002). *Stronger Than a Hundred Men: A History of the Vertical Water Wheel.* Vol. 7. Baltimore, MD: Johns Hopkins University Press.

Sieferle, Rolf Peter, and Michael P. Osman. (2001). *The Subterranean Forest: Energy Systems and the Industrial Revolution.* Cambridge, UK: White Horse Press.

Spera, David. (2009). *Wind Turbine Technology: Fundamental Concepts in Wind Turbine Engineering,* 2nd ed. Washington, DC: American Society of Mechanical Engineers Press.

Tissandier, Gaston. (1882). "Utilisation de la Chaleur du Soleil." *La Nature* 10(2) No. 482 (August).

Wailes, Rex. (1954). *The English Windmill.* London: Routledge and Kegan Paul.

Wilburn, David R. (2011). *Wind Energy in the United States and Materials Required for the Land-Based Wind Turbine Industry from 2010 Through 2030.* Washington, DC: U.S. Department of the Interior, U.S. Geological Survey.

Ziegler, Lisa, Elena Gonzalez, Tim Rubert, Ursula Smolka, and Julio J. Melero. (2018). "Lifetime Extension of Onshore Wind Turbines: A Review Covering Germany, Spain, Denmark, and the UK." *Renewable and Sustainable Energy Reviews* 82: 1261–1271.

CHAPTER 10

Suburban Practices of Energy Descent

Samuel Alexander and Brendan Gleeson†*

Abstract. This article proceeds on the basis that the cost of energy will rise in coming years and decades as the age of fossil energy abundance comes to an end. Given the close connection between energy and economic activity, we also assume that declining energy availability and affordability will lead to economic contraction and reduced material affluence. In overconsuming and overdeveloped nations, such resource and energy "degrowth" is desirable and necessary from a sustainability perspective, provided it is planned for and managed in ways consistent with basic principles of distributive equity. Working within that degrowth paradigm, we examine how scarcer and more expensive energy may impact the suburban way of life and how households might prepare for this very plausible, but challenging, energy descent future. The article examines energy demand management in suburbia and how the limited energy needed to provide for essential household services can best be secured in an era of expensive energy and climate instability. After reviewing various energy practices, we also highlight a need for an ethos of sufficiency, moderation, and radical frugality, which we argue is essential for building resilience in the face of forthcoming energy challenges and a harsher climate.

Introduction

Cities are humanity's most intricate creations. They are the metaformations within which other expressions of human creativity emerge and develop, and this complexity, like life itself, depends on energy for its sustenance and development (Smil 2017). Energy is not just another resource or commodity: it is the key that unlocks access to all other resources and commodities, thereby giving shape to the physical boundaries within which human societies must take form. Responding to urban problems and pursuing societal goals almost always involve energy investment, yet the more problems that are faced or goals that are pursued, the more energy a society needs to maintain its way of life. This is how civilizations take form and evolve, both enabled and constrained by

*Research Fellow, Melbourne Sustainable Society Institute. Lecturer, Office for Environmental Programs, University of Melbourne. Research areas: degrowth, permaculture, voluntary simplicity, "grassroots" transition. Author: *Degrowth in the Suburbs: A Radical Urban Imaginary* (2019); *Carbon Civilisation and the Energy Descent Future* (2018); and *Art Against Empire: Toward an Aesthetics of Degrowth* (2017). Website: samuelalexander.info Email: samuelalexander42@gmail.com

†Director, Melbourne Sustainable Society Institute, University of Melbourne. Founder and former director, Urban Research Program at Griffith University. Research areas: urban and social policy, environmental theory and policy. Author: *Heartlands: Making Space for Hope in the Suburbs* (2006). Co-author: *Degrowth in the Suburbs: A Radical Urban Imaginary* (2019). Recipient: John Iremonger Award. Email: brendan.gleeson@unimelb.edu.au

their energetic foundations (Tainter 1988). Indeed, a society must be able to meet and afford ongoing energy requirements if its specific socioeconomic form is to persist. If energy needs cannot be met or afforded, the society will transform or be transformed, voluntarily or otherwise.

Never has this energy dependency been truer than in the low-density urban landscapes of suburbia, predominantly comprised of stand-alone houses and generally inhabited by high-impact, energy-intensive households, which are both creatures and creators of the growth economy (Alexander and Gleeson 2019). Suburban affluence is the defining image of the good life under globalized capitalism, often held up as a model to which all humanity should aspire. The dominant development model has seen the global consumer class expanding as more economies industrialize and urbanize. But every aspect of this industrial mode of existence has been shaped by the cheap and abundant fossil energy supplies that have become accessible in the last two centuries (Smil 2017).

This dependency on fossil fuels has given rise to an energy crisis with two main dimensions (Moriarty and Honnery 2011). First, fossil fuels are finite resources that are being consumed at extraordinary rates (IEA 2018), such that their supply will one day peak and decline even as demand threatens to grow (Mohr et al. 2015). Second, the combustion of fossil fuels is also the leading driver of climate change (IPCC 2018), meaning that humanity must decarbonize by choice even before we are forced to do so through geological depletion. Further to those challenges, it remains highly uncertain whether renewable energy technologies will be able to fully replace the energy services provided by fossil fuels in an energetically or financially affordable way (Moriarty and Honnery 2008; 2016; Alexander and Floyd 2018). Thus, the future will be defined by increased energy scarcity not energy abundance, which implies an "energy descent future" with rising energy costs relative to today (Odum and Odum 2001; Holmgren 2012).

Rather than further diagnosing these problems, we assume the energy predicament outlined above and proceed on the basis that the cost of energy will rise in coming years and decades as the age of energy abundance comes to an end. We also take as given the close connection between energy and economic activity (Keen et al. 2019; Ayres and Warr 2009). On that basis, we assume that declining energy availability and affordability will lead to economic contraction and reduced material affluence. In overconsuming and overdeveloped nations, such resource and energy "degrowth" is desirable and necessary from a sustainability perspective, provided it is planned for and managed in ways consistent with basic principles of distributive equity (Hickel 2017). A large literature has emerged over the last decade that defends and examines the various complex issues surrounding such planned degrowth (Weiss and Cattaneo 2017; Kallis et al. 2018; Trainer 2020). We are broadly sympathetic with that paradigm. It informs the analysis below. Of course, scarce and expensive energy may well arrive *without* sufficient planning and in inequitable ways. This means that societies may need to prepare for economic contraction that looks and is experienced more like recession, depression, or even collapse—an unplanned economic contraction. But whether economic contraction arrives through design or disaster—or some mixture—this profound turning point in industrial civilization will be experienced very differently depending on context, including the vast array of suburban settings that now exist in the global urban age (Gleeson 2014).

In this article, we examine how scarcer and more expensive energy may impact the suburban way of life and how households might prepare for this very plausible, but challenging, energy descent future. While we acknowledge various structural challenges (especially access to land and the problem of carbon-dependent urban infrastructure), our analysis focuses primarily on the social or "grassroots" responses that may be available within those existing structural constraints. In addressing this theme and context, we acknowledge a tradition of prior commentary on "peak oil" adaptation (Heinberg 2004; Greer 2008; Hopkins 2008; Holmgren 2018; Piercy et al. 2010). However, we do not fall into the catastrophism of some suburban analysts of energy descent (Kunstler 2005). Our aim is to provide an up-to-date exploration of the energy challenges facing suburbanites in a carbon-constrained world. We also feel that our scholarly analysis and review of the issues are worthwhile contributions in an age where energy descent futures remain neglected and on the fringe of academic literature. We believe that scholarly neglect owes primarily to widely held techno-optimistic assumptions about renewable energy transitions. (For a critical review of those assumptions, see Alexander and Floyd 2018.)

Our article involves an examination of energy-demand management in suburbia and how the limited energy needed to provide for essential household services can best be secured in an era of expensive energy and climate instability. After reviewing various energy practices, we highlight the need for an ethos of sufficiency, moderation, and radical frugality, which we argue is essential for building resilience in the face of energy challenges. We begin, however, with an energy focus, and then explore the broader implications for urban material culture.

In order to delimit the scope of our analysis, we focus specifically on what we call "New World" suburbia—the suburban contexts of the United States, Australia, and New Zealand, which share many cultural and geospatial characteristics. Often poorly designed in terms of energy efficiency, these extensive suburbs will not all be knocked down for them to be built again in "greener" or more efficient ways. Built environments are highly fixed capital that evolve relatively slowly. Replacement rates occur at less than 5 percent per annum in Australia, and more like 1–2 percent in the United Kingdom (Gleeson 2014; Dixon et al. 2018). Instead of rebuilding, we argue that the task is to *resettle* the suburbs according to a new imaginary (Alexander and Gleeson 2019). We agree with permaculture theorist and practitioner David Holmgren (2018) and simplicity theorist Ted Trainer (2010) that when approached creatively, these low-density suburban landscapes show themselves to be a promising place to start a grassroots, transformative retrofit of the built environment in an age of rising energy costs and broader environmental crises. In what follows, we consider and outline the social practices and values needed to effect this deep suburban transformation, drawing on various literatures, including degrowth, permaculture, voluntary simplicity, urban studies, and critical energy analysis.

Unlearning Abundance: Energy Descent in the Suburbs

What, then, might energy descent look like at the level of the suburban household? What does it mean for a household to plan for economic contraction and embrace a context of rising energy costs? Does this necessarily imply hardship, deprivation, and sacrifice? If negotiated wisely, could such a managed descent give rise to an alternative, less materialistic form of prosperity? This raises practical questions about what suburban households can do to begin building a post-carbon economy within the shell of the old, but it also highlights the question of what role sociocultural transformation needs to play in reclaiming the suburbs for a new era of energy scarcity.

Some of the practices and attitudes reviewed in this article will come as no surprise, such as retrofitting a house for increased energy efficiency; a material ethics of frugality and sharing; household investment in solar panels; mending and making things rather than always buying; radically reducing waste; cycling; relocalizing food production via backyard gardening and urban agriculture; and connecting with local farmers and producers. Such "old ideas" will not excite those who fetishize "the new," but we argue that such practices deserve cursory restatement because they have a necessary and significant role to play in creating the sociocultural conditions needed for an energy-descent future to be managed well. If growth and consumerism cannot be maintained in a high-cost, energy-scarce future, it is important to understand what material and energy sufficiency would look like in suburban contexts that are currently so resource and energy dependent.

We also review other potential features of a retrofitted suburbia that have received far less attention in mainstream sustainability and resilience discourse, including domestic biogas production, disconnecting from fossil gas, composting toilets, solar ovens, peer-to-peer sharing, the gift economy, and re-commoning public and private space. Many of these practices are particularly suited—sometimes *only* suited—to the suburban landscape, in ways we will explain. We do not present such a brief survey as a universalizable or complete blueprint to be applied independent of context. By considering a range of such practices, and highlighting their underlying principles of motivation, it is hoped that we can begin to discern a new, post-carbon suburban imaginary that outlines a constructive and positive response to forthcoming energy descent.

Our underlying assumption is that sustainability in the suburbs (and more broadly) cannot be achieved merely through techno-efficiency improvements and the decarbonization of consumer lifestyles (Hickel and Kallis 2019). The extent of decoupling required is simply too great. Of course, all societies need to exploit appropriate technologies and design innovations in order to produce and consume more efficiently. But to have any positive effect, efficiency must be grounded in an ethics, economics, and, ultimately, a politics of sufficiency and self-limitation (Alexander 2015). In overconsuming and overproducing societies, that means a radical, but voluntary, demand-side reduction in energy and resource use. Efficiency without sufficiency is lost, as demonstrated by the increasing resource demands of growth capitalism over recent centuries (Kallis 2017).

A demand-side reduction will involve the ethical renegotiation of our relationships with the material world, as well as a vast and growing politics of collective action to support and realize it (Read et al. 2018). The rejection of materialistic values and practices is generally referred to as voluntary simplicity, otherwise known as "downshifting" or just "simple living" (Alexander 2009). That means unlearning consumerist cultures of consumption that are so easily taken for granted and normalized in developed nations (Hamilton and Denniss 2005). It also means relearning the lost arts of creative frugality that were commonsensical in previous eras of relative scarcity. But it also means creating the range of societal structures to support rather than inhibit post-consumerist, sufficiency-based ways of living. Even though it is currently out of intellectual and political fashion, we maintain that there is an utterly indispensable literature on sufficiency, moderation, self-limitation, and frugality that must inform any coherent sustainability-justice agenda, especially in anticipation of rising energy costs and climate instability (Westacott 2016; Alexander and McLeod 2014).

Recall that "economy," according to Aristotle, meant the good management of the household, and, for him, the household was the foundation of the *polis*. In our age of governmental paralysis and failure of nerve, this Aristotelian perspective might again highlight the necessity of a social strategy that begins with the intentional transformation of daily life in the suburbs.

A Necessary Caveat: Energy Descent for Whom?

At once we need to highlight a critical tension raised by our approach to retrofitting suburbia—a tension that speaks to the complexity of any praxis and politics of suburban transformation. On the one hand, the new energy context of scarcity and higher prices that may soon dawn categorically entails a significant reduction in the energy and resource demands of the wealthiest societies, so it is important to grasp what such downscaling might look like in terms of lived experience. The forthcoming analysis considers that question in some detail. On the other hand, it is clear that there are many people, even in affluent societies like Australia (from where we write), who are in precarious financial situations, struggling simply to feed and clothe their families, and who certainly do not experience their consumption practices as being excessive and superfluous (Bauman 2004). Degrowth and energy descent for whom, one might ask?

This raises structural and distributive issues concerning class, privilege, and property ownership. These issues entail a critique that has been leveled at the permaculture, ecovillage, sustainable consumption, and "simple living" movements regularly

(Frankel 2018). Although the practices reviewed in this article will need to be a part of any post-carbon future, many (but not all) of the practices depend on the ownership of land or access to secure housing, which are privileges far from being universally provided.

Access to affordable land and housing is fundamental (Nelson and Schneider 2018). This draws the analysis into radical and controversial territory because broadening societal access to land and housing implies a revision of property rights and market structures, which sit at the conceptual heart of capitalism. Options for radical "top-down" reform have been considered elsewhere, including the following: design new measures of growth to replace GDP, establish limits to resource use, reduce work hours, design public budgets for more public goods, invest in renewable energy, transform the financial system, and guarantee the right to housing (Alexander and Gleeson 2019: 181– 195). For now, the point is simply that some of the practices reviewed below are not easily embraced by those unable to secure ownership of, or secure access to, housing and land. As populations grow and put more pressure on cities, this problem of ownership and access to affordable housing threatens to intensify, unless there are some bold policy interventions aimed at broadening the distribution of wealth, power, and property in society (Nelson and Schneider 2018).

Similarly, tenure is profoundly important. There are obvious reasons why people renting will not invest in solar panels or water tanks in a transient or insecure rental property. That is, renting implies what urban theorist Anitra Nelson (2018: 102) calls an "unsettled temporariness." Even digging up the lawn and growing food can depend on the permission of landlords. Furthermore, retrofitting a house can be expensive and many households may not have discretionary expenditure to invest in solar panels, efficient appliances, or water tanks, especially if trying to get into the housing market, which may imply oppressive mortgage obligations.

It would be naïve, therefore, to suggest that personal or household action alone can resolve the problems suburbanites face in an energy descent future. But the following program of action still remains a necessary part of the picture of transformation. It just means that there are deep structural, financial, and cultural obstacles that lie in the way of such a grassroots transition scaling up.

Nevertheless, we also recognize the latent transformative potential of those who have the agency to downshift their material living standards (Holmgren 2018). These relatively high consumption suburbanites—relatively prosperous working and middle classes—may have to play a lead role in creating the social conditions needed for a politics of energy descent to emerge. This article will focus predominately on the capacity of that class to act within existing structural constraints. But this focus on suburban homeowners can only be the start of any response to energy scarcity and rising energy costs, and ultimately this constituency must commit to and collaborate with broader social movements of solidarity, resistance, redistribution, and transition.

Suburban Practices of Energy Descent

Our survey of household actions and attitudes begins by focusing on the central question of energy: how suburbanites can practice, and, in some instances, have already practiced energy descent (Holmgren 2018). After reviewing these practices, we consider some broader homesteading activities consistent with an energy descent future, including the practice of voluntary simplicity, relocalizing food production, and participation in alternative economies outside the market.

The Necessity of Demand Reduction

The most important thing any household can do to decarbonize energy use and prepare for energy scarcity is simply to reduce energy demand. After all, a transition to 100 percent renewables will be proportionately easier to achieve and more affordable if demand is significantly reduced. Since the Industrial Revolution, energy has been so cheap relative to its rewards that it has been easy to be wasteful and careless in energy use (Smil 2017). That very wastefulness provides a source of grounded hope, however, because it means there are huge opportunities for demand reduction in ways that do not imply any reduction in well-being. In ways we will now outline, trimming superfluous energy use requires both behavioral changes and investments in household retrofitting activities for increased efficiency and self-provision (Sorrell 2015).

In terms of behavior change, households can practice a range of important, but unexciting, energy rituals, including: turning lights off when leaving the room; taking short showers; never using (or having) a clothes dryer; only judiciously using air-conditioning (more for health than comfort); washing clothes only when genuinely needed; closing curtains and windows on really hot days to keep the heat out; putting warm clothing on in cool temperatures before turning any heating on (and only heating the rooms being used); watching TV or online entertainment sparingly; unplugging appliances when not in use; and a long list of tiny other things too mundane to mention. One Australian study estimated that these types of behavioral responses could reduce average in-house energy use in a household by half (Alexander and Yacoumis 2018). That study did not exhaust the range of practices available. Mainstream environmentalism has been on top of this behavioral advice for decades, and it should not be dismissed. But while such practices are necessary, they are far from enough to achieve sustainability, given the systemic embeddedness of consumption practices and the problem of structural "lock in" (Trainer 2012; Sanne 2002). Nevertheless, they begin building household resilience by anticipating reduced energy availability through voluntary energy demand reduction. In terms of retrofitting a house, options include:

- investing in efficient appliances (like a small fridge) and solar panels, and progressively electrifying all gas appliances;
- putting extra insulation in the walls and roof to minimize the need to heat and cool the house;
- closing gaps around doors and windows;
- planting a west-facing grapevine or deciduous tree that shades the house with its foliage in summer, keeping it cool, but lets the sun hit the house in winter by dropping its leaves;
- installing thick curtains to keep heat in (or out) as needed; and
- other equally mundane but useful things of this nature.

A range of small and more significant changes can add up to surprisingly large demand-side energy reductions (Holmgren 2018). All of them increase resilience in anticipation of energy becoming scarcer and more expensive. In short, if energy becomes increasingly unavailable or unaffordable in a context of energy descent and economic contraction (whether planned degrowth or unplanned recession), being able to manage with as little energy as possible becomes an essential household skill.

While there is obviously a privilege implied by owning a house—roughly 65 percent of Australians own their home—frugal financial practices and minimizing superfluous consumption can, to some extent, free up income to invest in a solar array, a biogas digester, heat-pump hot water system—all reviewed below—amongst other retrofitting investments. Within the permaculture (Holmgren 2018), voluntary simplicity (Alexander and Ussher 2012), and "transition towns" (Hopkins 2008) movements, households have been taking these types of actions and practicing energy descent here and now, whilst governments have been relatively inactive. Alexander and Ussher (2012) conducted what remains the most extensive empirical examination of the downshifting movement, and conservatively concluded that as many as 200 million people in Western nations are practicing voluntary simplicity, even if this subculture entails a wide range of practices, from light green consumerism to more radical expressions of simple living. Could this constituency yet radicalize, mobilize, and organize to become a social movement of transformative import? Journalist George Monbiot (2007: 42) famously declared that people never "riot for austerity," but rioting for a new vision of frugal abundance no longer seems quite so implausible, even if this broad movement remains in its infancy as a political project.

While the systemic and structural challenges cannot be analyzed in any depth in this article, the research and practices reviewed suggest that, in some suburban contexts, much can be done within existing structures to decarbonize the suburban household. Several suburban cases studies are reviewed in Holmgren (2018), with similarly promising and inspiring examples analyzed in Nelson (2018). The structural problem of carbon "lock in" is very real for some households (Sanne 2002). Nevertheless, for many households, a significant portion of their carbon footprint is largely a *choice* or *habit* that could be modified. This highlights a cultural or normative challenge, which arguably can be best resolved incrementally through ongoing grassroots activities and the evolution of new cultural practices and norms "from below." To talk of "incremental change" and "evolution," however, should not be interpreted as downplaying the urgency of change that is needed.

The behavioral practices are free but involve the challenge of changing habits, which humans are not very good at without nudging or other incentives (De Young 2014). The investments in efficiency or renewable energy production will cost money, and the challenge in that regard is about creating an ethos of sustainability that sees such investments as more important than other consumer commodities or experiences. That said, the economics of solar are becoming more attractive (Creutzig et al. 2017). Household solar is becoming less of a "cost" and more of an "investment," even though the upfront expense can still be a barrier. Expensive housing and rent will also make such investments difficult for many, although financial resources could become available for some households if more frugal and mindful spending practices were adopted (Domingeuz and Robins 1992). This is a point to which we will return.

Making the changes reviewed above obviously requires the *desire* or *incentive* to take energy demand reduction seriously, which is lacking in many affluent cultures today. This lack is primarily because the dominant paradigm of techno-optimism pushes the message that we can just buy "green" goods and services rather than reduce demand. Our counter-message is that significant demand reduction is achievable in many suburban households, and it is important that decarbonization in the city begins with these changes wherever they are available. As more households take these small, but cumulatively transformative, steps, we contend new cultural norms would arise, in relation to which current political and macroeconomic goals would be reevaluated and, in time, potentially revised (Alexander 2013). Without dedicated demand-side action, any transition to sustainable and more resilient energy systems will fail.

Some political economists, such as Frankel (2018), will be quick to dismiss such "lifestyle" changes as being of little consequence, not recognizing that the structural changes that are certainly needed will never arrive until there is progressive culture that demands them. Practicing energy descent at the household level is an indispensable part of that cultural r/evolution, representing a prefigurative politics that is necessary to any post-carbon or post-growth transition (Alexander 2013). The rest of the household actions reviewed in this article should be judged in that light also—not as direct, consumption-based "solutions" to the problems of overproduction, but as necessary groundwork for creating the new culture of sufficiency that will need to precede any new politics or macroeconomics of sufficiency.

Solar PV

On the path of household decarbonization, the second-best thing to do—after significantly reducing demand—is to invest in solar photovoltaics (PV), a strategy most suitable for suburbanites with their typically low-density, stand-alone houses and private roof space. There is still academic controversy over the best ways to decarbonize economies (Jacobson et al. 2017; Heard et al. 2017; Alexander and Floyd 2018; Heinberg and Fridley 2016). Still, few deny that solar PV will need to play a greatly increased role in energy production. Most governments around the world (notably Australia and the USA) are failing to take the lead on a clean energy transition and initiate deep decarbonization (IPCC 2018). Therefore, by force of logic, there is an increased burden on households and communities to invest in their own renewable energy, even if this may not always be the most efficient way to do it (Borenstein 2017). Household solar energy production is certainly more desirable than waiting while governments do little or nothing. In any case, it is likely that a renewable energy future will be one that moves towards greater decentralization of energy generation, especially if battery technology continues to advance (Liaros 2019; Palmer and Floyd 2020). The tide of household solar installations is strengthening this pattern, and grid architecture will need to evolve to adapt to changing patterns of generation and use.

Using the sun more directly through solar ovens is another practice highlighting the elegance of simplicity (Alexander and Yacoumis 2018). This is obviously climate dependent. While unable to completely replace an inside oven, solar ovens can reduce electricity for cooking several days a week in the warmer months, while also teaching households important lessons about the art of living in accordance with solar energy flows.

An Electric "Heat Pump" Hot Water System

One of the key features of deep decarbonization involves electrifying energy services previously provided by fossil energy. This presumes that electric appliances are powered by renewable electricity, since electric appliances running on coal-generated electricity can be more carbon-intensive than fossil gas appliances. Electric hotwater systems once cost much more than gas systems to operate, but developments in heat pump technology mean that electric systems are now up to 80 percent more efficient than they used to be (Gehl et al. 2012). Without going into the technicalities, a heat pump absorbs heat from the air and transfers it to the water, minimizing the need for further heating with electricity. This is a form of solar heating since the sun heats the air, and that heat gets transferred to the water, effective even in winter. Best of all, these heat pump units generally have a timer, which means that they can heat the water when the solar panels have maximum sun exposure. For this reason, heat pumps can be conceived of as a battery of sorts, with the sun and solar panels "charging" the water when the sun is up and storing the energy in an extremely well-insulated tank. Residents can use the hot water in the mornings or in the evenings, when the sun is down. This minimizes grid demand in ways that make a 100 percent renewable energy transition more affordable and manageable.

Biogas in the Suburbs

Most suburban blocks would have space for a domestic biogas digester, although this highly promising alternative technology is all but unknown in developed regions of the world. In this regard the so-called developing nations have much to teach, with China having 27 million biogas digesters and India having 4 million (Bond and Templeton 2011). With irony, blindness, and paradox, the discourse of "development" can barely conceive of the possibility that "advanced" nations might have things to learn from the "less developed" nations.

Biogas is produced when organic matter biodegrades under anaerobic conditions (without oxygen). The primary benefit of biogas is that it is a renewable energy source with net-zero emissions. Whereas the production of oil and other fossil fuels will eventually peak and decline, humans will always be able to make biogas so long as the sun is shining and plants can grow. Biogas has net-zero emissions because the carbon dioxide that is released into the atmosphere when the methane burns is no more than what was drawn down from the atmosphere when the organic matter was first grown (Alexander, Harris, and McCabe 2019).

There are other benefits, too. The organic matter used in biogas digesters is typically a waste product. By producing biogas, households can reduce the amount of food waste and other organic materials being sent to landfills, which also means less methane in the atmosphere. Furthermore, biogas digesters produce a nutrient-rich sludge that can be watered down into a fertilizer for gardens, homesteads, or farms. All this helps increase energy independence, build resilience, and save money.

The level of food waste in affluent New World nations is alarming, around AU$8 billion worth in Australia alone each year (ABC 2013). It makes sense to divert that waste from landfills to produce clean energy in the suburbs. Research by Reynolds et al. (2014) indicates that there would easily be enough food waste in Australia for all suburban households to cook on biogas without exhausting food waste streams, even if food waste was significantly reduced. New research on domestic biogas production suggests that putting approximately 1.5 kilograms of food waste per day in a domestic-scale biogas digester can produce on average 38 minutes of cooking per day, which is enough to cover most household cooking requirements (Alexander, Harris, and McCabe 2019). Coupled with a solar hot water system this can allow for complete disconnection from fossil gas and minimize electricity demand.

Biogas has the potential to be a disruptive alternative technology that could contribute to the deep decarbonization and increased energy security. We maintain that suburban households should exploit this innovation on the path to a post-carbon and resilient society. Although it can seem like an energy miracle—clean energy from food waste—biogas is really nothing other than an elegant example of permaculture: working with nature and natural processes, rather than fighting against them.

Post-Carbon Transport

Suburbia was built with cheap oil and designed primarily to be car dependent. Electric vehicles will inevitably play some role in the transformation of transport in the near- and long-term future. We argue, however, that it is a mistake to think they can solve the problem of the carbon- and resource-intensity of private automobiles (Alexander and Gleeson 2019: Ch. 2). Any genuine transport solution will not be accomplished by electrifying the world's currently growing addiction to private motor vehicles but by finding ways to avoid the need for such vehicles altogether (Moriarty and Honnery 2008, 2016). The alternatives are walking, cycling, and electrifying public transport, which have many environmental and health benefits (Higgins and Higgins 2005).

Electric bikes are also likely to be of transformative significance, providing a kind of "middle way" between electric cars and the human-powered bicycle. Electric bikes retain most of the benefits of the human-powered version, while extending ranges and load capacity to cope adaptively with settlements and economies structured to suit cars and trucks. By making cycling lower impact on the rider and much more accessible, electric bikes could be a linchpin technology for managing energy descent and initiating a degrowth transition, at least as an enabler that gets many more people engaged with post-car transport and gives people their first taste of the personal benefits and freedoms available to the cyclist.

Walking or cycling will be nonviable in certain contexts, and even public transport is not always available. These structural problems are well known and not easily or swiftly resolvable, even if the solution is relatively clear: build more infrastructure to support these low-carbon or post-carbon alternatives. Nevertheless, there is also vast scope for replacing many car trips with alternative modes of transport that are less carbon-intensive, especially through a cultural embrace of cycling.

In Australia it has been estimated that three-quarters of all personal car journeys are less than 10 kilometers, with half being less than 5 kilometers, and one-third less than 3 kilometers (Alexander and Yacoumis 2018). It is reasonable to assume that a significant proportion of those trips could be replaced with cycling without hardship, although disability, heavy freight, or other complexities would mean a full substitution would be difficult or impossible. Nevertheless, a study in the United States by Higgins and Higgins (2005) has shown that substituting walking and cycling for short car trips, based on recommended daily exercise, could reduce U.S. domestic oil consumption by up to 34.9 percent, while also having huge health benefits and leading to reduced health care costs. No doubt other oil-dependent nations could also achieve significant savings through this "simple," low-tech strategy.

Recent research by Laskovsky and Taylor (2017) in Melbourne, Australia, also bears consideration: the vast amount of urban and suburban space dedicated to cars, roads, and parking is deeply wasteful, especially when it is understood how inefficiently that space is used in terms of irregular occupation. Reclaiming this land for other purposes is an exciting urban prospect, as it would open up vast tracts of land for an array of retrofitting activities limited only by our imaginations.

Low-Meat Diets and Population Issues

We close this section on energy with a brief consideration of decarbonizing diets and family size. While not limited in relevance to the suburban context, these issues have significant implications for energy demands and thus deserve comment.

The production of animal products is hugely energy (and carbon) intensive and there is absolutely no way that average Western levels of meat consumption could possibly be globalized in a sustainable way (Poore and Nemecek 2018). While there are some prospects for efficiency improvements in the production of animal products (which might come at the expense of animal welfare), the necessary but rarely acknowledged part of the equation is drastically reducing (or, for some, eliminating) meat and dairy consumption in diets (Hadjikakou 2017; Hadjikakou and Wiedmann 2017).

Nevertheless, this issue ought to be approached with the subtlety it deserves. Global averages can mislead, and a localized economy necessarily means shortening the chain between production and consumption in ways that demand context-dependent analysis (Holmgren 2018). To provide an extreme example, it is no good asking the Inuit people to reduce meat consumption, given that eating sea mammals is their primary means of sustenance, and there are communities around the world similarly dependent on animal agriculture to survive. Much land is not suitable for cropping, in which case the distinction between grain-fed and pasture-fed animals is important. Reducing the former could certainly open up more land for lower-carbon, non-meat food production, which would be far more energy efficient on account of feeding food to humans instead of that food to animals and then eating the animals. The role of grazing animals in landscape restoration and regeneration is also an important consideration, too often overlooked by those ignorant of land management and food production (Massy 2017).

None of this changes the fact, however, that in many affluent societies significantly reducing meat and dairy consumption is one of the most significant things people can do to decarbonize their lives (Wynes and Nicholas 2017). Having small families is the other issue deserving of note, and, indeed, the growth paradigm treats population as a driver of growth and therefore presumptively a good thing. Yet both strategies (reduced meat consumption and lower fertility) scarcely get a mention in mainstream environmental or political discourse. This willing blindness is a major cultural obstacle to any post-carbon transition and one that is not easily overcome. The best that can done is to show by example that low or no meat diets can be healthy, cheap, and delicious, and that small family size accrues many benefits (financial, increased free time, more sleep) aside from the environmental ones. Climate activist Bill McKibben (1999) suggested a good starting question for the next generation of parents-to-be: "Maybe one?" As for diets, it is hard to improve upon the simple advice offered by food guru Michael Pollan (2007): "Eat [fresh, unprocessed] food. Not too much. Mostly plants."

Toward a Post-Carbon Suburban Homestead: Reimagining the Good Life

Beyond direct energy considerations, the emergence of expensive energy and a contracting degrowth economy will require a revaluation of values and practices in other domains of life, too. Any consumerist culture is going to require a growth economy to meet its demands for ever-rising material living standards. The flip side of that coin is that a degrowth economy will depend on and require a material culture of sufficiency that embraces a post-consumerist existence of relative scarcity of energy and resources. The dual value of embracing this strategy is that it moves the culture of consumption in a more sustainable direction, and it prepares the household for disruptive and unstable economic times in which reduced consumption is enforced rather than voluntarily chosen. That is, downshifting prepares the household for times of crisis or unplanned economic contraction, and thus increases resilience, even if the primary or initial motivating goal is sustainability.

By "voluntary simplicity," we are talking about more than taking shorter showers, turning the lights off, and recycling. A degrowth culture of consumption in an energy descent context must assume a far more radical form of downshifting. According to the Ecological Footprint analysis, humanity would need four or five planets if the Australian or U.S. way of life were globalized. If Australian living standards were attained by the projected global population of 2050, then humanity would need 10 planets (Trainer 2012).

Few analysts of the global predicament seem to appreciate the magnitude of this challenge: it requires a 75–90 percent reduction in ecological impacts compared to living standards in the wealthiest regions of the world, even if sustainable living will always be a context-dependent practice (Trainer 2012, 2020). As Hickel and Kallis (2019) have shown, efficiency, technology, and the decoupling strategy are failing to bring the global economy within sustainable bounds. It follows by force of logic and evidence that globalizing Western-style material living standards is a recipe for catastrophe—both ecological and humanitarian. A just and sustainable world necessarily involves some radically transfigured practices of consumption and production compared to the ecocidal forms that have emerged in the West, and that means, among other things, embracing the all-but-forgotten wisdom of frugality, moderation, and sufficiency (Princen 2005; Westacott 2016).

Enlightened Material Restraint: The Practice of Sufficiency and Self-Limitation

What might this alternative suburban ethics of consumption look like in practice? As always, context is everything, but some broad comments may offer some general insight into how consumption practices may need to be transformed in and for an energy descent future. Above, we addressed energy specifically, with the clear, but often complex, prescription being to radically reduce energy demand and invest in localized renewable energy production. In affluent societies of the "developed" world, some of the funds for such investment could be found simply by reducing expenditure elsewhere. Voluntary simplicity or downshifting implies being extremely mindful with one's money and being aware that numerous small expenses (magazines, clothes, takeout food, that extra beer) over months and years can add up to considerable sums (Domingeuz and Robins 1992). In a recessionary or depressed economy, of course, such downshifting may be enforced rather than voluntarily chosen, in which case it makes sense to anticipate the more austere material culture that lies ahead in an energy descent future. One thinks of the Depression-era slogan: "Use it up, wear it out, make do, or do without."

This should not be presumed to imply hardship necessarily (Kasser 2017; Lockyer 2017). At the least, how well an individual or household manages economic contraction is partly a function of the values and attitudes one brings to experience (Burch 2012). Once sufficiency in material living standards is achieved (through basic provision of food, housing, clothing, and energy), voluntary simplicity implies resisting the dominant cultural pressure to seek ever-higher incomes and instead seeking the good life in a range of non-materialistic sources of meaning and fulfilment (Alexander 2009). This essential insight is supported by a vast body of social and psychological research showing that money and possessions have diminishing marginal returns; the richer people get, the less money contributes to quality of life (Lane 2000; Kasser 2002, 2017).

In pursuit of voluntary simplicity, households will discover a number of practices that can reduce impact while also saving thousands of dollars every year:

- buying second-hand clothes;
- avoiding the lure of fancy possessions;
- growing a portion of household food;
- capturing water in tanks;
- making or mending rather than purchasing;
- developing cheap and low-impact leisure activities;
- sharing and borrowing;
- brewing one's own beer or cider; and
- minimizing waste and avoiding packaging.

In these ways, creating a surplus can be directed into the clean energy revolution, or allow for reduced working hours, which can open up more time to dedicate to community action, home-based production, or simply more time for family, friends, and private passions (Read et al. 2018).

Of course, the usual proviso applies: many households even in affluent societies are living from paycheck to paycheck, with little room for voluntary downshifting. But in consumer cultures, there are many households that have normalized abundance with no conception of "enough" (Hamilton and Denniss 2005; Jackson et al. 2004; Lane 2000). In anticipation of an energy descent future, such a normalization of abundance must be unlearned. The less people need to purchase to maintain their way of life, the less they are obliged to work to pay for that market consumption. By thus reimagining the good life beyond consumer culture, voluntary simplicity offers a path to maximizing freedom and advancing genuine well-being, a transition that Soper (2008) calls "alternative hedonism" and Raser-Rowland and Grubb (2016) refer to as "frugal hedonism." (This rightly implies that self-interest is an incentive beyond environmentalism or concern for the world's destitute, and empirical research verifies that voluntary simplicity offers this hedonic reward [Alexander and Ussher 2012; Kasser 2017].)

Even the most radically downshifted suburban households, however, are probably still overconsuming on a global scale, so the practice of sufficiency must remain an ongoing context-dependent process, not a static destination to arrive at or achieve once and for all (Princen 2005). This again points to the systemic nature of global crises, since it can be very hard or even impossible to consume less within societal structures that have been created to promote limitless growth and unbounded consumerism (Sanne 2002). Nevertheless, the structural transformation will never transpire until there is a post-consumerist culture that is prepared to embrace material sufficiency. Accordingly, new cultures of voluntary simplicity are required both to provide the social conditions needed for a degrowth economy to emerge systemically and to build resilience if economic contraction occurs through recession or depression rather than through planned design (Alexander 2013).

The political significance of the voluntary simplicity movement is most apparent in how it can carve out *more time for people to create the new (suburban) economy.* The politics of voluntary simplicity is typically conceived of in terms of "political consumers" who express their values through what they buy and where they spend (Stolle and Micheletti 2013). That is fine as far as it goes, but it misses the more significant matter of freedom and time. Building a new economy from the grassroots up in an energy descent future will take time, and currently most households are "time poor," locked into a work-and-spend cycle (Robinson 2009). By rethinking consumption levels, embracing frugality, and exchanging superfluous stuff for more free time, voluntary simplicity provides a pathway that can enable grassroots activism and suburban homesteading, while also being directly in line with the post-materialist values of degrowth and permaculture.

Eating the Suburbs

We have been exploring some of the practices and values that may be needed in order to build suburban resilience in the face of an energy descent future and a contracting economy. Having reviewed direct energy considerations and the ethos of sufficiency that informs the voluntary simplicity and downshifting movements, we turn now to the relocalization of food production and increased self-sufficiency through home-based production (Gaynor 2006).

There is a flourishing "local food movement" in many cities today (Norberg-Hodge 2019). However, its full potential has not yet been fully realized (Trainer 2019). Digging up backyards and front yards and planting fruit and vegetables, keeping chickens, and composting are important practices, reconnecting people with the seasons, the soil, and the food on their plates. To borrow the phrase often spoken in Australian permaculture circles, we should "eat the suburbs."

There are lessons here from the Cuban experience in the early 1990s. When the USSR collapsed, Cuba quickly found itself having to manage with greatly decreased oil imports (Friedrichs 2010). Despite this so-called special period being a time of considerable hardship, a key strategy for dealing with energy descent in Cuba was to relocalize and decarbonize food production by scaling up organic food production in and near cities, deeply influenced by permaculture theory and practice (Viljoen 2005: Chs. 17–18).

Furthermore, in an age characterized by what Louv (2008) has called "nature deficit disorder," the rewards of home or community gardening go well beyond the environmental and physical health benefits of eating local, fresh food. Getting into the garden and out of our cars offers mental health rewards, too (Soga et al. 2017). There might be silver linings to more austere material futures where home-based production and cycling become necessary, due to rising energy costs and tightening household budgets in a contracting economy.

Recent scholarly analyses demonstrate the productive potential of suburban blocks. Ted Trainer has undertaken a detailed quantitative analysis of East Hills, an outer suburb of Sydney, Australia, where he lives. Trainer (2019: 25) demonstrates through quantitative analysis that urban and suburban agriculture has highly significant productive capacity, concluding that "most, and possibly almost all food could come from within settlements, that is from home gardens, community gardens, neighbourhood commons, and very small farms." Similarly, promising analyses have been published by the Melbourne-based Victorian Eco-Innovation Lab (VEIL 2018; Trainer, Malik, and Lenzen 2018).

Nevertheless, few suburban households, if any, could be fully self-sufficient in fruit and vegetables, let alone in other things like wheat, oats, and rice, as well as any number of other foodstuffs like salt, sugar, nuts, and milk. But producing as much as possible saves money, increases self-sufficiency, builds resilience, and as noted, reconnects people with the land and soil. Trainer's analysis, just noted, also highlights the importance of moving beyond mere "self-sufficiency," and working toward a "collective sufficiency," wherever possible. This would involve reclaiming underutilized public land, especially roads and car parks, and sharing private land for food production (Laskovsky and Taylor 2017).

In terms of creating soil, the suburban composting toilet may also have a place in a degrowth economy, as households stop exporting nutrient-rich waste in potable water and instead treat their own waste onsite. Michael Mobbs (2010) of Sydney is among the early adopters. A composting toilet helps close the nutrient cycle; it creates fertilizer for fruit trees; and minimizes or avoids the need to import fertilizers for the garden, saving money. Human waste needs to be respected for safety reasons but it need not be feared, as explained and scientifically justified by Joseph Jenkins (2005).

Home-based food production also offers a means of escaping the market, to some extent, thereby undermining the industrial food industry by withdrawing financial support for it, and redirecting that support, when necessary, toward local farmers markets (Norberg-Hodge 2019). Over time, we can imagine food production crossing beyond household boundaries, too, re-commoning public space. This is already under way, as people reclaim nature strips for food production, plant fruit trees in the neighborhood, establish community gardens, and cultivate unused land through "guerrilla gardening." Decarbonizing food production generally means relocalizing production—shortening the space between production and consumption. Urban agriculturalists are not waiting, and should not wait, for governments to lead this transition (Holmgren 2018; Trainer, Malik, and Lenzen 2019).

Escaping the Market: Sharing, Gift, and the Urban Peasantry

We close this incomplete survey of energy-descent resilience practices by highlighting the importance of sharing, gift, and home-based production, all of which have untapped prospects for decarbonization, dematerialization, and relocalization. These are topics that also highlight how degrowth and energy descent involve an upscaling of informal, non-monetary, and "post-capitalist" modes of economy, as well as increased economic localization (Albert 2004; De Young and Princen 2012; Gibson-Graham et al. 2013; Holmgren 2018).

By sharing more between households—facilitated by the Internet or by traditional community engagement—less energy- and resource-intensive production needs to occur to meet society's needs. Indeed, even in a contracting economy (whether contraction is by design or by crisis), households can still secure access to the tools and other things they need, provided a culture of sharing emerges. This is the revolutionary reinterpretation of "efficiency" implicit in the degrowth paradigm: produce less; share more; thrive. Nelson (2018) explores the potential of sharing land and housing as a promising means of overcoming some of the access barriers to this fundamental need.

On a similar note, degrowth also arguably implies an incremental reemergence of the gift economy—to some extent, at least (Eisenstein 2011). If living standards are forever expected to rise, long working hours required to support that ongoing material advance will generally leave people "time poor," making it difficult for people to gift their skills and resources in the spirit of community and neighborly support. By consuming less and carving out more time for practices outside the formal economy, downshifting can also enliven the informal gift economy.

As this culture of decommodification emerges, it becomes increasingly self-supporting: one household is liberated from the market economy to some extent by practicing voluntary simplicity, allowing more time to gift skills and resources outside the market; but as other households do that, too, the benefits and rewards of the gift economy return, reducing reliance on the market economy and making voluntary simplicity increasingly viable, which further supports the gift economy in a symbiotic loop of mutual support. Paradoxically, then, financial frugality enables generosity, solidarity, sharing, and redistribution (Gibson-Graham et al. 2013). Over time, a new economy could emerge from within the shell of the old economy.

Finally, degrowth and permaculture in the suburbs implies turning the household into a place of production, not merely consumption (Holmgren 2018; Alexander and Gleeson 2019; Trainer 2019). On this point, some inspiration can be found in the past. Mullins and Kynaston (2000) assessed what they call the "urban peasant thesis," and their review of the evidence shows that up until the middle of the 20th century, Australian urban households had operated a highly developed, subsistence-based, domestic economy. This included the production of foodstuffs in suburban backyards, but extended to the manufacture of other household goods, including clothes, furniture, and even owner-built housing. Thus, the dwelling and the yard were seen primarily in utilitarian, rather than aesthetic, terms. This "urban peasantry" declined, however, in the postwar boom, as the rise of mass consumer capitalism enabled households to purchase goods previously produced within the household. This suggests that any degrowth or energy descent future of reduced productive capacity in the formal economy may well see the reemergence of an "urban peasantry" in this sense, albeit one shaped by different times and concerns.

Conclusion

Some of the practices, attitudes, and approaches reviewed in this article are not new, and draw from modes of living that homesteaders, eco-villagers, permaculturalists, hippies, and other counter-culturists have been doing for decades or more (Alexander and McLeod 2014). We contend that the wider urban application of these practices is well justified in the face of a contracting economy and declining access to cheap energy, even if still often marginalized by dominant energy and consumption cultures. The social-scientific evidence we have presented and reviewed is emerging to support these earlier practices of exploratory and radical sustainability and resilience.

There are also a few new and emerging features, like domestic biogas and peer-to-peer sharing facilitated by the Internet, whose cultural potential is highly promising but remains largely untapped. Most of the practices, such as solar PV, biogas, food production, solar-oven use, and water collection, are also enabled by the suburban context. A separate analysis could determine if those practices would be impossible, impractical, or at least significantly different in high-density urban contexts.

These household practices and values are not a panacea to today's problems, but it is likely that managing an energy-descent future is going to require more suburbanites embracing them, albeit in context- and household-dependent ways. Granted, things like second-hand clothes, biogas, composting toilets, home-based production, and sharing offer a humbler vision of the future than the eco-modernist visions defended today (Bastani 2019). But we contend that our humbler vision is much more coherent when the challenges of climate change and peak oil are taken seriously and the limits of techno-optimism are understood (Hickel and Kallis 2019). "Greening" the supply of energy and resources is necessary but insufficient; high-impact, energy-intensive societies also need to radically reduce demand.

Promising and necessary though these practices of suburban downshifting are, things are not as rosy or free from contradiction as they might first seem. We opened this article by acknowledging the deep structural obstacles of class, privilege, and property ownership that lie in the way of any degrowth transition. Although space has not permitted a "top-down" political analysis of energy-descent planning in the national and/or international domains, there are myriad policy options available to assist with this transition, such as greater government funding of renewable energy, a strong price on carbon to quickly phase out fossil fuels, the development of broader networks of bike lanes, and exploration of distributive options (within and between nations) to ensure equity in a contracting economy (Alexander and Gleeson 2019: Ch. 7). Without diminishing the importance of a "top-down" response, the regressive state of contemporary national and global politics prompted us to focus on the social or grassroots strategies available, which we hold up as the most promising spaces for transformative change in an age of widespread political paralysis.

We are also disconcertingly aware of how many of the efforts to transition beyond fossil fuels depend, to date at least, on the very fuels those efforts are trying to transcend, as well as the globally integrated supply chains that are enabled by fossil fuels (Alexander and Floyd 2018). Solar panels, biogas digesters, heat pumps, and bicycles are currently a product of fossil fuels, and the same goes for nails, screws, steel sheet, and windows, as well as all the commodities that make households function, from pots and cutlery, to furniture and musical instruments. Indeed, even households with vast net surpluses of renewable energy production will, in the absence of expensive battery storage, still draw from and depend on the fossil-energy grid at night to keep the refrigerator running and the lights on after dark.

These critical reflections should not be interpreted as undermining the strategy or importance of retrofitting suburban households in the manner and spirit outlined in this article. They only point to the complexity of the predicament. Existing suburbanites can and should get to work building new, low-energy forms of life within existing structures. As this article argues, there is a huge amount that could be done in that space. The household may not be the world economy, but changing the world will require changing the household. We contend that a resilient suburban future will embody many, if not all, of the values and practices reviewed.

References

Albert, Michael. (2004). *Parecon: Life After Capitalism.* London: Verso.

Alexander, Samuel, ed. (2009). *Voluntary Simplicity: The Poetic Alternative to Consumer Culture.* Whanganui, New Zealand: Stead and Daughters.

________. (2015). *Sufficiency Economy: Enough, for Everyone, Forever.* Melbourne: Simplicity Institute.

________. (2013). "Voluntary Simplicity and the Social Reconstruction of Law: Degrowth from the Grassroots Up." *Environmental Values* 22(2): 287–308.

Alexander, Samuel, and Brendan Gleeson. (2019). *Degrowth in the Suburbs: A Radical Urban Imaginary.* Singapore: Palgrave Macmillan.

Alexander, Samuel, Phillip Harris, and Bernadette McCabe. (2019). "Biogas in the Suburbs: An Untapped Source of Clean Energy?" *Journal of Cleaner Production* 215: 1025–1035.

Alexander, Samuel, and Josh Floyd. (2018). *Carbon Civilisation and the Energy Descent Future.* Melbourne: Simplicity Institute.

Alexander, Samuel, and Amanda McLeod, eds. (2014). *Simple Living in History: Pioneers of the Deep Future.* Melbourne: Simplicity Institute.

Alexander, Samuel, and Simon Ussher. (2012). "The Voluntary Simplicity Movement: A Multi-National Survey in Theoretical Context." *Journal of Consumer Culture* 12(1): 66–88.

Alexander, Samuel, and Paul Yacoumis. (2018). "Degrowth, Energy Descent, and 'Low-Tech' Living: Potential Pathways for Increased Resilience in Times of Crisis." *Journal of Cleaner Production* 197: 1840–1848.

Australia Broadcast Corporation (ABC). (2013). "Do Australians Waste $8 Billion Worth of Edible Food Each Year?" *ABC* October 8. https://www.abc.net.au/news/2013-10-08/food-waste-value-australia/4993930

Ayres, Robert, and Benjamin Warr. (2009). *The Economic Growth Engine: How Energy and Work Drive Material Prosperity.* Cheltenham, UK: Edward Elgar.

Bastani, Aaron. (2019). *Fully Automated Luxury Communism: A Manifesto.* London: Verso.

Bauman, Zygmunt. (2004). *Wasted Lives: Modernity and its Outcasts.* Cambridge, UK: Polity.

Bond, Tom, and Michael Templeton. (2011). "History and Future of Domestic Biogas Plants in the Developing World." *Energy for Sustainable Developmen*t 15(4): 347–354.

Borenstein, Severin. (2017). "Private Net Benefits of Residential Solar PV: The Role of Electricity Tariffs, Tax Incentives, and Rebates." *Journal of the Association of Environmental and Resource Economist*s 4(S1): S85–S122. https://www.journals.uchicago.edu/doi/10.1086/691978 or https://pdfs.semanticscholar.org/2994/e6255314c3011f5ae90b8788af85e18d7777.pdf

Burch, Mark. (2012). *The Hidden Door: Mindful Sufficiency as an Alternative to Collapse.* Melbourne: Simplicity Institute.

Creutzig, Felix, Peter Agoston, Jan Christoph Goldschmidt, Gunnar Luderer, Gregory Nemet, and Robert C. Pietzcker. (2017). "The Underestimated Potential of Solar Energy to Mitigate Climate Change." *Nature Energy* 2: 17140. https://doi.org/10.1038/nenergy.2017.140

De Young, Raymond. (2014). "Some Behavioural Aspects of Energy Descent: How a Biophysical Psychology Might Help People Transition Through the Lean Times Ahead." *Frontiers in Psychology* 5: 1255. https://doi.org/10.3389/fpsyg.2014.01255

De Young, Raymond, and Thomas Princen, eds. (2012). *The Localization Reader: Adapting to the Coming Downshift.* Cambridge, MA: MIT Press.

Dixon, Tim, Simon Lannon, and Malcolm Eames. (2018). "Reflections on Disruptive Energy Innovation: Methodology, Practice, and Policy." *Energy Research and Social Science* 37: 255–259.

Domingeuz, Joe, and Vicki Robins. (1992). *Your Money or Your Life: Transforming Your Relationship with Money and Achieving Financial Independence.* London: Penguin.

Eisenstein, Charles. (2011). *Sacred Economics: Money, Gift, and Society in the Age of Transition.* Berkeley: North Atlantic Books.

Frankel, Boris. (2018). *Fictions of Sustainability: The Politics of Growth and Post-Capitalist Futures.* Melbourne: Greenmeadows.

Friedrichs, J. Jörg. (2010). "Global Energy Crunch: How Different Parts of the World Would React to a Peak Oil Scenario." *Energy Policy* 38: 4562–4569.

Gaynor, Andrea. (2006). *Harvest of the Suburbs: An Environmental History of Growing Food in Australian Cities.* Perth: University of Western Australia.

Gehl, Anthony, Jeffery Munk, Philip Boudreaux, Roderick Jackson, and Gannate Khowailed. (2012). *Campbell Creek Research Homes: FY 2012 Annual Performance Report.* Oak Ridge, TN: Oak Ridge National Laboratory, U.S. Department of Energy. https://www.tva.gov/file_source/TVA/Site%20Content/Energy/Technology%20Innovation/CampbellCreekReport2012.pdf

Gibson-Graham, J. K., Jenny Cameron, and Stephen Healy. (2013). *Take Back the Economy: An Ethical Guide for Transforming Our Communities.* Minneapolis: University of Minnesota Press.

Gleeson, Brendan. (2014). *The Urban Condition.* London: Routledge.

Greer, John Michael. (2008). *The Long Descent: A User's Guide to the End of the Industrial Age.* Gabriola Island, BC, Canada: New Society Publishers.

Hadjikakou, Michalis. (2017). "Trimming the Excess: Environmental Impacts of Discretionary Food Consumption in Australia." *Ecological Economics* 131: 199–128.

Hadjikakou, Michalis, and Thomas Wiedmann. (2017). "Shortcomings of a Growth-Driven Food System." In *Handbook on Growth and Sustainability.* Eds. Peter A. Victor and Brett Dolter, pp. 256–276. Cheltenham, UK: Edward Elgar.

Hamilton, Clive, and Richard Denniss. (2005). *Affluenza: When Too Much Is Never Enough.* Crows Nest: Allen & Unwin.

Heard, Benjamin P., Barry Brook, Tom Wigley, and Corey Bradshaw. (2017). "Burden of Proof: A Comprehensive Review of the Feasibility of 100% Renewable-Electricity Systems." *Renewable and Sustainable Energy Reviews* 76: 1122–1133. https://doi.org/10.1016/j.rser.2017.03.114

Heinberg, Richard. (2004). *Powerdown: Options and Actions for a Post-Carbon World.* Gabriola Island, BC, Canada: New Society Publishers.

Heinberg, Richard, and David Fridley. (2016). *Our Renewable Future: Laying the Path for 100% Clean Energy.* Washington, DC: Island Press. http://ourrenewablefuture.org/

Hickel, Jason. (2017). *The Divide: A Brief Guide to Global Inequality and its Solutions.* London: William Heinemann.

Hickel, Jason, and Giorgios Kallis. (2019). "Is Green Growth Possible?" *New Political Economy.* https://doi.org/10.1080/13563467.2019.1598964

Higgins, Paul, and Millicent Higgins. (2005). "A Healthy Reduction in Oil Consumption and Carbon Emissions." *Energy Policy* 33(1): 1–4.

Holmgren, David. (2012). "Retrofitting the Suburbs for the Energy Descent Future." *Simplicity Institute Report* 12i: 1–19.

_______. (2018). *Retrosuburbia: The Downshifter's Guide to a Resilient Future.* Hepburn, Victoria, Australia: Melliodora Publishing. https://melliodora.com/product-tag/melliodora-publishing/

Hopkins, Rob. (2008). *The Transition Handbook: From Oil Dependency to Local Resilience.* White River Junction, VT: Chelsea Green Publishing.

Intergovernmental Panel on Climate Change (IPCC). (2018). "Summary for Policymakers." In *Global Warming of 1.5°C.* Geneva, Switzerland: IPCC. https://www.ipcc.ch/site/assets/uploads/sites/2/2019/05/SR15_SPM_version_report_LR.pdf or https://www.ipcc.ch/sr15/download/#chapter

International Energy Agency. (2018). *World Energy Outlook 2018: Executive Summary.* Paris: International Energy Agency. https://webstore.iea.org/download/summary/190?fileName=English-WEO-2018-ES.pdf

Jackson, Tim, Wanger Jager, and Sigrid Stagl. (2004). "Beyond Insatiability—Needs Theory, Consumption, and Sustainability." In *The Ecological Economics of Consumption.* Eds. Lucia Reisch and Inge Røpke, pp. 79–110. Cheltenham, UK: Edward Elgar.

Jacobson, Mark Z., Mark A. Delucchi, Zack A. F. Bauer, Savannah C. Goodman, William E. Chapman, Mary Cameron, Cedric Bozonnat, Liat Chobadi, Hailey A. Clonts, Peter Enevoldsen, Jenny R. Erwin, Simone N. Fobi, Owen K. Goldstrom, Eleanor M. Hennessy, Jingyi Liu, Jonathan Lo, Clayton B. Meyer, Sean B. Morris, Kevin R. Moy, Patrick L. O'Neill, Ivalin Petkov, Stephanie Redfern, Robin Schucker, Michael A. Sontag, Jingfan Wang, Eric Weiner, and Alexander S. Yachanin. (2017). "100% Clean and Renewable Wind, Water, and Sunlight All-Sector Energy Roadmaps for 139 Countries of the World." *Joule* 1: 108–121.

Jenkins, Joseph. (2005). *The Humanure Handbook: A Guide to Composting Human Manure,* 3rd ed. White River Junction, VT: Chelsea Green Publishing.

Kallis, Giorgos. (2017). "Radical Dematerialization and Degrowth." *Philosophical Transactions of the Royal Society A.* 375:20160383: 1–13.

Kallis, Giorgos, Vasilis Kostakis, Steffen Lange, Barbara Muraca, Susan Paulson, and Matthias Schmelzer. (2018). "Research on Degrowth." *Annual Review of Environment and Resources.* 43: 4.1–4.26.

Kasser, Tim. (2002). *The High Price of Materialism.* Cambridge, MA: MIT Press.

________. (2017). "Living Both Well and Sustainably: A Review of the Literature, with Some Reflections on Future Research, Interventions, and Policy." *Philosophical Transactions of the Royal Society A.* 375: 20160369.

Keen, Steve, Robert Ayres, and R. Standish. (2019). "A Note on the Role of Energy in Production." *Ecological Economics* 157: 40–46.

Kunstler, James. (2005). *The Long Emergency: Surviving the Converging Catastrophes of the Twenty-First Century.* New York: Grove/Atlantic.

Lane, Robert. (2000). *The Loss of Happiness in Market Democracies.* New Haven: Yale University Press.

Laskovsky, Jonathan, and Elizabeth Taylor. (2017). "A Lot of Thought: The Space of Car Parks and Shopping Centres in Australian Cities." In *Proceedings of Automotive Historians Australia, Vol. I: Driving Futures.* Eds. Harriet Edquist, Mark Richardson, and Simon Lockrey, pp. 1–18. Melbourne, Victoria, Australia: Automotive Historians Australia, Inc. https://researchmgt.monash.edu/ws/portalfiles/portal/276977661/276977531.pdf

Liaros, Steven. (2019). "Implementing a New Human Settlement Theory: Strategic Planning for a Network of Regenerative Ecovillages." *Smart and Sustainable Built Environment.* https://doi.org/10.1108/SASBE-01-2019-0004

Lockyer, Joshua. (2017). "Community, Commons, and Degrowth at Dancing Rabbit Ecovillage." *Journal of Political Ecology* 24(1): 519–542.

Louv, Richard. (2008). *Last Child in the Woods: Saving Our Children from Nature Deficit Disorder.* New York: Workman Publishing.

Massy, Charles. (2017). *Call of the Reed Warbler: A New Agriculture —A New Earth.* Brisbane, Australia: University of Queensland Press.

McKibben, Bill. (1999). *Maybe One? A Case for Smaller Families.* New York: Plume.

Mobbs, Michael. (2010). *Sustainable House*, 2nd ed. Sydney: New South Wales Press.

Mohr Steve et al. (2015). "Projection of World Fossil Fuels by Country." *Fuel* 141: 120–135.

Monbiot, George. (2007). *Heat: How to Stop the Planet from Burning.* London: Allen Lane.

Moriarty, Patrick, and Damon Honnery. (2008). "Low-Mobility: The Future of Transport." *Futures* 40: 865–872.

________. (2011). *Rise and Fall of the Carbon Civilisation: Resolving Global Environmental and Resource Problems.* London: Springer.

________. (2016). "Global Transport Energy Consumption." In *Alternative Energy and Shale Gas Encyclopedia.* Eds. Jay Lehr, Jack Keely, and Thomas Kingery. New Jersey: John Wiley and Sons.

Mullins, Patrick, and Chris Kynaston. (2000). "The Household Production of Subsistence Goods: The Urban Peasant Thesis Reassessed." In *A History of European Housing in Australia*, 9th ed. Ed. Patrick Troy, pp. 142–163. Cambridge, UK: Cambridge University Press.

Nelson, Anitra. (2018). *Small Is Necessary: Shared Living on a Shared Planet.* London: Pluto Press.

Nelson, Anitra, and Francois Schneider. (2018). *Housing for Degrowth: Principles, Models, Challenges, and Opportunities.* London: Routledge.

Norberg-Hodge, Helena. (2019). *Local Is Our Future: Steps to an Economics of Happiness.* Byron Bay: Local Futures.

Odum, Howard, and Elizabeth Odum. (2001). *A Prosperous Way Down: Principles and Policies.* Colorado: University of Colorado Press.

Palmer, Graham, and Joshua Floyd. (2020). *Energy Storage and Civilization: A Systems Approach.* Singapore: Springer.

Piercy, Emma, Chris Granger, and Rachel Goodier. (2010). "Planning for Peak Oil: Learning from Cuba's 'Special Period'." *Urban Design and Planning* 163(4): 169–176.

Pollan, Michael. (2007). "Unhappy Meals." *New York Times Magazine* January 28. https://www.nytimes.com/2007/01/28/magazine/28nutritionism.t.html

Poore, Joseph, and Thomas Nemecek. (2018). "Reducing Food's Environmental Impacts Through Producers and Consumers." *Science* 360(6392): 987–992.

Princen, Thomas. (2005). *The Logic of Sufficiency.* Cambridge, MA: MIT Press.

Raser-Rowland, Annie, and Adam Grubb. (2016). *The Art of Frugal Hedonism: A Guide to Spending Less While Enjoying Everything More.* Hepburn, Victoria, Australia: Melliodora Publishing.

Read, Rupert, Samuel Alexander, and Jacob Garrett. (2018). "Voluntary Simplicity: Strongly Backed by All Three Main Ethical-Normative Traditions." *Ethical Perspectives* 25: 87–116.

Reynolds, Christian, Vicki Mavrakis, Sandra Davison, Stine Bordier Høj, Elisha Vlaholias, Anne Sharp, Kirrilly Rebecca Thompson, Paul R. Ward, John Coveney, Julia Pintadosi, John W. Boland, and Drew Dawson. (2014). "Estimating Informal Food Waste in Developed Countries: The Case of Australia." *Waste Management and Research* 32(12): 1245–1258.

Robinson, Tim. (2009). *Work, Leisure, and the Environment: The Vicious Circle of Overwork and Overconsumption.* Cheltenham: Edward Elgar Publishing.

Sanne, Christer. (2002). "Willing Consumers—Or Locked In? Policies for a Sustainable Consumption." *Ecological Economics* 42(1): 273–287.

Smil, Vaclav. (2017). *Energy and Civilization: A History.* Cambridge, MA: MIT Press.

Soga, Masahi, Kevin Gaston, and Yuichi Yamaura. (2017). "Gardening Is Beneficial for Health. A Meta Analysis." *Preventative Medicine Reports* 5: 92–99.

Soper, Kate. (2008). "Alternative Hedonism, Cultural Theory and the Role of Aesthetic Revisioning." *Cultural Studies* 22(5): 567–587.

Sorrell, Stephen. (2015). "Reducing Energy Demand: A Review of Issues, Challenges and Approaches." *Renewable and Sustainable Energy Reviews* 47: 74–82.

Stolle, Dietlind, and Michelle Micheletti. (2013). *Political Consumerism.* New York: Cambridge University Press.

Tainter, Joseph. (1988). *The Collapse of Complex Societies.* Cambridge, UK: Cambridge University Press.

Trainer, Ted. (2010). *The Transition to a Sustainable and Just World.* Sydney: Envirobook.

________. (2012). "Degrowth: Do You Realise What it Means?" *Futures* 44: 590–599.

________. (2019). "Remaking Settlements for Sustainability: The Simpler Way." *Journal of Political Ecology* 26(1): 202–223.

________. (2020). "De-Growth: Some Suggestions from the 'Simpler Way' Perspective." *Ecological Economics* 167.

Trainer, Ted, Arunima Malik, and Manfred Lenzen. (2019). "A Comparison Between the Monetary, Resource, and Energy Costs of the Conventional Industrial Supply Path and the 'Simpler Way' Path for the Supply of Eggs." *Biophysical Economics and Resource Quality* 4(3): 1–7.

VEIL. (2018). *Publications List.* https://veil.msd.unimelb.edu.au/#publications

Viljoen, Andre, ed. (2005). *CPULs: Continuous Productive Urban Landscapes.* Oxford: Architectural Press.

Weiss, Martin, and Claudio Cattaneo. (2017). "Degrowth—Taking Stock and Reviewing an Emerging Academic Paradigm." *Ecological Economics* 137: 220–230.

Westacott, Emrys. (2016). *The Wisdom of Frugality: Why Less Is More—More or Less.* Princeton, NJ: Princeton University Press.

Wynes, Seth, and Kimberly Nicholas. (2017). "The Climate Mitigation Gap: Education and Government Recommendations Miss the Most Effective Individual Actions." *Environmental Research Letters* 12(7). https://iopscience.iop.org/article/10.1088/1748-9326/aa7541

CHAPTER 11

What Makes a Good Cargo Bike Route? Perspectives from Users and Planners

George Liu, Samuel Nello-Deakin†, Marco te Brömmelstroet‡, and Yuki Yamamoto§*

ABSTRACT. Cargo bikes—bicycles made to carry both goods and people—are becoming increasingly common as an alternative to automobiles in urban areas. With a wider and heavier body, cargo bikes often face problems even in the presence of cycling infrastructure, thus limiting their possibilities of route choice. Infrastructure quality and the route choices of cyclists have been well studied, but often solely based on a quantitative approach, leading to tools such as BLOS (bicycle level of service). With various designs of cargo bikes being used for a wide range of purposes, the route choice of cargo bike users is difficult to generalize. This study combines quantitative and qualitative approaches in order to explore what is important for cargo bike users' route choice, and how this knowledge can be effectively used for planning. Our results suggest that while some general preferences exist, route choice involves complex dynamics that cannot be fully explained by quantitative measures alone: in addition to understanding "what" is important for cargo bike users, we need to understand "why" it is important. Furthermore, route choice is also influenced by the city context, making a study tailored to the local context essential.

Introduction

Citizens around the world are recognizing that the energy efficiency and spatial compactness of the bicycle provides a transportation solution for cities looking to improve the quality of their public space. At present, per capita vehicle use is 6,000–7,000 kilometers per year in Western and Northern Europe, and around 13,000 in the United States (Lewis 2020). In order to meet the European target for reduced greenhouse gas emissions from transportation, Europeans will need to cut auto travel by about 66 percent; Americans will need to reduce driving

*Doctoral Researcher, Dept. of Geography, Planning & International Development, University of Amsterdam; Doctoral Researcher, Dept. of Built Environment, Eindhoven University of Technology, Netherlands; Faculty, Urban Cycling Institute, Amsterdam.

†Doctoral Researcher, Dept. of Geography, Planning & International Development, University of Amsterdam; Faculty, Urban Cycling Institute, Amsterdam.

‡Professor in Urban Mobility Futures, Centre for Urban Studies, AISSR, University of Amsterdam; Faculty, Urban Cycling Institute, Amsterdam.

§Researcher, Urban Cycling Institute, Amsterdam, Netherlands.

by nearly 90 percent (European Cyclists Federation 2011).

Many current urban trips include the need to carry more than the rider. Parents may need to take their young children to school or to the doctor. Cars and trucks currently carry groceries, equipment, and other goods in quantities that exceed what an ordinary bike can carry, even with luggage racks and a backpack on the rider.

For these uses, the "cargo bike" may be key to enabling the widespread use of active transportation and enable cyclists to carry larger loads, yet it is unclear if current bicycle infrastructure is designed to accommodate these larger vehicles. Maximizing the use of cargo bikes and reducing deliveries by heavy vehicles can pay dividends in terms of carbon emissions, air quality, safety of street users, and better use of urban space. Lightweight cargo bikes that can carry up to 250 kilograms are already used in various cities, and constitute a reliable, fast, and cheap way of delivering goods (Maes and Vanelslander 2012). However, there has been relatively little attention paid to the factors that make some routes much better than others for cargo bikes. Conscious consideration of these questions by transportation planners can promote more rapid growth of cargo bike transport.

In this article, we conduct interviews in two cities—Amsterdam and Stockholm—with cargo bike riders as well as planners to illuminate the factors that are particularly important for cargo bike use. The two cities have similarities in that urban cycling is a significant factor in local transportation, though the mode share of cycling in Amsterdam is much higher. There are also significant differences in topography, spatial layout, and weather. Therefore, these two cities offer useful comparisons and contrasts that may be valuable to planners and activists in other cities as well. While we do not know the total number of cargo bike users in these two cities, it is estimated

Figure 1
Examples of Cargo Bikes (Left: two-wheel model; Right: three-wheel model)

Source: Photographs by authors.

that light electric freight vehicles can replace 10 to 15 percent of delivery-vehicle movements (Ploos van Amstel et al. 2018). For personal use, we already see about 2 percent of Amsterdam households owning a cargo bike, with families incorporating cargo bikes into their daily routine of transporting children and large amounts of groceries (Boterman 2018). Figure 1 shows two popular forms of personal cargo bikes found in Amsterdam.

It is expected that more than 80 percent of the population of Europe will live in urban areas by 2050, so cargo bikes are receiving an increasing amount of attention as an alternative means of urban mobility. A key advantage of cycling compared to motorized transport is that it allows for greater and more flexible route choices, thereby reducing travel distances to destinations (Manum and Nordstrom 2013). Cyclists can also minimize their exposure to air pollution by choosing an appropriate route (Hertel et al. 2008). While the route choices of cyclists and e-bike users have been extensively studied, no study has explored the route choices of cargo bike users (Plazier et al. 2017; Ton et al. 2017). The greater size and poorer maneuverability of cargo bikes, for instance, might result in cargo bike users avoiding narrow or zigzagging routes that they would normally choose on a regular bike. Similarly, cargo bike users may be more inclined to avoid routes with steep gradients or excessively busy cycle paths.

In order to address the lack of existing knowledge on the preferences of cargo bike users, we investigate the route choice preferences of cargo bike users, and consider how this knowledge can be effectively used in the planning process. Our main research question can be summarized as follows: How does infrastructure quality relate to the route choices of cargo bike users, and how can this knowledge be used to inform planning? Our article explores three subquestions:

1. What are the stated route choice preferences of cargo bike users?
2. How do these stated preferences relate to the actual route choices of cargo bike users?
3. How can this knowledge be used for planning?

Route Choice and Cycling Suitability Evaluation

The route choices of cyclists and the motivation behind them have been widely discussed in the field of transportation planning, as well as in other fields such as psychology (Ma et al. 2014; Stefansdottir 2014), sociology (Garrard et al. 2008), and engineering (Callister and Lowry 2013; Ehrgott et al. 2012; Priedhorsky et al. 2012). Route choice is often associated with the motivation for cycling; lack of route choice may result in reduced destination accessibility, possibly discouraging bicycle trips (Winters et al. 2010). Various attempts have been made to understand why cyclists choose certain routes, but there seems to be no agreement among researchers. Caulfield et al. (2012), and Suzuki et al. (2012), for instance, claim that directness and short travel times are the strongest motivation, but Krenn et al. (2014) found that the route that is actually used is 6 to 16 percent longer than the shortest possible route, based on research in various cities in the world.

While Koh and Wong (2013), Li et al. (2012), and Menghini et al. (2010) have focused on external factors such as the cycling environment, infrastructure, and legal system, Bernhoft and Carstensen (2008) examine user characteristics, and Garrard et al. (2008) consider trip purpose. Other studies combine both internal and external factors (Caulfield et al. 2012; Ehrgott et al. 2012; Krenn et al. 2014; Segadilha and Sanches 2014; Sener et al. 2009). Broach et al. (2012), for example, found that the purpose of the trip also matters in route choice and that commuter cyclists have a stronger preference for the shortness of the route than cyclists with non-utilitarian purposes.

Safety is another important aspect of route choice, and numerous studies have been conducted on this issue. Segadilha and Sanches (2014) argue that safety-related factors such as traffic speed, the number of heavy vehicles, and street lighting are the first priorities to cyclists. The presence of dedicated cycling facilities has been found to be important (de Sousa et al. 2014), as is the width of these facilities (Jensen 2007; Kang and Lee 2012). As might be expected, cyclists are found to prefer cycling facilities separated from car traffic (Caulfield et al. 2012; Hull and O'Holleran 2014). In Amsterdam, however, Ton et al. (2017) found that cyclists do not value separation as much. Other important factors to consider include traffic lights (Broach et al. 2012) and passing distances between cyclists and cars (Stewart and McHale 2014).

Comfort and the experience of cycling also play a role in route choice. Comfort is partially related to safety: relatively safer routes tend to be more comfortable, and relatively dangerous routes tend to be less comfortable. Congested spaces, intersections, and frequent turns all contribute to decreased comfort, since they require much more attention of cyclists, while a combination of continuous space and calm traffic with moderate complexity gives comfort to cyclists (Stefansdottir 2014). According to Koh and Wong (2013), cyclists prefer a route that is comfortable, close to roadways, with other cyclists and pedestrians, flat terrain, and good scenery. Road condition—including state of maintenance and surface material—is also a factor often discussed (Kroll and Sommer 1976). On-street parking facilities also affects cyclists' route choice (Sener et al. 2009; Winters and Teschke 2010). In addition to infrastructural elements, Liu et al. (2018) observe that the types of bicycle used and the carriage of people and cargo also affect the social, sensory, and spatial aspects of cycling experience.

How cyclists make trade-offs between route attributes is an important aspect to consider in route choice, since cyclists generally travel longer in order to avoid certain road attributes (Scarf and Grehan 2005; Tilahun et al. 2007). Cyclists have to accept trade-offs among various aspects of the route, and a holistic analysis needs to be done to understand this complex dynamic. Cyclists, for instance, are usually happy to take a moderate detour in return for a better environment for cycling (Broach et al. 2012).

Over the last decades, various methods and measures have been developed in order to holistically understand the route choices of cyclists. One such measure is the concept of *level of service* (LOS). With its origins in the field of civil engineering, LOS aims to measure the quality of infrastructure and can be defined as a "qualitative measure that needs to reflect user perceptions of the quality of service, comfort and convenience" (Zhang and Prevedouros 2011). LOS was originally developed in the United States as a tool to analyze the quality of roads for automobiles, but it has since been modified and applied to other modes of transportation (Hull and O'Holleran 2014). LOS for automobiles is too narrowly focused and fails in evaluating road quality for cyclists, and therefore bicycle level of service (BLOS) was created (Huff and Liggett 2014). BLOS can be defined as "the level of satisfaction that a bicyclist would experience while riding on a bicycle road" (Kang and Lee 2012). In practice, however, BLOS indicators rely on a number of simplifications and assumptions that tend to fail to reflect the actual preferences of cyclists (Callister and Lowry 2013). Many BLOS studies consider bicycles as equal to vehicles (Asadi-Shekari et al. 2013). The studies do not take into account potential varieties in bicycle types. Lack of validation of BLOS leads to questionable results, and the inability to accommodate various types of bicycles reduces the power of this indicator. At the same time, attempts to include personalized preferences and take into account the changing environments surrounding cycling infrastructure can be resource intensive and time consuming (Huff and Liggett 2014). BLOS or similar types of approaches are often used for route prediction, but they usually take into account only time and distance. Incorporating personal preferences would make the prediction more accurate (Priedhorsky et al. 2012). In this study, we seek to provide a first step in this direction by exploring cargo bike users' route choice preferences.

Research Design

Our study takes the form of a comparative case study focusing on two cities with different cycling contexts: Amsterdam and Stockholm. With the only possible exception of Copenhagen, Amsterdam is known as the world's leading cycling city, with a high level of cycling usage and extensive provision of cycling infrastructure rarely seen elsewhere

(Nello-Deakin and Nikolaeva 2020). Cycling in Amsterdam does not involve many geographic constraints in terms of route options, since the city is flat and there are not many topographical barriers. Stockholm, on the contrary, is a city where route options are often significantly limited by water and varying terrain. The number of cyclists in Stockholm has risen rapidly during the last decade, and there exist a sufficient number of existing cargo bike users in Stockholm to enable a study of this topic. Nevertheless, Stockholm's cycling infrastructure and culture are by no means as well developed as in Amsterdam. In addition, Stockholm has more extreme weather, being much colder and snowier than Amsterdam in the winter. By studying the two cities, we are able to compare a mature cycling city and a developing cycling city with slightly different geographical and climatic contexts. This allows us to explore the extent to which the route choices and preferences of cargo bike users are common to both cities and therefore generalizable (at least to a certain degree), or, on the contrary, specific to each city.

Overall Preferences

In order to answer our first subquestion about the stated route choice preferences of cargo bike users, we conducted an online survey. We decided to focus on stated preferences rather than observed preferences (such as traffic volume of cyclists) because cyclists only start using a route if its condition is perceived as safe and comfortable; as a consequence, observed route choices may not necessarily reflect cyclists' true preferences (Ma et al. 2014). Anyone who used a cargo bike (defined as any type of bicycle that is larger than a normal bicycle) in each city was able to participate. The survey link was distributed during approximately six weeks in each city. The survey consisted of two parts. The first part involved the usage of cargo bikes: type, trip purpose, and frequency. The second part asked questions about route choice preferences. Route choice preferences were investigated quantitatively, and the importance of each infrastructure element was surveyed with a 10-point Likert scale. (See Table 1.) At the end of the survey, several open-ended questions were included to allow for more flexible answers. These questions focused on infrastructure issues that people face while using a cargo bike, and were included both to expand the scope of this survey as well as to identify relevant issues for the subsequent interviews. (See the subsection below on the dynamics of actual route choice.)

Survey variables were selected based on previous studies, and refined based on the local context in each city.

The survey was conducted online in order to facilitate participation. The survey link was distributed both online and in person. In the former case, dissemination took place through social media, cargo bike shops, businesses using cargo bikes, and bike-related organizations. For the surveys carried out in person, intercept surveys were carried out on streets with large numbers of cyclists, as well as schools where many parents pick up their children by cargo bike. In total, we collected 206 valid responses in Stockholm and 121 in Amsterdam.

The results of the survey were analyzed with SPSS. General route choice preferences were analyzed using the questions based on the Likert scale.

Table 1
Variables in the Study (# = number)

Variable	Abbreviation
Type of infrastructure	Type
Width of cycling space	Width
Smoothness of road surface	Smoothness
Straightness	Straightness
Absence of vehicle parking	No parking
Traffic volume (car)	# Cars
Traffic volume (heavy vehicle)	# Heavy vehicles
Traffic volume (bicycle)	# Bicycles
Traffic volume (pedestrian)	# Pedestrians
Speed limit	Speed limit
Number of traffic lights	# Traffic lights
Intersection design	Intersection
Brightness	Brightness
Upward steepness	Steepness

The importance of each variable was ranked using measurements of central tendency (mean, median) and rates of high-score answers (those who selected "8" or higher out of 10 alternatives from 1 to 10). Our intention in combining these three measurement methods was to reduce the potential bias resulting from relying on a single method of summarizing Likert scores.

Dynamics of Actual Route Choice

In order to answer our second subquestion, cargo bike users were interviewed. Our aim was to better understand the main trade-offs faced by cargo bike users when making route choices. Interviewees were selected from the survey respondents based on their willingness to participate in an interview. The interview took the form of a semi-structured interview where the topics were standardized, but the phrasing of each question depended on the context of each interviewee's cargo bike usage.

The interview included four main topics, which are summarized in Table 2. Each interviewee was asked to submit route information prior to the interview; subsequently, the road condition along each route was checked by the interviewer either by cycling the route or by observing the route virtually through Google Street View. Seven cargo bike users were interviewed in Stockholm and four in Amsterdam, with a mixture of different types of cargo bikes and usage purposes.

Knowledge Transfer to Planning

For our third subquestion, we interviewed city planners working on cycling policy and/or traffic infrastructure issues in order to explore how the knowledge acquired in the surveys and the interviews might be translatable to practice. Two planners in Stockholm and one in Amsterdam were interviewed; interviews were semi-structured, and the details of the questions were tailored to the expertise of each planner.

As shown in Table 3, the interview consisted of

Table 2
Questions Cargo Bike Users Were Asked

Topic	Question
Usage information	When do you use a cargo bike, and for what purpose? What kind of cargo bike do you use?
Route information	Which route do you take? (asked prior to the interview) Why do you take this route? What do you like and dislike about this route? Does the route differ sometimes? When and why? Are there road segments you try to avoid?
Normal bike—cargo bike difference	Do you also use a normal bike? Do you choose a different route? What kinds of difficulties do you face even with a normal bike? What are the problems specific to your cargo bike?
Application of preferences	Which road segments in the city are best/worst for your cargo bike (as examples)? Why are they good/bad?
Other	What are other important aspects of your route choice?

four parts. The first part of the interview was an exercise designed to provide a starting point for a discussion on the topic of route choice. Prior to the interview, each planner was asked to guess the route taken by one of the cargo bike users interviewed in the previous research phase, based on the start/end points of the trip on a map. Subsequently, planners were asked about the reasoning behind their guess; this was followed by the revelation of the actual route taken by the cargo bike user, leading to a discussion of potential issues on the route. The second part of the interview focused on the process of infrastructure planning for bikes, with the aim of understanding how it is evaluated in each city. The idea of BLOS was then introduced in the third part, and the quantitative results of the survey with cargo bike users were presented and discussed with planners. The last part of the interview consisted of a global reflection of the three previous parts, leading to a discussion of potentials and limitations of trying to evaluate the quality of road segments using a quantitative approach.

Results and Analysis

Survey Results: Overall Preferences

In Table 4 (Stockholm) and Table 5 (Amsterdam), we report survey responses regarding the importance of each element in shaping the route choices of cargo bike users. The relative importance of each element is ranked based on mean, median, and percentage of high score answers.

Regardless of the method used, there is considerable overlap in the most important elements for each city, even though there are differences in the exact ranking. The traffic volume of heavy vehicles is the most important element in both cities. These results suggest that the method used here (Likert scale) can produce informative results in terms of which elements have high importance without a detailed consideration of statistical operations, even though it may not enable us to ascertain their precise order of importance.

In both cities, the type of infrastructure, smoothness, traffic volume of cars, and traffic volume of

Table 3
Interview Topics and Questions (City Planners)

Topic	Question
Case study	Based on the start/end points indicated in the map, which route do you think the cargo bike user takes? Why do you think this route is chosen? What kind of problems do you think the cargo bike user may face on this route? How surprising were the reasons behind the route choice?
Planning procedure	What is the process of planning for bicycles like? How are roads evaluated? What are the criteria of evaluation?
BLOS	Do you think BLOS is useful for bicycle planning in Stockholm/Amsterdam?
Reflection	Do you think map making is useful for planning? What kind of difficulties does map making involve? What kind of planning for cargo bikes do you think works best?

Table 4
Ranking of Overall Preferences in Stockholm

(*N*=206)	Mean	Rank	Median	Rank	% High score (8-10)	Rank
# Heavy vehicles	7.65	1	8	1	65.5	1
No parking	7.24	2	8	1	51.9	4
Type	7.20	3	8	1	59.2	2
# Cars	7.09	4	8	1	52.4	3
Smoothness	6.87	5	7	2	45.1	5
Width	6.82	6	7	2	44.7	6
Intersection	6.19	7	7	2	33.5	8
# Pedestrians	5.92	8	6	3	31.1	9
# Traffic lights	5.84	9	6	3	34.5	7
Straightness	5.82	10	6	3	29.6	10
Brightness	5.64	11	6	3	28.6	11
Steepness	5.26	12	5	4	23.8	13
Speed limit	5.17	13	5	4	24.8	12
# Bicycles	4.82	14	5	4	13.6	14

Table 5
Ranking of Overall Preferences in Amsterdam

(*N*=121)	Mean	Rank	Median	Rank	% High score (8-10)	Rank
# Heavy vehicles	7.38	1	8	1	56.2	1
Smoothness	7.08	2	8	1	51.2	2
# Cars	6.79	3	7	2	47	4
# Traffic lights	6.66	4	8	1	50.4	3
Type	6.64	5	7	2	46.3	5
Width	6.52	6	7	2	40.5	6
Intersection	6.45	7	7	2	38.9	7
Brightness	5.98	8	6	3	33.9	10
Steepness	5.94	9	6	3	37.1	8
No parking	5.83	10	6	3	34.7	9
# Bicycles	5.23	11	6	3	13.2	14
# Pedestrians	5.16	12	5	4	19	12
Speed limit	5.14	13	5	4	28.1	11
Straightness	4.84	14	5	4	16.6	13

heavy vehicles are among the five most important elements. The existence of car parking in Stockholm and number of traffic lights in Amsterdam are considered important in that city, but are ranked low in the other city. All other elements have similar ranking in both cities, and significant differences between the two cities can be observed only for these two elements.

Tables 4 and 5 show preferences on the type of infrastructure, which was measured with a Likert scale with five alternatives from very favorable to very unfavorable: "1" represents "very favorable" and "5" represents "very unfavorable." The result supports the well-known finding that cyclists value physical separation of cycling space from automobiles (Caulfield et al. 2012; Hull and O'Holleran 2014) and that the higher the level of separation is, the more cyclists tend to prefer it.

Cargo Bike User Interviews

Seven people were interviewed in Stockholm. Reasons mentioned for choosing a specific route included time, distance, scenery, safety, and infrastructure. Many of the interviewees were still not happy with their chosen route, mainly complaining about car traffic and infrastructure quality. While car traffic was mentioned as a safety issue by parents carrying children, many interviewees also pointed out that, with a cargo bike that is larger than a normal bike, it is often impossible to overtake cars waiting in traffic, forcing cargo bike users to stay behind cars. Several people stated that bike paths with physical separation can be a problem or an obstacle for a wide cargo bike with high volumes of bike traffic; accordingly, some cargo bike users preferred bike lanes without a hard separation. Unclarity as to where to cycle, infrastructure inconsistencies, rough surfaces, hills, and bicycle traffic were also mentioned as obstacles encountered when moving around by cargo bike.

In some cases, there were also conflicting preferences in terms of infrastructure types and traffic lights. One section of Fleminggatan (a main street in the city) has a bus lane that is shared with bicycles. One respondent mentioned it as an example of the worst road segment because carrying children on a cargo bike while sharing a road with buses is scary, but another interviewee called it the best segment because there is a lot of space thanks to the bus lane. Another conflict of opinion was observed in relation to the "green wave"—a coordinated set of traffic lights designed to allow cyclists to bike through consecutive intersections without stopping. For one interviewee whose cargo bike does not have a motor, the speed of green wave was too fast, while it was mentioned in a positive light by another interviewee who uses a cargo bike with a motor.

As an example of route choice in Stockholm, Figure 2 displays the route choice of a father who carries his children from home to school on a trailer attached to a road bike. Even though the total distance is only about 1 km, there are several route options. The blue route goes through woods and is comfortable to bike on, but it is longer, and he takes this route only when he has enough time. The orange line represents a cycling path in the middle of a main road (Valhallavägen), which is almost completely separated from car traffic with grass and trees on both sides. However, one section of this route (marked in red) also functions as a parking area for cars, forcing cyclists to go through the middle of parked cars. In the evening when visibility is low, he tries to avoid the route while transporting children. The pink route is a bike path along a main road and is the shortest option of all, but the road has a lot of traffic and is not pleasant to cycle along, so he only uses this route when he is in a hurry. Another option is to use sidewalks, indicated with green. This is technically illegal and can take longer when there are pedestrians, but is a safe option without the need to make a long detour. Whether he uses the sidewalk on the northern side or southern side of the road depends on the timing of traffic lights.

In Amsterdam, four cargo bike users were interviewed. In three of the four interviews, the intensity of motorized traffic and the frequency of traffic lights were mentioned as the main reasons for selecting the chosen route. Interviewees noted that being unable to move quickly and make sharp turns gives cargo bike users less opportunity to move around cars in case the road is shared, and thereby diminishes their comfort when cycling on a main road. Three interviewees also mentioned the difficulties created by the blockage of roads, whether on a bike path or a shared road, by construction and by motor vehicles, especially delivery trucks. One interviewee also noted that he cannot overtake bike taxis, which are significantly wider than normal bikes. Poles at the entrance of a bike path to prevent cars from entering were also mentioned as irritating, even it is generally still possible to pass with a cargo bike through the poles. Speed bumps and rough surfaces were also noted as problematic for carrying fragile cargo. All in all, however, interviewees generally appreciated the cycling infrastructure of Amsterdam and considered that most of the city is accessible by a cargo bike. Many of the problems they faced, such as the presence of traffic lights, tourists, and confusing intersections, are not necessarily attributable to the usage of cargo bikes as opposed to normal bikes.

An example of a route in Amsterdam is shown in Figure 3. This cyclist uses a traditional large cargo bike with three wheels. The black line indicates the route taken, and the colored lines are the segments he tries to avoid. The green segment is the official

Figure 2
Example: A Route Choice in Stockholm

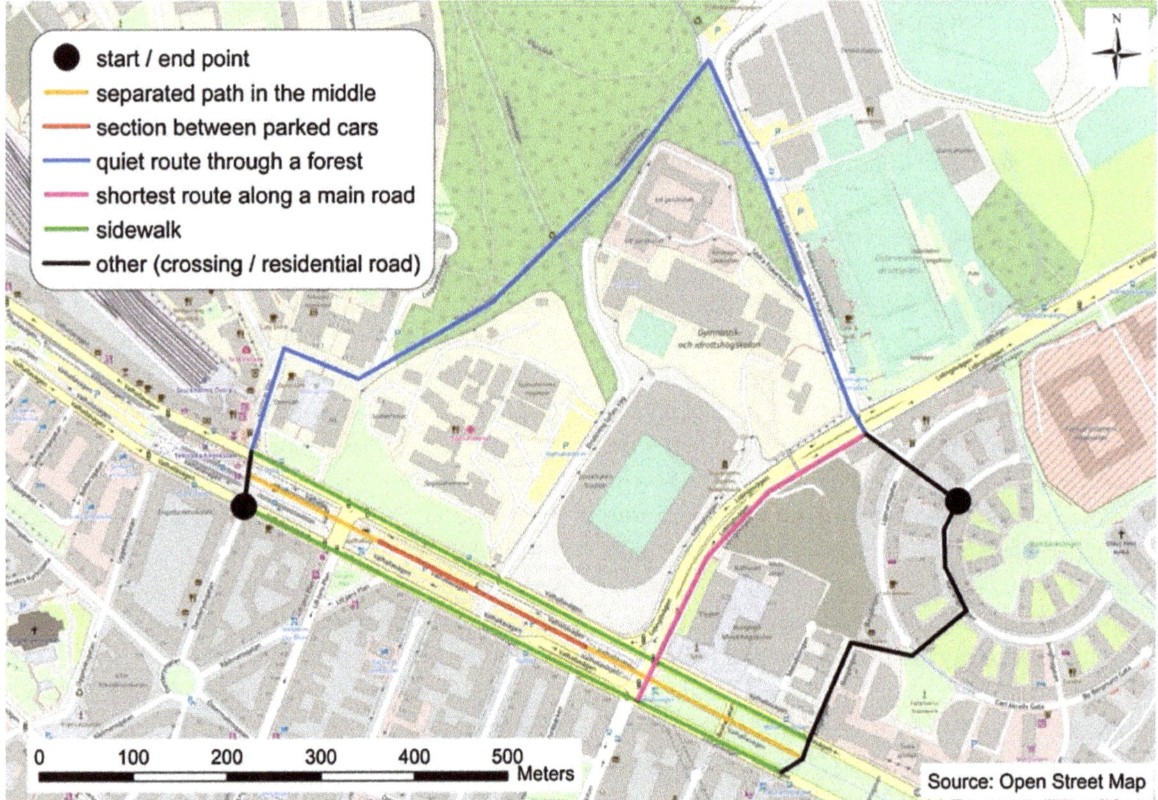

Source (cartography): OpenStreetMap ©OpenStreetMap contributors. Copyright: Creative Commons Attribution-ShareAlike 2.0 license (CC BY-SA). Added material in Figure 2 is made available under the Open Database License: http://opendatacommons.org/licenses/odbl/1.0/. Any rights in individual contents of the database are licensed under the Database Contents License: http://opendatacommons.org/licenses/dbcl/1.0/.

route to the park for bicycles, but because there are many pedestrians, traveling on this segment with his large cargo bike is difficult and instead he uses a path officially made for pedestrians. The orange segment has no dedicated cycling infrastructure, and has many cars parked on the road. The red section has a separated bicycle path, but the surface is not smooth due to tree roots, and he prefers not to use this route especially with fragile cargo. The last part of his trip requires him to stay on the right side of the road and make two left turns, as indicated in blue, but he prefers to avoid the detour and stay on the left side, as the traffic volume of bicycles is low and is usually not a problem.

City Planner Interviews

Two planners in Stockholm and one planner in Amsterdam were interviewed. In Stockholm, we used the route shown in Figure 2 for discussion, and in Amsterdam we used Figure 3.

In both Stockholm interviews, planners found it difficult to guess the route taken by the cyclist because there were several options and some parts of the routes involved usage of private roads or illegal

Figure 3
Example: A Route Choice in Amsterdam

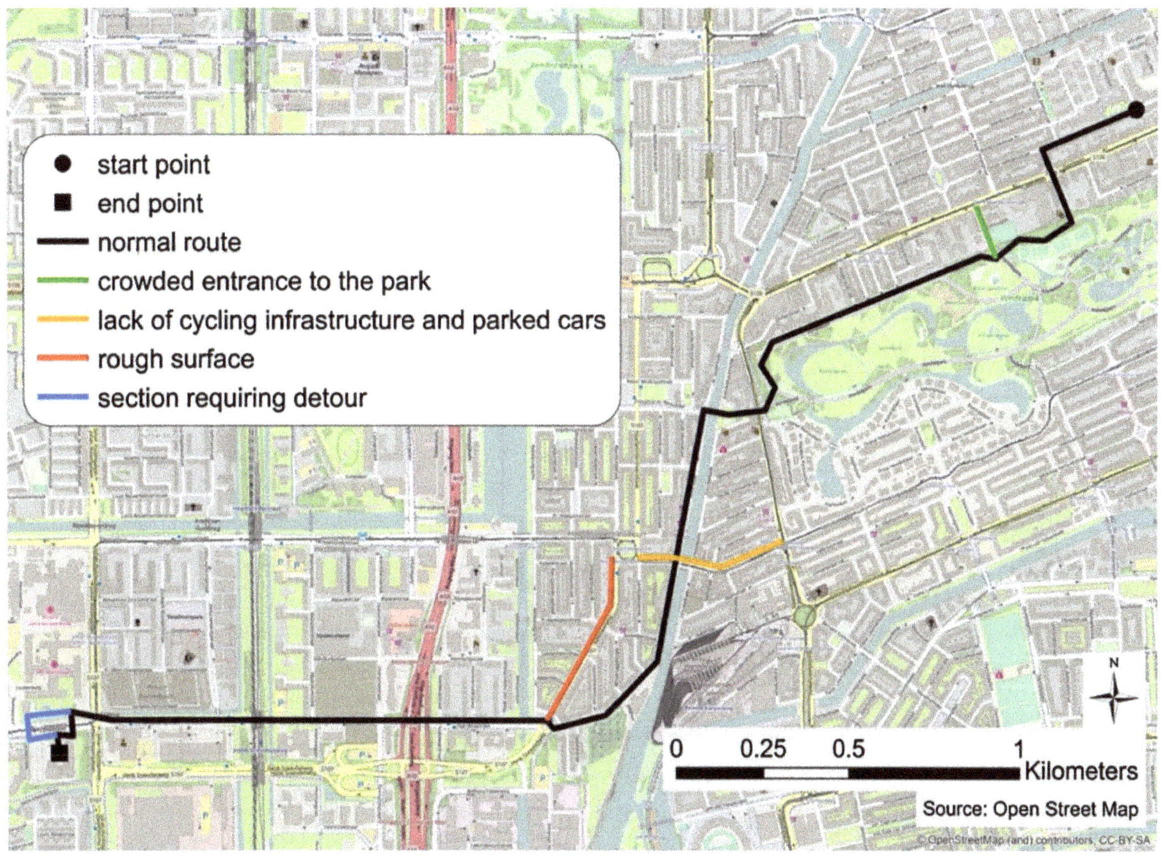

Source (cartography): OpenStreetMap ©OpenStreetMap contributors. Copyright: Creative Commons Attribution-ShareAlike 2.0 license (CC BY-SA). Added material in Figure 3 is made available under the Open Database License: http://opendatacommons.org/licenses/odbl/1.0/. Any rights in individual contents of the database are licensed under the Database Contents License: http://opendatacommons.org/licenses/dbcl/1.0/.

usage of roads, such as cycling on the sidewalk. The main problem faced by the cargo bike user along that route—that the segment of a bike path also used for car parking is not comfortable to cycle on, especially in the evening—was only spotted by the interviewees after the interviewer hinted at this issue. This exercise worked as a lesson that all kinds of bicycles need to be considered in the planning process. Road evaluation for cyclists in Stockholm is done based on several factors, such as traffic volume of bicycles, category of roads (commuting route, main route, local route), and safety of cyclists. However, safety is difficult to measure, and there is no clearcut way to holistically evaluate roads. Maps are actively used in the planning process in Stockholm, and the idea of BLOS was favored by both planners interviewed as a straightforward way to evaluate roads and provide information for planning. While both agreed that map making is useful in planning, they pointed out technical difficulties such as coordination with other departments and making changes to existing maps.

The interview in Amsterdam used the route shown in Figure 3 as a basis for the discussion. While the western side of the route was not familiar to the city planner interviewed, the route and the reasoning behind it were not surprising to him. He considered route choice of a cargo bike less complex than that of a normal bike because the cyclist is likely to avoid smaller roads due to its larger size. In Amsterdam, evaluation of roads involves the width of the cycle paths, with a goal of a certain percentage of roads being equipped with a wide (more than 2.5 meters) cycling space; in addition, the speed of cycling is also monitored. There are also surveys about the level of satisfaction for cycling, with both general and specific questions. The interviewee called cyclists "pedestrians with wheels," and because the usage of bicycles in the Netherlands is different from that in other countries, he did not think BLOS would be useful at all in the Netherlands. He also pointed out that even if a BLOS map can be made, the map can lose its meaning because combining different criteria makes it difficult to see what the map is about. A large part of infrastructure improvement in Amsterdam depends on public opinions through complaints and suggestions, and the city takes a more qualitative approach to improve infrastructure.

Conclusion

In this research, a survey was used to explore the stated route choice preferences of cargo bike users in Stockholm and Amsterdam. In both cities, four of the five most important infrastructure elements guiding route choice were the same: type of infrastructure, width of cycling space, traffic volume of heavy vehicles, and traffic volume of cars. The survey suggests that the traffic volume of heavy vehicles is the most important factor guiding the route preferences of cargo bike users. According to the subsequent interviews with cargo bike users, the reasons behind this finding are somewhat different in the two cities. In Stockholm, people often raised concerns about the safety of cycling alongside heavy vehicles; in Amsterdam, on the contrary, interviewees often mentioned the difficulty of passing large parked vehicles. Streets in Amsterdam are much narrower than those in Stockholm, and cargo bike users need to take into account the possibility of getting stuck around parked vehicles.

Cycling planning has long emphasized the need for physical separation of cycling space from motor vehicles (Caulfield et al. 2012; Hull and O'Holleran 2014). While our survey results support this assumption, our interviews reveal that some cargo bike users prefer to share a bus lane with buses because of its greater width. The difficulty of being flexible with a cargo bike—which is potentially more difficult to maneuver in relatively narrow, physically separated cycling paths—is an important aspect that needs to be considered before automatically advocating the physical separation of cycling space. As our findings suggest, a large enough road width is a key element for the convenience and safety for users of wide cargo bikes.

Our interviews also revealed that route choice of cargo bike users is a complex process that involves many considerations that cannot be easily quantified using measures such as BLOS. Even though quantification of infrastructure quality is possible to some degree, there are factors that remain difficult to measure and factor into a route choice model, such as pleasantness, darkness, the time that the cyclist has available, the timing of traffic lights, and the direction of travel, as can be seen in the examples of route choice. Despite the goal of tools such as BLOS, namely, generalizing route choice preferences or cycling suitability, our results suggest that there is no simple way of generalizing preferences: despite sharing some characteristics, the route choice preferences of cargo bike users are not universal, but depend on a multitude of individual and place-specific factors. As the planner in Amsterdam stated about cyclists in Amsterdam, this is particularly true for cargo bike users, who are perhaps even more varied than "regular" cyclists in terms of their bicycle types, cycling styles, and purposes.

These results suggest that planning of cycling infrastructure for cargo bikes requires a study tailored to the local context, preferably combining a quantitative approach that allows us to understand "what" cargo bike users want, with a qualitative approach that allows us to understand "why" they want it. Whether it is possible to provide infrastructure that is favored by all cargo bike users is difficult to say, considering the varying individual cyclist's preferences. However, one can conclude that it is necessary to consider the local context and adjust the methods to optimize the analyses and avoid misinterpretation of the results. The extent to which this statement is applicable to normal bikes cannot be judged directly from this study, but it suggests that varying preferences of cyclists make it difficult for planners to provide infrastructure that is favored by everyone. With the complexity and varying preferences of route choice for cargo bikes, an attempt to improve the cycling environment for normal bicycles could be counter-productive for cargo bikes, and additional considerations should be made for the safety and comfort of cargo bike users. With the appearance on the streets of more and more innovative unconventional types of bicycles and other vehicles using cycling infrastructure, there is an increasing need for inclusive planning of cycling infrastructure. The proposed planning strategy of focusing on both "what" and "why" can be beneficial not only for cargo bikes but also for a wider range of cycling infrastructure users.

Limitations and Discussion

Our method of selection for survey participants may have potentially resulted in biased results in terms of some infrastructure preferences. In Stockholm, many of the participants were targeted along streets with a high volume of bicycles, i.e., main roads. This may have resulted in the overrepresentation of those who prefer to cycle on main roads, which tend to have particular infrastructure qualities such as separated bike paths and high traffic volume of cyclists. Most interview recruiting took place during commuting hours, and therefore people who only cycle during off-peak hours may have been underrepresented. In Amsterdam, much of the participant collection was done at primary schools due to high usage of cargo bikes among parents with young children, leading to a potential bias in terms of trip purpose.

The research did not include a systematic comparison between cargo bikes and normal bikes, and the extent to which the route choice preferences observed in this research are determined by the usage of cargo bikes specifically is unknown. Even though differences between normal bikes and cargo bikes were explored in the interviews, including normal bikes in the survey could have provided an objectively comparative result. Such data, we suggest, could be collected in future studies. One of the planners interviewed in Stockholm noted that this is precisely the kind of research that the city needs to conduct because planners do not know what cargo bike users want. Knowledge of differences between normal bikes and cargo bikes might then be applied to the planning process, which currently is focused mostly on normal bikes, even in Amsterdam, where usage of cargo bikes is very common. Since more and more types of unconventional bikes are appearing these days, taking into account the different preferences and requirements of different kinds of bicycles is likely to become an issue of growing importance for city planners worldwide.

Acknowledgments

Special thanks to Professor Luca Bertolini for his critical eye in reading earlier drafts of this article. The authors appreciate the help of those who helped with distribution of the survey: Ronin in Stockholm, and Dr. Byke, Urban Arrow, Henry (WorkCycles), and Fietsersbond in Amsterdam. This work is part of the VerDuS program Smart Urban Regions of the Future with project number 438-15-160, which is (co) financed by the Dutch Research Council.

References

Asadi-Shekari, Zohreh, Mehdi Moeinaddini, and Muhammad Zaly Shah. (2013). "Non-Motorised Level of Service: Addressing Challenges in Pedestrian and Bicycle Level of Service." *Transport Reviews* 33(2): 166–194. https://doi.org/10.1080/01441647.2013.775613

Bernhoft, Inger Marie, and Gitte Carstensen. (2008). "Preferences and Behaviour of Pedestrians and Cyclists by Age and Gender." *Transportation Research Part F: Traffic Psychology and Behaviour* 11(2): 83–95. https://doi.org/10.1016/j.trf.2007.08.004

Boterman, Willem R. (2018). "Carrying Class and Gender: Cargo Bikes as Symbolic Markers of Egalitarian Gender Roles of Urban Middle Classes in Dutch Inner Cities." *Social and Cultural Geography* 21(2): 1–20. https://doi.org/10.1080/14649365.2018.1489975

Broach, Joseph, Jennifer Dill, and John Gliebe. (2012). "Where Do Cyclists Ride? A Route Choice Model Developed with Revealed Preference GPS Data." *Transportation Research Part A: Policy and Practice* 46(10): 1730–1740. https://doi.org/10.1016/j.tra.2012.07.005

Callister, Daniel, and Michael Lowry. (2013). "Tools and Strategies for Wide- Scale Bicycle Level-of-Service Analysis." *Journal of Urban Planning and Development* 139(4): 250–257. https://doi.org/10.1061/(ASCE)UP.1943-5444.0000159

Caulfield, Brian, Elaine Brick, and Orla Thérèse McCarthy. (2012). "Determining Bicycle Infrastructure Preferences—A Case Study of Dublin." *Transportation Research Part D: Transport and Environment* 17(5): 413–417. https://doi.org/10.1016/j.trd.2012.04.001

de Sousa, Adriana, Suely P. Sanches, and Marcos A. G. Ferreira. (2014). "Perception of Barriers for the Use of Bicycles." *Procedia—Social and Behavioral Sciences* 160(Cit): 304–313. https://doi.org/10.1016/j.sbspro.2014.12.142

Ehrgott, Matthias, Judith Y. T. Wang, Andrea Raith, and Chris Van Houtte. (2012). "A Bi-Objective Cyclist Route Choice Model." *Transportation Research Part A: Policy and Practice* 46(4): 652–663. https://doi.org/10.1016/j.tra.2011.11.015

European Cyclists Federation (ECF). (2011). *Cycle More Often 2 Cool Down the Planet! Quantifying CO_2 Savings of Cycling.* Brussels: ECF.

Garrard, Jan, Geoffrey Rose, and Sing Kai Lo. (2008). "Promoting Transportation Cycling for Women: The Role of Bicycle Infrastructure." *Preventive Medicine* 46(1): 55–59. https://doi.org/10.1016/j.ypmed.2007.07.010

Hertel, Ole, Martin Hvidberg, Matthias Ketzel, Lars Storm, and Lizzi Stausgaard. (2008). "A Proper Choice of Route Significantly Reduces Air Pollution Exposure—A Study on Bicycle and Bus Trips in Urban Streets." *Science of the Total Environment* 389(1): 58–70. https://doi.org/10.1016/j.scito tenv.2007.08.058

Huff, K. Herbie, and Robin Liggett. (2014). *The Highway Capacity Manual's Method for Calculating Bicycle and Pedestrian Levels of Service: The Ultimate White Paper.* Los Angeles: University of California, Institute of Transportation Studies. http://www.lewis.ucla.edu/wp-content/uploads/sites/2/2014/09/HCM-BICYCLE-AND-PEDESTRIAN-LEVEL-OF-SERVICE-THE-ULTIMATE-WHITE-PAPER.pdf or https://merritt.cdlib.org/d/ark:/13030/m5281nrv/1/producer/891678314.pdf or https://trid.trb.org/view/1326489

Hull, Angela, and Craig O'Holleran. (2014). "Bicycle Infrastructure: Can Good Design Encourage Cycling?" *Urban, Planning and Transport Research* 2(1): 369–406. https://doi.org/10.1080/21650020.2014.955210

Jensen, Søren Underlien. (2007). "Pedestrian and Bicyclist Level of Service on Roadway Segments." *Transportation Research Record* 2031(1): 43–51. https://doi.org/10.3141/2031-06

Kang, Kyungwoo, and Kyeora Lee. (2012). "Development of a Bicycle Level of Service Model from the User's Perspective." *KSCE Journal of Civil Engineering* 16(6): 1032–1039. https://doi.org/10.1007/s12205-012-1146-z

Koh, P. P., and Y. D. Wong. (2013). "Influence of Infrastructural Compatibility Factors on Walking and Cycling Route Choices." *Journal of Environmental Psychology* 36: 202–213. https://doi.org/10.1016/j.jenvp.2013.08.001

Krenn, Patricia Jasmin, Pekka Oja, and Sylvia Titze. (2014). "Route Choices of Transport Bicyclists: A Comparison of Actually Used and Shortest Routes." *International Journal of Behavioral Nutrition and Physical Activity* 11(1): 1–7. https://doi.org/10.1186/1479-5868-11-31

Kroll, Bonnie, and Robert Sommer. (1976). "Bicyclists' Response to Urban Bikeways." *Journal of the American Planning Association* 42(1): 42–51. https://doi.org/10.1080/01944367608977703

Lewis, Sherman. (2020). *Transportation Statistics by Country.* Hayward, CA: International Comparisons. http://internationalcomparisons.org/environment/transportation.html

Li, Zhibin, Wei Wang, Pan Liu, and David R. Ragland. (2012). "Physical Environments Influencing Bicyclists' Perception of Comfort on Separated and On-Street Bicycle Facilities." *Transportation Research Part D: Transport and Environment* 17(3): 256–261. https://doi.org/10.1016/j.trd.2011.12.001

Liu, George, Sukanya Krishnamurthy, and Pieter van Wesemael. (2018). "Conceptualizing Cycling Experience in Urban Design Research: A Systematic Literature Review." *Applied Mobilities.* https://doi. org/10.1080/23800127.2018.1494347

Ma, Liang, Jennifer Dill, and Cynthia Mohr. (2014). "The Objective Versus the Perceived Environment: What Matters for Bicycling?" *Transportation* 41(6): 1135–1152. https://doi.org/10.1007/s11116-014-9520-y

Maes, Jochen, and Thierry Vanelslander. (2012). "The Use of Bicycle Messengers in the Logistics Chain, Concepts Further Revised." *Procedia—Social and Behavioral Sciences* 39: 409–423. https://doi.org/10.1016/j.sbspro.2012.03.118

Manum, Bendik, and Tobias Nordstrom. (2013). "Integrating Bicycle Network Analysis in Urban Design: Improving Bikeability in Trondheim by Combining Space Syntax and GIS-Methods Using the Place Syntax Tool." *Proceedings of the Ninth International Space Syntax Symposium.* Eds. Y. O. Kim,

H. T. Park, and K. W. Seo. Seoul: Sejong University. https://pdfs.semanticscholar.org/0494/4ce51d3304746b522b008230a5d165240f19.pdf

Menghini, G., N. Carrasco, N. Schüssler, and K. W. Axhausen. (2010). "Route Choice of Cyclists in Zurich." *Transportation Research Part A: Policy and Practice* 44(9): 754–765. https://doi.org/10.1016/j.tra.2010.07.008

Nello-Deakin, Samuel, and Anna Nikolaeva. (2020). "The Human Infrastructure of a Cycling City: Amsterdam Through the Eyes of International Newcomers." *Urban Geography.* https://doi.org/10.1080/02723638.2019.1709757

Plazier, Paul A., Gerd Weitkamp, and Agnes E. van den Berg. (2017). "'Cycling Was Never So Easy!' An Analysis of E-Bike Commuters' Motives, Travel Behaviour and Experiences Using GPS-Tracking and Interviews." *Journal of Transport Geography* 65(June): 25–34. https://doi.org/10.1016/j.jtrangeo.2017.09.017

Ploos van Amstel, W., S. Balm, J. Warmerdam, M. Boerema, M. Altenburg, F. Rieck, and T. Peters. (2018). *City Logistics: Light and Electric: LEFV- LOGIC: Research on Light Electric Freight Vehicles.* Amsterdam: Centre for Applied Research Technology.

Priedhorsky, Reid, David Pitchford, Shilad Sen, and Loren Terveen. (2012). "Recommending Routes in the Context of Bicycling: Algorithms, Evaluation, and the Value of Personalization." *Proceedings of the ACM Conference on Computer Supported Cooperative Work, CSCW*: 979–988. https://doi.org/10.1145/2145204.2145350

Scarf, Philip, and Paul Grehan. (2005). "An Empirical Basis for Route Choice in Cycling." *Journal of Sports Sciences* 23(9): 919–925. https://doi. org/10.1080/02640410400023282

Segadilha, Ana Beatriz Pereira, and Suely da Penha Sanches. (2014). "Identification of Factors that Influence Cyclists' Route Choice." *Procedia—Social and Behavioral Sciences* 160(Cit): 372–380. https://doi.org/10.1016/j.sbspro.2014.12.149

Sener, Ipek N., Naveen Eluru, and Chandra R. Bhat. (2009). "An Analysis of Bicycle Route Choice Preferences in Texas, US." *Transportation* 36(5): 511–539. https://doi.org/10.1007/s11116-009-9201-4

Stefansdottir, Harpa. (2014). "A Theoretical Perspective on How Bicycle Commuters Might Experience Aesthetic Features of Urban Space." *Journal of Urban Design* 19(4): 496–510. https://doi.org/10.1080/13574809.2014.923746

Stewart, Kathryn, and Adrian McHale. (2014). "Cycle Lanes: Their Effect on Driver Passing Distances in Urban Areas." *Transport* 29(3): 307–316. https://doi.org/10.3846/16484142.2014.953205

Suzuki, Kiyoshi, Yusuke Kanda, Kenji Doi, and Nobu Tsuchizaki. (2012). "Proposal and Application of a New Method for Bicycle Network Planning." *Procedia—Social and Behavioral Sciences* 43: 558–570. https://doi.org/10.1016/j.sbspro.2012.04.129

Tilahun, Nebiyou Y., David M. Levinson, and Kevin J. Krizek. (2007). "Trails, Lanes, or Traffic: Valuing Bicycle Facilities with an Adaptive Stated Preference Survey." *Transportation Research Part A: Policy and Practice* 41(4): 287–301. https://doi.org/10.1016/J.TRA.2006.09.007

Ton, Danique, Oded Cats, Dorine Duives, and Serge Hoogendoorn. (2017). "How Do People Cycle in Amsterdam, Netherlands?: Estimating Cyclists' Route Choice Determinants with GPS Data from an

Urban Area." *Transportation Research Record: Journal of the Transportation Research Board* 2662(1): 75–82. https://doi.org/10.3141/2662-09

Winters, Meghan, Michael Brauer, Eleanor M. Setton, and Kay Teschke. (2010). "Built Environment Influences on Healthy Transportation Choices: Bicycling Versus Driving." *Journal of Urban Health* 87(6): 969–993. https://doi.org/10.1007/s11524-010-9509-6

Winters, Meghan, and Kay Teschke. (2010). "Route Preferences Among Adults in the Near Market for Bicycling: Findings of the Cycling in Cities Study." *American Journal of Health Promotion* 25(1): 40–47. https://doi. org/10.4278/ajhp.081006-QUAN-236

Zhang, Lin, and Panos D. Prevedouros. (2011). "User Perceptions of Signalised Intersection Level of Service Using Fuzzy Logic." *Transportmetrica* 7(4): 279–296. https://doi.org/10.1080/18128601003667460

CHAPTER 12

Winds of Trade: Passage to Zero-Emission Shipping

*Nicola Cutcher**

ABSTRACT. The shipping industry needs to decarbonize over the coming decades, but there are competing visions about how that will happen. While major shipping companies are looking to potential new fuels, including ammonia, other disruptors are already shipping small quantities of boutique goods, emission free, on sailboats harnessing the power of the wind. They are a reminder that all global trade used to travel by sail. Can wind propel us back to the future? There is a role for wind power in shipping as both a primary means of propulsion and a way to provide wind assistance to reduce a vessel's fuel use. This article examines the possibilities and challenges for wind-based sea transport.

Introduction

Imagining zero-emissions shipping is often presented as a technological challenge for the future, rather than a feat accomplished in the past. Global trade used to travel under sail before steamships and fossil fuels displaced masts and canvas. Can the power of the wind propel us back to the future?

Today, 80 percent of everything we buy travels by sea for part of its journey (UNCTAD 2018). Shipping is the facilitator of globalization, the lifeblood of our modern economy. It is responsible for roughly 2–3 percent of global greenhouse gas emissions (IMO 2015).

Ships burn the dirtiest oil. Residual fuel oil, known as bunker fuel, is a waste product from the refinery process, the scrapings from the bottom of the barrel, the crud in crude. It is so thick that you could walk on it at room temperature, so filthy that it is illegal to burn on land.

A small group of sailors, brokers, and entrepreneurs are already turning away from the black stuff and hoisting sails once more to carry produce across oceans. One of the first companies to pioneer the return of sail cargo was Fairtransport in the Netherlands. In 2009, its magnificently restored 70-year-old minesweeper, the *Tres Hombres,* undertook its maiden voyage. The company has since also revived a wooden ketch called *Nordlys* dating back to 1873. These beautiful boats have inspired others to join Fairtransport's vision for clean transport. Operating on a boutique scale, a handful of small sailing ships are now moving quality exotic ingredients such as coffee, chocolate, rum, and olive oil to serve conscientious consumers who are increasingly concerned about sustainability.

These companies are offering nearly-zero-emissions shipping right now. "Nearly" means most of these vessels have auxiliary engines for maneuvering into ports or rely on other motorized boats to assist them. Meanwhile, they urge the wider shipping industry to clean up its act.

---

*British freelance investigative journalist, writer, and documentary producer. Worked on flagship BBC programs, including *Panorama* and *Newsnight.* Co-produced the BAFTA-nominated documentary *Syria's Disappeared.* She has written for the *Guardian, Telegraph, Independent,* and *New Statesman.* Email: nicola@cutcher.co.uk

The Goal: Cutting Emissions

They may be ahead of the tide, but the tide is changing in their direction. The U.N. International Maritime Organization (2018: 5) aims to cut shipping emissions by "at least 50 percent" by 2050. The world's largest shipping company, Maersk (2020), has gone further, pledging to be carbon neutral by 2050. Maersk's Chief Adviser for Climate Change, John Kornerup Bang, says: "Our announcement itself was a key part of our strategy." For shipping to fully decarbonize, lots of actors will need to mobilize simultaneously, and Maersk wanted to send a clear signal to the market that it foresees transitioning to a zero-carbon future.

Whilst there is a consensus that shipping needs to cut its carbon footprint, there are competing visions about how it will do it. The sail cargo revivalists argue that transitioning to a zero-carbon future requires a wholesale social, cultural, and philosophical transformation. They add that shipping goods by sail is part of a practical solution and emblematic of some of the wider adjustments that will be needed. For example, their vision suggests we should move less cargo more slowly and pay more for the service. But they argue that there are benefits to this too, beyond saving emissions and improving our air quality and marine environment, as these changes could also help us to reconnect with our localities and the natural world. By contrast, companies like Maersk and the wider industry predict ongoing rising demand for shipping, and they are searching for new fuels that can enable a continuation of business as usual for the sector. There is a role for wind power in both scenarios.

The amount we ship has been increasing dramatically for decades. In 1840, back in the age of sail, total seaborne trade amounted to 20 million tons (Stopford 2009: 24). In 2019, it exceeded 11 billion tons (UNCTAD 2019). That represents an increase by a factor of 550.

Jorne Langelaan (2020), a co-founder of Fairtransport, is one of the visionaries in the shipping industry:

> Number one, and this might sound like a funny thing to say as a ship owner and broker, we need to ship way less stuff. We need to buy what we can locally and stop transporting what we can produce ourselves. Then for the other things that we really want, for example things like coffee which are grown far away, we should be shipping them sustainably.

Langelaan believes that we are at the start of a new industrial revolution, where innovations such as artificial intelligence and 3D printing will make it cheaper for companies to manufacture goods in their local economies again. The world will pivot from globalization back towards localization, vastly reducing demand for shipping. One of the mantras of the sail cargo movement is: "Buy less, buy better, buy local, or by sail."

Yet current industry projections are for shipping demand to continue rising, with international maritime trade expected to expand at an average annual growth rate of 3.5 percent over the 2019–2024 period (UNCTAD 2019). Shipping expert Dr. Tristan Smith (2020) cautions:

> Many developed economies only became rich because of trade. Many developing economies are seeing significant economic development because of trade. Dramatic reduction in trade would have dramatic impacts on developing economies. Whereas a zero-emission shipping fleet could enable sustainable global economic development.

The Purists: Wind Alone

The amount currently transported purely by wind is just a drop in the ocean compared to total shipping demand. The restored sailing ships currently carrying cargo are small; the *Tres Hombres*, for example, can take 35 tons. But sail cargo has much larger ambitions and potential. Langelaan (2020) says: "At Fairtransport, we started with small boats because the market was not ready for more, but now we need bigger ships and more ships running more routes more regularly."

In the jungle of Costa Rica, Danielle Doggett (2019) is building a new ship called *Ceiba* that looks set to become the largest operating sailing ship in the world. *Ceiba* will be able to carry 250 tons of cargo, equivalent to around 10 containers, and she is being made from locally and sustainably sourced wood.

Langelaan is working to scale up the sail cargo movement and recently formed a new company called EcoClipper to develop a logistics system to facilitate emission-free shipping worldwide. He is also working on designs for a new prototype vessel, the EcoClipper, that takes its inspiration from the original line drawings of a successful Dutch clipper ship called *Noah*, built back in 1857. The EcoClipper would carry 500 tons of cargo. Langelaan (2020) acknowledges:

> This is still too small for the regular cargo shipping logistics system, and that is why we are putting up an alternative logistics system to operate alongside the status quo. We are thinking outside the box, outside the container in fact.

Langelaan's EcoClipper will not have an engine, so the captain "must use that sail, day and night, fair weather or foul." He fears that having an engine raises the temptation to use it to maintain speeds at times of low wind, and that would be an inefficient use of fuel for transporting cargo because the largest modern ships achieve greater efficiencies per cargo load when burning fossil fuels. He knows that he could build a larger clipper ship by replicating the design of the *Cutty Sark*, for example. It would carry over 1,000 tons, but rather than build the largest possible sailing ship, he prioritizes getting several EcoClippers on the water to enable multiple crossings a year to most usefully serve customers in need of a regular supply.

In France, Transoceanic Wind Transport (TOWT) is also thinking the time is right to launch a small fleet. TOWT's manager Guillaume Le Grand (2020) is planning four new smart sailing cargo ships, each able to carry 1,000 tons.

Cornelius Bockermann founded Timbercoast, a German sail cargo company that runs the *Avontuur*, a stunning restored schooner from 1920. Bockermann (2020) dreams of building new vessels the size of the old Flying P-Liners, which were some of the largest sailing cargo ships in history, carrying around 5,000 tons, equivalent to around 350 containers. Nonetheless, even those giants of the ancient seas are dwarfed by the largest modern container ships, which can carry more than 20,000 units, and the biggest bulk carriers, which take more than 300,000 tons (IMO 2020).

Will Templeman (2019), founder of shipping broker Shipped by Sail, observes that the largest shipping companies are working to make their gigantic fleets more energy efficient, but his approach is different:

> We're coming from the opposite direction and offering emission-free shipping right now, whilst asking what sail shipping could have been with another 100 years of development.

The Hybrids

Dr. Tristan Smith is a leading academic analyst of how the shipping industry can transition to a zero-carbon future. Smith (2019) says: "The cheapest option is lots of wind power plus another fuel." This means more hybrid vessels, not necessarily using the wind as their primary means of propulsion, but enabling the wind to assist the vessel in reducing fuel usage wherever possible. There are multiple possibilities for wind assistance, with different technologies tailored to different types of ship.

Gavin Allwright is Secretary of the International Windship Association, promoting wind propulsion in commercial shipping. He suggests that retrofitting various wind-assistance technologies onto the current fleet can typically offer fuel and emissions savings of 5–20 percent, with the potential to save up to 30 percent. Allwright (2020) says significantly higher savings are possible with newbuild wind-assist vessels because they can be fully optimized to take advantage of the wind. "For primary newbuild wind, this is well over 50% savings in wind tunnel testing, however not yet proven at sea."

What are these wind-assistance technologies? A central contender is the Flettner Rotor. Another technology from the past, this was designed by German inventor Anton Flettner in the 1920s. Rotors are large rotating columns operated by low-power motors. The propulsion principle is based on the Magnus effect, whereby the difference in air pressure on different sides of a spinning object generates thrust. It is the same reason that spinning balls curve in flight. Rotors lack the aesthetic romance of sails—instead resembling factory chimneys—but they are effective. A number have already been installed on a range of ship types, with proven success.

Two Norsepower Rotor Sails installed onboard the long-range tanker *Maersk Pelican*, as shown in Figure 1, led to an annual fuel saving of 8.2 percent, equivalent to approximately 1,400 tons of carbon dioxide (Maersk Tankers 2019). Norsepower claims that fuel costs are typically reduced by 5–20 percent without lowering the operating speed of the vessel. On certain routes during the trial, the *Maersk Pelican* achieved far higher savings, demonstrating the potential of the rotors to achieve higher fuel savings on routes with more favorable wind conditions. Gavin Allwright (2020) adds:

> This vessel could easily have taken four rotors, which while not necessarily doubling that savings level, would give a substantially higher level (say 12–15 percent). Also, … these savings were derived on a vessel that did not adjust anything else. If a vessel was to adopt weather routing to

Figure 1
Norsepower Rotor Sails Onboard Maersk Pelican: Largest Flettner Rotors in the World

SOURCE: Wilsca (2018). License: Creative Commons Attribution-Share Alike 4.0 International license. LICENSE SOURCE: https://creativecommons.org/licen ses/by-sa/4.0/deed.en

> maximize wind propulsion input and potentially slowed speeds to increase the percentage delivered by wind, then we could be seeing much higher savings, but potentially delivering the fuel a couple of days later.

In addition to rotors, other offerings include hard sails, suction wings, and kites. The kites are just as you might imagine—a giant kite tied to the front of a ship. (See Figure 2.) Airseas is manufacturing kites to tow commercial ships and promising fuel and energy savings of 20 percent. Kites are potentially a great wind-assist solution for container ships that do not want sails or rotors because they use most of their deck space for cargo. Maersk says it is considering retrofitting kite-type sails on container ships trading on windy routes (Maersk 2020).

In 2020, Neoline will start building two RoRo ships (Roll-on, Roll-off vessels) with soft sails for transporting vehicles. The company has backing from major partners, including Renault. These RoRo ships are intending to sail from the west coast of France to the east coast of the United States, carrying around 500 cars. Neoline's Managing Director Jean Zanuttini (2020) says the objective is to save around 80 percent of fuel, by slowing down to use the sails to maximum effect:

Figure 2
Skysail

Source: Horn (2008). License: Creative Commons Attribution 3.0 Unported.
License source: https://creativecommons.org/licenses/by/3.0/deed.en

> We will go slow, at a commercial speed of 11 knots. Similar vessels typically run at 15–17 knots. Whilst these numbers are currently theoretical, we believe we'll use 35 tons of gasoline for the Atlantic Crossing. Another boat of the same size, running at 11 knots, would use 120 tons, though in reality they'd never go that slow. When they run at 15 knots, they use 230 tons. We are currently 30 percent more expensive to build than our classic counterpart, and moving around 30 percent slower, but we will save 80 percent of fuel.

The Neoline RoRo ships should hit the water in 2022.

Slowing down saves energy and cuts emissions by enabling wind to contribute a greater share of a ship's power. The Energy Institute at University College London estimates that reducing ship speeds by 20 percent below their 2012 values would reduce carbon dioxide emissions by 24–34 percent (Faber et al. 2019: 10). Thus, if the U.N. International Maritime Organization (IMO) introduced speed limits for ships, emissions from shipping could be cut by a quarter overnight, possibly a third. This figure takes account of the fact that more ships would be required to transport the same number of goods.

Several possible regulatory measures are being considered by the IMO to create a framework to incentivize further emissions reductions. The possibility of imposing speed limits is one option on the table. Other proposals would introduce an emissions-reduction objective without stipulating how that should be met. This would allow ships flexibility to determine their own course, so some might choose to slow down, whereas others might invest in new wind-assist technologies or new fuels to cut their emissions without reducing speed. A focus on operational efficiency might better incentivize technological developments.

Wind power has its challenges. Some routes are more favorable than others because engines allowed ships to depart from routes governed by trade winds. Relying on wind power demands more flexibility with schedules as speeds are dependent upon weather conditions. That could have ramifications for other parts of the supply chain, requiring more warehouses to store goods rather than relying on just-in-time deliveries. Some ships lend themselves more to wind than others. Allwright (2020) explains:

> Wind propulsion is certainly a good fit for tankers and bulkers as they have a lot of deck space, travel at relatively slow speeds, and their cargos are taken from stockpiles and generally delivered to stockpiles, thus not time sensitive, or less so.

All possibilities for low-emissions shipping have their own challenges. The shipping industry is searching for the new fuels of the future, of which ammonia is a leading candidate, but there are many hurdles to jump before they get to market. For Maersk, alcohol, ammonia, and biofuels are the primary options under consideration. Biofuels are controversial because, if used at scale, they require a huge amount of land, pitting fuel in competition with food (Lloyds Register and UMAS 2019: 17). Other sectors are likely to be in competition for the fuel as the entire economy scrambles to decarbonize as quickly as possible. In addition, new fuels like ammonia require energy for their creation, so there is a danger of pushing emissions impacts upstream.

Those uncertainties show why it is wise for shipping to harness as much wind as possible to minimize its demand for fuel of any type. As Le Grand (2020) puts it: "One simple physical observation: on the open sea, the only renewable and abundant source of power is the wind." Bockermann (2020) adds:

> The main advantage of sails over any new technology, be it CO_2 neutral fuels or other means of propulsion, is that wind is free for all and available almost anywhere in the world at no cost and no requirement of any primary energy or resource to produce it. Any type of new fuel, be it hydrogen, ammonia, methanol or whatever, will need primary energy or resources.

Langelaan (2020) summarizes the situation succinctly: "Sail is the proven technology."

There is also a lot of market uncertainty right now. Following the polluter-pays principle, governments should impose fees on carbon-based fuel to reflect environmental costs and to encourage a shift to new technologies. A long-term agreement on full-cost energy pricing would make investment in wind technologies and new fuels more stable and competitive. In the meantime, we can be sure that wind energy will always be free. As Allwright (2019) points out:

> Wind propulsion solutions lock in a percentage of fuel costs at zero, creating certainty where there is none. We can't foresee future fuel prices, policy frameworks, carbon pricing or rationing. All of these can't be predicted, but we can predict that all of these areas will be volatile and not risk free. However, one thing we can depend on is that the cost of the wind today and the cost in 30 years when you come to replace your vessel is fixed, helping to future proof your fleet in a period of great uncertainty in almost all other aspects of the shipping industry.

If ships slow down and get smaller, we will have to pay more for the service. Bockermann (2019) acknowledges that his method of shipping entails significantly higher freight costs, but stresses that industrial shipping is only cheap because it fails to pay the environmental costs:

> What you normally pay a shipping company doesn't account for the damage to the environment, pollution or health—these are all externalized costs. Our costs are comparatively high but if you had to pay for the damage of conventional shipping then we wouldn't seem expensive.

Langelaan (2020) thinks that shipping has become too cheap, adding:

> Currently the costs of shipping are so low that it does not matter anymore where a company produces, where the raw materials are sourced, where the markets are, and in which country the garbage is dumped.

We have been paying for high-speed shipping for many years without knowing it because environmental costs did not show up in the market price. In the future, cost and price will likely be more closely aligned.

Conclusion

As the days of cheap, abundant fossil fuels draw to a close and as concerns about climate change mount, every sector of the economy is shifting to renewable energy sources. Oceanic shipping is no different.

A number of companies are already experimenting with methods of shipping cargo with reduced use of carbon-based fuels. The more radical method involves an almost complete shift to wind power, using sailing ships as cargo vessels. The second method involves hybrid technologies that use wind energy as a supplement to fuel. This has the potential to significantly reduce fuel usage, with larger reductions possible if ships also slow their speeds.

There are many uncertainties surrounding the future of shipping and its energy sources and controversies about the best approach. On one point, however, everyone agrees: the average lifetime of a ship is around 30 years, which means that vessels built today will likely still be in use in 2050. New vessels hitting the water ought to be capable of sailing emission-free. The transition is upon us so we had best lean into the wind.

References

Allwright, Gavin. (2019/2020). "Wind Works." *Bunkerspot Magazine* 16(6): 83–87. http://wind-ship.org/wp-content/uploads/2019/12/Wind-works.pdf

________. (2020). Email correspondence with author. January 27.

Bockermann, Cornelius. (2019). Telephone interview with author. August 26.

________. (2020). Email correspondence with author. January 25.

Doggett, Danielle. (2019). Telephone interview with author. August 23.

Faber, Jason, Dagmar Nelissen, Hary Shanthi, UMAS, Lloyd's Register, and Öko-Institut. (2019). *Study on Methods and Considerations for the Determination of Greenhouse Gas Emission Reduction Targets for International Shipping.* Luxembourg: Publications Office of the European Union. https://www.cedelft.eu/en/publications/2297/study-on-methods-and-considerations-for-the-determination-of-greenhouse-gas-emission-reduction-targets-for-international-shipping

Horn, Ursula. (2008). *Skysails* [image]. https://commons.wikimedia.org/wiki/ File:Skysails1.JPG

International Maritime Organization (IMO). (2015). *Third IMO Greenhouse Gas Study 2014.* London: International Maritime Organization.

________. (2018). *Initial IMO Strategy on Reduction of GHG Emissions from Ships.* Resolution MEPC.304(72). London: International Maritime Organization. http://www.imo.org/en/OurWork/Documents/Resolution%20MEPC.304%2872%29%20on%20Initial%20IMO%20Strategy%20on%20reduction%20of%20GHG%20emissions%20from%20ships.pdf

________. (2020). *Sulphur 2020—Cutting Sulphur Oxide Emissions.* London: International Maritime Organization. http://www.imo.org/en/MediaCentre/HotTopics/Pages/Sulphur-2020.aspx

Kornerup Bang, John. (2020). Telephone interview with author. January 17.

Langelaan, Jorne. (2020). Telephone interview with author. January 31.

Le Grand, Guillaume. (2020). Messaging correspondence with author. January 28.

Lloyd's Register and University Marine Advisory Services (UMAS). (2019). *Zero-Emission Vessels: Transition Pathways.* London: Lloyd's Register.

Maersk. (2020). Press office email correspondence with author. January 27.

Maersk Tankers. (2019). *Norsepower Rotor Sails Confirmed Savings of 8.2% Fuel and Associated CO2 in Maersk* Pelican *Project.* Press Release. October 24. https://maersktankers.com/media/norsepower-rotor-sails-confirmed-savings

Smith, Tristan. (2019). Telephone interview with author. November 28.

________. (2020). Email correspondence with author. January 29.

Stopford, Martin. (2009). *Maritime Economics,* 3rd ed. London: Routledge.

Templeman, Will. (2019). Telephone interview with author. July 25.

U.N. Conference on Trade and Development (UNCTAD). (2018). *Review of Maritime Transport 2018.* New York: United Nations Publications. https://unctad.org/en/PublicationsLibrary/rmt2018_en.pdf

United Nations Conference on Trade and Development (UNCTAD). (2019). *Review of Maritime Transport 2019.* New York: United Nations Publications. https://unctad.org/en/PublicationsLibrary/rmt2019_en.pdf

Wilsca (photographer). (2018). *Norsepower Rotor Sails Modern Version of Flettner Rotor* [image]. https://en.m.wikipedia.org/wiki/File:Norsepower_rotor_sails_modern_version_of_flettner_rotor.jpg

Zanuttini, Jean. (2020). Telephone interview with author. January 30.

CHAPTER 13

Energy-Transition Education in a Power Systems Journey: Making the Invisible Visible and Actionable

Jonee Kulman Brigham and Paul Imbertson†*

ABSTRACT. We describe an approach to educating for systemic change in energy systems by integrating technical knowledge of solutions with reflection on paradigms and norms, facilitated by experiential and art-based forms of learning. The course, "Power Systems Journey: Making the Invisible Visible and Actionable," is part of the University of Minnesota interdisciplinary grand-challenge curriculum. Students take on the challenge of public science communication about how to change the electric-grid system (from power generation to consumption) as part of an energy transition to respond to climate change. The course integrates electrical engineering, history of science and technology, systems thinking, design thinking, paradigms, art, humanities, science communication, storytelling, experiential learning, and the creation of GIS story-maps and museum exhibits. The design context and elements of the course are described and include: the grand challenge of the energy transition itself, the context of energy-transition education, the nature of the grand-challenge curriculum, the collaborative and teaching philosophy, the role of students, the interdisciplinary course framework, the special focus on the role of arts and humanities in energy education, and the course-curricular structure, which uses the "Earth Systems Journey" curriculum model. The centerpiece of the article describes the "Power Systems Journey" experience in narrative form to match the pedagogical approach of the course using artwork examples from students as they investigated the grid. The article concludes with reflections from students and teachers on what the course offers and where to go from here.

*Senior Research Fellow, Minnesota Design Center, College of Design, University of Minnesota. AIA, LEED O+M. Interdisciplinary architect, artist, and educator. Specializes in sustainability and human-nature relationships. Her Earth Systems Journey curriculum model for art-led experiential environmental education has been applied across grades, from pre-K through higher education. Her work engages human and natural infrastructure, systems thinking, paradigm, story, GIS, and participatory art. Email: Kulma002@umn.edu

†Teaching professor, electrical and computer engineering, University of Minnesota. Immediate and near family includes five electrical engineers, all with connections to electric power and energy. Currently teaches electrical engineering, focusing on energy issues from a systems viewpoint including technical, historical, societal, and metaphorical framings. Works to promote sustainability both at home and across the globe. Email: imberts@umn.edu

Conflict of Interest Management: Jonee Kulman Brigham is the owner of Full Spring Studio, LLC, which owns the Earth Systems Journey curriculum model referenced in this article. This relationship has been reviewed and managed by the University of Minnesota in accordance with its conflict of interest policies.

Introduction

As the urgency of the climate crisis heightens, there is an increasing necessity to find effective means to catalyze a rapid energy transition. While an energy transition away from fossil fuels seems more inevitable with every coal plant closure, and ever-falling prices for renewable energy, it is not clear if this transition will occur in time to meet the Paris Agreement goals for keeping global temperature from rising 1.5 degrees Celsius. Research-based scenarios for the needed drawdown to achieve goals, such as outlined in Project Drawdown, show that there are currently available solutions that could meet the goal. While research on solutions needs to continue, the largest barrier to achieving rapid drawdown is not a lack of solutions, but a lack of deployment of solutions. Why? According to systems analyst Donella Meadows (2008), there are many levers of systemic change, and while it depends on the situation, she holds paradigms amongst the highest levers of change. Behavioral psychologists point to the power of social norms, meaning, and story. This article discusses a university course that integrates technical literacy, systems thinking, paradigms, story, and meaning-making as a path to addressing the grand challenge of how to change our electric system as part of an energy transition toward addressing climate change. The course, which is part of a grand-challenge curriculum, is interdisciplinary and combines electrical engineering, history of science and technology, design thinking, art, humanities, science communication, storytelling, and experiential learning. In this article, we will show an approach to educating for systemic change by integrating technical knowledge of solutions with reflection on paradigms and norms, facilitated by experiential and art-based forms of learning.

Overview

This article is organized into four main sections. The Overview provides an orientation to the topic and the content.The Course Design Elements section lays out the factors that make the course possible and shape its structure. The Power Systems Journey Experience is the centerpiece and longest portion of the article and describes the course experience in narrative form to match the pedagogical approach of the course. Finally, Next Journey/Going Forward concludes with reflections from students and teachers on what the course offers and where to go from here.

The following official course description provides a useful summary of the elements and methods of the course, which will be addressed in more detail in sections that follow.

> GCC 3027/5027: Power Systems Journey: Making the Invisible Visible and Actionable
>
> An energy revolution is underway, and needs to accelerate to support climate and economic goals. But the general citizenry does not understand our current energy systems, particularly the seemingly invisible phenomena of electricity, and its generation, distribution, and use. Technical knowledge is only half the solution, however. It is through human decisions and behaviors that technical solutions get applied and adopted, and the importance of communication and storytelling is being recognized for its relevance to making change. How can science literacy and behavior-motivating engagement and storytelling be combined to help make systemic change? This course explores the integration of science-based environmental education, with art-led, place-based exploration of landscapes and creative map-making to address this challenge. How do we make electricity visible, understandable, and interesting—so we can engage citizens in energy conservation with basic literacy about the electric power system so that they can be informed voters, policy advocates, and consumers. In this class, you will take on this challenge, first learning about the electric power systems you use, their cultural and technical history, systems thinking, design thinking, and prior examples of communication and education efforts. With this foundation, you will

then apply your learning to create a public education project delivered via online GIS story maps that use a combination of data, art, and story to help others understand, and act on the power journey we are all on. All will share the common exploration of power systems through field trips and contribute to a multi-faceted story of power, presented in a group map and individual GIS story maps. No prior knowledge of GIS story maps or electricity issues is needed. The study of power systems can be a model for learning and communicating about other topics that explore the interaction of technology and society toward sustainability. (Brigham and Imbertson 2018)

Course Design Elements

There are many elements that determined or influenced the design of the course. In this section, we will outline each: the grand challenge of the energy transition that the course addressed, the context of energy-transition education, the nature of grand-challenge curriculum as it is practiced at the University of Minnesota, the collaboration and teaching philosophies of the teaching instructors, the students and their role in the course, the course's interdisciplinary framework, and the curricular structure and model for the course.

The Grand Challenge: An Energy Transition

The first design element of the course is the challenge it takes on: our energy transition. We are on the verge of a major energy transition forced upon us by scarcity, environmental concerns, and climate change, with all the attendant negative consequences. New energy technologies, the plummeting cost of renewable energy, and growing public interest will enable and power this transition. The energy transition is in some ways a societal design response to climate change. But our response is also subject to consequences of climate change that are already happening, increasing the vulnerability of our energy systems.

The focus of the course is on a part of the energy transition relating to the electric grid. The electric grid interfaces with the story of the energy transition in multiple ways. If we are to shift to an energy system that reduces or eliminates contributions to climate change from our fossil-fuel-dominant energy sources, we need two major shifts related to the electric sector, and they need to happen together. First, we need an electric grid that is powered by sources that do not emit greenhouse gases. This is currently understood to include increasing the portion of the grid powered by renewable energy, such as wind and solar, as well as some nuclear energy as part of the solution, at least until we can provide stable base-energy supply and energy storage. The second shift relating to the electric grid is to electrify the economy, meaning that, wherever possible, energy uses that have been provided by fossil fuels, such as transportation and heating, will now be supplied by electricity. This puts new load and demand quantities and patterns on the current electric grid, which can provide both challenges and opportunities. At the same time, the electric grid needs to shift its power-generation sources and accommodate increased utilization; it also needs to respond to increasing vulnerability due to threats from extreme weather and flooding made worse by climate change.

While the electric grid is commonly thought of as a topic for electrical engineers and energy-policymakers, the need for wholesale changes demands that all sectors of society engage with the transition. The grid can no longer remain effectively invisible to society, for every sector of society is affected by the transition and has a role to play in accelerating its implementation. But this is not the first time humankind has faced an energy transition, and it is useful to examine previous transitions in order to more fully comprehend the possible strategies and consequences of our current energy transition and get some sense of the systemic forces that interact to support or to shift our energy systems. The course experience section elaborates on the history of our energy transitions as told to the students.

Energy-Transition Education

University-level education in energy, sometimes related to the energy transition, exists in a number of disciplines. Electrical and mechanical engineering programs teach about the engineering of energy-consuming systems as well as ways to generate energy and transport it. Architecture students learn how to reduce the energy use of their building designs. Law students learn energy law, and so forth in departments of public policy, environmental science, arts, and more. But the energy transition and its role in climate change is a wicked problem—a grand challenge that cannot be solved one discipline at a time.

In exploring the challenges of interdisciplinary energy education, Blockstein, Middlecamp, and Perkins (2015) note that less than 10 percent of colleges and universities in the United States have interdisciplinary energy programming. The same article identifies dual difficulties for the interdisciplinary education needed, with some students challenged by technical content and others by the contextual content around energy. Many universities are looking to project-based learning as a way to address the interdisciplinary skills and experience needed to address real-world problems (Rangel 2018).

It is not just the interdisciplinary challenges that energy education faces, but also a need for shifts in focus. In a recent review of research in energy education, Jorgenson, Stephens, and White (2019) found that environmental education about energy and climate is often focused on individual actions that do not address the systemic change needed. They recommend that environmental education on energy and climate better address issues of political and social action and understanding of the role of policy. They also point to the need for energy education to engage students with "new narratives and guiding visions" that help students learn about advances in new energy systems as part of visualizing a sustainable future.

The growing trend of "grand-challenge" education programs can serve energy-transition education needs through approaches that are interdisciplinary, project-based, oriented to systemic change, and solutions-focused.

Grand-Challenge Curriculum

Another design element of the course is determined by the Grand Challenge Curriculum approach at the University of Minnesota (2015). This grand-challenge curriculum is one part of a larger movement in higher education to better address the challenges that society faces, such as the energy transition and climate change. Many of these grand challenges are wicked problems in complex systems that require collaboration across many disciplines working together. The complexity of the systems means that the aim is less to develop "solutions" (final and definitive answers) than to design effective interventions from which we learn and adapt in an ongoing process of adjustment and response. But effective for whom? One of the characteristics of wicked problems is that there may never be any ideal solution that resolves the problems for all the stakeholders. One of the challenges for today's students is to learn how to meaningfully engage with such situations in a collaborative, interdisciplinary way. The skills and capacities that a grand-challenge course could offer to students to build their agency and effectiveness in addressing these types of challenges include: a tolerance of ambiguity, an ability to collaborate across disciplines, listening skills, practicing empathy, cultural competency, perspective-taking, systems literacy, and the ability to communicate across disciplines, cultures, and to the public.

The University of Minnesota Grand Challenge Curriculum (GCC) is structured to support many of these goals. There are common elements to the courses, which are proposed by instructor teams and reviewed and approved by a GCC committee. The courses have their own "GCC" course designator outside of any single department, signaling that this is a different type of course. The program includes: at least two instructors from two or more departments or, preferably, colleges, financial structures to enable buyout of teaching staff time, and promotional support to recruit students across the university for a well-balanced, interdisciplinary class. The GCC courses are aimed at undergraduates in their sophomore year or later, but they are often cross-listed to include graduate students. Each course identifies the grand challenge it is addressing and brings an interdisciplinary approach, integrating each of the instructor's areas of expertise, but also wider considerations, including what students bring from their own disciplines.

The courses spend roughly a third to a half of the semester becoming familiar with the challenge, including ways of understanding it and tools to address it. The remainder of the semester shifts to an emphasis on hands-on project work, where students propose and, in some cases, create work that is meant for real application as a system intervention, whether it is a design for a new program, a product, a communication piece, or another authentic effort at making a real impact. The project is important for a sense of making a difference in the world but also as a means of inquiry. By actually trying to put a solution together, the many complex factors in the system become apparent.

Collaboration and Teaching Philosophy of Instructors

The course design was also driven by the teaching philosophy of the instructors and their collaboration on common interests. The GCC co-taught curriculum is not meant to be two half-courses, or alternating lectures, but truly interdisciplinary co-teaching. To create this kind of collaboration to design and teach in a truly interdisciplinary way takes time. Besides intersecting interests in a grand challenge, it is helpful to have experience with interdisciplinary work and, ideally, prior shared experiences to draw from. That was the case here. Both of us had interdisciplinary tendencies and had met each other in our roles as faculty advisors to an interdisciplinary student Solar Decathlon team in 2009. We are also both affiliates of the Institute on the Environment, a hub for interdisciplinary networking and research at the University of Minnesota. It was at an Institute event where we started the conversation about forming a GCC course together. Jonee had wanted to try her Earth Systems Journey curriculum model on the electric grid after having applied it to water systems, and Paul had wanted to do more with integrating the arts with teaching about the electric grid. The common interdisciplinary interest in similar topics, as well as compatible teaching philosophies, shaped the collaboration. A course design grows from the instructor's ideas and collaboration, but it is incubated and supported by university structures that foster connections and support alternative, joint-teaching approaches.

Co-instructor Paul Imbertson's teaching philosophy is centered on the belief that students have an inherent drive to learn and that inherent drive will shine if the instructor can get out of the way. He believes that deep understanding only comes after viewing issues from multiple frameworks and that what each student takes from educational experiences differs depending on their prior experience, openness, and interest, and so the most effective teaching comes from exposing students to new environments and experiences, not expecting that everyone will experience it the same, but knowing that each student will come away with new insights that are uniquely their own.

Co-instructor Jonee Kulman Brigham's teaching philosophy is to put the educational content in a context of personal and shared social meaning. She designs course work to invite the students to bring their whole selves, and their perspectives to the material. Her goal is to help students increase their sense of agency in the world, even when they may not specialize in a topic or, like this class, when the challenge is immense. She wants them to feel they can contribute. She encourages students to build their teamwork skills beyond task-sharing, to learn from each other, and to form a team where each student's strengths can be used. Besides these capacities, a learning objective that permeates her work and teaching is systems understanding of the interconnectedness of humans as a part of the rest of life on earth.

In addition to the co-instructors, the course benefited from teaching assistants who contributed ideas and GIS teaching skills to help shape the course. In Spring 2019, the teaching assistant (TA) was history

PhD student Christopher Saladin. In Fall 2019, the TA was Masters of GIS student Anders Hopkins. Also, in Spring 2019, PhD student Juliette Lapeyrouse-Cherry contributed a unit on Energy Humanities and helped shape ideas for potential research on the course.

GCC courses often have guest lectures and, in the case of this course, a hallmark of the journey was to meet "place guides" along the way. Over the two semesters, place guides and guest lecturers included professionals from an interfaith climate justice organization, engineering firms, lighting design, sustainability education, energy transition research, architects, zero-energy homeowners, and more.

The Students

We consider the students another course design element. In a GCC course, the students come from many disciplines and will return to those disciplines. Therefore, while the course needs to cover some topical information to provide a common understanding, it is the skills of navigating grand challenges, systems thinking, interdisciplinary group work, and communication that many are most likely to take with them after the course. The course was also listed as a technical elective for electrical engineers, who made up about half the students, and so some depth of content needed to be covered as well, while not alienating non-engineering majors. Across the two semesters that have been taught at the time of this writing, student majors have included: electrical engineering (about half of students), graphic design, architecture, neuroscience, environmental sciences, political science, biology, and more. The majority of the students are undergraduates, with a handful of graduate students and adult learners. There were approximately 50 students in Spring 2019 and 26 in Fall 2019. The students are also a design element for the course because they have agency in the course; they are not just recipients of knowledge. Their interests shape their projects, and their participation is essential to the total course experience. The challenges they take on form a second layer of curriculum in which they all learn from each other in team meetings and symposia. In terms of the Hero's Journey structure of the course, the students play the role of the "heroes," leaving the familiar world of their disciplines and venturing into interdisciplinary challenges of climate change and reinventing our energy system in a short time span. Their experience as heroes in this adventure is the primary medium of the course design; in a way everything else (knowledge, tours, projects) is props and stage sets all acting in support of their own journey of learning.

Interdisciplinary Course Framework

The design element that gave the course its breadth was what we called the "Interdisciplinary Course Framework." To reflect a whole-systems view of the role of the electric grid in the energy transition, the course integrated many ways of seeing the content and the challenge. These ways of seeing were represented by a variety of disciplines in the course framework. Themes in the course framework included *contextual frames*, such as the nature of grand challenges, systems and systemic change, theories of change, and the overall climate crisis, in which and to which the energy transition responds. *Energy-related themes* in the course included an understanding of energy transitions, past and present, the culture and history of technology, and some background in energy policy. The technical focus of the class, *the electric grid*, included understanding of grid engineering and grid components, electricity end use, financial and regulatory aspects of the grid, and smart grids. Finally, the framework also includes ways of seeing related to *communications and humanities*, including art, story, geographic thought, geographic information science (GIS), GIS story-maps, design thinking for systemic change, environmental and energy humanities, environmental justice, communications design, and behavioral psychology. While all of these elements were important, this article focuses on a subset of these themes that illuminates the integration of technical knowledge with experiential and art-based forms of learning that stem from the humanities.

Environmental and Energy Arts and Humanities: Experience and Reflection. By engaging art and story, poetry, ceremonial activities, props, and narrative, the course curriculum integrates technical knowledge with the discipline of environmental arts and humanities, particularly with energy-arts and humanities. While the arts are often considered part of the humanities, we distinguish them here because the course intentionally engaged with three dimensions of the arts and humanities. The arts, in the form of creating a work to be perceived aesthetically was incorporated in the class through student sketching assignments, the creation of displays for a pop-up exhibit, and the creation of visual GIS story-maps as major projects where visual expression and storytelling were emphasized in integration with technical issues.

The second dimension of the arts was an experience of artistic works as participants. Philosopher John Dewey ([1934] 2005) says that artworks are not the artifacts of art, but the personal experience of the artifact, and that it is "recreated every time it is esthetically experienced." In this sense, for every student experiencing an art object, a new artwork was created. An art object is experienced as an artwork to the extent it is experienced and, in our society of commoditization of aesthetic experiences, artworks as experiences can be diminished when the participants are passive and not engaged. The course emphasized interactive artworks that could be considered participatory theater or "social practice," in which art creates an altered interaction or perception and the people experiencing the art are part of the artwork (Finkelpearl 2013). Here, there is little opportunity for students to remain passive observers since they are cast as participants and effectively actors in artworks that blur the boundary between normal expected tours and lectures and ceremonial and performative elements.

The third dimension of how arts and humanities were integrated in the course is through the process of critical reflection on a student's own and others' creations. The humanities look for patterns and insights to the human experience as reflected in literature, philosophy, and—especially in environmental-and-energy humanities—the interplay of humans, technology, and nature. Reflection was woven into every element of the class. Students were asked to reflect and respond to questions exploring the tensions and synergies between paired readings from different disciplines. Students were asked to reflect on their firsthand experiences traveling through the power system using both sketching and journal prompts for what they noticed, wondered, and what ideas the experience prompted. In all student projects, from the exhibits they created to the GIS story-maps they made, they were asked to create a design statement that accompanied the created work, articulating its intentions and assumptions and reflecting on the process and result.

Environmental-and-energy humanities are scholarly disciplines fostering dialog about energy and the environment across humanities disciplines and with the natural or social sciences. They reflect on culture and cultural artifacts with an environmental or energy focus. In contrast, environmental art and literature (and other art forms) are direct creative works engaging with environmental or energy themes. But arts and humanities are often blended, and that may be where the most effective education takes place. John Dewey ([1938] 1997) promotes an approach to education that alternates between doing (direct experience) and reflection. That is the spirit of this course. The course was not driven directly by Dewey's philosophy, but his focus on experience and reflection in both education and art provides a good theoretical reference point for the approach of the course.

Arts and Humanities in a Theory of Change. Even though it is recognized that our major grand challenges or "wicked problems" need interdisciplinary solutions and systems thinking, why would a course focused on solutions place such a high emphasis on the arts and artistic ways of knowing? The answer lies in a theory of change that underlies the course: our paradigms and culture are not just receiving contexts for how we use technology but are drivers. David Nye

(2006), historian of science and technology, argues that technology does not drive or determine culture, but rather that culture shapes the way we use and adapt technology. As instructors, we both subscribe to Nye's "contextualist" approach to the history of technology that focuses on the cultural role in technology adoption, use, and meanings. Accordingly, the primary text for the course was *The Grid* by Gretchen Bakke (2017), a cultural anthropologist who puts past and current energy transitions into their cultural, social, and political contexts. Our first reading, however, was from Donella Meadows (1999), who views the beliefs or paradigms of a culture or system as the source of that system. She positions those cultural beliefs near the highest point of leverage in changing that system. The arts and humanities have always played a role in navigating a culture's paradigms, whether retaining or changing them to reflect new understandings. In this time of transition, it is important that we critique the paradigms that have led us to the climate crisis and carefully consider which paradigms will lead us to a habitable future.

Curricular Structure: A Journey Through the Electric Grid

The course design is organized around a curricular structure that is one of the most distinctive differences between this and other GCC courses at the University of Minnesota. Although there are common elements to grand-challenge curriculum, each course is different, reflecting the collaborative course design of the interdisciplinary instructors. In the case of Power Systems Journey, we organized the course as an experiential journey, using a curriculum model developed by Jonee called Earth Systems Journey.

Earth Systems Journey Curriculum Framework. Earth Systems Journey (ESJ) is a model for art-led, experiential, interdisciplinary environmental education. It combines the resonant power of story using the pattern of the hero's journey, as described by Joseph Campbell ([1949] 2008), with the insights of systems thinking. Here is the description from the website for the model:

> Earth Systems Journey (ESJ) is a curriculum framework for art-led, experiential, place-based environmental education about environmental flows, (such as water, air, energy or material) through the school building and grounds. ESJ is an approach that teaches ecological and environmental content, principles, analysis and decision skills in a way that shows how human-engineered systems are integrated with natural systems. At its core, the design of an Earth Systems Journey is to make a special journey starting from a place of personal experience, following a flow of interest to its source and destination, as far as you can, so that when you return to where you started, your view of that place and its flows is transformed by knowing the larger story that runs through it and the places and people and natural elements that live in relation to it. What makes the journey "special" is its composition as a transformative experience paying attention to props, interactive and expressive activities, [and] participatory storytelling, and [taking] time to reflect and integrate the experience into a personal story. By using the natural learning form of story, complex systems can be made both engaging and comprehensible. (Brigham 2014)

Earth Systems Journey is related to STEAM curriculum that integrates science, technology, engineering, arts, and math, except that STEAM curriculum is often centered on STEM curriculum and supplements it with arts to enhance understanding and engagement with STEM content. In contrast, Earth Systems Journey (ESJ) is centered on a journey of meaning-making, using art and story, and enhances this journey of meaning with STEM content. This has the inherent effect of putting STEM content into the personal, social, and emotional context of a quest for meaning and relevance. (See Figure 1a and b.)

In the case of Power Systems Journey, the flow that was followed was electricity. In the next section, we describe an overview of the journey, followed by a detailed description of each stage, showing examples of how the journey integrated technical, social, and artistic ways of knowing.

The Power Systems Journey Experience

Students start the Power Systems Journey at the Bell Museum, which is the interpretive hub (or "Home Place" in Figure 1). They engage with the flow of electricity and light in a particular place in the museum, and prepare for the journey by learning tools, preparing supplies (like a travel journal), and forming teams. The adventure starts upstream. But what is upstream of a light switch? Which power plant? Indeed that is the narrative challenge of telling the story of the electric grid and a barrier to understanding how it works. So the students travel to multiple upstream elements of the grid, including several power plants and transmission lines, until they hit a "confluence" at a nearby substation, where they follow the grid further along distribution lines, to a transformer, through the museum's electrical system, and finally to the light switch and the light that they first experienced. They follow the electricity as it is used to generate light, that bounces off the specimen they have been viewing and into their eye, through the pupil to the retina, optic nerve, and finally to their mind and perception. Along the way, they use a travel journal to reflect, sketch the grid, and create public online communication pieces about Minnesota Power Histories.

But that does not end the journey, which is not over until the heroes (participating students) return from their adventures with something to offer back to the community. This launches the second part of the course, where students create additional public communications to help increase understanding and motivation to improve the electric grid.

The students gain insights about the grand challenge in their journey through grid history as embodied in the physical grid they explore, from readings, lectures, and the Project 1 story-maps. As the heroes return to the present, they reencounter the scale of the challenge we are facing through use of a climate-simulation role-playing exercise. They contribute to public understanding and motivation

Figure 1

(a) Earth Systems Journey (b) Power Systems Journey Concept Diagram

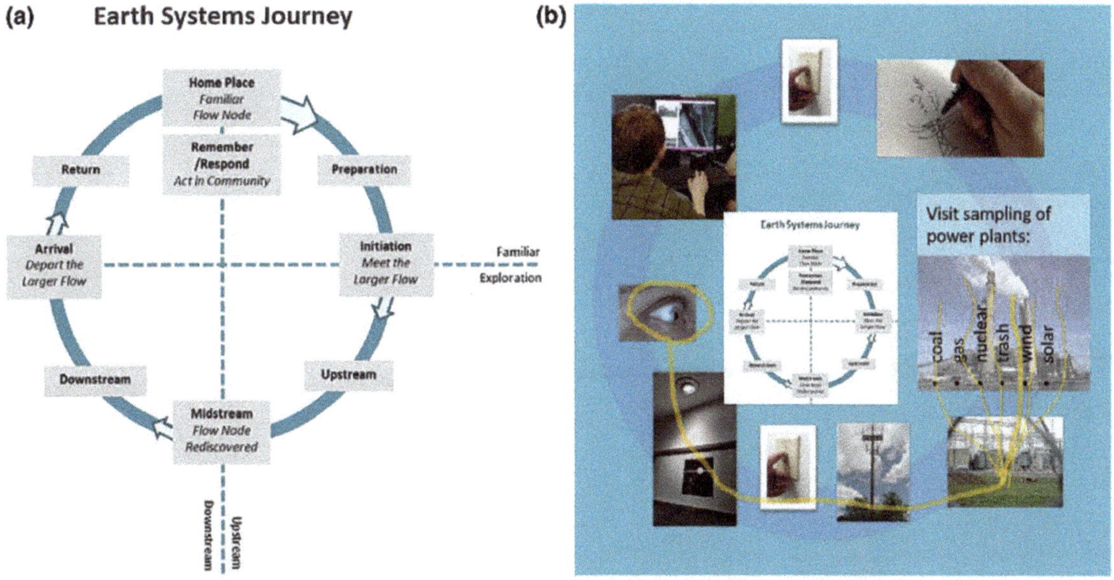

Source: © Full Spring Studio, LLC, and Power Systems Journey Models (Brigham 2012, 2018).

for solutions by creating and presenting interactive exhibits for families at the Bell Museum and by generating a set of story-maps on Minnesota power futures. These exhibits and story-maps are described in the sections below that follow each stage of the journey, representing a composite of experiences from spring and fall semesters in 2019.

The Setting of the Journey

The Power Systems Journey takes place in the Twin Cities of Minneapolis and St. Paul, Minnesota, and surrounding suburbs. There are three campuses within the University of Minnesota-Twin Cities: two in Minneapolis, across the Mississippi River from each other, and the other "St. Paul Campus," which is in Falcon Heights, a suburb of St. Paul. While the classroom was located on the Minneapolis campus, the interpretive hub of the journey was on the St. Paul campus at the Bell Museum of Natural History, which is part of the College of Forestry and Natural Sciences. The choice of Bell Museum as an interpretive hub and starting point of the power journey was based on it being a point of meaning for many on and off campus, so that the public story of the journey would have wide relevance. The other reason is that the story of the electric grid is presented in the context of humans and our creations existing within larger earth systems. The Bell Museum focus—telling the story of humans in relation to the natural world—was a perfect fit, and our partners at the Bell Museum became mentors to the students in how to communicate science to the public in an informal education setting.

An Earth Systems Journey chooses an even more particular point of departure than a building or property. The "flow node" in Figures 1a and 1b is a particular point of resource flow within an environment that creates an iconic location for the journey to begin. In this case, it was a light switch in the "Collections Cove," a room devoted to hands-on access to specimens: from taxidermy bats, to birds, to rocks, and skulls. The hands-on nature of this room represents one of the pioneering innovations of this museum, and it was a fitting point to launch the journey.

The preparation for this encounter began back in the classroom with a Call to Adventure.

Call to Adventure: Energy-Transition Stories

The grand challenge of our energy transition did not come out of the blue. Our ancestors have been here before, albeit facing different technological changes. In order for students to be able to fulfil their mission to tell stories that help our current energy transition, they need to understand the larger history of the many energy transitions we have already lived through.

The epic story of our ever-changing relationship with energy kicked off the journey. As individuals, groups, and societies, humans have always been power-limited; the availability of power has always dictated what we could accomplish. The story is more easily understood if we group all power into one of two self-explanatory categories: 1) heat and light and 2) mechanical power. Heat warms us, and light is for the long, dark nights, while mechanical power is for anything that needs to be moved or physically changed. In our earliest times, heat and light (when not available from the sun or seasons) came primarily from wood; mechanical power came from human muscle.

This was the state of our energy picture for countless years—wood for heat and light, and human muscle for mechanical power—and this left us severely power-limited and placed hard constraints on what we could achieve. Thomas Hobbes described this condition as nasty, short, and brutish, although recent thought on the subject is that the lives of these ancestors were closer to Eden than Hades.

The first energy transition came with the Neolithic Revolution. In particular the domestication of draft animals gave us a new source of mechanical power: animal muscle.

Following this transition, heat and light still came primarily from wood, but we now had a potent and compact power source, animal muscle, enabling new possibilities in addition to human labor. We embarked on great projects unthought of before—the Great Wall of China, where 1 million people worked and half of them died on the job, and the Grand Canal of China, where over 6 million people worked and again half of them died on the job. They were great accomplishments, although at the cost of many lives.

However, this new power source was limited by the simple fact that we needed to feed these animals. Many thousands of acres of farmland were dedicated to providing the fuel to feed our animals. Just as effort and land were needed to feed the human muscle, so, ultimately, animal muscle gave humans new capabilities, but we were still power-limited (although it might be more precise to say energy-limited).

Wood shortages brought on the next major energy transition. There had been many periods of wood scarcity over the years, for example, in ancient Greece and in the Roman Empire, but those shortages did not change our basic energy picture. However, when England experienced wood shortages, it embarked on an energy transition that fundamentally changed our energy story and every aspect of our lives.

The solution to England's wood shortages was to transition from wood to coal for heat. Mining operations ramped up throughout England, as the miners dug deep into the ground to extract the coal that was replacing wood for heat. Soon, many of these mines were deep enough that they reached the water table, flooding the mines and halting operations. To continue mining, elaborate water pumping mechanisms were devised to drain the mines to allow deeper extraction. These water pumps were powered by human and animal muscle, as that was the primary source of mechanical power, but things changed when Thomas Savery developed the vacuum pump, powered by burning coal, which replaced human and animal muscle as the source of power to drain the mines. It did not matter that these machines were less than 1 percent efficient because they ran on coal, and, being at a coal mine, the one thing they had in abundance was coal. Thomas Newcomen improved the system with his atmospheric pump. However, it, too, was less than 1 percent efficient.

At less than 1 percent efficiency, these machines were impractical for use anywhere except at a coal mine, but this would all change with James Watt's improvement on these technologies that ultimately led to the development of the coal-powered steam engine.

James Watt's improvement was the addition of a simple device, the condenser, which increased the efficiency of his machine to 10 percent, a substantial improvement. At that efficiency, the steam engine became a viable replacement for water turbines at textile mills and opened the possibility of having nearly unlimited mechanical power available anywhere in England. Coal was now replacing human and animal muscle for mechanical power, and this new source of mechanical power, unlike animal muscle, was virtually unlimited.

It did not take long before high-pressure steam engines were developed that were far more power dense and because of their compact size could be mounted on wheels on rails, the birth of locomotives and railways. Thus, coal mines powered by coal fed rail cars powered by coal that delivered coal to factories that were powered by coal, and this entire system was powered by the virtually unlimited energy of the enormous coal veins.

Rail lines spread across England, Italy, Germany, and the young United States, ushering in the unification of Tuscany, the unification of the German states, and with the final Golden Spike at Promontory Point, Utah, linking the entire North American continent.

Political boundaries changed, transportation changed, distribution changed, and manufacturing changed, all because we were forced to transition from wood to coal. Completely unplanned and unexpected, this energy transition changed everything.

Our next energy transition was initiated by a simple plan to replace whale oil for light with kerosene. The transition involved Col. Edwin Drake (not a real colonel), John D. Rockefeller, and a host of players from the new class of "captains of industry."

Kerosene is a petroleum product. Derived through fractional distillation, kerosene is less volatile than its cousin gasoline, another product of distillation, which was considered a waste product and often disposed of in rivers. Kerosene rapidly became the light of the world, displacing whale oil and spawning a vast industry to support its extraction, distillation, and distribution. When the electric lightbulb began to displace kerosene as the preferred source of light, these industries looked for a new market, and found one in the gasoline, which now would be used for automobiles and trucks. While this obviously transformed the transportation sector, gasoline would soon find a new use, fueling wars.

World War I has been described as a battle between trains and trucks. Trains were powered by coal and trucks by gasoline. The trucks won. This fact was not lost on people of the time, and it prompted one French senator to say shortly after the war "oil, the blood of the earth, became the blood of war, and will become the blood of peace." It is quite evident that oil has become the blood of war, but it is less clear whether oil has, or ever will, become the blood of peace. However, from that time until today, nations look at oil as a strategically vital commodity, a necessity to successfully wage war.

This is the energy world we live in today: heat and light provided by fossil fuels and mechanical power also provided by fossil fuels. Efforts to move away from fossil fuels are confounded by an enormous energy appetite and by the strategic importance of oil.

We know that we are on the verge of a dramatic energy transition, as we need to move away from our dependence on fossil fuels, but what will this transition look like? Each of our previous transitions has resulted in consequences that were not planned and were completely unexpected. Our task for the coming energy transition is to make a plan and to avoid the unexpected.

In making this plan, it is expected that a major player will be electricity, as there is a growing consensus that we need to do three things: 1) improve efficiency, 2) take the carbon out of the electric grid, and 3) electrify everything possible. The electric-power grid is at the heart of all of these efforts—the invisible machine that must now become visible.

Preparing for the Journey

The stage of "preparing for the journey" orients students to the topics, establishes tools and methods for recording impressions, and builds anticipation.

Students were instructed to obtain a sketchbook for recording observations on the journey. Why a sketchbook in this era of easy digital photography? It is an old habit and tool of engineers to sketch whatever they are working on. They do this to deepen their understanding and to force themselves to see things that they did not see before. We asked the students in this class to engage in much the same way and for the same reasons. They were asked to seek out parts of the grid and simply sketch what they saw. In the process, the students discovered unnoticed elements that were hiding in plain sight, and, at times, they also discovered the beauty and metaphor of the grid.

The students updated their travel journal weekly for the same reason that any traveler would. They were on a journey of discovery, visiting unfamiliar sites and meeting people in their natural habitats, with limited signposting to help them to make sense of the journey. Travelers have always found that keeping a travel journal is the best way to make sense of their journey and build new insights. So, the students kept a travel journal as well. Students uploaded their sketches and responses to travel-journal prompts of: What did you notice? What did you wonder? and What ideas did you have? These sketches and observations were collected in a story-map, and the sketches were also featured in an exhibit about the class (Brigham and Imbertson 2019).

Initiation

The initiation stage of the journey is when the travelers leave the world of the familiar and enter the world of exploration. It is one of the milestones of the journey.

We arrived at the Bell Museum and were greeted in a grand lobby by museum staff who welcomed the students as special guests and project partners. The first exhibit we went to was the "Collections Cove," part of the touch-and-see area, and a point of historical pride of the museum. We talked about how the experience of the specimens in the room was made possible by light, and noted that while there were some views, the majority of the light was provided by the light fixtures. We turned the light switch off and on to make note of the impact the light had on the experience of the space.

Next the student teams were asked to find a specimen that they were fond of and sketch the object, as part of forming a bond with the museum and its function to connect visitors with natural history. While students were sketching the specimens, we went to each group, asked them to pose with their specimen, and made photo portraits of each group that we called "Receiving Light from the Grid." Making the light tangible was the foundation for next questions. Where does it come from? What makes it possible? That was our quest.

Then, we held up a piece of amber and told a story to mark the students' initiation into the journey. Amber holds a special place in the history and understanding of electricity. Amber is derived from fossilized tree sap from trees that thrived 250 million years ago. Much like shellac, which is also derived from tree sap, amber has the unique property that, when rubbed, it can generate a static electric charge. Based on this phenomenon, it is quite likely that some of the first experiments in electricity were performed with amber. But there is more to this gem that makes it special in the world of electricity. The word for amber in ancient Greek is elektron, and amber (elektron) is the gem from which we get the word and meaning of electricity. Each student received a piece of amber as a symbol of the start of the journey, as a token to keep them mindful of their task, and as a binding stone for the entire group.

Upstream

The first part of the journey took students to many places "upstream" of the light switch at the museum.

Transmission Lines. The class first discovered the grid by looking out the classroom window. There it was, far away across the Mississippi, hidden in plain sight, an artistic transmission-line power pole that they would later learn was a 115 kV, three-phase line capable of delivering 200 MW of electric power to downtown Minneapolis. (See Figure 2.) But the class first met the grid up close the following week on a walking tour around campus.

On their walking tour of the grid, the class followed power lines and learned how to estimate voltages and power levels. They sketched what they saw and discovered aspects of power lines that they had never noticed before: Stockbridge dampers, grounding cables, and more.

Main Energy Plant. Hidden away below the banks of the Mississippi River is the university's Main Energy Plant (MEP). Formerly a coal plant, MEP was recently converted to a combined-heat-and-power natural-gas plant. Visiting this plant was eye-opening for most of the students, in part because this plant was literally within a stone's throw of their daily walking commutes but they had never seen it. Also eye-opening were the progressive and ecologically attuned attitudes of the plant engineers who they met here. Many of the cutting-edge technologies they had read about were being implemented right there in the plant, hidden in plain view, and

Figure 2
Student's Sketch of Transmission Lines by Neva Hubbert

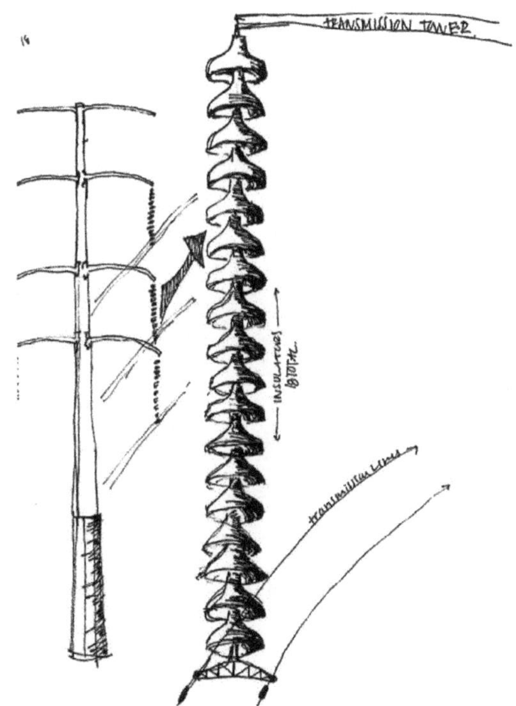

Figure 3
Student's Sketch at Main Energy Plant by Philip Hult

Figure 4
Student's Photo of Transmission Lines Near Prairie Island Nuclear Plant by Amethyst O'Connell

championed by traditional power engineers. (See Figure 3.)

Net-Zero Home and Shiloh Temple. In a grid with increasing amounts of distributed energy resources, even a solar home can be "upstream," feeding energy back into the grid in times of abundance and drawing it back out at night. Students visited the "Ohm Sweet Ohm" project near campus and got a personal tour from the owners and the architect at SALA Architects (Sloot 2016). This net-zero home is all electric, with batteries and grid interconnections. It produces more energy than it consumes in a year, even accounting for the electric-car charging. It also demonstrates efficiency and conservation, including just-right sizing to meet owner needs in a compact and attractive home. Students noted that, like any new construction, this form of energy responsibility is still economically out of reach for many households.

Affordable and equitable participation in the green-energy economy is a feature of the Shiloh Temple project, a community solar garden that is pioneering in its subscription availability for low-income residents as well as its green-job-creation strategies (McKnight Foundation 2018). (Students had a virtual tour of this project, by representatives from Minnesota Interfaith Power and Light, due to climate-changed-influenced severe weather on the day planned for the original tour.)

Prairie Island Nuclear Plant, Solar Farm, and Wind Turbine. It was easy to find the Prairie Island nuclear plant. (See Figure 4.) We simply followed the high-voltage power lines, of which there were many. Twenty-three insulator bells told us that these were very-high-voltage lines, 345 KV, and capable of delivering vast amounts of power. At 950 MW, the Prairie Island nuclear plant is a major source of electric power for the area. Since its construction in 1974, it has been at the center of many interesting stories.

Perhaps the best-known story is how the question of dealing with spent nuclear fuel at the plant spawned the rapid growth of wind power in Minnesota, but no less important are the many stories of the interactions of the power plant and the Prairie Island Indian Community who share this land. A stark reminder of this shared ownership is found on a gravel road dividing the plant and the tribal community. On one side of the road is a sign declaring that this land is the property of Xcel Energy; on the other side of the gravel road is a nearly identical sign declaring that this land is the property of the Prairie Island Indian Community. Being in this space, which is steeped in ancient traditions and now populated with modern technology, the students realized the wide-reaching effects of the electric-power grid, stretching in all directions from this mighty plant.

It was easy to find our way back by just following the power lines. We followed those lines past a solar farm to a lone wind turbine situated in the flat farmland south of the Twin Cities. (See Figure 5.) It was cold and snowy when we trudged to the wind turbine and craned our necks to see the top, realizing that this turbine, the solar farm, and the nuclear power plant share the same grid.

MISO (Midcontinent Independent System Operator) and Hydro Power. As we collected experiences of the many upstream power sources, the question arose about how all these power plants are coordinated. We had learned that the electrical grid needs to have a fine-tuned match of supply and demand in order to function. To see where it happens, we traveled to the Midcontinent Independent System Operator (MISO). Students learned about the process of communication and pricing between MISO and the many power plants and how decisions are made about which plants need to increase or decrease their power output. (See Figure 6.)

As with other lessons about the power grid, we use metaphor to help make the complexity tangible. For example, the grid is like a vast collection of bicycles connected by strong rubber bands. Some of the bicycles have pedals and are generators, while others have brakes and are loads. With changes in braking (loads) and pedalers trying to maintain a constant speed, the rubber bands stretch and shrink, constantly oscillating and trying to find equilibrium. The entire Eastern Interconnect of the grid, from Florida to

Figure 5
Student's Sketch at Eolos Wind Turbine by Allison Chang

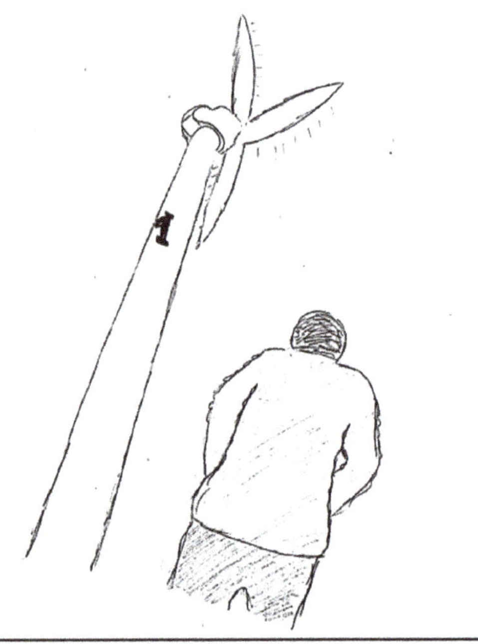

Manitoba, is like these bicyclists together trying to maintain a steady speed, "60 hertz," transmit power, and avoid breaking any of the rubber bands, that is, power lines.

On the way back, we stopped by the Ford Hydro plant, formerly used to supply power for manufacturing and now a feature of a new sustainable-housing development taking place on the old industrial site.

Allen S. King Coal-fired Power Plant. The Allen S. King Plant is an 800 MW coal plant. It has the tallest chimney within several hundred miles, although many claim to have never noticed this enormous structure. (See Figure 7.) The plant is nestled on the banks of the St. Croix River and hidden by hills. As students walked the perimeter of the plant, they discovered the reason for the plant's location.

Here we found a massive mountain of coal brought in by the trainload from Gillette, Wyoming. The tall chimney spews gases into the atmosphere, and the many cooling towers take water from the St. Croix River. The interplay of technology,

Figure 6
Student's Sketch of Midcontinent Independent System Operator (MISO) by Marie Wulff

infrastructure, and ecology were all on display here, a short distance from the river town of Stillwater.

Built in 1965, the Allan S. King power plant is scheduled to burn its last trainload of coal within the decade, ushering in a new chapter in the story of the electric-power grid.

Transmission Lines. We followed the power lines out of the King plant, noticing them for the first time, although they were in plain sight on the journey to the plant. We can learn a great deal by examining power lines. For example, we can recognize high-voltage lines, which indicate that the power is meant to travel long distances. Doubled or tripled conductors, called bundles, indicate even higher power flows.

We followed the lines until they left us to go to the Kohlman Lake Substation, but we rejoined the lines where they turned south to enter the Terminal Substation. From the Terminal Substation, which at one time was used for aircraft and lightning research, we follow the lines to the Gopher Substation and ultimately to our classroom on campus.

Although the power lines were massive, we did not notice them until our journey back from the King plant, and, in following the lines, we discovered something else, a solid connection from Gillette, Wyoming, to the St. Croix River, and, ultimately, to our campus.

Figure 7
Student's Sketch of the Allen S. King Coal Plant's Chimney by Hannah Bodmer

Terminal Substation and Story of Coal. We next visited the Terminal Substation, which we had previously viewed from the windows of the bus on our transmission-line journey. Here, the power leaves the high-transmission lines and drops down to ground level, creating what would be a dangerous situation except for the ubiquitous cyclone fence that surrounds every substation. (See Figure 8.)

The students met three utility power engineers who helped them suit up into protective gear and enter the substation. The engineers showed the students how to recognize the high-voltage areas of the substation, widely spaced equipment and bus bars, and the lower voltage sections of the substation where things were more closely packed. They explained the very real danger of voltage arcing and were careful to explain where it was safe to walk and where it was not.

The engineers explained the operation of circuit breakers, sectionalizers, current transformers, and at the heart of it all, the transformers. Transformers are the queen bees of the power grid. Most of the equipment in the substation is there primarily to protect the transformers, and the ability of transformers to change voltages is the primary reason that we now utilize alternating-current (AC) power rather than direct-current (DC) power in our electric grid. In power plants, transformers raise the voltage to transmission levels. Substation transformers bring the voltage back down to more usable levels.

Power leaves the substation underground or on tall power poles, safe from possible contact with humans, on its way to factories, businesses, and residences.

Since only half of the class could safely tour the substation at one time, we had two shifts. While one was touring the substation that was transmitting electricity partly made possible by coal, the other half joined in a discussion of the history and cultural dimensions of coal. We started with a reading from Barbara Freese ([2003] 2016). She brings a perspective to the cultural perception and function of coal over time, the dual nature of our dependence on it, and our distaste for its messy consequences, from sooty cities to black lung disease. We listened to a speech from Van Jones (2016), invoking a metaphor of death associated with fossil fuels, including coal. We also listened to an old coal mining song in which coal and life, and even the coal miner's body itself, are all intertwined, inseparable (Travis 1947).

Distribution Lines to the Switch. The next week, we picked up where we left off near the substation. We followed the 13.8 kV distribution lines from the Terminal Substation to the perimeter of the Bell Museum property where the power lines went underground, lost to sight. At this point we met one of the engineers who was responsible for the design of the Bell Museum electrical system. Together we got back on the scent of the power lines by the simple mechanism of dangling a copper wire in the air, connected to a handheld oscilloscope. There on the face of the oscilloscope was the fingerprint of the power line: a 60-hertz sine wave. We followed the signal

Figure 8
Student's Sketch from the Terminal Substation by Corey Bracken

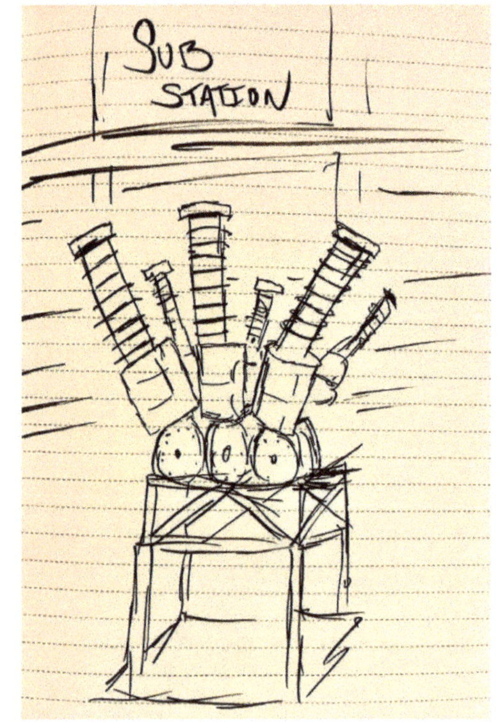

to the far side of the Bell Museum where, through an artful screen, we could see the transformer that brings the 13.8 KV voltage down to a manageable level for the building. (See Figure 9.)

From there, the power entered the building and made its way to the distribution center where, behind metal panels, switches and circuit breakers routed the power to the far corners of the building. Following conduit pipes containing wires we traced the power from the distribution room to the Collections Cove where our journey had begun.

We had finished our journey, and now the source of the light was no longer invisible; we had traveled the whole path, arriving back where we started.

Midstream—The Switch

We gathered in the Collections Cove, and we pointed out the light switch where the journey began. In silence, we turned the light off, paused, then on again. We remembered: all the coal, all the natural gas, solar, wind, and hydropower; all the transmission lines, and the substation where the power gets stepped down, safe for distribution lines that follow along our streets and alleys; then the transformer, the electrical room, and the conduit leading to this light switch in the Collections Cove; all for this simple action of switching a light on.

Downstream—Light to Vision

But where does it go? What is downstream of the switch? The light fixtures in the Collections Cove, which are LED, send out light that falls on our specimens of birds and rocks and skulls, and bounces off and enters our eyes through the pupil. We held up a diagram showing how the light continues to the retina, the optic nerve, and from there to the brain, the mind, perception—vision! Our desire to see, to learn about the specimens is one purpose of the grid. The grid only exists to serve our needs. We are the grid too, part of the continuum of energy. The students drew this last downstream leg of the journey, sketching their partner's eye and imagining the light's destination behind the pupil. (See Figure 10.)

We noted that there is another path of light to vision at the Bell Museum. A photovoltaic array on the roof converts light into energy, which also powers the lights and other electric uses and helps the Bell Museum achieve its energy-saving and environmental-responsibility goals.

Arrival

In a hero's journey and Earth Systems Journey, the point in the story that represents "arrival" signifies a transition from the world of exploration back to the world of the familiar—but not the end of the journey. It is a threshold point that, like the "initiation" stage, marks the transition from the world of the familiar into the world of exploration.

The students received another token, reminding them of the token of amber they had received at the beginning of this journey. This new token was a piece of jet—a semi-precious gemstone—more

Figure 9
Student's Sketch of Distribution Lines by Elizabeth Levang

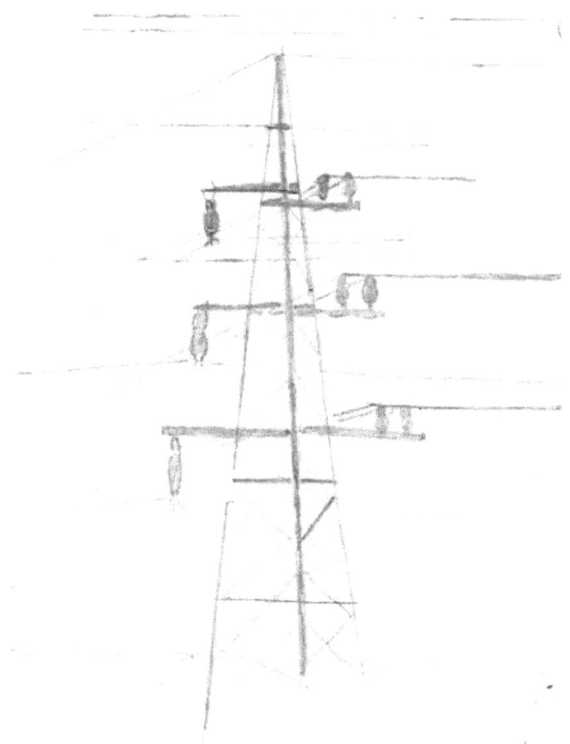

Figure 10
Student's Sketch of Light to Vision by Hannah Bodmer

formally called jet lignite and informally known as black amber. It is in fact a form of coal, lignite coal.

The amber, which the students had carried with them everywhere, reminded them of the origin of the story of electricity, and the jet that they now held in their hands reminded them that coal was the source of much of that electricity. But there was more to the story of amber.

The word for amber in the ancient Greek was *elektron*, but to the ancient Greeks elektron did not mean electricity, it meant beaming sunlight. In Greek mythology, the fossilized tree sap, which is amber, was the tears of the daughters of Helios, the sun god, despondent at the death of their brother. So electricity to the ancient Greeks is sunlight, and electricity for us will now become sunlight as well. The solution has been there in plain sight all along, electricity is sunlight. The solution was just lost in translation, but we could not find the translation without first taking this long journey.

Return—Reconnecting with the Climate Crisis

The "return" stage of the journey has participants returning to the familiar world and community from which they left. Here, it is important to put the local journey back into its global context. The context of the climate crisis generated the call to adventure and the need for the energy transition. Now students return to the climate context again via experiencing a "World Climate Simulation" process developed by Climate Interactive (2019). Guest leaders lay out the scenarios in which student teams represent countries or groups of countries that negotiate their emission reductions and their contributions to the U.N. Green Climate Fund. Each team has a profile of the concerns, history, and particular issues of the countries or country groups they represent.

To remind the students of the human reality behind the simulation "game" they were to play, we preceded the simulation sessions by watching Swedish youth-climate-activist Greta Thunberg (2018) implore them to make the drastic changes needed to protect the future for today's children. We viewed a spoken word video by Isabella Borgeson, recounting trauma in the Philippines after a typhoon (2015). As the games began, the atmosphere was exploratory and a bit competitive. The tensions rose with each round in which the goal of preventing a 1.5°C rise was not met.

Once we ran out of time, the guest guides announced two other players that were haunting the game, unnoticed. Jonee played the role of Time personified alternately by Greek gods Chronos, Kairos, and Ananke. The gods serve as symbols to question the paradigms of time at play during the simulation. Paul concluded, playing Gaia, Greek god representing Earth. He issued this warning: "I am Gaia, I am nature. Now that you have finished your negotiations, I have one final proposal for you. This proposal is nonnegotiable: Come back to me and I will save you. Ignore me and you are doomed." Then we dimmed the lights and sat quietly together.

Remember/Respond

The journey of heroes is complete only if they come back with something to share or offer: a story to tell or an insight to improve their community. This part of an Earth Systems Journey is about stories and service.

The students had already created one set of stories: Minnesota Power Histories. This collection of group projects took the form of GIS story-maps, exploring how the existing grid came to be. These stories served a purpose and were a public service by educating people about the electric grid so that they could be more informed voters and energy consumers.

To face the challenge of our current energy transition, the students took on new storytelling tasks. First, they created an interactive display for a special temporary exhibit at the Bell Museum, the "Power Pop-Up." This exhibit took place on a Saturday morning for the public, where the students were the exhibit guides, engaging the public of all ages with concepts about electricity through various devices and models. Topics ranged from the opportunities of combining pollinators with solar panels, to battery-powered demonstrations of wind power, to cartoon characters championing the energy transition with their special powers, inspired by the old power mascot, "Reddy Kilowatt."

They also created a suite of GIS story-maps, paired with the first set, called "Minnesota Power Futures." Here they responded to the pressures of climate change by educating the public about various aspects of the strategies for the energy transition, from how a homeowner can put solar on the roof, to the role of smart-grid technologies, to the use of behavioral psychology to increase adoption of energy-conserving practices.

The course concluded with a student symposium in which they shared their projects with each other and guests. The Minnesota Power Histories and Minnesota Power Futures were published on a public-facing website, reinforcing the authentic, real-world storytelling work the students had contributed. The story-maps are available at www.powersystemsjourney.net.

Next Journey/Going Forward

One journey ends and another begins. For the students, this means different things. Some of the students in electrical engineering decided or strengthened their prior decision to pursue renewable energy or power systems design that addresses issues of the energy transition. Some of the students already in environmental fields or with environmental leanings in their own field brought greater context with them back to their home disciplines as well as some new skills. Some of the students expressed that they had become much more conscious consumers of electricity and energy and were being more efficient. (See Figure 11.)

In a final exercise to add to our class story-map, we asked: "What will you take with you from Power Systems Journey? What new journey(s) will you take that relate to any of the themes of this course? What ideas, beliefs, insights, or interests will guide your next Journey?" Here are some of the answers from the students, our heroes.

> Before taking Power Systems Journey, I didn't know much about the grid or energy production, but now I have a better understanding of our grid's social, economic, political, and

technical context. I'll be taking my understanding of systems thinking and how energy is a piece of a much larger system that feeds into our lives.—L.A.

The number of problems with the grid this course brought to light was alarming since I considered myself well educated on the changes happening in the power industry. I will move forward, knowing the need to explain these problems to the public so we can solve these problems. The general public seems unaware of the issues facing the grid today, so there will be a great challenge of informing them as all these changes are occurring. –M.A.

The Power Systems Journey opened my eyes to the beauty and complexity of the grid and changed the way I see it in the environment around me. For many of us, the grid is difficult to understand due to its vastness and technicality. Through the power of storytelling, this complexity can be broken down so that more people can begin to see the grid in a new light.—N.H.

I am thinking I should improve people's knowledge about the effect of their daily decisions on the earth, and I believe all of us should start with our family members and friends in the kindest way that is possible.—P.M.

In the future, I hope to contribute my skills in graphic design and communication towards initiatives to stop climate change.—W.O.

Figure 11
Closing Image: Student Facing the Story of Power by Sheila Peyraud

I believe each of us have the power to make a change and should use our passion, knowledge, and devotion to help people feel the same way about sustainable, clean, and green energy. This course has been an eye opener about how much we can do but are being negligent towards problems our world is facing. I also learned from folks who took this class, it only made me see various other perspectives people brought to the table. I walk out of this course with immense amount of motivation and zeal to help make a difference.—P.S.

I believe that the grid can enhance our natural and human world, and it is our responsibility to address the negative impacts we have as individuals, communities, states, nations, and humanity on the planet. This class emphasized the power of storytelling, and I think when we have the ability to narrate the future we want to create, we can change anything.—H.B.

The Global Journey

For our current energy transition, the journey is still in progress. We have passed certain hurdles that make the destination seem more assured, as energy prices for renewables fall, coal plants close in the United States, and the pressure to address the climate crisis increases. But the speed of this transition and the resulting outcomes are neither clear nor inevitable, and the consequences of delay are grave. The urgency for systemic change—to complete our clean energy transition in an equitable process—is high and we need to press all the levers for change from technological innovation, to policy understanding, to public energy literacy. Behind it all, we need to consciously choose the paradigms that will guide us. We can learn from our history of energy transitions in the past, and we can acknowledge the role of culture and values in this process of creating a vision for where we want to go. Technical literacy about the complexities of the electric grid, integrated with arts and humanities, can provide both the means and the meaning that guide us to our future.

References

Bakke, Gretchen Anna. (2017). *The Grid: The Fraying Wires Between Americans and Our Energy Future.* Bloomsbury USA.

Blockstein, David E., Catherine H. Middlecamp, and John H. Perkins. (2015). "Energy Education: Easy, Difficult, or Both?" *Journal of Sustainability Education* 8 (January). http://www.jsedimensions.org/wordpress/wp-content/uploads/2015/01/Blockstein-et-al-JSE-Vol-8-Jan-2012.pdf

Borgeson, Isabella. (2015). "Yolanda Winds" [poem]. *Spoken Word for the World Competition.* https://www.youtube.com/watch?v=w4d8uM1H7pI

Brigham, Jonee Kulman. (2012). *Downstream/Upstream: A Systems Journey for Experiential Education and Placemaking.* Minneapolis: University of Minnesota.

________. (2014). "About." *Earth Systems Journey.* http://earthsystemsjourney.com/about/.

________. (2018). "The Role of Art and STEAM in Energy Education." Presented at the 3rd National Energy Education Summit, January 25, Washington, DC.

Brigham, Jonee Kulman, and Paul Imbertson. (2018). "GCC 3027/5027 | Grand Challenge Curriculum." *Grand Challenge Curriculum.* http://gcc.umn.edu/gcc-30275027

________. (2019). "PowerSystemsJourney." *Power Systems Journey.* www.power systemsjourney.net

Campbell, Joseph. ([1949] 2008). *The Hero with a Thousand Faces.* Novato, CA: New World Library.

Climate Interactive. (2019). "World Climate Simulation." *Climate Interactive.* https://www.climateinteractive.org/tools/world-climate-simulation/

Dewey, John. ([1934] 2005). *Art as Experience.* New York: Perigee.

________. ([1938] 1997). *Experience and Education.* New York: Simon & Schuster.

Finkelpearl, Tom. (2013). *What We Made: Conversations on Art and Social Cooperation.* Durham, NC & London: Duke University Press.

Freese, Barbara. ([2003] 2016). *Coal: A Human History*, revised and updated edition. New York: Basic Books.

Jones, Van. (2016). "Water Is Life. Oil Is Death." *News2Share.* https://www. youtube.com/watch?v=L_6rSQSAl7c

Jorgenson, Simon N., Jennie C. Stephens, and Beth White. (2019). "Environmental Education in Transition: A Critical Review of Recent Research on Climate Change and Energy Education." *Journal of Environmental Education* 50(3): 160–171.

McKnight Foundation. (2018). "Powering Neighborhoods." *The Power of Minnesota.* https://www.powerofmn.com/stories/poweringneighborhoods/

Meadows, Donella H. (1999). *Leverage Points: Places to Intervene in a System.* Hartland, VT: Sustainability Institute. http://www.donellameadows.org/wp-content/userfiles/Leverage_Points.pdf

________. (2008). *Thinking in Systems: A Primer.* Ed. D. Wright. White River Junction, VT: Chelsea Green.

Nye, David E. (2006). *Technology Matters: Questions to Live With.* Cambridge, MA: MIT Press.

Rangel, Nicole. (2018). *Why Interdisciplinary Project-Based Learning? Assessing the Benefits and Challenges at U.S. Institutions of Higher Education.* Berkeley: Blum Center, University of California. https://blumcenter.berkeley.edu/deveng/why-interdisciplinary-project-based-learning/

Sloot, Marc. (2016). *Ohm Sweet Ohm* [design project]. Minneapolis and Stillwater, MN: SALA Architects. https://salaarc.com/project-types/featured/ohm-sweet-ohm/

Thunberg, Greta. (2018). "The Disarming Case to Act Right Now on Climate Change." *Ted Talk.* https://www.ted.com/talks/greta_thunberg_the_disarming_case_to_act_right_now_on_climate_change/transcript

Travis, Merle. (1947). *Dark as a Dungeon* [song]. Hollywood, CA: American Music, Inc. https://www.youtube.com/watch?v=9CP8FgkmBpA

University of Minnesota. (2015). "Grand Challenges Curriculum." *Strategic Planning.* https://strategic-planning.umn.edu/grand-challenges-curriculum

CHAPTER 14

Solar Commons: A "Commons Option" for the 21st Century

*Kathryn Milun**

ABSTRACT. Private ownership of nature's gifts—water, air, sunlight—stands in the way of solving the collective problems of the 21st century. In the case of sunlight, common ownership through community solar trusts can overcome both the inequities and the inefficiencies of investor-owned utilities (IOUs) with legal monopolies. Those monopolies function with the same arrogance as aristocrats did in the past, but now the stakes are higher: the future of the planet. This essay describes the Solar Commons Project by which a team of inspired citizens and public scholars joined to create a form of community-trust solar-energy ownership, in which multiple stakeholders benefit. The goal is to make this "Solar Commons" model an iterable, scalable, model of community solar that empowers low-income neighborhoods in the United States. An integral part of the project is a process of creating community-engaged public art to communicate the nature of community ownership. Artistic and theatrical presentations can help involve the public in dialogues around questions of utility management that are normally couched in technical language designed to obfuscate the political power of electric utilities. One role citizens can play is unmasking utilities when they publicly promote themselves as providers of clean energy, even when they are actively engaged in protecting the interests of fossil-fuel companies. Ultimately, however, creating a Solar Commons involves more than criticizing the failed institutions of the past. It requires us to think innovatively about ways to draw upon the history of the commons to design new modes of sharing sunlight and other common goods to create a more equitable, sustainable future.

*Associate professor of anthropology and Director of the Center for Social Research, University of Minnesota, Duluth. Founded and directs the Solar Commons Research Project, which innovates and prototypes community trust ownership of solar energy for low-income communities. Her students from the Energy, Culture, Society course run the annual Duluth Power Dialog, bridging academic research with public policy and citizen engagement. Email: kmilun@d.umn

> Common wealth, properly organized, provides a way to address the two greatest flaws in contemporary capitalism—its relentless destruction of nature and widening of inequality—while still keeping the benefits that markets provide. ... Common wealth—that is, wealth belonging to everyone equally—includes the gifts of nature, societal creations, and economic synergies. It is immense and in some cases imperiled, yet it remains invisible to markets because it is poorly organized and lacks clear property rights. Organizing common wealth so that markets respect its co-inheritors and co-beneficiaries requires the creation of common wealth trusts, legally accountable to future generations. These trusts would have authority to limit usage of threatened ecosystems, charge for the use of public resources, and pay per capita dividends. Designing and creating a suite of such trusts would counterbalance profit-seeking activity, slow the destruction of nature, and reduce inequality. (Barnes 2015)

Introduction

In 2007, I was a new member of the Tomales Bay Institute (TBI) in northern California. The founder of TBI, Peter Barnes (2006), had just published a book that laid out the economic argument for building a "commons" sector of the U.S. economy, geared to managing and equitably distributing common wealth from shared resources, such as the atmosphere, water, and wildlife—sources of life whose value have been diminished by market and state-sector management (or lack of management). The climate crisis, water pollution, and massive species extinction provided more than enough evidence to warrant new governance strategies based on a "common property" status of air and the public trust status of water and wildlife. Furthermore, the growing disparity in wealth in the United States called for new economic tools that would better distribute wealth accumulated from nature's gifts, such as minerals, wind power, and wildlife. Barnes had gathered a diverse group of activists and public scholars to brainstorm how new uses of trust ownership could more sustainably capture and more equitably distribute common wealth from nature as common property. How could new, enduring institutions for a commons sector be created, and what experiments were needed to test common wealth trust ownership? These were the thoughts I took back with me to Arizona, where I was living at the time, a legal anthropologist newly out of work from the university. With the sun beating down on my head and my brain emancipated from my academic discipline, I was free to imagine how solar radiation, with its distributed abundance and scalable photovoltaic technologies, could be claimed as common property and inspire a local ownership model to direct the common wealth benefits of the sun's energy to those most in need. With that, the idea of a Solar Commons was born.

It was not until 2018, after 10 years of creative, collaborative, legal, and financial work as well as pavement pounding for partners and sites, that the first Solar Commons Project was interconnected to the grid: a community-trust-inspired model that allowed solar panels on the roof of a building in one part of Tucson, Arizona to send a 20-year income stream to weatherize homes in a low-income neighborhood across town. The community-based research team wanted to make sure that no Solar Commons Project would recede into the same siloed, technical, and financial obscurity that has hidden the ownership, equity, and pollution issues of 20th-century energy infrastructure. As a result, we were joined by a team of artists who worked with the Solar Commons beneficiary community to co-create public art that could make visible how this neighborhood was claiming its common property right to gather the sun's common wealth for the well-being of the community.

This essay uses a description of the Solar Commons Project to demonstrate why commons economic thinking presents a transformative approach to the ecological and economic inequities of our historical moment. Imagine a portion of the U.S. electric grid providing a "commons option" for communities to access their gathering rights to the sun's common wealth. Low-income neighborhoods or depressed rural communities could capture their share of the sun's energy with photovoltaic panels, send that electricity directly to the electric grid, and have grid owners pay for it with deposits into a community trust fund that would support much needed community programs and projects. If the panels were installed on the roof of a neighborhood factory or warehouse, the roof owners would use the electricity on site and would pay for it with deposits to a community trust fund. The beneficiaries of these solar commons trust funds would be programs supporting affordable housing and homeless shelters, sustainable community agriculture projects, paid internships for low-income high school students to work with community newspapers, job training programs, and much more. In short, Solar Commons would be an economic tool of the energy transition, supporting community-empowerment projects that local partners deemed useful for their community's well-being.

In 2019, the Solar Commons Project was a finalist in the U.S. Department of Energy's "Solar in Your Community Challenge." A 2018 analysis by the Rocky Mountain Institute of the financial model and scalability potential of the Solar Commons Project found that it presented a positive net present value to funders and could be quickly scaled to provide 10 gigawatts (GW) on the U.S. electric grid (Brehm and Lillis 2018a, 2018b). As of 2018, "cumulative operating solar photovoltaic capacity now stands at 62.4 GWdc, about 75 times more than was installed at the end of 2008" (Runyon 2019). Indeed, applying commons design principles to solar energy, the Solar Commons Project aims to demonstrate a variety of economic uses and scaling techniques that can make Solar Commons a robust institution in a commons (as opposed to market or state) sector, connecting solar energy to the broad array of solutions proposed to better steward natural and community resources for ecological and economic equity in the 21st century.

Beyond its practical potential, the Solar Commons Project provides a conceptual intervention into the dominant ownership structures of the U.S. electricity sector. Electric utilities are resistant to decarbonization, compromised by conflicts of interest, and lacking in innovation and incentives to spark and share the benefits of the green energy revolution. Solar Commons brings a "commons" framework to the U.S. electricity grid. From a commons perspective, energy ownership can be analyzed, critiqued, and transformed beyond the private/public duality that has dominated 20th-century energy infrastructure.

In what follows, I consider the ownership and economic issues of the current U.S. power sector from the perspective of commons. I begin with a historical introduction to the type of trust ownership that underlies the Solar Commons model. Trust ownership is one of the oldest forms of property in the common law tradition. It arose as a corrective to inequities in the feudal property regime and has continued to evolve over time, often as a way around limitations of the dominant property regimes of its day. Going back to a time before the existence of the kind of private and public property regimes that have been naturalized in 20th-century energy infrastructure, we can more easily see the limits of our current energy ownership and the potential for legal innovation. Following this historical perspective, I consider how today's investor-owned utilities have much in common with feudal-ownership structures. For that reason, they will not be leaders in creating a democratic, just energy transition. We can learn from our nonmodern legal ancestors a practical and conceptual work-around of our current carbon-intensive ownership regime in taking up a commons perspective.

Finally, I return to a practical description of the Solar Commons Project, outlining how it works behind and in front of the meter to produce a community income stream. The basic economic principles and governance structures of the Solar Commons protect against failures of market logic and conflicts of interests in state political sectors. I explain why the Solar Commons model requires, as a feature of its Creative Commons license, the use of community-engaged public art to communicate community ownership. Solar Commons demonstrates the work of a new civic imagination in our energy system, one that is connected to other social movements currently forming around the creative use of trust ownership to protect our common wealth in nature's bounty and ensure that that wealth is nourishing all communities (Kelly 2012; Weston and Bollier 2013).

We Once Were Commoners: Feudal Energy Infrastructures

As an anthropologist, I view economic and property systems as cultural developments, embedded in the historical circumstances where they arose. An ancient ownership vehicle like the trust, when applied centuries later to new material circumstances, carries a capacity to "remember" that past and to leverage its residual elements for innovative purposes. Trust ownership is the cornerstone of Solar Commons. Understanding how the trust vehicle arose to address structural inequities of feudal land ownership in the past offers creative insight into how community trusts might contribute to more equitable and local ownership of renewable-energy assets today. Such historical thinking shines a much needed light on the taken-for-granted corporate ownership model of today's fossil-fuel infrastructures and their for-profit investor-ownership networks that must be decarbonized before midcentury.

Ancient, Residual, and Emergent Trust Ownership

In the English common law tradition that governs the U.S. electricity grid today, the most ancient form of ownership is found in the vehicle of trust property. Simply put, trust ownership allows one party to own the "legal title" to an asset while another party owns the benefits of that asset in the form of an "equitable title." Importantly, trust ownership arose as a property "corrective" from the feudal era when peasants had no legal title to the land that held the energy resources on which their lives depended: fields for agricultural production, rivers for fishing, pastures for grazing, forests for gathering wood and game, and bogs for peat (turbary) provisions (Scott 1922; Scott and Fratcher 2000). The feudal property regime, instituted in England after the Norman invasion of 1066, allowed only monarchs and their managerial hierarchy of dukes, earls, and barons to own legal title to land in medieval England. This new legal arrangement undercut the customary land use practices of local villagers and peasants, who were left without the right to access the sources of their livelihood. English courts recognized and corrected the inequity of the dominant legal order by allowing local peasants to exercise an "equitable title" in the energy resources of lands, even when the legal title belonged to the king and lords. These lands with equitable title access rights were often called "commons" (Bravo and De Moor 2008) (Figure 1).

The history of the English common law tradition shows that rights in commons were secured in various ways. For example, sometimes the equitable title to access bogs, forests, and pastures would reside in "hearths" of cottages that sat on the estate of a feudal lord. This way, the equitable title for local subsistence land use would be passed on intergenerationally to peasants who lived in those households and worked on those lands (Birtles 1999). It is an enduring testament to the durability of commons practices and trust ownership that today, in the 21st-century English countryside, there are still local residents who practice their equitable title rights to access local forests and wetlands to gather their customary portion of wood and peat for household heating or to access local pasture to graze their customary number of sheep. These residents do not have legal title to the forest or turbary commons, which may be legally owned by private estates or county governments. But the evolution of the common law tradition has provided that the equitable title rights of local residents persist despite a transfer of legal title to a private or public landowner. Today in the United Kingdom there are also land trusts set up to manage these lands on behalf of present and future generations of equitable title holders, still known as "commoners" (Short 2008). Regardless of the legal structures that protect them, similar energy provisioning practices endure to this day in locations around the world where commoning is still recognized (Dietz et al. 2003).

Another way to view the idea of equitable title as a corrective to the inequities of the dominant laws of feudal England is to see it as a limit on the power of the legal property owner: agricultural and peat commons represented a limit on the landowners' rights to exclude peasants. The Forest Charter of the Magna Carta of 1215 spelled out the limits on the king's authority to exclude local villagers from gathering wood and other provisions in the king's forests (Linebaugh 2008).

While, in some places, peasants enjoyed equitable title rights through the end of the feudal era and the rise of the modern capitalist state, in much of England, commons were enclosed and turned into private property during the 17th and 18th centuries. Private landowners worked with English legislators to extinguish equitable title access to common lands on their property, preferring to use the property to generate more commodity value for trade. Thus, lands that once supported subsistence crops for local consumption were privatized to produce surplus grains for export or to provide pasture for sheep whose wool was sold in expanding commodity markets. As the new class of private landowners and merchant traders shifted the economy from local agrarian production to large-scale industrial production, peasants migrated to the expanding towns and cities to find work in factories and provide for their households by exchanging their labor in the new wage economy of the Industrial Revolution. The peasant revolts of the 17th and 18th centuries demonstrated commoners' resistance to the loss of their customary subsistence property rights in commons (Thompson 1971). English historians note that the peasant revolts were civic demonstrations that the new economic order was overstepping the limits of a "moral economy," economic practices long established in customary commoning activities and once secured and protected in equitable title of trust property arrangements (Götz 2015). The ancient moral economy had indeed found intergenerational

Figure 1
Turbary: Harvesting Peat as a Traditional Commons Right

Source: Photo licensed from ALAMY. Photographer: H. & D. Zielske. Original title: "A farmer with a donkey cart peat cutting, Doo Lough Pass, County Mayo, Ireland, Europe.

Contributor: Image Professionals GmbH/ Alamy Stock Photo; Image ID: BH11JN.

legal expression in the Forest Charter of the Magna Carta and in the uses of equitable title to limit the power of the feudal landowner. With the waning of the feudal era, however, the norms of the moral economy were eroded by new laws protecting the surplus production values of private property owners and the emerging capitalist merchant class.

Applying Trusteeship Today

Today, the idea of trust law serving the equitable interests of the poor has mostly faded from memory in North America. Many U.S. citizens are familiar with the legal term "trust" from antitrust legislation. At the beginning of the 20th century, antitrust laws were used to break up large monopolies like Standard Oil and U.S. Steel, companies that had used trust ownership during the Gilded Age of U.S. capitalism to control markets and accumulate enormous wealth (Trachtenberg [1982] 2007). Trusts are also familiar today as a more personal legal vehicle, used, for example, when grandparents set aside money for the benefit of their newborn grandchildren. In a trust agreement, the grandparents can set out the terms and arrange for bankers to act as the "trustees" of the assets until the grandchildren (the beneficiaries of the trust) turn 18. Thus the trust has become popular as a practical, do-it-yourself legal tool to hold an asset—money—in trust for the benefit of another who will inherit that money at some time in the future. But even in this personal use of trust ownership, the technical legal terms carry the historical remnants of the "corrective" that the courts provided to the inequities of the feudal property regime. In the process of splitting ownership of the monetary asset, the trustees will hold the legal title to the property and the beneficiaries will own the equitable title to the asset. Today the beneficiary is still called the "equitable" title owner.

The community-trust model of ownership in the solar commons revives the more ancient idea of "equity" in trust ownership. By splitting the ownership of a solar array into a legal and an equitable owner and making that equitable owner a local low-income community beneficiary, a Solar Commons directs wealth created by electricity generation into low-income communities. Importantly, it does this not by saving pennies on individual low-income households' electricity bills while passing on surplus wealth to corporate owners to be accumulated as profit. Rather, the Solar Commons trust functions as a social wealth fund that allows communities to aggregate a large portion of the economic benefits from the renewable-energy transition and to direct those benefits to local neighborhoods as a whole. Thus, the economics element of solar commons functions as a community empowerment tool, even as it helps close the "solar income gap" with those who benefit from the current private, investor-ownership structure of the electric grid (Mueller and Ronen 2015). Solar Commons also invokes the moral economy arguments of common property owners embedded in the Magna Carta and other common law traditions: solar commoners claim their share of the sun's free and abundant common wealth in solar energy. They are like the landless peasants of yore, exercising an equity claim to energy benefits in a property structure that would otherwise exclude them. Ancient, residual, and emergent trust ownership creatively persists as a legal vehicle for solar commoners to work around contemporary inequities in modern fossil-fueled energy infrastructures.

We Still Are Serfs: Managerial Feudalism in Investor-Owned Monopoly Electric Utilities

Drawing from the practical solutions of our historical past, the Solar Commons framework was built from several key lessons about energy use in premodern times. When the dominant property regime, protected by legal title, had no ownership structure for the local laborers to control energy resources in wood, peat, and pasture land, they invoked a common property solution and protected it by equitable title. When elites accumulated wealth by blocking common access to forests and peat bogs, moral outrage and resistance helped institute limits on the power of the dominant regime (encoded in principles of the Magna Carta's Forest Charter) (Linebaugh 2008). Using common property forms and taking up collective action to define the limits of tyrants, landless peasants left a legacy of civic action before the rise of the modern state or the capitalist marketplace. Solar Commons uses many of these legal and economic strategies. Applying "commons thinking" to today's energy landscape, we can better understand the appeal of Solar Commons trust ownership. It can also help us unpack the complex ownership problems that impede decarbonization and economic equity in our energy system today. As it turns out, our modern power sector employs legal, ideological, and managerial strategies that greatly resemble what our commoner, trust-strategist ancestors faced in our shared English, common law past.

Modern Managerial Feudalism

Let us begin by considering how much the investor-owned monopoly utility that dominates the U.S. electric grid today is like the feudal landowner of yore. The most obvious comparison is that both feudal property regimes and modern structures of utility ownership give owners rights to exclude competitors in their jurisdictions. This is why today's utilities are called "monopolies." Feudal kingdoms and for-profit electric utilities are both safe from competition when it comes to their legal rights to govern and own energy infrastructure in their jurisdictions. (Remember, the aristocratic landowner was the one who held legal title over the forests and peat bogs in the "wood economy" of medieval England [Radkau 2012].) Why is it now a problem for American electric utilities to function as noncompetitive monopolies by owning systems of power generation, transmission, distribution grids, rights-of-way energy corridors, and electricity billing? It is a problem because the U.S. power industry is notoriously inefficient as well as environmentally toxic.

Since the 1960s, the U.S. electric-power sector has not upgraded its technology to automate and digitize in ways that we have seen in the rest of the economy. These upgrades are necessary for the electric grid to function as a "smart grid" that can integrate variable electricity generation from renewable-energy sources like solar rooftops. Smart grids also allow utilities to more efficiently balance customers' electric loads by, for example, setting time-of-day use controls on high-energy appliances like automatic dryers so that they can only turn on in the evening, after peak electricity need is over.

Why is the U.S. power sector so resistant to upgrades and to change? First, the equipment is old:

> About one-fifth of the power plants in America's generation fleet are more than fifty years old, and much of the nations' high-voltage transmission network was designed for an era when there was very little interstate commerce in electricity. (Jones and Zoppo 2014: 1–2)

Second, electric-utility owners do not invest in research and development. Other major industries spend as much as 3 percent of total revenues on research and development, but the electric-power sector spends less than 1 percent. The U.S. electric-power sector is arguably the nation's largest industry with over $600 billion in physical assets and annual sales of over $260 billion (Jones and Zoppo 2014: 2, 3). It is fueled predominantly by coal, gas, and nuclear sources. When states allow these investor-owned-utilities (IOU) to function as monopolies in a given region, they face no competition and submit to public oversight by politically appointed or elected state authorities (generally called public utility commissions). Throughout the 20th century, this ownership structure guaranteed investors a good return on long-term, costly investments in power plants (first coal, then expensive nuclear, and now increasingly gas) and on an extensive network of transmission lines. The investors' return rate was set by the public regulators and was recovered by charges to customers in their monthly electric bills. For the last century, the investor-owned electric-utility monopoly was one of the most stable forms of investment, despite its increasingly known inefficiencies and pollution problems. Certainly, lack of competition and guaranteed return on investment partially explain why this large, profitable, and essential industry sector managed to protect itself from change.

What other explanations can help us understand why and how the electric-power industry remains immune to change? It is often easier or more cost-effective to continue along an already set *path* than to create an entirely new one. This is called "path dependency theory" (Stein 2016). But, from a commoner's perspective, we can consider a more materially relevant response to the question of industry inefficiency: ownership. In fact, a commoner's perspective explains not only inefficiency but also the industry's market failure and its inability to respond to the looming dangers of the climate crisis.

Here again, the feudal analogy is enlightening. Both monarchs and modern corporate shareholders are the distant owners of their vast realms. But they cannot exercise their monopoly ownership powers without the intricate network of locals who make up a managerial class so well embedded in the local economy and government that political, economic, and technical power become indistinguishable. Political economists call such ownership structures "managerial feudalism" (Brenner and Brenner-Golomb 1996; Graeber 2018). They note that decision-making and jobs in such regimes owe less to economic need and efficient practices than to maintaining a social network of obligations based on status and power that will secure the distant owners' investments and the managers' high-paying jobs. Just as our ancestors recognized the medieval nobility presiding over the charity halls and religious festivals throughout their local countryside, we captive utility ratepayers have also seen corporate utility vice presidents, community outreach personnel, and communications specialists show up at civic meetings, county fairs, and university stages. We may even be aware of the revolving door between private industry and public-sector employment. Who has not seen their utility's logo on the back of neighborhood Little League jerseys and on the backboards of high school hockey tournament arenas? Corporate utility employees are recognizable as they repair downed electric lines and even advertise clean-energy aspirations on local television stations.

It is far more difficult to recognize the myriad ways electric monopolies use their local political power to avoid making the urgent transition to clean energy. This is their secret power: the power of modern managerial feudalism resides in its complex invisibility. It is like the invisible energy infrastructure—distant power plants, extensive transmission lines, and gas pipelines—that we unconsciously engage when we turn on a light switch or turn up our thermostat. When we consciously acknowledge the cultural embeddedness of the power industry's managerial feudalism, we can see that its power is more pervasive and more complex than anything that could be dealt with upfront by voter ballots or academic debates over policy contradictions. Utility managerial feudalism obfuscates the conflicts of interest in our carbon-invested utility corporations. But even more importantly, it undermines the effectiveness of the legal and political institutions available for local energy users (whom we should call "commoners" rather than "consumers" or "ratepayers") to push for more renewable energy on their local distribution grids.

I can highlight the structures of managerial feudalism in corporate utilities even further by using my own electricity jurisdiction as a case in point. In fact, I have the undergraduate anthropology students in my Energy, Culture, Society course do this as an "ethnographic" exercise every year. They study the managerial feudalism of our local corporate-monopoly utility, Minnesota Power, which rules over electricity generation and distribution in the city of Duluth and areas surrounding Lake Superior in northern Minnesota. My students study the utility's conflicts of interest and consider what remedies exist for local citizen action toward a more just and democratic energy transition. But instead of writing papers about their findings, the students are tasked with a much more difficult mission: they have to create a civic discussion about their findings by hosting an annual "Power Dialog" at a local community theater and inviting local experts to come on stage to answer their questions regarding utility investments in fossil fuels and contradictory utility messaging around renewable energy (Theater of Public Policy 2019). When anthropology students study the energy industry, they look at social, legal, and political structures as well as the cultural embeddedness of these structures. Thus, they design their Power Dialog to include policy and technical experts as well as artists and improvisational comedy theater actors who can be onstage to "translate" the energy-policy-speak of experts into compelling images and comedy skits. Outbreaks of audience laughter keep the local energy transition discussion resistant to capture by technical policy-speak. Technical jargon is a secret power of modern managerial feudalism.

In the Duluth Power Dialog 2019, students foregrounded several obfuscated relationships of their for-profit utility corporation, Minnesota Power. They pointed out that Minnesota Power is a "vertically integrated" utility, which means that it owns the generation, transmission, and local distribution infrastructure of the region's entire electricity system. Minnesota Power uses a fuel mixture that is approximately 60 percent coal, a key contributor to the climate crisis. Students had to work hard to uncover how much of Minnesota Power's electricity is, in fact, coal-generated since this information is not clearly available on Minnesota Power's website. Students looked into the utility's report to the U.S. Securities and Exchange Commission (2019), which notes that 27.2 percent of its power comes "from market purchases in the MISO market and from Other Power Suppliers," where the fuel mixture is not given. In clarifying the utility's ownership relationships, students pointed out that Minnesota Power is a subsidiary of Allete, Inc., whose other subsidiary, ALLETE Clean Energy, leases its rights-of-way for electricity-transmission lines to gas and oil pipeline companies. The contradictions and apparent conflicts of interest are thus not lost on the audience, as students make visible with maps and graphics how ALLETE Clean Energy helps move gas from the North Dakota Bakken shale oil fields through our region using an electricity-transmission corridor (paid for by Duluth ratepayers). Minnesota Power promotes the corridor as its vehicle for bringing "clean" hydropower from our distant Canadian neighbor, Manitoba Power. Indeed, deep in the archives of Minnesota Power's website, students discovered statements like this:

> A top priority of the ALLETE Energy Corridor is to develop an extension of the existing energy delivery path some 60 miles westward to the burgeoning Bakken shale oil fields of west-central North Dakota. ... ALLETE Clean Energy has been working diligently with potential partners to study the co-location of facilities and assess the capital needs for the Bakken link. It is envisioned that various lengths of the corridor would be used for different purposes. (Allete 2013)

Thus, shareholder wealth of Minnesota Power is closely tied to fossil-fuel industries. Embedded investments in fossil-fuel industries are not uncommon in electricity-transmission corridors (Klass and Meinhardt 2014).

Students also pointed out that the local managers of this utility are interwoven in a back-scratching network embedded in our city's political, social, and cultural institutions. The executive officers and employees of Minnesota Power sit on the boards of public and private institutions around our region. Minnesota Power's executive vice president is also the head of the board of regents of the University of Minnesota; employees of Minnesota Power sit on the Duluth City Council, on the board of the Duluth Chamber of Commerce, and other private-sector regional economic development institutions. Employees of Minnesota Power also fund and work in local organizations, such as "Better in Our Backyard" (2020), that favor mining and pipelines for oil and gas, even as they present themselves as being grassroots organizations that are based in the community. The CEO of Allete, Inc. is also on the board of directors of many local institutions, including Essentia Health Systems, the region's largest health care complex, and PolyMet Mining Corporation, which has proposed a controversial sulfide-mining project for copper-nickel in the watershed of the St. Louis River and Lake Superior (Karnowski 2020). When students interview on stage a member of the Duluth Climate/Energy Network (DCEN), a local citizen action group aiming to bring more renewable energy to the region, that person attests to the frustration of

DCEN members seeking to move forward an agenda to promote a renewable-energy democracy in the jurisdiction of this political, economic, and technical swamp of Minnesota Power's managerial feudalism.

Beyond Managerial Feudalism to Divine Right

Besides being materially embedded in local government, education, and community institutions, investor-owned utilities also enjoy a transcendental status when it comes to their reason for being. This makes them look more like feudal institutions than modern companies. Like medieval aristocrats, who enjoyed their power as a divine right, utilities represent themselves as systems governed by "natural" principles rather than by social conventions. Electric utilities are called "natural monopolies," which means they have a *logical right* to exist without competition because of the high start-up costs and economies of scale in their industry. Of course, this 20th-century logic is contradicted by the nature of the new 21st-century renewable-energy technologies like solar and wind that individuals and community groups can now competitively finance, install, and own with great advantage to their local economies (Cole and Grossman 2003; Heiman and Solomon 2004).

Another material fact of 21st-century life eroding the logic of monopoly ownership comes from the climate crisis. It is no longer rational to argue that carbon-intensive electricity produced cheaply by a utility, based on its economies of scale, is a compelling justification for allowing that utility to own exclusive rights to generate electricity in a given region. If one factors in the existential threat of fossil-fuel-induced global warming, the social cost of producing "cheap" electricity is quite high. In the 21st century, we should expect that external costs to public health and to the stability of the climate system will be internalized to provide a true price of power from coal, gas, solar, or wind generated by a utility.

Despite profound changes in the natural world, the irrational legal legacies and institutional protections of natural monopolies remain baked into the 21st-century advantages afforded the monopoly utility. These advantages give monopoly corporations invested in fossil-fuel infrastructure an incentive to ignore local benefits from clean-energy ownership and to slow down effective citizen participation in energy policy. Progressive states, such as New York and California, have started to break up utility monopolies (Zaccour 2012). However, many states continue to protect the right to monopolize by employing the logic of the "consumer welfare standard." This is a Reagan-era economic argument that values the right of consumers to obtain the lowest cost goods above the rights of competitors—or, for that matter, the rights of citizens to a stable climate system (Orbach 2011). Cheap electricity, which assigns zero value to environmental impacts, thus becomes a kind of sacred economic value that utility regulators, ostensibly ruling in the interest of the public good, are loathe to rule against. In these ways, utilities are protected by law against competition. Like the consumer kingdoms of Amazon and Walmart, utilities distribute cheap (and polluting) goods, while depressing local economic activity in clean energy.

We Are Still Serfs

Indeed, in many ways, we citizens are still serfs in our energy landscape. For the most part, we are at the mercy of our one electricity provider, and we pay electricity rates determined by the investments that a monopoly utility makes. As captive, long-term ratepayers we are valued for the risk-free market we provide for utilities' investments in large, distant power plants and transmission grids. But, as rate-payers, we have little, if any, say about the kind of power plants investors finance. If our federal or state governments change air pollution standards, investor-owned utilities will need to decide how to transition away from carbon-intensive, coal-powered plants. But if utility owners commit to a 30-year investment in a gas plant rather than a wind farm or a solar installation, and if regulators affirm that choice as the cheapest source of electricity, then ratepayers will be forced to pay, regardless of their preference to see their money invested in clean-energy infrastructure. This will significantly slow down an energy transition.

Minnesota Power is currently doing exactly this. It would have ratepayers pay for a new, 550-megawatt plant, powered by natural gas, located near Duluth (Olsen 2019). Customers have not first been offered an option to pay for a local solar installation or to aggregate our money to build and own a community solar facility or to purchase clean power from a wholesale grid operator. None of these options exist in Minnesota Power's fiefdom.

The managerial feudalism of an investor-owned utility (IOU) creates a swamp where there should be transparent, public accounting and citizen participation in decision-making. Two examples from Duluth's utility jurisdiction again illuminate the case. IOUs often sell a portion of their power to a wholesale grid market. Ostensibly, this arrangement improves efficiency by engaging in competition that discriminates only on the basis of price and not according to fuel source: coal, gas, solar, or wind. But the timing and costs of IOUs selling that power to the grid is considered proprietary information and is not readily shared with customers. In early 2020, Minnesota Power ratepayers discovered that our utility has been selling its coal-generated electricity power to the wholesale grid at a loss of millions of dollars and recovering those losses on ratepayers' monthly electric bills (Lyden 2020). Theoretically, we customers should receive a rebate if our IOU is making a profit selling its expensive (and dirty) electricity on a wholesale market when it could be purchasing cheaper (and cleaner) electricity wholesale for us. The proprietary aspect of the utility's wholesale operations makes it hard for ratepayers to get the facts they need about the true costs of running coal plants today and the profits and losses made by utilities.

It has also recently been revealed that Minnesota Power, along with many of the country's largest investor-owned utilities, is a member of a lobbying group called the Utility Air Regulatory Group (UARG), an opaque industry group with a long history of lobbying and suing to undermine clean air and public health rules issued by the U.S. Environmental Protection Agency. My students are astounded to learn that here in the beautiful northlands of Minnesota, our utility's dirty, coal-generated power is often more expensive than wind or solar and that our utility has been paying lobbyists to advocate subsidies for coal and gas, lowered air pollution standards, and fewer environmental regulations. (Once news broke about Minnesota Power's membership in UARG, our utility withdrew from that organization [Kasper 2019]). When I ask students to bring in their monthly electric bills so I can teach them how to decipher the byzantine fees they are charged for their electricity, they rightly wonder if they are also paying the lobbyist fees to advocate lower public health standards. Given the murkiness of these accounting and billing arrangements, my students can only discern a general outline of how the current energy ownership system is forcing them to participate in their own oppression.

The way things are set up now, it appears unimaginable that a ratepayer in a corporate monopoly-owned-utility jurisdiction would have an incentive to be an owner of her own clean-electricity generation, just as it was unthinkable for a serf to be an owner of her own land. The feudal ownership system was not built to recognize deeds of title for serfs, and the modern monopoly utility has no incentive for electricity customers to become independent energy generators and owners. Even energy efficiency is outside the algorithms of the 20th-century investor-owned utility. Less electricity use (through better insulated buildings, energy-efficient appliances, and overall more conscientious energy use) means less corporate revenue. Even in states where government inducements to renewable-energy ownership exist through tax incentives and rebates, investor-owned utilities place higher fees on solar users to reduce the incentives for solar ownership (Tabuchi 2017). The IOU business model works best when IOUs themselves, not smaller-scale users, are the owners of any renewable-energy assets. But IOUs have deep attachments to fossil-fuel infrastructure, not only in their investment portfolios, but also in the way they hold power through relationships of managerial feudalism. For these reasons, it is highly improbable that our monopoly investor-owned utilities will be leaders in the clean-energy transition we need. But if smaller-scale solar users—cities, local business owners, individual households, and communities—also become owners of solar assets and have incentives to use energy more efficiently, what might that energy ownership system look like? What institutions might emerge to support these new local ownership models? This is where commons thinking provides insight.

Solar Commons: A New Civic Institution for Our Energy Future

In international law, the earth's climate system appears as one of our largest global commons (Milun 2011; Edenhofer, Flachsland, and Lessmann 2015). However, it lacks institutions—either in the public or private arenas—to protect and manage its complex gifts. To mitigate climate change, we need commons-sector institutions and a new civic imagination that connects our climate commons to our energy infrastructure, which itself is trapped in public/private, petroculture institutions of the 20th century. In particular, our electricity sector needs to be re-imagined technologically and politically as we follow the imperatives of the energy transition by moving our transportation sector from oil to electric vehicles and by transitioning our electric grid onto renewables (Latour 2018). We need 21st-century ways of thinking about how to own the grid and govern the atmosphere, both of which are material sources of life, as opposed to "resources" of industrial society. Increasingly we hear that policies governing the electric grid should be in sync with the public-trust property concepts that 21st-century international law uses to define our atmospheric global commons (Wood 2013). Invoking public-trust property is a sign that we are talking about commons.

Practically speaking, what do well-managed commons look like in the 21st century? Our experience with the commons of our pre-modern past has left us some tools to answer this question. In England's feudal era, subsistence commons for food and energy were protected by the legal innovation of trust ownership. Trust ownership arose as a way to work around the feudal property regime that justified land ownership by the divine right of kings. The body of rules and legal entities that make up trust law—trustees as legal title owners; beneficiaries as equitable title owners; trust agreements as constitutive governance documents; trust funds as economic tools—continue to be available in the English common law tradition today. Trust ownership is protected by our courts and recognized by our markets. It is as if our new, modern commons, whether given by nature or technology, had a persistent body of law waiting in the wings to help us work around the inequities of our current, albeit managerially feudal, fossil-fuel regime. Why not consider trust law as a toolbox for creating the governing institutions and ownership models to manage the intricately related commons aspects of our climate system and energy infrastructures?

Solar Commons in Practice: Common Wealth, Community Trusts, Local Governance

For the past several years I have directed the Solar Commons Research Team, a group of community-engaged scholars and legal practitioners building a community-trust-law toolbox for solar energy (Solar Commons Research Project 2020).* Our first grid-interconnected success is the Tucson Solar Commons prototype, which generated its first kilowatts on October 31, 2018, following the outline of the Solar Commons basic model in Figure 2. A fuller explanation of the underlying principles and legal structures

* Over the years, the Solar Commons Research team has been invigorated by many, including the following legal thinkers and practitioners:

- Tim Walsh, Maria Pitner (Henson & Efron), Jeannie Oliver and Kevin Jones (Vermont Law School Energy Clinic), Pilar Thomas (Lewis Roca Rothberger) and these architects, engineers, and artists:
- Kirby Spitler, Michael Jackson, Tom Fisher, Kathleen Crowson, Cole Carlson, Paul Krumrich, Arshia Kahn, Ellen McMahon, Dorsey Kauffman and community scholars and activists:
- Kathleen Fluegel, Kitty Stratton, Valerie Rauluk, David Bollier, Julie Ristau, Marlise Riffel, Randel Hanson.

of the Solar Commons Community Trust Ownership model can be found in the law review article written by members of our legal research team (Milun, Walsh, and Pitner n.d.). The section below offers a general overview of our prototyping work and a description of the Tucson Solar Commons prototype, which informs our current work in Minnesota.

Three key features of our work distinguish our prototypes as emergent institutions of the commons sector:

1. *The commonwealth of the sun.* The Solar Commons uses sunshine, a gift of nature that belongs to everyone, to generate monetary value through solar energy panels that create savings on the electric bills of a host;

2. *The community wealth fund.* Net solar savings from the host's electric bill become the trust property of a social wealth fund that delivers money into the low-income beneficiary neighborhoods for local community-empowerment programs. This feature denaturalizes electricity-infrastructure ownership from its corporate monopoly realm and demonstrates an economic algorithm beyond the modern classic supply/demand logic of the marketplace (Lansley, McCann, and Schifferes 2019); and

3. *The Solar Commons governance agreement.* Community partners co-create institutional rules for transparent and equitable management of their solar assets and the funds they generate through a Solar Commons agreement. This feature links community ownership to community governance as Solar Commons agreements are informed by more general principles of commons governance that include social trust, transparent

Figure 2
Solar Commons Basic Model: Trustee Model of Ownership

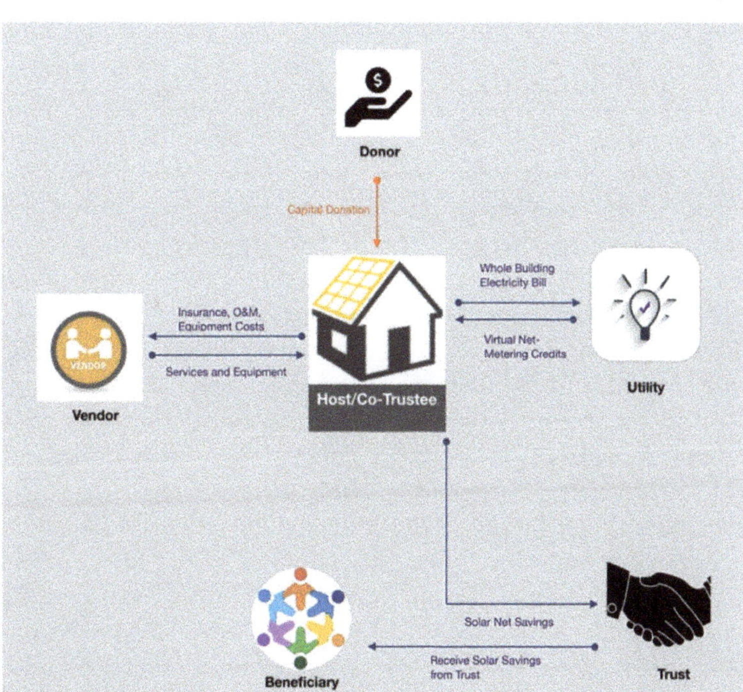

Source: Brehm and Lillis (2018a: 3).

rule-making, and equitable distribution of benefits (Ostrom 1990).

Using principles of community-trust-based ownership for solar energy assets, our research team understands that we are following the path of our medieval energy-commons ancestors, working around the inequities of our current (public/private) ownership regime, and establishing the institutional framework for a "commons-sector option" for solar energy. The Solar Commons Research Team works with community partners to design and implement Solar Commons prototypes across the United States with the aim of producing free, open-source, legal templates and do-it-yourself community guides so that communities themselves can eventually take the lead in using Solar Commons to fund their specific community empowerment projects.

The Tucson Solar Commons is a small, but first, Solar Commons in the United States. Lessons learned from the design and implementation of this prototype are ongoing and provide a window on how solar commons ownership and governance can work in practice. The Tucson Solar Commons is a 14.5kW solar array located on the roof of a nonprofit community center in the center of Tucson, Arizona, a state whose solar capacity is among the greatest in the United States. The money for the array was donated by an Arizona charitable foundation. The community center helped bring together trusted community partners and signed a Solar Commons agreement that laid out the details of how it should take the solar savings on its electricity bill, deduct costs of operations and management (an industry standard amount was used) and the cost of adding an insurance rider, and send the remaining savings to an escrow trust account held by a local community finance development institution (CDFI). CDFIs exist in low-income neighborhoods across the United States. They are designed to serve those communities and are thus a logical financial partner to help with the trust responsibilities of a Solar Commons agreement. In Tucson, the CDFI sequesters a small amount from the solar savings it receives in order to create a separate fund that can be used by the community center in year 10 of the agreement to pay for a new inverter, a necessary technology upgrade. The CDFI will deliver the remaining funds across town to the solar commons beneficiary, the Tucson Urban League (TUL). TUL is located in one of Tucson's poorest neighborhoods, the Garden District, which is home to many new immigrants and refugees. TUL runs several neighborhood programs, including after-school programs. Following Solar Commons design principles, the beneficiary program supported by the Solar Commons fund is a weatherization program run by TUL so that low-income households can see their electricity bills decrease by plugging up leaky windows and by investing in other energy-efficiency measures that will support the long-term sustainability and community-empowerment practices associated with the Solar Commons name. Solar Commons design principles require that partners choose beneficiaries carrying out regenerative ecological practices that empower low-income communities. (Solar Commons are licensed under a Creative Commons License—3.0: attribution, non-commercial, no-derivatives—to ensure that general commons principles are adhered to when using the Solar Commons name and model.) There is flexibility in the agreement for reassigning the beneficiary funds to other such programs if needed. As the Solar Commons model is further prototyped, the role of a "trust protector" will be developed to work with trustees and beneficiaries to manage changes over time in Solar Commons agreements. Also, the Solar Commons Research Team is developing digital tools that can provide a transparent community platform to register solar electricity generated, solar savings going to the trust, and neighborhood programs that benefit.

The Tucson Solar Commons is small. It puts around $40,000 into the trust fund over 20 years at a fixed rate of 14 cents a kilowatt hour (which was the net-metering rate in Tucson when the Solar Commons was interconnected in 2018). The Solar Commons agreement puts no cost increases into this electricity rate and thus, over the 20 years of the agreement, the community center will see an overall savings of about $10,000 as overall electric costs, according to industry standards, will rise by around 3 percent a year. After the 20-year agreement is up, the community center will keep all the remaining savings from the solar panels, which will likely keep generating clean electricity for 10 or more years. Solar Commons agreements should distribute the benefits of the sun's commonwealth to all parties—the hosts, trustees, and neighborhood beneficiaries.

With this first, small Solar Commons prototype, our research team has proven that community-trust solar ownership can work successfully behind the meter even at a small scale. We would like to see larger, 500-kilowatt Solar Commons panels sitting on the roofs of big-box stores and factories, fulfilling their corporate social responsibility to their neighborhoods by donating their metered solar savings to Solar Commons trust funds that maintain community gardens, job training programs in clean-energy industries, and other community empowerment and well-being programs. The Solar Commons Research Team is also in the process of designing in-front-of-the-meter Solar Commons in the state of Minnesota, which has a successful solar-garden program allowing third parties to generate solar electricity directly into regional distribution or transmission grids. In these cases, we imagine large Solar Commons systems, appropriately designed and placed in rural or urban settings, that could annually deliver substantial sums to local programs serving low-income community needs. Such successful scaling was indeed the finding of the Rocky Mountain Institute's analysis (Brehm and Lillis 2018b). Our research team is currently prototyping Solar Commons with interested donors in order to build the institutional design of a robust community-trust-solar-ownership model. But in the future, there is no reason why Solar Commons could not be funded by green-bank financing or local investment dollars, paying back the upfront capital with early years of solar savings and sending the savings of later years back into community-empowerment projects.

The New Civic Consciousness of Solar Commons

To be successful as a robust socio-legal commons institution, Solar Commons also needs to raise the cultural consciousness of U.S. energy users. Thus, in Tucson, the Solar Commons beneficiary neighborhood is also the site of a collaborative public art project that we see as the public-facing "deed of title" to the neighborhood's equity stake in the sun's commonwealth. For the research team, the innovative legal, economic, and governance structures of Solar Commons represent the civic institution that we are building with our research project; but it is the public art, co-created in the neighborhood of the Solar Commons beneficiary, that represents the new civic imagination that will breathe life into Solar Commons institutions in the United States. In Tucson, our legal research team was fortunate to work with art faculty and students at the University of Arizona and community leaders and kids in the Garden District to design and implement the public face of community-trust solar ownership.* The artists suggested that Garden District kids could best deliver the message of Solar Commons—that sharing the sun's commonwealth benefits through community-trust solar ownership was linked to caring for the broader commonwealth benefits of the earth; that Solar Commons were linked to earth commons and that both of these required neighborhoods to engage in *the activity of commoning*. Input from kids at the Garden District's elementary school led to the creation of the Solar Commons Game, a beautiful tile board game that could teach the principles of both earth commoning and solar commoning. In 2020, we are refining the game, adding a teaching curriculum, producing the game, and giving it to libraries

* I want to thank, in particular, Prof. Ellen McMahon, Dorsey Bromwell-Kaufmann, and the undergraduate students in Dr. McMahon's Environmental Art class for their work on the Solar Commons Game. The beautiful artwork, conceptual design, and gaming features come from a year of their work with the Solar Commons Project team.

Figure 3
Solar Commons Game: Sun and Earth Hub Tiles

Source: Author.

Figure 4
Adding Nature Tiles Around the Earth Hub to Create a Nature Commons in the Solar Commons Game

Source: Author.

in the Garden District's elementary school and after-school programs. We will also have a large mural of children playing the Solar Commons Game painted on the expansive outdoor wall of the elementary school, a central signpost of the Solar Commons beneficiary neighborhood.

How the Solar Commons Game Works

Figure 3 shows the sun and earth hub tiles, around which solar and nature commoning is organized. The game starts with a distribution of nature tiles: sun, water, minerals, plants, air, and animals. Players get more or fewer nature tiles by drawing cards that tell them how nature commoning works: "You took a long shower this morning; give back two water tiles." "You planted trees in your park, take three plant tiles." Figure 4 shows how nature tiles can be placed around the earth hub to create an earth commons in your neighborhood. Players also get fossil-fuel tiles, which are shown in Figure 5. The aim is to get rid of them. Doing so requires building a Solar Commons in the neighborhood, as shown in Figure 6.

Solar Commons tiles line up like this: agreement, gathering, electricity, trust, community. You get Solar Commons tiles by drawing from cards to learn the rules of solar commoning: "You are working with your neighbors to find a strong roof for solar panels; take one agreement tile." The goal is to build a beautiful neighborhood full of nature commons and Solar Commons. (See Figure 7.)

Figure 5
Solar Commons Game: A Fossil-Fuel Tile

Source: Author.

Figure 6
Adding a Solar Commons to the Nature Commons Starts with a Sun Hub Tile

Source: Author.

A player gets rid of her last fossil-fuel tile when that player connects her neighborhood to another player's neighborhood by building a Solar Commons together. See Figure 8 for an example of several neighborhoods joined together by collectively built Solar Commons.

The Solar Commons Game and the neighborhood mural showing the kids of the Tucson Garden District playing the game act as the public-facing "deed of title" to the neighborhood's equity stake in the sun's commonwealth. As we prototype Solar Commons in the United States, we imagine that the associated public art will look different in each community; Solar Commons public art should look like the neighborhoods that it serves.

Conclusion: Solar Commons and Our Common World

> Common wealth, properly organized, provides a way to address the two greatest flaws in contemporary capitalism—its relentless destruction of nature and the widening of inequality. Barnes (2015)

The sun is the common source of all energy on earth (Crosby 2006). By gathering the sun's common wealth through thoughtfully designed and well-placed solar panels and organizing that wealth in community trusts to serve those most in need, Solar Commons can be more than a gift of technology, more than a legal gift from our clever peasant

Figure 7
Building a Neighborhood with Solar Commons and Nature Commons

Source: Author.

ancestors. Solar-powered community trusts are indeed more than a tool to work around the inequities of the managerial feudalism that keeps fossil-fuel-invested monopolies and corporations in charge of our electric grids and right-of-way corridors.

As part of a new civic imagination, Solar Commons can contribute to how we go about creating what the anthropologist Bruno Latour (2018) has called "the progressive composition of a common world." Latour is referring to how democracy could evolve beyond its modern, Eurocentric institutions to include the earth as an active partner in building equitable ways of living together. For Latour, this involves listening differently to scientist-ecologists who measure earth impacts at global and microscopic scales and tell us our limits; redesigning our modern infrastructures accordingly; repairing the harms of colonialism; and redefining citizenship and politics to value care and mutuality. These are features of a 21st-century world Latour hopes will emerge … in time. Solar Commons aspires to contribute to this world, not by adding solar energy to feed the current high-energy lifestyle of modern, industrialized societies, but rather by envisioning renewable-energy ownership as a way to redesign, repair, and better care for communities. A solar-powered "commons option" for the 21st century connects nature commoning and solar commoning; it is a humble tool to imagine community ownership and build common wealth that serves the needs of a common world.

Figure 8
Joining Neighborhoods by Building Solar Commons Together in the Solar Commons Game

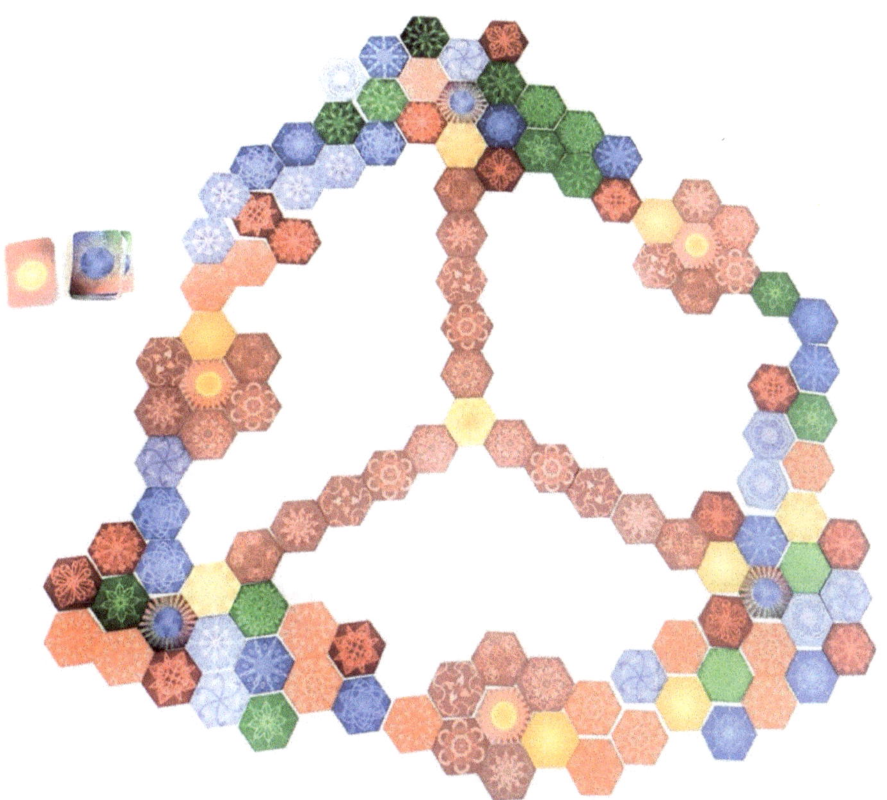

Source: Author.

References

Allete. (2013). "ALLETE Energy Corridor Would Offer Efficient Movement of Multiple Products, from Flared Gas to Water to Carbon." *Allete.* https://investor.allete.com/news-releases/news-release-details/allete-energy-corridor-would-offer-efficient-movement-multiple

Barnes, Peter. (2006). *Capitalism 3.0: A Guide to Reclaiming the Commons.* San Francisco: Berrett-Koehler Publishers.

________. (2015). *Common Wealth Trusts: Structures of Transition.* Great Transition Initiative. Cambridge, MA: Great Transition Initiative, Tellus Institute. https://greattransition.org/publication/common-wealth-trusts

Better in Our Backyard. (2020). *About Us.* Duluth, MN: Better in Our Backyard. https://www.betterinourbackyard.com/

Birtles, Sara. (1999). "Common Land, Poor Relief and Enclosure: The Use of Manorial Resources in Fulfilling Parish Obligations 1601–1834." *Past and Present* 165: 74–106.

Bravo, Giangiacomo, and Tine De Moor. (2008). "The Commons in Europe: From Past to Future." *International Journal of the Commons* 2(2): 155–161. https://www.thecommonsjournal.org/articles/10.18352/ijc.98/

Brehm, Kevin, and Genevieve Lillis. (2018a). *Solar Commons Financial Analysis Results: Solar Commons Project Analysis Phase 1 of 2.* Snowmass, CO: Rocky Mountain Institute. https://static1.squarespace.com/static/5855aade3e00be1ae0b98fb2/t/5cce0a76eef1a108d731746b/1557006971 607/RMI_SolarCommonsReportPhase1_.pdf

________. (2018b). *Solar Commons Scalability and Constraints Analysis Results: Solar Commons Project Analysis Phase 2 of 2.* Snowmass, CO: Rocky Mountain Institute. https://static1.squarespace.com/static/5855aade3e 00be1ae0b98fb2/t/5cce0ab4e2c4833aaec0c78d/1557007034233/RMI_SolarCommonsReportPhase2_.pdf

Brenner, Y. S., and Nancy Brenner-Golomb. (1996). "The New Feudalism: Managerial Oligarchy." In *A Theory of Full Employment*, pp. 7–12. Dordrecht, Netherlands: Springer.

Cole, Daniel H., and Peter Z. Grossman, eds. (2003). *The End of a Natural Monopoly: Deregulation and Competition in the Electric Power Industry.* New York: Routledge.

Crosby, Alfred W. (2006). *Children of the Sun: A History of Humanity's Unappeasable Appetite for Energy.* New York: Norton.

Dietz, Thomas, Elinor Ostrom, and Paul C. Stern. (2003). "The Struggle to Govern the Commons." *Science* 302(5652): 1907–1912.

Edenhofer, Ottmar, Christian Flachsland, Michael Jakob, and Kai Lessmann. (2015). "The Atmosphere as a Global Commons: Challenges for International Cooperation and Governance." In *The Oxford Handbook of the Macroeconomics of Global Warming.* Eds. Willi Semmler and Lucas Bernard. New York: Oxford University Press.

Götz, Norbert. (2015). "'Moral Economy': Its Conceptual History and Analytical Prospects." *Journal of Global Ethics* 11(2): 147–162. https://doi.org/10.1080/17449626.2015.1054556

Graeber, David. (2018). *Bullshit Jobs.* New York: Simon & Schuster.

Heiman, Michael K., and Barry D. Solomon. (2004). "Power to the People: Electric Utility Restructuring and the Commitment to Renewable Energy." *Annals of the Association of American Geographers* 94(1): 94–116.

Jones, Kevin B., and David Zoppo. (2014). *A Smarter, Greener Grid: Forging Environmental Progress Through Smart Energy Policies and Technologies.* Santa Barbara, CA: Praeger.

Karnowski, Steve. (2020). "Minnesota Court Rejects 2 Major Permits for Polymet Mine." *Kare11News.* https://www.kare11.com/article/news/local/minnesota-court-rejects-2-major-permits-for-polymet-mine/89-71f1d078-302b-4887-9ec1-8092c6395d55

Kasper, Matt. (2019). *As Utilities Flee Newly Scandalous UARG, Remaining Members Make Dishonest Claims About its Purpose.* San Francisco: Energy and Policy Institute. https://www.energyandpolicy.org/utilities-flee-utility-air-regulatory-group-amid-scandal-and-investigations/

Kelly, Marjorie. (2012). *Owning Our Future: The Emerging Ownership Revolution.* San Francisco: Berrett-Koehler Publishers.

Klass, Alexandra B., and Danielle Meinhardt. (2014). "Transporting Oil and Gas: U.S. Infrastructure Challenges." *Iowa Law Review* 100(3): 947–1053.

Lansley, Stewart, Duncan McCann, and Steve Schifferes. (2019). "The Case for Citizens' Wealth Funds." *International Journal of Public Policy* 15(1/2):136–152.

Latour, Bruno. (2018). *Down to Earth: Politics in the New Climatic Regime.* Hoboken, NJ: John Wiley & Sons.

Linebaugh, Peter. (2008). *The Magna Carta Manifesto: Liberties and Commons for All.* Berkeley: University of California Press.

Lyden, Tom. (2020). "Last Gasp of Coal: Plants Running When Cheaper, Cleaner Energy Available." *KMSP FoxNews.* https://www.fox9.com/news/last-gasp-of-coal-plants-running-when-cheaper-cleaner-energy-available

Milun, Kathryn. (2011). *The Political Uncommons: The Cross-Cultural Logic of the Global Commons.* New York: Routledge.

Milun, Kathryn, Tim Walsh, and Maria Pitner. (n.d., manuscript under review). "Bringing New Light to One of the Oldest Forms of Property Ownership: An Innovative Solution for Benefitting Underserved Communities Using the Solar Commons Community Trust Model."

Mueller, James A., and Amit Ronen. (2015). *Bridging the Solar Income Gap.* Working Paper. Washington, DC: GW Solar Institute, George Washington University. https://solar.gwu.edu/bridging-solar-income-gap

Olsen, Tom. (2019). "Minnesota Court of Appeals Orders Further Review of Proposed Superior Natural Gas Plant." *Duluth News Tribune.* https://www.duluthnewstribune.com/business/energy-and-mining/4835783-Minnesota-Court-of-Appeals-orders-further-review-of-proposed-Superior-natural-gas-plant

Orbach, Barak Y. (2011). "The Antitrust Consumer Welfare Paradox." *Journal of Competition Law and Economics* 7(1): 133–164.

Ostrom, Elinor. (1990). *Governing the Commons: The Evolution of Institutions for Collective Action.* New York: Cambridge University Press.

Radkau, Joachim. (2012). *Wood: A History.* Cambridge, UK: Polity.

Runyon, Jennifer. (2019). "U.S. Solar Market Tops 10 GW in 2018, Again." *Renewable Energy World.* https://www.renewableenergyworld.com/2019/03/14/us-solar-market-tops-10-gw-in-2018-again/#gref

Scott, Austin W. (1922). "The Trust as an Instrument of Law Reform." *Yale Law Journal* 31(5): 457–468.

Scott, Austin W., and William F. Fratcher. (2000). *Scott on Trusts*, 4th ed. New York: Aspen Publishers.

Short, Chris. (2008). "The Traditional Commons of England and Wales in the Twenty-First Century: Meeting New and Old Challenges." *International Journal of the Commons* 2(2). https://www.thecommonsjournal.org/articles/10.18352/ijc.47/

Solar Commons Research Project. (2020). *Home.* Beverly Hills, CA: Solar Commons Research Project. http://solarcommonsproject.org/

Stein, Amy L. (2016). "Breaking Energy Path Dependencies." *Brooklyn Law Review* 82(2): 559–604. https://brooklynworks.brooklaw.edu/cgi/viewcontent.cgi?article=1535&context=blr

Tabuchi, Hiroko. (2017). "Rooftop Solar DIMS Under Pressure from Utility Lobbyists." *New York Times.* https://www.nytimes.com/2017/07/08/climate/rooftop-solar-panels-tax-credits-utility-companies-lobbying.html

Theater of Public Policy. (2019). *Duluth Power Dialog.* Duluth, MN: University of Minnesota. https://cla.d.umn.edu/students/learning-experiences/anth-3300 or https://www.youtube.com/watch?v=aTAy_6jsxSA

Thompson, E. P. (1971). "The Moral Economy of the English Crowd in the Eighteenth Century." *Past and Present* 50(1): 76–136.

Trachtenberg, Alan. ([1982] 2007). *The Incorporation of America: Culture and Society in the Gilded Age.* New York: Hill & Wang.

U.S. Securities and Exchange Commission. (US-SEC). (2019). *Allete Inc.: Form 10-K for Fiscal Year Ended December 31, 2018.* February 13. Washington, DC: US-SEC. https://sec.report/Document/0000066756-19-000023/ or https://www.sec.gov/Archives/edgar/data/66756/000006675619000023/ale12312018-10k.htm

Weston, Burns H., and David Bollier. (2013). *Green Governance: Ecological Survival, Human Rights, and the Law of the Commons.* Cambridge, UK: Cambridge University Press.

Wood, Mary Christina. (2013). *Nature's Trust: Environmental Law for a New Ecological Age.* Cambridge, UK: Cambridge University Press.

Zaccour, George, ed. (2012). *Deregulation of Electric Utilities.* New York: Springer Science & Business Media.

Index

W

Y

Z

About Post Carbon Institute

Founded in 2003, Post Carbon Institute's mission is to lead the transition to a more resilient, equitable, and sustainable world by providing individuals and communities with the resources needed to understand and respond to the interrelated ecological, economic, energy, and equity crises of the 21st century.

www.ingramcontent.com/pod-product-compliance
Lightning Source LLC
Chambersburg PA
CBHW051719210326
41597CB00032B/5541

* 9 7 8 0 9 8 9 5 9 9 5 6 6 *